SELF-ASSESSMENT
AND
CAREER DEVELOPMENT:
A SYSTEMATIC APPROACH
TO THE
SELECTION AND MANAGEMENT
OF A CAREER

SELF-ASSESSMENT AND CAREER DEVELOPMENT: A SYSTEMATIC APPROACH TO THE SELECTION AND MANAGEMENT OF A CAREER

John P. Kotter

Victor A. Faux
Harvard University

Charles McArthur
Management Consultant

PRENTICE-HALL, INC., *Englewood Cliffs, New Jersey 07632*

Library of Congress Cataloging in Publication Data

KOTTER, JOHN P. (date)
  Self-assessment and career development.

  Bibliography: p.
  1. Vocational guidance. 2. Self-evaluation.
I. Faux, Victor A., joint author. II. McArthur,
Charles,   joint author. III. Title.
IV. Title: Career development.
HF5381.K67   331.7′02   78-4150
ISBN 0-13-803148-7

Printed in the United States of America

10   9   8   7   6   5

Case material of the Harvard Graduate School of Business Administration is
made possible by the cooperation of business firms who may wish to remain
anonymous by having names, quantities, and other identifying details dis-
guised while maintaining basic relationships. Cases are prepared as the basis
for class discussion rather than to illustrate either effective or ineffective
handling of administrative situations.

PRENTICE-HALL INTERNATIONAL, INC., *London*
PRENTICE-HALL OF AUSTRALIA PTY. LIMITED, *Sydney*
PRENTICE-HALL OF CANADA, LTD., *Toronto*
PRENTICE-HALL OF INDIA PRIVATE LIMITED, *New Delhi*
PRENTICE-HALL OF JAPAN, INC., *Tokyo*
PRENTICE-HALL OF SOUTHEAST ASIA PTE. LTD., *Singapore*
WHITEHALL BOOKS LIMITED, *Wellington, New Zealand*

Contents

Part Two
CAREER DEVELOPMENT

A POSTSCRIPT TO PART TWO

SELF-ASSESSMENT AND
CAREER DEVELOPMENT WORKBOOK   *255*

Acknowledgments

This book is the result of six years worth of work that was enthusiastically supported by the administration at Harvard Business School. We owe particular thanks in this regard to John McArthur, Larry Fouraker, and Jay Lorsch.

Over the developmental history of this book, numerous people contributed ideas of importance to the authors: Rod Hodgins, Warren Wilhelm, Eileen Morley, Frank Leonard, Alan Frohman, and Ron Tagiuri. In addition, a group of people who remain anonymous generously gave their time and effort in helping us to create the case materials in the book. We are in debt to all these people.

Special thanks are due to the creative force who launched this project—Tony Athos. To him, we dedicate this book.

SELF-ASSESSMENT
AND
CAREER DEVELOPMENT:
A SYSTEMATIC APPROACH
TO THE
SELECTION AND MANAGEMENT
OF A CAREER

1

Introduction

> "Cheshire Puss," she began, rather timidly, as she did not know whether it would like the name; however, it only grinned a little wider. "Come, it's pleased so far," thought Alice, and she went on. "Would you tell me, please, which way I ought to walk from here?"
>
> "That depends a good deal on where you want to get to," said the Cat.
>
> "I don't much care where," said Alice.
>
> "Then it doesn't matter which way you walk," said the Cat.
>
> "—so long as I get *somewhere*," Alice added as an explanation.
>
> "Oh, you're sure to do that," said the Cat, "if only you walk long enough!"
>
> —*Alice in Wonderland*

This book is about job and career decision making. Its purpose is to help people develop concrete skills for managing their own careers—skills at assessing themselves, assessing opportunities, making career- and job-related choices, and managing this process in both the short and long run.

When we speak of job- and career-related decision making, we are talking about a wide range of important choices that people out of necessity make during the course of their lifetimes. Such decisions include:

1. The selection of what type of career to seek.
2. Selection of what job to seek next.
3. Selection of a strategy for getting a particular type of job.
4. Selection of a job offer from among alternatives.
5. Selection of assignments, locations, etc., within a job when options are offered.
6. Selection of an approach to a job.
7. Selection of career goals or a sequence of desired promotions.

It is our observation that people often make these types of decisions with considerably less care and expertise than they use in the selection of a television or a vacation. Even people who have professional training in analysis and decision making often spend a great deal of time making decisions that, in the context of their lives, may be of little significance, while slipping semiconsciously into major life decisions whose implications are not at all clear to them. Compared to less important decisions, their data-collection methods tend to be less thorough, their analyses more superficial, and their choice processes more random.

There are undoubtedly many, often complex, reasons why people behave in this way. For most people, assessing something ''outside'' themselves is a great deal easier psychologically than assessing themselves. The latter creates discomfort, which people often deal with by avoiding the subject altogether. At the same time, our educational institutions have historically provided courses for helping us learn how to make "good" management decisions, legal decisions, engineering decisions, financial decisions, medical decisions—but not career and job decisions.

Some people, of course, manage to go through life quite happily without ever seriously assessing themselves, assessing opportunities, or making explicit job and career choices. Whether because of luck, or very good intuitive decision-making capabilities, they do very well. At the same time, however, many other people behave that way but find the results highly unsatisfying. They often semiconsciously slip into boring or frustrating careers. They sometimes find themselves faced with conflicting job and family demands that are unreasonable. Many discover, to their horror, that they will never achieve the position or professional reputation they had been seeking for years. Some go through the trauma of being fired. Others find themselves securely locked into a job and life style that is no longer satisfying, but from which escape seems impossible. In the words of one 49-year-old individual—"I woke up one day and just sat in bed thinking, how in the hell did I ever get myself into this mess?"

This book has been written for people who, for whatever reason, wish to consciously and explicitly manage their careers. While it offers no panaceas, it does try to bring to bear the best technology and insight that exists today on that subject. Like any management task in which the manager does not have absolute control of all the relevant variables, success is not guaranteed 100 percent of the time. Nevertheless, our experience over the past six years with the materials and approach presented in this book has convinced us that they are effective, and that they can be of *significant* help to most people.[1]

The following comments are typical of the written feedback we have received from our students:

1. The course, within the rubric of enforced dedication of time and effort, compelled me to address those issues which can often be ignored until a personal crisis arises.

   I have been able to achieve a better knowledge of myself, my motivations, and my goals-at-large. Furthermore, I have been forced to think about the causal links between these factors and my past achievements. In essence, I have been able to prioritize my personal needs and objectives in order to provide me with a basis for choosing a job and career which will be ultimately satisfying.

   Furthermore, I have developed some rudimentary awareness of the external forces which tend to impact the career development process in an unacceptable way. Given this knowledge, I can attempt to develop a personal strategy for anticipating, and dealing with, problems which tend to arise at different points in one's life.

   Finally, I have become acutely aware of the interdependence of various factors in one's life. The relationship between career and lifestyle is the most obvious example. As well, and of equal importance, are the other "constituencies" which command my time and attention. If the interdependencies are ignored, the strain which can develop might prove ultimately disastrous. I realize now, for instance, that both my wife and I must grow together.

2. Understanding now that everyone has strengths and weaknesses due to cognitive style, value systems, etc., I've become less judgmental of myself and others in areas of intelligence, and put more emphasis on what a person would be good at doing because of the person's (or my own) cognitive style, values, etc.

3. I gained a fantastic understanding of the *criteria* upon which I will make my job decision. I learned a great deal about what I *really* want out of a job. I learned a great deal about the potential pitfalls of the job hunt and later career development.

4. I have been forced to formalize a previously semiconscious awareness of myself. This has forced me to acknowledge certain characteristics as important enough to choose a career around. Before taking this course I was boxed into a narrow idea of what were acceptable careers, and viewed incompatible characteristics as sources of tension and discontent that I would just have to live with. Now I've reassessed my priorities, and am taking a much more imaginative approach to finding a job.

5. I feel like I've gained a whole lot from the course. I was very confused and worried about the job-hunting process at the beginning of this year. Now, I feel I have a good focus and a lot more *self-confidence* in dealing with the whole career selection process.

6. Frankly, I had never taken any psychological or even "interest orientation" tests before, so I really enjoyed taking the course for just this aspect. But I think I gained a *focus* on what I think I already knew about myself, too. I see now a necessity to continue this process over time, notwithstanding the difficulty and the competing demands on my time and emotions. Also, I think I learned a methodology which I will apply to myself and hopefully accurately to others too.

7. I have been able to confirm a lot of feelings I've had about the kind of work I've always thought I've wanted to do. The course has made me realize that it is in fact practical for someone with my background, desires, abilities, and personality. In that respect it has given me the push to go out and actively pursue these options.

---

[1]Well over 80 percent of the people who have been students in our Self-Assessment and Career Development course have reported it to be a very helpful experience. In a survey of people who took the course in 1973, seven months after they had left school and started full-time employment, 45 percent said that the course was either the best or one of the best courses they had while in graduate school.

The first part of this book deals with the process of self-assessment. It is designed both to help you learn how to assess yourself effectively for career and job decision-making purposes, and to help you actually produce a usable self-assessment. The second part of the book focuses on career development. It is designed to help you assess job and career opportunities, get a job, and deal with the challenges and problems encountered in different stages of a career. The final part of the book is made up of four appendices and a workbook. Two of the appendices contain examples of the kind of written self-assessments and career plans that result from using this book. The other two appendices contain references to other sources of information that are relevant to career planning. The workbook section contains instructions for a number of exercises that are described in parts one and two of the book. The workbook pages are perforated so they can be torn out and put in a three ring binder. That binder can also be used to store your responses to the exercises, and to serve as a working tool to help you use the methods described in this book to better manage your career.

Part One

SELF-ASSESSMENT

II

The Self-Assessment Process

The self-assessment method presented in the first part of this book is a systematic process designed to generate the type of accurate self awareness needed to make rational job and career decisions. This approach is similar to that used by many professional career management consultants, with one important exception. The process described here is not just a human assessment process, it is a *self*-assessment process. You will not only acquire skills in assessing people for career decision making purposes, you will learn how to assess yourself.

In this chapter, we will briefly describe the basic steps in the method. Chapters III through X will then explore those steps in more detail.

Generating Useful Data

Rational assessment, of necessity, begins by generating or gathering information. This book contains and describes a number of different mechanisms that can elicit potentially useful information about a person. These include devices we have specifically created for use here, as well as some standard psychological instruments. None of these methods alone can come close to capturing all there is to know about a person. But as a group, they will usually capture all that is relevant for our purposes.

Throughout the first stages of the self-assessment process you will be asked to use the devices in the workbook to generate useful data about yourself. Most of these exercises will require only 30-60 minutes of your time. (The exception is the Written Interview, which will require considerably more time and effort.) You will probably find some of the exercises fun, or at least interesting. And you will probably find some of the exercises boring, or anxiety producing. These feelings can be useful data too, and a space is provided in the workbook for you to record them.

One of the reasons people often feel anxious while using these devices is because they assume these mechanisms are evaluating them. They consciously, or more often unconsciously, believe that the devices are going to tell them if they are "dumb" or "smart," whether they have any chance at all of becoming a C.P.A., or whether or not they are "sane." And as a result, they approach using these devices with ambivalence, and they find using them to be somewhat anxiety producing.

It is very important for you to recognize, at the onset, that these data generating mechanisms *DO NOT ANALYZE YOU*. They don't tell you what you can or cannot do with your life or how good a person you are. All they do is supply potentially relevant information which you can use to create a self-assessment, which then can help you make better job and career related decisions. *You* have to make sense out of the information. *You* have to do the analysis. *You* are in charge. That's what *self*-assessment is all about.

Understanding the Data Generating Devices

In order to utilize the information supplied by any data generating device, it is crucial that you understand the device itself. As any physical scientist knows, in order to interpret information provided by an instrument on a subject, one needs to first understand the instrument itself and how it is used. When trying to use a photograph for "scientific" purposes, it might be very important that one know, for example, that the lens in the camera that produced the photo tends to distort the image within 3 mm of the edge, and that the picture was taken with the subject's knowledge. The same is true of the devices we shall be using.

Chapters III, IV, V, VII, VIII and IX are written to help you understand the data generating devices that we will be using, as well as some other alternative devices. These chapters are not designed to make you an instant expert in those measuring techniques; instead they are designed only to provide you with enough information so that you can reasonably and intelligently interpret the output of those devices.

As you go through the first part of this book you will be repeating the following cycle a number of times:

1. First, you will use some data generating device that is in the workbook.
2. You next will read the chapter that discusses that instrument.
3. You then will practice your understanding of how to interpret the data supplied by that instrument using data from one or more cases.
4. Finally, you will then do an initial interpretation of your own data.

The third step in the cycle is particularly important. To develop your skills at assessment requires practice. The case material in the first part of the book is carefully chosen with that requirement in mind.

Identifying Themes

It is important to keep in mind that our purpose here is to use a self-assessment as an aid in making the kind of career and job decisions listed in the previous chapter. That is, we seek to create a product that can help to discriminate among a set of potential or real career and job related options. We need something that can be used to help "predict" what might happen if a person chooses various job/career/lifestyle options: Will the individual be happier with job one or job two? be promoted quicker at company A or company B? perform better approaching the job this way or that way? feel more family/job conflicts with offer 1, 2, or 3?

A self-assessment that can help answer these types of questions must focus on a person's more central and stable characteristics. An assessment that says that an individual likes X, or tends to behave like Y, is not very useful if both X and Y can change unpredictably within a month. Although human beings do change rather drastically in some ways in a short period of time, all people tend to change slowly or not at all in other ways. It is this latter set of characteristics that one searches for in the data.

To get at these more stable, central, and important aspects of a person that in daily conversation we often call "interests," "values," "skills," "motives," etc., we will be helping you develop skills at thematic analysis (mostly in Chapter VI). In this type of analysis, one sorts through data from various devices looking for recurring ideas (themes). The underlying logic behind this kind of analysis is straightforward and compelling; if evidence pointing to a particular theme, such as "entrepreneurial tendencies," is found a significant number of times in data generated from numerous devices, then it is probably justifiable to conclude that it is saying something important about the person who generated the data. With the systematic use of this type of analysis, you can find virtually all of the important

themes in your life and be well on your way toward a sound self-assessment.

Thematic analysis is fundamentally a process of inductive logic. That is, it starts by focusing on specifics (data generated by the various devices) and from that slowly develops generalizations (themes). This is in contrast to a deductive process, in which we would begin with a set of generalizations (a model) about the behavior of all human beings, and then use them to generate more specific generalizations about a specific person. (For example, if a model says that "all people with red hair have strong affiliation needs," and Joe has red hair, then we would deduce that Joe has strong affiliation needs.[1])

This inductive process of thematic analysis is, in a sense, systematic detective work. It involves sifting through large amounts of information looking for clues (to potential themes), drawing tentative conclusions (about themes), and then testing those conclusions against still more data. And like detective work, it can be intellectually fun.

Identifying Implications

The final step in the self-assessment process is to identify the basic job and career related implications of the themes you have located (Chapter X). This step essentially involves translating that which you have found in the data into a form and format that is not only accurate, but easy to use in job/career decision making.

An example of a set of implications from a self-assessment paper can be found in the last few pages of Appendix A. You may find it helpful at this point to briefly examine Appendix A in its entirety, as it represents a tangible output of our self-assessment process.

Two exercises are built into the learning process in the first part of this book to help you develop your skills at identifying themes and implications. The first is a case in Chapter X, which asks you to critique someone else's self-assessment effort. The second is an exercise in the workbook (the dyad exercise), in which you will actually do a complete self-assessment of someone else.

Emotionally Demanding

Learning self-assessment is intellectually demanding just as is learning marketing, or finance, or art history. But unlike most other subjects, self-assessment can also be emotionally demanding. And it is useful to explicitly recognize this aspect of the process from the beginning.

It is relatively easy to be objective and calm when we are

---

[1] It would be nice if we could use a deductive approach to self-assessment, particularly because most of us have been educated more in deduction than induction. Unfortunately, however, we cannot. There exists today no single model of human behavior that is of the quality necessary for our purposes. The very best psychological or behavioral models are very limited in their scope and applicability. The behavioral sciences might some day create a truly general-purpose model of human behavior, but it most certainly does not exist today. An alternative method that would still allow deduction would be to study *all* the current models of human behavior and how and when each can be useful. But that is a task far beyond our scope here.

asked to evaluate someone else's strengths and weaknesses. But when it comes to assessing ourselves—that is quite a different matter. Virtually everyone finds engaging in self-assessment somewhat anxiety producing. It's only natural to worry about how the assessment will turn out. It's normal for many people to find themselves occasionally mad at one of our data generating devices or our cases. It's common for people to sometimes see nothing but "good," or nothing but "bad," things in their data, and to feel either very high or very low. That is just the way we are.

Have faith. Close to 1000 of our students have learned and utilized self-assessment as of December 1977. And none of them have found the process too emotionally demanding to learn or to apply usefully to themselves. Most of them, in fact, have enjoyed learning and applying the process.

The Written Interview

NOTE:
DO NOT READ THIS UNTIL YOU HAVE COMPLETED THE
WRITTEN INTERVIEW ASSIGNMENT IN THE WORKBOOK

Most people who engage in individual assessment as a vocation (e.g., as career counselors) begin data collection with a long interview of the person to be assessed. In one way or another, they say, "Tell me about yourself," and then they shut up and take notes, usually intervening only when the interviewee stops talking. Usually this open-ended background interview turns out to be the most important source of information for the assessment.

We begin the self-assessment process with a written version of such a background interview. The Written Interview Exercise from the workbook is very similar to a good introductory counseling interview. And like such an interview, it will be our most important data source.

The Interview's "Output"

To use one's responses to the Written Interview for assessment purposes, we need first to consider what type of information those responses provide. But stop and think for a moment; the most obvious answer is not correct.

If a person claims to have been born March 26, 1948, and to have one sister, it is probably reasonable to assume these assertions are true. That is, they are probably verifiable "facts." But if you examine a typical Written Interview, you will find that only a small percentage of its content represents clear-cut "facts" about the person's background. More important, if you examine the interviews of three or four people, you will find considerable variety in the *type* of

"facts" they have expressed. Unlike a more directive interview, in which a person is asked a series of very specific "fact-eliciting" questions, this type of interview allows the interviewee great latitude in deciding what to talk about. Which is, of course, the whole idea.

In talking about one's background, any person, given the time, could quite literally write at least one book. (Some autobiographies stretch across three or four volumes.) But because of the context in which the Written Interview is conducted, one gets instead the equivalent of one or two chapters. And the task of selecting what goes into the two chapters is left to the interviewee.

Of course, people being interviewed do not sit down and visualize all their history and then develop conscious criteria for "editing." They just talk or, in the case of our written equivalent, write. The result, however, is hardly a random selection. Two Written Interviews produced by the same person a month apart will look remarkably similar (and quite different from most other people's Written Interviews).

This type of data-generating instrument assumes that, given considerable latitude in responding to questions, a person must consciously or unconsciously choose what and how to answer, and those choices might tell us something important about that individual. What is said, what is left out, how it is said, the order in which it is said—all of this is potentially useful information about the individual.

Potentially!—for some of these data may say more about the manner and the context in which they were generated than they do about the person.[1] But there are ways to guard against that, which we will discuss later.[2]

Interpreting the Output

To make sense of this "potentially useful information," to decide what, if anything, the data tell us about the more central aspects of the interviewee we need to use a technique that we often use to "interpret" information in our everyday lives. That technique involves drawing inferences based on patterns we see in the data.

Drawing inferences is something that literally everyone engages in almost constantly. A person takes one or more pieces of data, makes one or more assumptions about the nature of things (often unconsciously), and then draws a conclusion that is (more or less) logically consistent with the data and the assumption. When Mr. Jones arrives at his new boss's home (which he has never seen before) for dinner, he notices that it has a circular driveway, a six-car garage, tennis courts, and a stable. He preconsciously makes a number of assumptions (about the cost of such a home and its upkeep, his boss's salary, his boss's previous work history, and so on) and quickly concludes that his new boss (or his wife) comes from a wealthy family. When Ms. Johnson is introduced to the manager of the Chicago office, she notices that he has a slide-rule tie clasp, a calculator on his desk, and a set of proceedings of an electrical engineering society on his shelf. She infers privately that he has a technical background and orientation.

Although we all are, in some sense, familiar with this technique for making meanings out of data, few people consciously think about the process and about how they tend to engage in it. And most of us often use it in a casual and sloppy manner in dealing with the more inconsequential aspects of our daily activities. For purposes of self-assessment, such casualness is inappropriate. In order to achieve as accurate an assessment as possible, we need to be very careful about how we make inferences.

Drawing Inferences

Figures 1 and 2 display some of the tentative inferences that two people independently drew after studying the Written Interview of a third person (Ms. Jones), along with the data on which those inferences were based. Look at each carefully and see if you can see how they are different.

---

[1]To take an extreme example: an interview conducted after a person has been kept awake for 72 hours undergoing physical punishment will look noticeably different from one conducted under more normal circumstances. This problem of contextual influence exists with all of the data-generating instruments we will be using.

[2]Briefly, one can successfully deal with these problems by taking three precautions. We have taken the first precaution for you by selecting data-generating devices that have been tested and shown to be not very sensitive to random contextual influence. As a second step, when interpreting data from any particular device, you can simply take into account any peculiar conditions that existed when the data were generated. Third, and perhaps most important, you can simply be conservative in your analysis and never rely solely on one datum or on data from one instrument alone in drawing any conclusions of importance.

FIGURE 1   Some Inferences Made from Written Interview Data

Data	Inference
Ms. Jones graduated from Stanford with honors	She is clearly very intelligent
Ms. Jones' writing style is very loose	She is probably an unorganized person
Ms. Jones is an only child	She is probably achievement oriented, socially withdrawn, and very tense
Ms. Jones talks a lot about the people in her life	She is a very people oriented and popular person

FIGURE 2   Some Inferences Made from Written Interview Data

Data	Inference
The five periods in Ms. Jones' life which she says were the most "dull and boring" (see page 2, paragraph 2; page 10, paragraph 1; and page 14, paragraph 2) all have one thing in common—she is not in contact with any or many people.	Interacting with people is probably an important source of stimulation for Ms. Jones
The only "hard" quantitative subject Ms. Jones says she took in high school or college was math, and she says she didn't like it at all (see page 5, paragraph 1; and page 16, paragraph 2).	Ms. Jones does not have strong quantitative skills
The four people Ms. Jones lists as being "the most influential" in her life are: her father, her tenth-grade teacher, one of her summer job bosses, and her grandmother (page 20).	Ms. Jones probably relates well to authority figures and can be influenced by them
Ms. Jones grew up in a middle-class family and twice makes references to "not wanting to be poor" (see page 1, paragraphs 3 and 4; and page 30, paragraph 1).	Money is not unimportant to Ms. Jones

Most people would agree that the analysis in Figure 2 seems a lot sounder than that in Figure 1. That is not to say that the inferences in Figure 1 are wrong or the inferences in Figure 2 are correct. We really don't have enough information to make that judgment. But there are a number of differences between Figures 1 and 2 that tend to give one more confidence in Figure 2.

First of all, the "data" in Figure 2 are a lot clearer and more specific than those in Figure 1. Figure 2 states, with some precision, exactly what it is in Ms. Jones' written interview that has led to such inferences. Figure 1 is more vague in this regard. One is left wondering how much "a lot'' of talk about people is, and what is meant by a ''very loose writing style.'' Is it not possible that Ms. Jones' writing style is fairly typical, but the person who created the inference in Figure 1 has a very structured writing style—so that what is perhaps typical looks ''loose'' to such a person?

It is easy to lose sight of the actual data in a Written Interview, and end up analyzing, instead, your own impressions of the data. We've seen people who, after expressing a strong belief in the validity of a set of inferences, were unable to point to a single specific piece of supporting information in the Written Interview. They had been performing a reasonably interesting analysis—but it was based mostly on their own impressions, not on the specific information provided by the other person.

A second obvious difference between Figures 1 and 2 relates to a number of questionable assumptions. All inferences are based on one or more assumptions, but some can contain many more assumptions than others. Figure 2's inferences seem more reserved and conservative (and reasonable!) because they assume less.

To get from ''Ms. Jones is an only child'' to ''She is probably achievement oriented, socially withdrawn, and very tense,'' one has to assume a great deal. Of course, the inference could be true, but only if a large number of implicit assumptions are also true.[3] Even the first inference in Figure 1, which assumes a great deal less, is still based on at least the following assumptions:

1. That Ms. Jones really did graduate from Stanford *with* honors.
2. That ''intelligence'' is a definable, measurable human attribute.
3. That one's ''intelligence'' is fairly stable over time—it doesn't go up or down drastically in a month, for example.
4. That the ''intelligence'' one displays does not vary greatly from situation to situation or task to task.

---

[3] Very often when people develop inferences that seem to be based on a lot of assumptions, the reason is that they carry a ''model'' (often preconsciously) around with them based on their own experiences or something they were taught in school. For example, the person who inferred that because Jones is an only child she is socially withdrawn, tense, and achievement oriented could have been applying a model of child development learned in school. Such a model might be represented as:

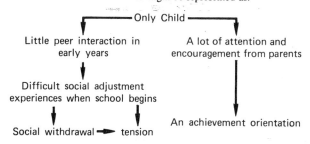

Such a simplified model of a complex phenomenon may be approximately true in some cases, but certainly not in all. Or then again, our data analyst might well have been an only child who had grown up socially withdrawn, tense, and achievement oriented! That is, the analyst could have been identifying with the data and projecting onto them without even being aware of what was happening. In either case, it would not be unusual for the analyst to believe the inference was ''obviously true'' and to vigorously defend it until forced to identify the assumptions implicit in the logic that led to the inference.

5. That to graduate with honors from Stanford, one *must be* intelligent. That is, that all the other possible explanations as to why one could graduate with honors (e.g., work hard, bribe the Dean) are impossible.

People often feel rather uncomfortable when forced to look at the assumptions implicit in their inferences. We often treat our inferences as if the assumptions were known truths, when they seldom are. All five of the assumptions implicit in the inference concerning Ms. Jones' intelligence have some probability of being accurate, but that possibility is significantly less than 1.0.

The more assumptions one makes that are not known truths, and the lower the probability that each of those assumptions is correct, the more one engages in what we might call an ''inferential leap.'' Starting with the datum about Ms. Jones graduating from Stanford, inferential leaps of various sizes are shown in Figure 3.

FIGURE 3 Inferential Leaps

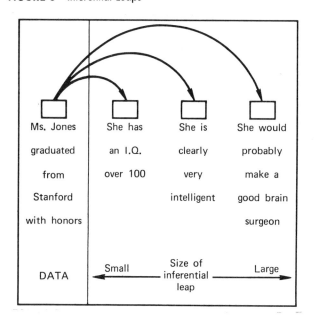

As that diagram implies, the larger the ''leap,'' the further it takes you from the data. Getting too far away from one's data can be dangerous in self-assessment.

A third difference between Figures 1 and 2 can be found in the nature of the data used. Figure 2 never starts with a single ''observation'' (such as ''Ms. Jones is an only child'') but with a number of observations that possibly identify a *pattern*. (''The five periods in Ms. Jones' life which she says were the most 'dull and boring' all have one thing in common . . .'') By starting with a set of data that possibly form a pattern, and by keeping the patterns relatively simple, the author in Figure 2 was able to draw nontrivial inferences without making a large number of questionable assumptions.

Perhaps the single most important part of analyzing a Written Interview involves looking for relatively simple patterns. Does the author of the interview repeatedly talk about any particular subject or person? Does the author always (or never) quantify things that can be measured? Does the author repeatedly use a certain type of verb or adjective?

Does the author always (or never) go into great detail in describing people? or objects? or events?

Through the identification of patterns we can really start to sort the peripheral and trivial from the more central and important. As any scientist recognizes, an event that occurs once tells us very little. But one that occurs again and again, in some pattern, may well tell us something central about whatever is being studied.

Identifying Patterns

Most people just "see" patterns—that is, the process of identification often occurs unconsciously. However, there are ways in which one can facilitate one's own preconscious processes. Understanding these can be helpful.

Perhaps the easiest technique to facilitate pattern identification is to underline or write on a separate sheet of paper anything that catches your attention when you read through the interview. On a second reading, you can begin to check more systematically whether some pattern is associated with any of those items.

Simple counting can be an important tool. If something "seems" to occur "a lot," count exactly how many times it does occur. You may find your "sense" was very accurate, or very inaccurate. In a similar vein, if something "seems" never to occur, carefully check that out. Does it really *never* occur?

Very speculative inferences (those based on lots of questionable assumptions), although not very useful as the product of an analysis, can occasionally be useful in the *process* of analysis. The major value of a highly speculative inference lies in its occasional capacity to point out an unseen pattern. Having made the inference, for example, that Ms. Jones is socially withdrawn, one might then notice *for the first time* how little she talks about her relationships with people in her Written Interview, and that she doesn't mention belonging to student organizations of any kind in high school or college. Or then again you might find just the opposite. In either case, the speculative inference led you to useful data that were previously unseen.

You will undoubtedly develop still other techniques yourself. Just keep in mind that pattern finding, like most good detective work, requires a combination of instinct, disciplined search, and time. And do not be surprised if, at first, you have some difficulty finding patterns. People often feel they don't know what to look for in the data, or

that they need a list of "typical patterns" to guide them.[4] Because most of us are better versed in deductive rather than inductive processes, such a response is natural in the beginning.

Recapitulation

In analyzing a Written Interview:

1. Stick closely to the data. Make sure you don't end up
2. Search for patterns. Remember that one datum alone tells you virtually nothing.
3. Be careful and explicit with your inferences. Make sure you are aware of your assumptions.
4. Treat all inferences as "tentative"—not as hard conclusions.
5. Try to be patient. Good analysis takes time.

analyzing something you've manufactured in your own head. "Let the data do the talking."

Exercise

On the next few pages you will find one person's responses to a Written Interview. This interview is typical of most Written Interviews we've seen, except that it is relatively short. To practice analyzing this type of material, we would suggest you do the following:

1. a. Read and study the replies to the first three questions only.
   b. Analyze just that portion of the interview.
2. a. Look at question 4, and try to guess how Murray will respond. Why have you guessed as you have?
   b. Look at Murray's response to question 4. How accurate or inaccurate were your speculations? Why? Draw any additional inferences you can from these new data.
3. Repeat steps 2a and 2b (above) with question and reply 5.
4. Read replies 6, 7, and 8. Analyze them.
5. Repeat steps 2a and 2b (above) with questions and replies 9, 10, and 11.
6. Now, do an analysis of the entire interview.

[4]There are literally an infinite number of patterns that are possible in a Written Interview. Creating a list of typical patterns is not possible.

Phillip Murray (A)

Question 1. For openers, we, your silent partners, need to hear something about the story of your life. As of this moment, we know nothing about you. What has happened to you thus far? What were the twists and turns in the winding road of your life?

What you are going to need is an account of your life more structured than free association, more personal than a resume or vita. The level of disclosure will be that of personal history—an overview of all those years' diaries that you didn't keep (or at least the parts suitable for public consumption).

Just let it flow. If you belatedly realize you've left something out, put it in when you think about it. This is a *rough* manuscript! Order and method come later.

How long should your story be? As long as it takes to tell. Although an autobiography is usually book length, you may be able to tell your story in the equivalent of a chapter or two.

Tell away!

Reply 1. The first years of my life all blend together somehow when thinking about significant events in my personal history. I grew up in a very close family—besides my parents, I have an older sister and a younger brother—and led a normal boy's life. My days were broken up with school, and after school I played stick ball in the school yard or "Ring o le vio" on the golf course. I think they were happy years—carefree mostly.

In junior high I learned about girls. I think it was in junior high also that I first showed signs that I was anything more than a C student. I had the opportunity to learn to play the violin and continued it through high school. Some of my proudest moments came playing the violin—in many orchestras and places—including Carnegie Hall.

In eighth grade I passed an admission test and went to Bronx High School of Science for ninth grade. It was a traumatic experience. The trip was an hour or more each way and turned out not to be worthwhile. I went there because I thought I wanted to be an engineer—a thought I did not put out of my head until second year of college.

The rest of my high school was spent at the local school—two blocks from my house—and all male. They too were good years, looking back. I was in all honor classes—yes, including language—and received what I consider to be a fairly good education. From my junior year on, though, school became a forum for all my activities. I was on the fencing team, wrote for the newspaper, acted in a play, was a representative to the N.Y.C. High School Press Council and a member of a religious youth group. In my senior year, I became head of *all* of those groups. I had all I could do to go to all of the meetings and prepare adequately. School became tenth priority.

Somehow I managed to make it through the year in one piece and graduated. I had been accepted to many schools. I decided to go to Europe for the summer. I didn't feel I was ready for college. My summer in Europe was fabulous!!

How can one describe in one paragraph what took scores of letters to tell about? I grew up a lot. I had my eyes opened by many things, but most of all, I think, by the different types of people in the world. I loved some and hated some. All in all, I prospered. The array of experiences I had could never be reproduced. I feel fortunate to have done it.

Coming back was hard—I had exactly 10 days to adjust before I was on my way to college. How weird everyone was there! It took quite a while to adjust, I remember. When I met people, I found myself really out of touch with what was going on. That changed quickly, though, and I was OK.

My first big setback in college was being turned down from the fraternity I really wanted. It was a crusher. I remember going to talk with a guy who was a good friend of the family. He was a senior and also a member of this fraternity. He took me in and we talked for hours. He convinced me to work for the all-campus musical—of which he was the chairman—and I did with all my heart. I got so into it, in fact, that during the second semester I almost flunked out. I managed to flunk 13 exams in a row and was pretty down and out. This also was the time, incidentally, that I gave up on engineering.

I ended up pulling the semester out of the bag by cramming for finals and pleading with teachers and went on to lead a distinguished average academic career. Activities were always more important than school, although I did

manage to learn a few things here and there. At the end of my freshman year I had done everything in the theatre group and tried to become the president. I was turned down—only being a freshman—for my second big defeat.

When I stopped brooding, I went to work on Homecoming, and managed to put together a parade for the next October. In the meantime, incidentally, I was accepted into the fraternity and ended up dying with it two years later. My whole college life could be measured by what activity I was working on. I always had to be doing something. Eventually, at the end of my junior year I was made Executive Vice-President of the Student Activities Council, and thus I reached the top. In this position I was kept busy 20–30 hours a week. School really suffered then.

Otherwise, college just went on. I had many close friends, got mildly into drinking, enjoyed going to concerts and demonstrations, and generally had a good time.

In my senior year I decided not to go to Med School, because that would be a huge commitment and I could not take that lightly. So I eliminated that. I took the LSAT and did well on it. I had written a book in my senior year, a book on the finances of nonprofit organizations, and that turned my thoughts to business school. That, plus my new girl.

I had a few connections at the business school of my Alma Mater, but one of the faculty of a more prestigious school was an alumnus of ours whom I had met during Homecoming committee work and he urged me to come there. It gave all my friends great grief! "Go to the West Point of Capitalism: It won't work with your life style. Look at the people who go there! Ech!"

Nevertheless, I spent two months chewing away at my application form and I was in agony another two months until I got the letter. They had let me in! So I decided to go.

The first day I was at business school—I always unpack my stereo the first thing, so I can have music while I'm unpacking—I had the real stuff going on the stereo and I was unpacking kind of dubiously when this guy runs in through the connecting door and says, "Thank God! It's good to know I have somebody here who shares my taste!" He became my best friend.

He helped. I found it unfathomable that so many people here my age were wholly unaware of the issues people were talking about: race, pollution, educational issues that I lived with. I laid into a number of them and I got into lots of trouble. I laid into professors, too. I'd ask them right out what they thought they were doing. I was ready to pack again the week before Thanksgiving but my friend told me to stick it out till the holiday and a chance to go home. So I stuck it out till Christmas and I made it through the rest of the year.

I'm happy I did. I've made a lot of close friends. We work together and play together. Once we knew how to do all the cases every night, it got better. I did well, though not so well as I wanted to. I didn't put in the hours to get honors. Some of the work made no sense for me to do it.

My second year here may turn out to be the best year of my life. A bunch of us took an apartment and really made it into a home. We got good furniture. There is a fireplace. The apartment has a formal dining room and we all sit down to a proper dinner five nights a week. Each night one guy cooks. We have tried some pretty exotic recipes! We have a "wine cellar" that might just be the best in town. After dinner we sit and talk. It is the way a fraternity ought to be.

School has even been good. It is more like living, to have more interesting topics coming up in the school day and after school to go home to a home, lie on the rug in front of the fireplace, eat a good meal, and talk.

Question 2. How late did you start your story? Most people get themselves born and then jump to age twenty, when they began their official "career." In a resumé, you would lump all the distant past into a few lines under "miscellany," but if you want to collect the facts that you'll need later to analyze your own career path, you should fill in some of the things that went on back before you were an adult.

Not that we care if you fell in love with your rocking horse at the age of four. But if your story begins with "I graduated from Michigan and . . . ," it probably leaves out some facts that are both public and pertinent—such as the years of secondary school. Or even primary school, at least its name and nature. Or early avocations. (Chemists and engineers receive their calling before their puberty.) Or those most cordially hated activities imposed by the community on the readily turned-off young. Or . . . you tell us. This is your life.

What else went on back there?

Set aside your rambling account of your life from Question 1 and go ahead and write some more about the beginning of your life story.

Unless you've already said all that need be said. If so, go on to the next question.

Reply 2. My first four years of school, I went to a parochial school. I was immediately segregated from my friends in the neighborhood. Although school was OK, I didn't like it. I remember so clearly one evening telling my father who was reading the paper, "Dad, I really don't like going away to school. I want to go to public school." He said OK, and I went to the public school the next year.

It took me a long time to adjust, to get back in the social swing. When I did, life was between the school and the playground and the golf course. We'd be out playing from morning to dark.

In school, I did not excel. I did not show my potential. Teachers kept telling my parents that they thought I had potential but I did not show it.

In junior high, I discovered the violin and that was important. I learned a lot fast, and played in a lot of orchestras. We even played one concert in Carnegie Hall!

I took the test to go to Bronx High School of Science. There were thousands of guys there, all with fairly good I.Q.s. I worked to meet the challenge and did very well but the ride was too much. By the time I got home it was dark.

Back at the nearby high school, I did OK. The real thing was that it was just very close to home. My sister and brother went there. I just really enjoyed being home and talking when we were all home together, all sitting down to dinner. My dad worked very close by, so he was always home for dinner. He regarded that as important.

I got into activities and organizations right from the beginning. I studied enough but that didn't occupy time

enough. I always wanted to do other things, extracurricular ones.

Question 3. Please fill in the cracks. Maybe you already have, but if you did you are unusually thorough. People's lives are full of temporariness. What went on during your summers? Was there a two-month gap between graduation and a first job? Did those four years at school include one spent abroad? Were there jobs that filled your evenings or weekends?

These odds and ends of living often teach lessons that matter. They often contain data you can use now, even though you saw no relevance in the experience back then.

Please set aside Question 2 and write some bits and pieces about the little odds and ends of living that got tucked in between the major activities that you already have described.

Of course, if you have already covered everything, you won't have much work to do for this step in our conversation.

Reply 3. I did things on my own very early. In the fourth grade, I went down to the UN on my own and did a research report. In junior high, I got a job delivering newspapers. It was a little route but there would be those days when it would snow and my dad would say, "No matter what, you're going outside!"

I started living in my present form when I changed to public school and I had the time to do all the other things I wanted to do. I lived just a block from the high school. I played sports at school. I wrote for the newspaper. I acted in the school play. I got into a Young People's Group that took a lot of time. We'd go to conventions on weekends and have seminars and things. Meetings were twice a week and there were committees. I was also on the fencing team.

My summers have basically been taken up with camp since I was eight. I went to several camps. I was a counselor later.

The summer I went to Europe was a real turning point. For the first time, I got into thinking about myself in terms of what others might think of me, people who were living a different kind of life from ours.

It was a well-organized program. The first weeks we studied languages and customs. Then we traveled a bit. I wrote home stacks of letters about all the things we saw. Then we had a sponsor family and lived with them. My "father and mother" were not affluent; my "father" showed up to pick me up in a horse and cart! But we lived right on a lovely lake. We'd work mornings in the fields, starting very early, then afternoons swim or just be on the lake and at four o'clock get together for tea and talk. I just loved it. It was an easy life. (I had a girl too, and that was nice.)

For the first time I started really reading. I'd read three books a week.

The last few weeks, everyone was supposed to go out and do some volunteer work or something. I got a paying job. I'd always thought I wanted to be an engineer, for some reason. I liked mechanical drawing. I got into things like chemistry and physics. (That's why I'd tried Bronx High

School of Science.) So I got a job with an architect. My boss was a pistol; he even gave me some lessons in scuba diving!

My first college summer was spent in the back office of a Wall Street house. I worked on the OTC Desk. The people were nice and I got along very well. I was able to live at home. It was a fairly good summer.

When I went back to school, I dropped out of engineering. That was quite a thing for me. It meant I had to change from the Engineering School to the Liberal Arts College. I had quite a time convincing two deans that I knew what I was doing. I just wanted to get into things like history and political science.

My sophomore summer, I worked for a brokerage firm in California. I worked in the cage as a trouble-shooter. I thought it was weird that people who had been there ten years didn't know what to do or even where the cage was. I knew more than they did in four weeks! I found out where the cage was and how it worked and saw that something had to be done. They had five million dollars in shorts. In three weeks I had found four and a half million and cleaned up those. They were amazed.

My junior summer I went back to camp. I taught a bunch of young boys in a gorgeous camp in the White Mountains. It was a nice summer. I went back there the next summer too.

Question 4. Talk a little, if you already haven't, about the people in your life. At least the public facts. Was Uncle Louie a graduate of this school? A drop-out? What has become of your brothers and sisters? Did your mother work, or go to school? What was your spouse doing before you married? How have you two arranged your lives since then? And your friends, what of them?

All these are data—later on, you will make use of them. We beg no conclusions about how, or even whether, all these folks mattered. But they were there.

Put them in the picture.

Reply 4. Earlier, there was my family. I could write on and on about my parents. The two were different and they built their differences into me.

My dad expressed his love by doing things with me—going to see the Mets or to football or basketball games or coming out and playing with us, doing Little League, etc. He had lots of time. His business didn't take all of it. He was very giving of himself.

My mother expressed her love by being helpful to us in school. Sometimes she was too "helpful." She'd get uptight about correcting all our homework. But she was the one we'd go to with big problems, like when a friend wasn't nice to us or something.

My sister and I were very close. We didn't do much together because we each had our school friends but we could talk to each other. As we got older, I got closer to my brother because we could play ball together. The whole family was close. Of course, when my sister grew up and went to college, we were no longer close.

I really liked my dad's family. He had a sagacious father, whom I just liked listening to.

Friends were very important. I had lots of them and we did all sorts of things together, sports and other things. As I grew older, my family became less central and my friends became more important because I was doing more things with them. I never had a *lot* of friends. None of my friends now are ones I used to run with as a kid.

I used to be able to become friends with teachers. I could get through the student-teacher relationship and really talk with them as people.

The other people that mattered to me were the people in various organizations.

Question 5. What about the future? Of course, that's the question we are both laboring to answer, but what reading do you take of your future now? Perhaps you've already said. If you haven't, please do. Or state the ins and outs of your uncertainty.

One subquestion surely deserves your attention: What future would be *ideal?* If all went as well as possible, what would be the Happy Ending?

Or maybe you could dream of more than one? Or more than two?

Reply 5. One thing is the image of a home life in the future, having a happy home and happy family, that whole thing. I also believe that what will make me happiest is having a vocation that I can really see, that I will really enjoy. You can do the scut work on any job if the general scene is right.

I do think that's possible! If I keep thinking about it steadily enough, I'll get to that point.

The immediate future is that I want to go to work right away. I've been to Europe and I've worked on the other side of the U.S.A. There's not much point in traveling this summer. I almost feel like my whole life has been a vacation and it's time to go to work.

I am developing two offers on Wall Street. One is with a big house that does nothing but institutional sales and is a hugely successful money machine. There I'd be doing corporate financing. The other offer is with a less well-known house of good quality. They want me as an administrative assistant to the vice-president in charge of operations.

I've talked to everyone who will listen to me about these two choices. Eveyone except one man says I should take the first company: they are the comers who have been growing like crazy; they pay extravagantly; everyone knows their name. My father says I could work for them 10 years and be rich enough to go do whatever I wanted to. Everyone in my class envies me for having the offer. Except the few guys who also do. The trouble is, I don't like those guys much. Generally speaking, I'm not sold on corporate finance types: they're pretty stuffy and ignorant of what is going on around them. There's one I know in class and from having some lunches together who also has an offer. I may rent an uptown apartment with him.

The one adviser who tells me not to take the first offer is one of my professors. He listened to me at length when I told him about my two offers and when I stopped talking he just laughed! He said that it was simple: I clearly had moved away from things and toward people.

I don't know. I've told both companies I want one more interview before I decide.

Question 6. If we read back over the exchanges in your written interview, we surely can find a series of moments when your situation changed. You left secondary school to go to college, college to go to graduate school, or to work, which at a later moment you left to go to graduate school. You may have entered one or another of the Armed Services, from which you subsequently departed, presumably making a decision not to stay when your hitch was over. Perhaps during your college years you transferred, took a year elsewhere, or dropped out. Or simply changed major field. At the very least, you picked a summer job or school or vacation spot. Some of these changes were in good part forced on you. Each put you into a new situation.

Before we go on with our written exchanges, please go back over your story and pick out these points of change. Make a list of them. Add some others we haven't discussed, if others now occur to you. This list will be the backbone of our discussion as we continue our written interview.

Reply 6

A Look Back—Requested List

From parochial school to elementary school.
From there to junior high.
*From junior high to Bronx High School of Science.
*From there back to high school.
*From there to Europe.
*From Europe to Engineering School.
*From Engineering to Liberal Arts.
*From there to the Business School.
And now.

That's a long list. I'll discuss particularly the ones I've starred.

Question 7. Even though you may have said something about them before, there is much to be learned by talking at greater length and in a more systematic way about the turning points you have listed.

For instance, at each point there were other options. Even in situations in which you thought you had no choice at all, in all likelihood you did. Maybe you applied only to one college; even so, what others did you consider? Did you have more than one acceptance? One's major field is not usually the one and only possibility ever thought about.

Please tell us about your discarded options. Go back systematically and write an account of how it looked back there at each of those times just before your road forked.

What were for you the paths not taken?

Reply 7. I could have stayed in the regular high school instead of going to Bronx High School of Science. I could

have stayed at B.H.S.S. afterwards. I was doing all right there.

If I hadn't gone to Europe I would probably have gone back to one of the camps as a counselor.

The choice of Ohio State was one of several possible universities that had both engineering schools and colleges of liberal arts. I eliminated M.I.T. and other places like that because they didn't offer the liberal arts option if I wanted to take it later. I could have gone to N.Y.U. but that would have been just like more of high school. I wanted to go away to a campus. I had friends who'd gone to Ohio and liked it.

There was really no option about changing to liberal arts. For me, that was an idea whose time had come. I just had to sell the deans on that idea.

Business school was at first a choice made by eliminating medicine and law. This school was chosen over Ohio State mostly on the basis of people I knew here and on its reputation for excellence even though it was really put down by all my friends in college.

Question 8. You may already have mentioned them, but it would be useful to review more thoroughly and to collect in one discourse the pros and cons that led to each of these decisions. The real reasons and the official reasons. Yours and other people's.

It usually wasn't entirely simple. "Why did you come to this school?" may evoke a blank stare and an astonished "Where else?" from some of us—but most of us can say a lot more. "My father got in and never had enough money to come and that influenced me a little, I guess, but the main reasons were what I wanted to get out of it for myself." Or, "The fact that my husband came from this part of the country was part of it," or "I liked what I saw when I visited. . . ." All these things can be threads in the story behind a decision—even one so apparently obvious. Thin threads, perhaps. You tell us what were the main ones.

Please write, then, a full description of the warp and woof from which *each* of your decisions was woven. (In part, you may want to refer back to what you've already said; in part, there's probably also more to each little story.) What were the important parts of the tale, what the trivial, as you look back now on the way it was spun?

Reply 8. The move to Bronx High School of Science was made even though all my friends were going to the local high school and so were all the people who played with me in the orchestras. I had always had the idea of becoming an engineer. So I took the test. When I passed, that was an honor. (I had not done so well in science in school.) It was a prestige school. My parents left the decision up to me, so I went.

Reversing the decision was easier. I just hadn't realized the effect commuting would have in eating up my time. I was not really living. I had no friends. I was missing things. I had nothing to do except science. The local high school had a good reputation academically. Besides, the education at B.H.S.S. was not all that exceptional. I would be getting more out of school if I went back.

I very much wanted to go to Europe. I'd been brainwashed by lots of friends who were going and who had gone on the same program the year before. They said it was a fun summer.

I really had to work to convince my parents. It was the one and only thing they were ever very much against. I finally got the tour manager to talk to them. I'm glad I did. I came back so much more mature.

I came back into the Engineering School and died! After that culture shock, I was once again doing physics, math, graphics and something or other called "Engineering English"! It was just a little choking. I wanted history and political science. That was one reason I put my energies into other activities instead of my courses. After a while I just had to face that engineering was not it. I wanted some humanities and they were going to allow me just eight electives in four years in engineering. I called "Time Out"!

So the decision was easy to make. I just had to have time to live. Convincing the deans to OK the transfer was the big problem. I wound up as an Ec. major, though I thought of philosophy and history. I took a lot of them and got just a generally good education. Useless, but good.

Choosing a graduate school was a hard decision. It was just sort of known that this one was about the best, but it also just blew the minds of my friends, who had a lot to say about the type of people who go to this school or who go into business. They couldn't see me conforming and being a company man. It seemed as though it would go against my grain.

But I wanted the best. I thought that if I was not happy I could go to work.

I had eliminated medicine and law and was going to go to work. So I wanted to learn to do it well. I felt I wouldn't want to go into a big corporation or maybe not even to be in a business, but I knew I wanted to administer—I'd been doing that in an amateur way—and I might as well learn how to do it right. Whatever I was going to administer, I would do it better and make a lot more money with an M.B.A. That's what it boiled down to.

Question 9. After each of these turning points, what was the transition like? What new things had saliency? How was the living different than it had been before? What new things stood out for you?

External circumstances presumably differed in obvious ways. A dormitory is not the same as your own home. But the point is, what changed *for you?* Was there in some ways a new you? More subtly, was there a new texture of living?

Perhaps a further question would be: are there any pieces of each of these new stages in your past life still living in you today?

Reply 9. The change after I got to Bronx High School of Science was that my life was no longer my own. I liked school, but I couldn't take getting home after it was too dark to do anything. I felt really lost. I was becoming a loner.

When I came back, at first I had a lot of void time but then the void time got taken up by activities as I reestablished relationships. I had friends, but then something else happened. I found my life again changing in that I was doing all these things but the people weren't that important because I was so busy that I didn't have time to spend reestablishing relationships with people.

That was a revelation!

In those two or three years I had only two or three close friends and they were not geographically close. One was over in Jersey, one up in Queens. I saw them once a week or once every two weeks. The people right around me were no longer very important to me.

My mother used to complain, "Why can't you find anybody right around home?" She meant especially girls.

I've told you about Engineering School. When I got over into liberal arts I had a reawakening and I was very close to a number of people. I was also a lot more aware of myself and aware of my interests. I began to read. I'd go into the bookstore and come out with 11 books. The bookstore lady thought I was some kind of a book nut and she even began giving me a discount!

Coming back from Europe was quite an adjustment. I saw things in American culture and society that I really did not like. Things people did and said and ways people acted. I found I consciously went about finding the people I could get along with, who believed like I believed.

I became more aware of my ability to do things and my ability to be independent. In some way, I was trying to collate people with things and somehow bring the two together so I wouldn't have to do one to the exclusion of the other. I was not entirely conscious of it, then, but it definitely was a pattern. That did not happen until I got to business school.

I've told you about how bad my first year here was and how my second year has been really excellent.

Question 10. What disillusionments did you suffer? Can you recall your expectations about college, or the Army, or a job and how these expectations contrasted with the event? Perhaps you were utterly realistic in advance—if so, that is a datum about you well worth recording!

Please cast your mind back—as you have already been doing—and set aside your 20-20 hindsight long enough to recreate what you (perhaps vaguely) thought each situation was going to be like before you confronted it, then how it in fact turned out. Perhaps your expectations were dead wrong, perhaps they were right on target. Likely there were aspects of the new situation that would never have occurred to you even in your wildest imaginings!

At any rate, please try a little retrospect on the before and after views of each listed event. Perhaps even a table is indicated: As Seen Before and After. But a little narrative will serve.

The emphasis here is on cognitive awareness, not on values. Did you know the facts?

Reply 10. I've already told you about what happened when I got to Bronx High School of Science.

Europe was in some ways a surprise. I had thought about it before I did it more than any other step I took. When I finally went, I was full of romantic expectations. It turned out that people here were just like people there, all struggling their way through life, all having their problems and not romantic figures at all. But Europe was also better in a lot of ways. I liked the idea of finding that everything was not as idealistic as I'd thought but only regular. I came out not nearly as idealistic. That was kind of cool.

College was different, too. As I've said. I thought I had a

lot going on before college but there I had no time to breathe! I found myself using my time all up. There was no laying in front of the fire. That was disappointing.

Graduate school has been worse than expected. Except for the status thing, it was disappointing. I had the overriding feeling that they were treating me like a child. I was going to a graduate school and I was supposed to be a graduate student now. Why did they have to say things like, "We can't give you a reading assignment because you can't do it and three cases"? Or, "There will be no class Friday, so you can do your WAC"? If I am interested, I will do it, anyhow. They don't have to regiment me.

They create work by fear. I resent an institution run so that you work because of fear; fear of being called on by the professor, fear of a quiz. They always talk about a "Pop Quiz." The idea is that otherwise you would concentrate all your work on one course.

As I've told you, I have found a way to make the second year much better.

Question 11. By now you must be aware of some repetition in what you've been saying. There probably are themes. In the past you have been basing your actions on certain kinds of considerations. What patterns do *you* see?

If you want to be systematic, you can make some tables showing the plus and minus factors—and perhaps also their weight—in each decision. What entries recur? Can you conceptualize a factor underlying apparently distinct entries? If you arrange the decisions chronologically, do the entries evolve with time?

This last point is of special interest, since being able to observe yourself acting as if you held consistent values and beliefs is one thing and deciding to base your next decision on these same considerations is quite another. There are two sides to a career: where it has been and where it is going.

Can the array of ins and outs of your actions in the past reveal to you something of the direction of time's arrow?

Reply 11. [Phillip Murray gave no answer to this question.]

IV

The AVL Study of Values

```
NOTE:
DO NOT READ THIS UNTIL YOU HAVE COMPLETED THE
AVL STUDY OF VALUES ASSIGNMENT IN THE WORKBOOK
```

The AVL Study of Values is a forced-choice questionnaire that asks you to indicate your personal preferences on 45 different questions. Originally published in 1931, it has been updated and refined on several occasions so that today it is still generally accepted as an instrument providing very interesting and useful information about a person. The instrument's output is a profile of the relative strengths of six "values" within you. These values are labeled: (a) theoretical, (b) economic, (c) aesthetic, (d) social, (e) political, and (f) religious. Each of these labels has a specific meaning, somewhat different from their everyday definitions, which you must thoroughly understand in order to use the data.

The Six Labels

Writing in 1921, Edward Spranger, a professor of Philosophy and Pedagogy at the University of Berlin, set out to develop, in a lengthy treatise, the "ideally basic types of individuality." The product of his philosophizing was six ideal types, which he called "Lebensformen" (life forms). The values involved were defined by Allport[1] as follows.

Theoretical

The dominant interest of the "ideal" theoretical person is the *discovery of truth*. In the pursuit of this goal a "cognitive" attitude is characteristically taken, one that looks for identities and differences, one that divests itself of judgments regarding the beauty or utility of objects, and seeks

only to observe and to reason. Since the interests of the theoretical person are empirical, critical, and rational, that person is necessarily an intellectualist, frequently a scientist or a philosopher. The person's chief aim in life is to order and to systematize knowledge.

Economic

The "ideal" economic person is characteristically interested in what is *useful*. Based originally upon the satisfaction of bodily needs (self-preservation), the interest in utilities develops to embrace the practical affairs of the business world—the production, marketing, and consumption of goods; the elaboration of credit; and the accumulation of tangible wealth. This type of person is thoroughly "practical" and conforms well to the prevailing conception of the average American business person.

Aesthetic

The aesthetic person sees *form and harmony* as the highest value. Each single experience is judged from the standpoint of grace, symmetry, or fitness. Life is regarded as a manifold of events; each single impression is enjoyed for its own sake. This person need not be a creative artist, nor need he or she be effete. Aesthetic here defines one who finds chief interest in the artistic episodes of life.

Social

The highest value for this ideal type is *love of people*, whether of one or many, whether conjugal, filial, friendly, or philanthropic. The social person prizes other persons as ends in themselves and is therefore kind, sympathetic, and unselfish.

---

[1] G. Allport, *Pattern and Growth in Personality*, 2d ed. (New York: Holt, Rinehart and Winston, 1961), pp. 279–299.

✓ Political

The political individual is interested primarily in *power*—not necessarily within the narrow field of politics. Whatever the vocation, such a person is seen as a Machtmensch (i.e., a powerful or power-oriented person). Leaders in any field generally have high power value. Since competition and struggle play a large part in all life, many philosophers have seen power as the most universal and most fundamental of motives. There are, however, certain personalities in whom the desire for a direct expression of this motive is uppermost, who wish above all else for personal power, influence, and renown.

Religious

The highest value for the religious person may be called *unity*. Mystical and seeking to comprehend the cosmos as a whole, this individual tends to relate to an embracing totality. Spranger defines the religious person as one "whose mental structure is permanently directed to the creation of the highest and absolutely satisfying value experience." Some people of this type are "immanent mystics"; that is, they find their religious experience in the affirmation of life and in active participation therein. A Faust with his zest and enthusiasm sees something divine in every event. The "transcendental mystic," on the other hand, seeks to unite with a higher reality by withdrawing from life. Such a person is the ascetic and, like the holy men of India, finds the experience of unity through self-denial and meditation.

The Instrument's Design

The authors of the Study of Values sought to create an instrument that would measure the relative strength of these six "values" within an individual. To do so, they identified a large number of famous people, activities, attitudes, and professions that most people tend to associate primarily with *one* of the Lebensformen. For example, mathematics, scientific apparatus, and Galileo were associated with the Theoretical value, while Beethoven, the color and pageantry of ceremonies, and *Arts and Decoration* magazine were associated with the Aesthetic value.

With an equal number of items to represent each of the "values," the authors constructed a series of questions that require the test taker to show a preference among a set of items, each representing a different value. The questions are designed so that if a person has no real preference between the "Social" items and the "Economic" items, the final scores on those two values will end up the same. If the person does have a preference, that value will have a higher score. The stronger the preference relative to the other values, the higher the score.

To accurately interpret a set of AVL scores, it is important to look "inside" the test at the items the authors have selected to represent each value. Most have face validity, but some don't. The religious items in the test booklet, for example, mostly have to do with valuing the rituals and artifacts of institutionalized religion (which is different from Allport's definition of the religious value). Similarly, the items in the Social scale emphasize one aspect of the broadly described social Lebensform—a concern for

the welfare of others, for altruism or philanthropy. These are essential ingredients of the broader social value system, but not the only ingredients. An understanding of these nuances can help you to get more out of the data supplied by the AVL.

Levels of Values

In reference to the Study of Values profile, Allport has remarked:

> The profile gives only the relative importance of the six values within the single life. No absolute levels can be inferred. In fact, the lowest value of a person who has high "value energy" might, in absolute terms, be more dynamic in his or her life than the highest value of a person who is generally apathetic and devoid of interest. The construction of the scale by the forced-choice method precludes the measurement of absolute magnitudes.[2]

That is, the Study of Values test is intended to bring to the surface the consistencies of pattern *within you*. It is not, in the usual overtones of the word, a psychological test. You are not being measured against a standard.

In Figure 1, for example, Jones and Smith both score 53 on Theoretical. This means that they both selected the theoretical option instead of one of the other five with the same relative frequency when taking the test. These identical scores are not, however, "equal" in the sense of their absolute value. Smith may well value theoretical concerns much more than Jones. Indeed, he might well value everything more than Jones, but the test itself can't tell us that. All the test tells us about the level of Jones' 53 score on Theoretical is that it is higher than his own 48 on Political, 42 on Aesthetic, and so on.

In short, what your Values Profile records is the answer to the question, "Given two or more alternatives, which did

FIGURE 1

	Jones' Profile	Smith's Profile
60		
55	— (53) Theoretical	— (53) Theoretical
50	— (48) Political	
45		— (43) Political
	— (42) Aesthetic	— (42) Aesthetic
40	— (39) Economic	
35		— (36) Economic — (35) Religious
30	— (30) Religious — (28) Social	— (31) Social
25		

[2]*Op. cit.*, p. 456.

you fairly consistently prefer?'' That is what a "value" is: an enduring and pervasive preference. Such beliefs are often strong enough to influence how one acts.

Interpreting the Profile

With a clear understanding of the meaning of the six values, of the absence of data on the absolute level of the values, and of the basic method of drawing inferences that we have used before in the previous chapter, interpreting an AVL profile is easy. Two profiles are shown in Figure 2.

In the first (A), we see that five of the six values cluster closely together. Only one value, aesthetic, clearly differentiates itself in a lower position. We might reasonably infer that this person does not, in decision making, consistently select either a "pragmatic" option, or a "moral" option, or one that pursues "truth," or "power." Indeed we might, very tentatively, expect that this person balances his or her choices fairly evenly over such options when faced with either/or choices. [It is tempting to infer that the pragmatic (economic) and moral (religious) options will receive more than equal attention, but it is questionable whether a four-point difference in scores (Economic = 43, Social = 39) is really significant.] One might also reasonably infer that this person's behavior and life are not highly aesthetic, relative to other standards.

Each of these inferences raises questions that can be checked against other data. Given this last inference, for example, what might you expect person A's Written Interview to look like? What type of activities would you expect such a person not to have participated in during high school and college? What about his or her hobbies? Your answers to these questions are clearly quite speculative, but they can be useful in the detective work of self-assessment.

Person B's profile is more highly differentiated. We see there a clearer first choice (Religious) and second choice (Social). We would expect that to be reflected in his or her behavior. As opposed to person A, we might infer that person B will more consistently choose a "religious" or "social" option over others.

In B's Written Interview, we might tentatively expect to

find relatively few activities directed toward the accumulation of power and wealth. While it is difficult even to guess whether person B went to college, if this person did, we would be surprised if he or she majored in engineering.

While we could make more inferences about persons A and B based on their AVL data, usually what we can say from AVL data alone is limited—and that's how it should be. Inferences to be drawn from the AVL alone are quite speculative. Yet the data can be valuable if used cautiously. AVL data can lead one to raise questions that otherwise would have been ignored. Such questions might help one discover something in other data sources that, until then, were not seen. AVL data can also be useful in supporting (or not supporting) tentative themes developed from other sources, particularly the Written Interview.

Group Norms

Although there is danger in comparing one individual AVL profile with another, a knowledge of group norms nevertheless can be useful in helping one get a feel for the information a profile is providing and how to interpret it. The two profiles A and B are not, in fact, those of single individuals. Profile A is an average score for 5,894 college men who took this test during the 1950s and 1960s. Profile B is the average score for 2,425 college women who took the test during the same period. All available evidence suggests that if the test were given to a large sample of college students today, the norms would be somewhat different, especially for the women. Do these profiles fit your image of the average male and female college student before 1970? Why? Why not?

In Figure 3 we show three more "average" profiles, all for business school students. Look them over carefully. Do they seem reasonable? Surprising? What common-sense inferences might you draw from these data about business school students?

Interpreting Your Own Profile

When interpreting your own profile, if some relatively high or low score doesn't make sense, go back to the test booklet and read the items that went into making that particular score. What aspect of yourself were you expressing when you gave those responses? The test booklet allows you to do your own value content analysis by attempting to break down the six basic values into subvalue scales.

If you find yourself reacting strongly to a particular score or the test itself, be sure to make a note of this. Your own reactions can be used later as data from which to draw inferences about yourself. Every little piece of information is potentially useful in this complex process.

Exercise

On the following page is Phillip Murray's AVL Profile. You can approach it with the procedure used previously:

1. Guess what the profile might look like. Be explicit about the basis of your guesses.
2. Examine the profile carefully. What does it mean? How does it support or not support the picture of Phillip Murray you created with your analysis of the Written Interview?

FIGURE 2

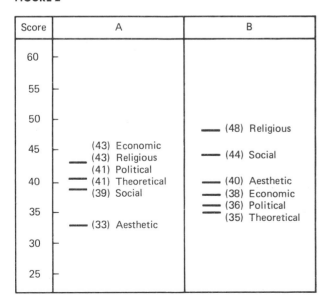

Score	A	B
60		
55		
50		— (48) Religious
45	(43) Economic (43) Religious	— (44) Social
40	(41) Political (41) Theoretical (39) Social	— (40) Aesthetic — (38) Economic — (36) Political (35) Theoretical
35		
	— (33) Aesthetic	
30		
25		

FIGURE 3

Score	508 Harvard Business School students (all men) (pre-1970)	173 students of Business Administration at Boston University (pre-1970)	72 Harvard Business School students in 1973 (66 men, 6 women)
60			
55			
50		─── (50) Economic	
45	─── (47) Economic ─── (44) Political	─── (44) Political	─── (46) Economic ─── (45) Political
40	─── (41) Theoretical ─── (39) Religious	═══ (40) Religious ═══ (39) Theoretical (38) Social	─── (41) Social ─── (39) Theoretical ─── (37) Aesthetic
35	─── (35) Aesthetic ─── (34½) Social		
30		─── (29) Aesthetic	─── (32) Religious
25			

Phillip Murray (B)

Profile of Values

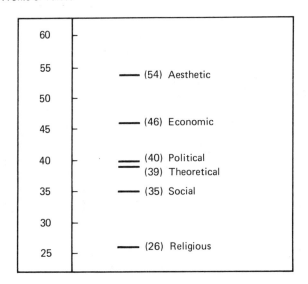

V

The 24-Hour Diary

NOTE:
DO NOT READ THIS UNTIL YOU HAVE COMPLETED THE
24-HOUR DIARY ASSIGNMENT IN THE WORKBOOK

As social scientists have discovered over the years, one useful way to learn about a person or a group of people is to obtain information regarding what they actually do on a daily basis. What type of activities do they engage in? How do they allocate their time among job, family, entertainment, sleep, and other activities? Who do they interact with, in what ways, and how often?

Even in situations that are highly structured by others (e.g., the Army), or on the most "atypical" days, the way in which an individual adapts and behaves says something about him or her. Regardless of the setting, we are always faced with choices regarding what to do, how to do it, and when. Patterns in those choices can tell us something about ourselves.

There are a number of different ways one can collect information about an individual's daily activities, but most are not useful for our purposes. An anthropological methodology, for example, in which a second "observer" follows the individual throughout the day, is impractical. Simply asking a person what he or she does on a daily basis is practical, but research has shown it to be not very reliable. People's impressions of what they normally do are often quite inaccurate.

A method we have found that is both feasible and reasonably reliable asks an individual to keep a log or diary of his or her activities throughout the day. It is not very difficult or time-consuming to pause every hour or so and to make a few notes regarding what you have been doing. (The entries do not have to be particularly lengthy.) Most people can remember in some detail what they have been doing for the past hour or two. While this method loses the "objectivity" of a second-person observer, it gains an additional type of

useful information. As with the Written Interview, one cannot record everything. Consequently, what a person chooses to record and how it is recorded becomes potentially useful information in itself.

Interpreting a 24-Hour Diary

A self-recorded diary can be treated for our purposes exactly like a Written Interview.[1] Taking into account how and why it was created, you can examine a 24-hour diary for patterns, and draw inferences from those patterns. You can also examine a diary for evidence to support themes that have emerged from other sources.

As in the case of the Written Interview, a large number of different types of patterns might be found. For example, some diaries have all their entries recorded at regular intervals (perhaps every 30 minutes), while others don't. Some diaries make entries at very specific times (e.g., 5:47, 8:54, 10:01), while others don't (e.g., 10:00, 10:15, 11:40). Some diaries will be full of human interaction. Others won't. A few might describe each person mentioned in the diary in great detail. Some won't mention any names. Some diaries are recorded in short cryptic phrases, while others read like a novel. Some describe an incredibly fast-moving, active person. Others don't. Some describe people who sleep exactly eight hours a night (invariably 11:30 P.M. to

---

[1] Although, obviously, it won't be nearly as rich a source of data as the Written Interview. Like the AVL, this device is most useful in corroborating or contradicting themes that have emerged elsewhere.

7:30 A.M.). Some describe people who jump from one activity to another, while others describe people who concentrate on one thing until the task is completed. And so on.

By identifying patterns in a diary and drawing careful inferences from those patterns, you can corroborate or contradict themes that have emerged in other sources, as well as identify new themes. All that is needed is some time, patience, and a modicum of skill.

Exercise

To help you develop some skill in using 24-hour diaries, we have included, on the following pages, the diaries of three different individuals. Study each of them carefully. What might those people be like? What types of jobs might they like?

Jon Williams

3:55 pm	Typed up handwritten comments on my life style and turned in copy.
4:30 pm	Ran two and a half miles, stretched, and took a shower.
5:30 pm	Studied Service Operations case while cooling down and letting hair dry.
6:00 pm	Dinner with Timothy Plain and Jim Falcone, discussed how students are motivated to study and how they decide the amount of time to commit.
6:45 pm	Watched news on Mideast and Watergate affair, ate an apple.
7:00 pm	Read and completed analysis of Service Operations case, Victoria Station Inc.
8:30 pm	Read first section of case for Marketing Mgt.
9:00 pm	Break for cookies and ice cream.
9:15 pm	Completed study first of two cases for Marketing.
10:10 pm	Studied second of two cases for Marketing.
10:40 pm	Rapped with roommate about Thanksgiving break plans and upcoming papers due.
11:00 pm	Continued study of second marketing case.
11:30 pm	Slept.
7:30 am	Woke up, showered, dressed and to Serv. Ops.
8:30 am	Management of Service Operations class.
9:50 am	Light brunch.
10:10 am	Completed reviewing appendix surveys for marketing.
10:30 am	Perused today's *Wall Street Journal*.
11:00 am	Chatted with roommate about something happening in his class and wrote out some thoughts on General Foods case.
11:30 am	Marketing Management class.
12:50 pm	Listened to professor chat with students after class.
1:05 pm	Lunch, alone.
1:40 pm	Begin reading Business Policy case for Thursday.
2:05 pm	Typed out this diary.
2:30 pm	Self-Assessment and Career Development class.

Stephie Rosenbloom

4:00 pm	Left Self-Assessment. Bopped down to Course Material Supply Room. Ran into Irv and got my creature contact (lots of nice pats while walking through the library). Dumped my overdue consumer behavior paper in Scott's office.
	Went to bookstore, ran into Jimmy Losick who told me Dick Nelson wanted to talk about the communication course I'm trying to develop. Ran into Jim Lane and Mac, talked about Danny Kirsch. Volunteered to go see him and Evelyn. Back to room. Beer. Reflected on the course I'm trying to get started, have to face fact the faculty members all seem to want to take my course development away from me. Called Dick, set up appointment. Should try to get to Miles first. Won't be able to. Plan tonight's studying. Not much today. Read USA news. Crud, won't be able to keep appointment with B.C. Allday & Co here tomorrow, will have to cancel.
4:30 pm	Cleaned desk. Filed today's cases, looking for tomorrow's. Can't find [expletive deleted] Self-Assessment assignment. Read Marketing Management for tomorrow. Can't find my felt tip marker either.
5:00 pm	Betsy called. Wants to play bridge tonight. OK. Not much work. More Marketing Management. Out to eat so I don't miss Betsy's return call. Borrowed dollar, went over to Galley. Eating hamburger on way back. Ran into Tony. Told him it didn't matter how "screwed up" he was as long as he was attractive that way. Marketing Management again.
5:30 pm	Marketing Management. Maureen going shopping, had to make list.
6:00 pm	Spent 15 minutes on phone trying to find fourth for bridge. Bridge off. Good. After you've spent so much time talking about it you don't want it. Marketing Management.
6:30 pm	Marketing Management. Helped Mo in with the groceries.
7:00 pm	Marketing Management. Betsy called back, found fourth. On her way to get me.
7:30 pm	Spent 10 minutes waiting for Betsy, 15 minutes to her place. Waiting for fourth to show up. Reading Marketing Management.
8:00 pm	Made 5 no trump. Still reading Marketing Management.
8:30 pm	Lost rubber. Still playing. Still reading Marketing Management. Betsy's a stewardess, so's Kathy. John's the fourth. We picked him up somewhere. Who cares where. News on. I think Nixon's psychotic.
9:00 pm	Still playing bridge. Both vulnerable.
9:30 pm	Just made 1,000 hand. Still playing. Betsy and I are having trouble at the two level. We're getting used to making slam.
10:00 pm	Still playing bridge. Have finished Policy.

10:30 pm	Still playing bridge.
11:00 pm	Still playing bridge.
11:30 pm	Finish the last rubber, we win by piles of points. John's taking me home.
12:00	Home. Talked to John about product management possibilities at Gilberts.
12:30 am	Continue talking to John. He left. Talked to Maureen about ESP possibilities. Would be great for bridge.
1:00 am	Still talking to Maureen. Munching on cheese and crackers.
1:30 am	Still talking with Mo. To bed at two.
2:00 am	Bed.
5:00 am	Wake up. Not sleepy. Bored. Nothing to do.
5:30 am	Go back to sleep.
8:30 am	Mo wakes me up. Get dressed.
9:00 am	Still get dressed. Walk over bridge to Admin. Center to negotiate loan terms. Always horrible ladies there.
9:30 am	Still at Center. Head down to bank.
10:00 am	Bank. Walk back across to dorm.
10:30 am	Spend about 5 minutes talking with maid. Drink some milk (breakfast and lunch).
11:00 am	Gather cases together. Head for class. Review marketing management with Ann. Call Dick Nelson's office. Cancel appointment.* Fool around with regular premarketing management group doing Al Pesky imitations. Hope Sonny brings his St. Bernard to class. Get coffee.
11:30 am	Ahah. There is no Self-Assessment assignment. Won't have to do it in class now. Spent first half hour of MM writing self-assessment diary. Writing note to Sonny, too.
12:00	Marketing Management.
12:30 pm	Marketing Management. I think I'm hung over, but it could be the class. Had case smashed. Good feeling.
1:00 pm	Business Policy, bored. This is a dumb course. Anyone who doesn't know about strategy, shouldn't be here.

*Can't get another one till Monday. And he wants to see me. What would happen if I wanted to see him? Can call Miles first then.

1:30 pm	Policy. Bored to death. Although cases better than usual.
2:00 pm	Policy. Bored to death again. Enjoy watching Dennis Anderson laugh.
2:30 pm	Self-Assessment.
3:00 pm	Self-Assessment. (There will be no editorial comments made in this class.)

Charles M. O'Brien

1600–1630	Went to store to buy a humidifier as recommended by doctor, to help my wife, who is sick. Had to drive to another building to pick up the humidifier—waited about ten minutes to find it.
1630–1700	Went to auto supply store to order a new water pump and muffler for my wife's car, which disintegrated over the weekend on our way back from Cape Cod. Traffic was heavy and driving was miserable.
1700–1730	Met an old friend on the way home—we both pulled over to the side of the road and chatted for awhile.
1730–1800	Wife sick—doesn't feel like eating—went out and got pizza.
1800–1830	Ate pizza and watched news. Wife ate some broccoli soup I made. Surprised that Nixon agreed to surrender tapes to Judge Sirica.
1830–0100	Studied. Got a few phone calls from friends—called a friend and asked for some information about installing water pump. Felt very sleepy so went to bed.
0630–0700	Woke up; morning ablutions; packed briefcase, made cheese sandwich for lunch.
0700–1130	Drove to Hyannis to pick up our cat in Animal Hospital. Cat has infected paw and had to stay in hospital after having two toes removed. My wife was told that the cat would be able to come home today but when I arrived in Hyannis I was told that the cat's paw still showed infection and she could not come home.
1130–1300	Got back to school in time for Starting New Ventures.
1300–1430	Personnel Administration—ate lunch in class. Almost fell asleep during guest's lecture.
1430–1600	Self-Assessment and Career Development.

VI

Identifying Themes

It is natural, after you have data from two or more devices, to begin to see some themes that seem to run through them. If, for example, (1) the Written Interview says that a person began college as a physics major, but switched to management, and (2) it also indicates that the person was elected president of a college fraternity, and (3) the AVL score for Political is significantly higher than four of the five other values, and (4) the Diary shows the person to be the head of a student consulting project team, then one might reasonably begin to see a theme developing here that we might label "enjoys being in charge." That is, the same idea runs through—i.e., could be legitimately inferred from—all the four pieces of data listed above.

As you may recall from Chapter II, our objective in identifying themes is to help separate the peripheral and trivial from the more central and important behaviorally related characteristics of a person. For job/career decision-making purposes, we ultimately need as accurate a statement of a person's central and stable characteristics as is possible. Developing themes is the key step in the creation of such a statement.

Locating Potential Themes

Locating themes is the work of detectives and researchers. Some people will find it easy to "see" themes without consciously thinking about how they do it. Others will find it difficult. That, in and of itself, is an interesting datum about a person.

Although there is no single standard method that works best in locating potential themes from multiple sources, most people seem to use the following procedure:

1. First, they do a thorough analysis or interpretation of the data from each device separately.

2. Then they take each of the patterns or potential themes developed in step 1 from one of the devices and look carefully for data that either support or refute it in the output from all the other devices.
3. Based on the support or lack of support that they find, they either accept, abandon, or modify the theme.
4. They repeat steps 2 and 3 with the patterns or potential themes developed in step 1 from each of the other devices.

The process of locating themes in the data from multiple instruments is much the same as the process of finding patterns in the Written Interview or the Diary. It is a fluid, iterative process.

Some of the initial thematic analysis done by one person on data from four devices is shown in Figure 1. Most of the themes look fairly promising, although we might wonder if they are all labeled correctly. An initial analysis of data from four devices can typically be expected to identify ten promising themes.

Labeling Themes

Figure 2 shows how three different people used labels to describe the same four themes they identified together in data made available to them on person A. It does not require much more than a glance to notice that the three sets of labels are different in some very fundamental ways. Look at the labels carefully. Which set do you think is probably most appropriate for our purposes? Why?

In labeling themes, it is important to try to be as descriptive (nonevaluative) as possible. That may sound easy, but for many reasons it often isn't. In daily conversations it is a rare person who uses language as precisely and nonevalua-

Philosophical

The word philosophical appears 12 times in the Written Interview (such as "I liked his philosophical approach to life").

High choice of "philosophy" options over others on AVL test (e.g., option 4b on page 8, options 9a and 11d on page 9).

Money

Money mentioned 17 times in the Written Interview (such as "I got a thrill out of making money").

Economic second highest AVL score.

No Interest in Sports/Athletics

Only mention of sports in the Written Interview was "I am not sports oriented."

Spends no time, in 24-Hour Diaries, watching or participating in sports.

Great Awareness and Concern with Time

There are 45 lengths of time (ranging from one hour to 50 years) referred to in the Written Interview.

In 24-Hour Diaries, all times are recorded to the minute. The Diary refers to how long it took the person to do something in six different instances.

Involvement

Large portions of time recorded in 24-Hour Diaries spent in situations with large numbers of people and lots of activity, even if little personal interaction (classes, restaurant, etc.).

The word "involved" appears 18 times in the Written Interview (such as "my biggest regret was not getting involved in a fraternity").

tively as person 2 (in Figure 2). Most people describe other people and events loosely and with a heavy evaluative overtone. If, for whatever reason, we "like" another person, our description often uses "positive" words (person 3), while for someone we don't like the opposite occurs (person 1).[1]

FIGURE 2   Labels Assigned to Four Themes by Three Different People

	Theme A	Theme B	Theme C	Theme D
Person 1's Labels	A bore	Machinelike	A workaholic	A nervous wreck
Person 2's Labels	Quantitative	Systematic	Energetic	Tense
Person 3's Labels	Numerical genius	Very well organized	"Able to leap tall build- ings . . ."	Intense

It is also important to be as precise as possible in labeling themes. Just as a good writer works hard to find the best word or phrase to express some meaning, you must expect to spend some time and effort considering what are often

subtle differences in labels. That effort is an important part of achieving our ultimate objective—as accurate a set of statements as possible about your more central and stable characteristics.

Contradictory Evidence

It is extremely important to look for, and keep track of, data that appear to contradict emerging themes. The tendency to ignore such data because they don't fit neatly must be resisted, because such information can be very useful. The great explorer and scientist, Charles Darwin, is alleged to have kept a small black notebook with him at all times in which he recorded every datum, no matter how small, that appeared to contradict his emerging theory of evolution. He then used that information, quite successfully, to help shape his ideas in sound, sensible, and creative ways.

A sensitivity to contradictory evidence can help one differentiate the more central and key from the more random and peripheral in an emerging analysis. Just as important, it can also help you to identify and label themes more precisely.

It is not unusual, for example, to have a theme in which three pieces of evidence seem to be supportive while another two are apparently saying the opposite. Sometimes one finds that by changing the label slightly, all five pieces of data can be taken into account. In other cases one cannot reconcile the evidence, suggesting that the theme should be abandoned.

On some occasions a modification of a label and the creation of a second theme will eliminate the contradictory evidence. Consider, for example, the case in which some

---

[1]This is the problem of "projection" of which we have spoken before (see pages 12-14). Persons 1 and 3 have probably based their labeling of themes on more than just the data—that is, on the data and on their projected feelings about some or all of them. As we have said before, the best solution to this problem is simply to try to be sensitive to its occurrence.

evidence seems to say that the person is very people oriented, while other data seem to say that that is not the case at all. Closer examination might reveal two compatible and supportable themes: one labeled "a few very close friends" and a second labeled "doesn't like groups of people."

An Example of a Set of Themes

Figure 3 shows a set of theme labels derived from analysis of data from six data-generating devices. These data were on Phillip Murray. Look over the themes carefully. Based on his Written Interview and the AVL, do these themes surprise you?

FIGURE 3 Phillip Murray's Themes

1. Social status, prestige, the best
2. Communication of words and ideas
3. Socializing with peers
4. Somewhat aesthetic and creative
5. *Active*—activities/project oriented
6. Not very entrepreneurial
7. Some variety of things
8. With people
9. Not deep affiliative relationships
10. Administrator of activities
11. Aesthetic/social activities
12. Financial activities
13. Not traditional businessman
14. "Home-family" orientation
15. Not averse to detail

Exercise

Now that you have data on yourself from a number of devices, try doing an initial thematic analysis of those data. Remembering that this is all very tentative, what themes do you see?

***

Since we will not be referring to Phillip Murray again, let's take a minute to put some closure on his "story."

We have modified Murray's Written Interview slightly to make it sound as if he went through the self-assessment process while he was still a second-year M.B.A. In fact, he did not. When we began developing these materials, and before we had ever taught the course, we needed a volunteer who would agree to let us disguise his data and make him a "case study." Through an intermediary we approached Murray, who at that time had been out of school for five months. He agreed to help. But let's go back now and take things chronologically.

In his second year in graduate school Murray lined up two basic job offers with (1) a prestigious Wall Street house that specialized in institutional sales, a highly successful "money machine," where Murray's job would have been concentrating in corporate finance; and (2) a less well-known, more diversified house of "good quality" where he

would have been an administrative assistant to the vice-president of operations. He liked the people more in the second company. Almost everyone advised him to accept the first company's offer. In fact, he chose the second company.

IN LIGHT OF WHAT YOU KNOW ABOUT MURRAY, AND WITH THE ADDITIONAL DATA IN FIGURE 3, HOW WELL WOULD YOU PREDICT MURRAY'S JOB CHOICE WORKED OUT FOR HIM? THINK ABOUT IT A MINUTE.

After five months on the job, he was not happy, which is one reason he agreed to take the SACD tests. (He spent two days in Boston taking the tests and talking to a counselor. He was reluctant to really go through the whole self-assessment process. He wanted some quick advice.)

At this time he was not happy with the people he was working with and he didn't like the "staff" job. At about this time, he had started to separate himself from his colleagues; he did not join them at lunch; on business trips he would make arrangements to see his own friends in the evening instead of going with his colleagues. After nine months he quit and took the job at the first Wall Street firm he had considered.

In light of the themes in Figure 3, these events are hardly surprising. Some of the themes suggest why Murray was drawn to a Wall Street investment banking organization (#1, #12). But others rather clearly indicate that he would have difficulty fitting in and being happy in an environment of very hard working, task oriented, aggressive and entrepreneurial, economically oriented people (#3, #4, #6, #7, #8, #11, #13). And none of his themes necessarily suggests an "assistant-to" job.

He stayed six months in this next job. It turned out to be no better. He still went to lunch by himself and got upset when others made subtle demands that he behave like everyone else. His attitude, he says, got worse and worse. He was eventually fired.

For his first year in New York City he lived with a fellow classmate who had a corporate finance job on Wall Street. He ended up spending little time in his apartment. He found he didn't like his roommate, his taste, or his friends. After a year he found an apartment by himself. But he was not really satisfied with that either (hardly surprising in light of themes #3 and #14).

After being fired, he came to Boston to see the counselor again, briefly. He was miserable. The counselor noticed that this time, as opposed to the first time they talked, Murray listened. He even went for a job interview (*not* with another Wall Street firm) on the counselor's suggestion. But he was confused and upset.

He found still another Wall Street job. He was becoming totally convinced that this was not his thing; however, he did it again. He reported for work one Friday morning and at 4:00 pm. that day he quit. In his own words, he was very unhappy and very confused.

And then there was his girl friend. Her father had a business in New York City. The whole issue of marriage and going into business came up (a package deal as he saw it). A second option that developed involved an older friend whom he admired and respected. This man was putting together some cable television deals in Connecticut. Still a third option he considered was "getting out of the jungle" and going to California. The cable TV deal fell through. And he "fled" to California.

On the way to California he stopped by to see us. He bragged to friends here in a very bravado kind of way that he felt able to leap buildings in a single bound. Even to the casual observer, however, this was clearly a front.

After three months in San Francisco, having looked through the "want ads" columns, having pushed all his contacts, having walked the streets, having gotten more and more frustrated, he nearly gave up and came back to New York. But then he had an interview with a man in a large, fast-growing bank. In his own words, Murray was very pushy about what he thought he wanted, and that was based mostly on his work with the Boston career counselor. He was hired on a one-month probation period with very much an open option in terms of how he would work out. For Murray, the job offered him the first real opportunity to manage something. He particularly liked the notion of trying to get things done under pressure—something he felt he was very good at.

He did reasonably well. He mentioned to friends that things were beginning "to make sense to him" regarding what kind of job he wanted. The work he had done with the career counselor in Boston was beginning to make sense. He began to make more decisions based on that assessment. And he started to become more proactive in managing his career.

After five months he moved into the budget/controllership function, at his initiative. He did well again and was promoted to the number two spot. He worked long hours (70 per week) getting the budget together in time for the year-end deadline. He began to like his job. To friends, he enjoyed describing the political and interpersonal dynamics of getting others to accept a budget.

On September 1, 1975, 18 months after joining the bank, he was promoted to vice-president in charge of cost analysis and profit planning. At 27, he was the youngest vice-president in the bank's history. He had 22 people working for him (mostly M.B.A.s). He was in charge of a special project dealing with organizational profitability—an internal budget type analysis of a very political nature, to be presented to the president and chairman, regarding the nature of bottom-line results through each division. Murray's task was to get all the overhead allocated back to the divisional profit centers. That is, he was attempting to establish a total overhead absorption system, which obviously had huge political ramifications for profit-center managers who would have to accept it. Murray said, "The thing I love about the work is that there is a very high human/political side to it. I really have to do all my work through people." On the other hand, there was also a lot of logistical number-crunching type management to be done—small detail work involved in getting to know the costs.

On the personal side, Phillip Murray was married in May 1975. He bought a house in a prestigious residential suburb, north of San Francisco. Referring back to his themes, it is not difficult to see why the job and life style he established in San Francisco worked well for him.

When we talked to him in October 1975, he said things were really humming and that he was just so in love with his work and his life that he thinks back to his past confusion and wonders at it. He said that his assessment makes a lot of sense to him now and that he is still using it in his job and career decision making. He also said that the assessment help he received was unquestionably one of the most important things that had occurred in his life.

VII

The Strong-Campbell
Interest Inventory

NOTE:
DO NOT READ THIS UNTIL YOU HAVE COMPLETED THE
STRONG ASSIGNMENT IN THE WORKBOOK

The Strong-Campbell Interest Inventory (SCII) is the recently updated version of an enormously respected "vocational guidance" instrument that was originally developed over 40 years ago. The output of this instrument, generally called the "Strong Profile," provides a great deal of potentially relevant information about a person. Indeed, our students have generally found the SCII to be second only to the Written Interview in its usefulness as a data generating device.

To use the Strong Profile for self-assessment purposes, we need, as always, a fairly thorough understanding of the instrument. This chapter has been written to provide you with that understanding.

The Design of the Test

The SCII asks a person over 300 questions that elicit his or her preferences (likes, dislikes, or indifferences) concerning various occupations, school subjects, activities, amusements, and types of people. The test's input, therefore, is data about what we generally call "interests" or "attitudes." The SCII does not elicit information regarding a person's intelligence, aptitudes, or skills.

The instrument uses this information about a person's interests to compute a number of "scores" which are gener-

ally presented in three parts, as shown in Figure 1. These parts are the (1) General Occupational Themes, (2) Basic Interest Scales, and (3) Occupational Scales. Each of these three sets of scores compares the test taker's interests with either men and women in general, or men and women in specific occupations (e.g., bankers, advertising executives, etc.). And, as we shall see, these comparisons can be very useful data.

The data presentation in the Strong Profile in Figure 1 is organized around six themes, based on the work of J. L. Holland[1] (e.g., all occupational scales related to each theme are grouped together). The addition of these themes as an organizing device in the Profile, as well as the general occupational theme scores, is new to this latest version of the Strong. And while the information is useful, it is not the most important part of the Profile. As such, we will delay a discussion of the themes and focus first on that part of the profile which is most important for our purposes—the occupational scales.

---

[1]In *Making Vocational Choices: A Theory of Careers* (Englewood Cliffs, N.J.: Prentice-Hall, 1973), Holland argues that it is useful for career decision-making purposes to conceptualize occupations, job-related-activities, and personality types in terms of the themes, which he labels realistic, investigative, artistic, social, enterprising, and conventional.

FIGURE 1 SVIB-SCII Profile

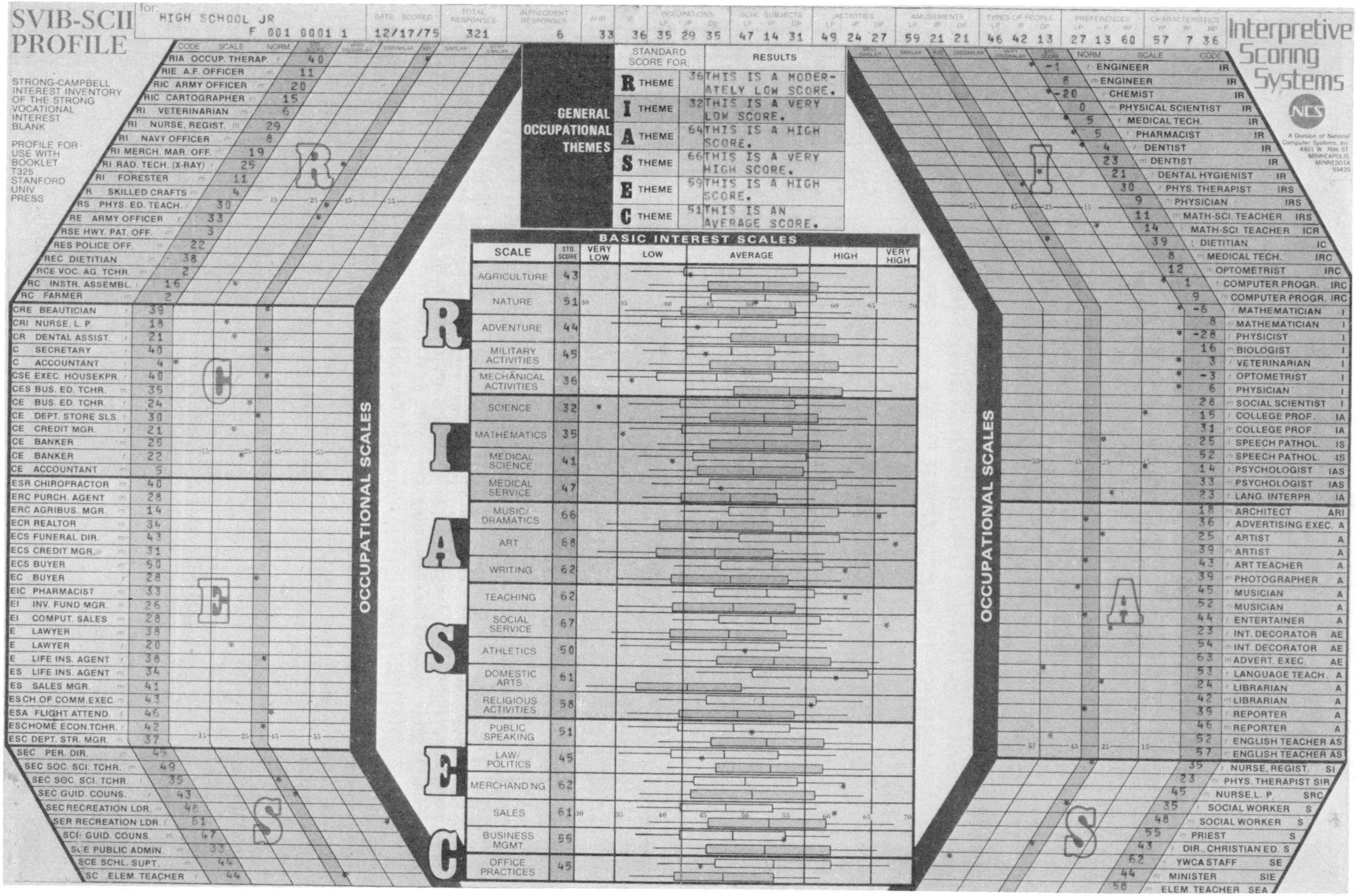

The Occupational Scales

The occupational scales have been created to inform the taker how similar his or her interests are to the interests that are somewhat idiosyncratic to a particular male or female occupational group (such as female bankers or male engineers). Specifically, each of the 124 occupational scales was created in the following manner:

1. A group of about 150–450 men or women were identified as being happily employed in an occupation and as having been in that occupation for more than three years (average tenure was usually 10–20 years).
2. These people were asked to answer the 325 questions on the SCII.
3. Whenever these people expressed some particular preference much more or less frequently than a large sample of "people in general," that alternative was used in creating the scale for that occupational group.
4. The scale was then normed so that the average person in the occupational group scored 50^2 on the scale while two-thirds of the group scored between 40 and 60.

As a result of this scale construction procedure, the more often a person using the SCII expresses preferences that distinguish a particular occupation, the greater the score he or she will receive on that occupational scale. For example, suppose you indicated in response to question 217 that you liked "living in the city." Suppose also that the criterion group of male architects happened to choose that option much more often than most other people. In that case, your score on the m architect scale would go up a notch. If time and time again you chose an option that had been chosen by male architects (liking, disliking, or being indifferent to an item) but not chosen by others, then your final score on the m architect scale would probably be high, usually considered to be a score of 45 or above. You and the criterion group of architects are indicating shared attitudes. You have something in common. You express the same preferences they do.

Sharing a large number of preferences with people in an occupation is important because research has linked such commonalities to people's decisions to go into and stay in an occupation.[3] It would appear that, given an appropriate

level of ability, those who tend to share the same preferences as other occupational members—those who "talk the same language"—are also more likely to get on, to be readily accepted, to enjoy their work, and to be successful.

To be able to effectively use your scores on the occupational scales, it is sometimes useful to have some supplementary information about the scale's occupation, the criterion group used to construct the scale, or the type of people that tend to score high on the scale. This information is given in Figure 2, and should be carefully taken into account when examining the profile. For example, in interpreting a high or low score on the male banker scale, it is probably important to recognize that the scale was based on a national sample of bank presidents and vice presidents, many of whom were employed in small commercial banks in small towns. One would suspect that such a group of people is significantly different from, say, a group of New York investment bankers.

It is also useful when interpreting a profile to recognize that the occupations that are grouped together in Figure 1 and marked with a single letter (either I, A, S, E, C, or R) all tend to share certain characteristics in common. According to John Holland, the R occupations (such as forester and veterinarian) tend to involve the explicit, ordered, or systematic manipulation of objects, tools, machines, and animals. The I occupations (such as physician and college professor) usually involve the observation and symbolic, systematic, and creative integration of physical, biological, or cultural phenomena. The A occupations (such as musician and reporter) involve ambiguous, free, unsystematized activities that create art forms or products. The S occupations (such as social worker and personnel director) all entail the manipulation of others to attain organizational or self-interest goals. And finally, the C occupations (such as accountant and secretary) usually entail the explicit, ordered, systematic manipulation of data.

The occupational scales on most profiles will have a number of "high" (45 or above) scores in both male and female occupational groups.[4] In addition to accepting at face value what those scores tell you (that you have interests and attitudes much like people in those occupations), it can be useful in interpreting a profile to list those occupations separately, and to try to identify what, if anything, they have in common. The same technique can be profitably used with particularly low scores.

The occupational scales on some profiles will be relatively flat; there will be few if any high scores. The raw datum here indicates that the test taker's values and attitudes have not crystalized around any of the occupational types for which the instrument is scored. The most common reason for this relates to culture. Flat profiles sometimes occur when the test taker was raised in an environment that was different from the white, middle class, American culture from which virtually all criterion groups come.

---

[2]One of the consequences of setting the occupational group's average score at 50 is that it is possible to get a negative score on many of the scales.

[3]For previous versions of this instrument, Strong verified the predictive values of the occupational scales for the 18 years after the test was taken [E. K. Strong, Jr., *Vocational Interests 18 Years After College* (Minneapolis: University of Minnesota Press, 1955)]; McArthur showed they predicted for 14 years (C. McArthur, "Long-Term Validity of the Strong Vocational Interest Test in Two Subcultures," *Journal of Applied Psychology* (1954), pp. 346–533). These and other research efforts have found that the odds that the following statements will turn out to be true range from 2 to 1 up to 5 to 1, with 3.5 to 1 being the commonest result.
1. People continuing in occupation X obtained a higher interest score in X than in any other occupation.
2. People continuing in occupation X obtained a higher interest score in X than other people entering other occupations.
3. People continuing in occupation X obtained higher scores in X than people who changed from X to another occupation.
4. People changing from occupation X to occupation Y scored higher in Y prior to the change than in any other occupation, including X.

---

[4]The Profile shown in Figure 1 marks, with an asterisk on the line graph, only the male occupation scores or the female occupation scores depending upon the sex of the test taker. Nevertheless, it presents both scores in the column marked STD score. Some people find it helpful when they work on a Profile to fill in by hand the missing asterisks.

FIGURE 2 Supplemental Data on Occupational Scales

Scale	Comments
Accountant (f)	Based on a national sample of women in the American Society of Women Accountants (1967).
Accountant (m)	Based on a sample of CPAs in Minnesota (1965).
Advertising Executive (f)	Based on a sample of women listed in Standard Directory of Advertising Agencies (1973), including media directors and buyers; creative, art, production, research, client service, and broadcasting directors; and account executives.
Advertising Executive (m)	Account executives listed in Standard Directory of Advertising Agencies (1968).
Agribusiness Managers (m)	Elevator managers, implement dealers, farm service supply managers, dairy processing-plant managers, nursery managers from Minnesota and North and South Dakota (1972).
Air Force Officer (m)	Line Officers, captains or higher (1960). Physically adventurous individuals sometimes score high on this scale.
Army Officer (f)	Captains, majors, and lt. colonels (1962). M.B.As often score high on this scale.
Artists (m) (f)	Noncommercial artists listed in *Who's Who in American Art* (1966).
Banker (f)	Members of the National Association of Bankwomen (1968).
Banker (m)	National sample of bank presidents and vice presidents. Many were in small banks in small towns.
Business Education Teacher (m) (f)	These and all other ''teacher scales'' are not college instructors but secondary school teachers.
Buyer (f)	Heads of merchandise departments in department stores (1967).
Buyer (m)	National sample of department store buyers (1969).
Cartographer (m)	Civilian employees of U.S. Army Topographical Command (1969).
Chamber of Commerce Executive (m)	Half are Chamber executives; half are managers of trade associations (1960). People who score high on this scale tend to be politically oriented.
Computer Sales (m)	From Control Data Corporation (1964).
Credit Manager (f)	Average education = 13 years (1973).
Credit Manager (m)	Average education = 15 years (1958).
Dentist (f)	Based on a sample from 1934-1947.
Department Store Manager (m)	From Penney's (1969).
Engineer (f)	A 1959 sample.
Farmer (m)	People who score high on this scale are often rather independent, solitary, and bored with speculative thinking.
Funeral Director (m)	These are mostly small businessmen and entrepreneurs.
Interior Decorators (m) (f)	Average education = 15 years.
Investment Fund Manager (m)	Average education = 17 years (1966).
Lawyer (m)	Over one-third the sample were federal judges.
Librarian (m) (f)	Average education = 17½ years. Often scholarly and well-organized people (male sample from 1959, female from 1967).
Life Insurance Agent (m) (f)	National sample (1973) of holders of the American College of Life Underwriters Certificate.
Merchant Marine Officer (m)	Deck officers and engineers, in ratings from third mate to captain.
Minister (m)	Protestant ministers from 13 denominations. Average education = 20 years. Tend to have strong ethical concerns, an attitude of seriousness toward problems of value, and sometimes a philosophical turn of mind.
Musician (m) (f)	People who score high on this scale often share a musician's penchant for solo performances, despite their lack of musical aptitude. The female sample is based on a 1952 sample, the male on a 1969 sample.
Personnel Directors (m)	Personnel directors and managers from companies with over 500 employees.
Public Administrator (m)	Chapter officers of the American Society of Public Administrators (1969). Average education = 17 years.
Purchasing Agent (m)	Member of Twin City Association of Purchasing Agents. Average education = 14 years.
Realtors (m)	Brokers and salesmen in Minnesota.
Sales Managers (m)	Vice presidents in charge of sales and marketing and small company owners in Minneapolis area.
YWCA Staff (f)	B.A. degree holders. Those scoring high on the scale tend to be gregarious organizers who can initiate and monitor a host of activities in any institutional setting.

SOURCE: Much of this information can be found in: David P. Campbell, *Manual for SVIB-SCII* (Stanford, Calif.: Stanford University Press, 1977).

The Basic Interest Scales

The basic interest scales, shown in the middle of the Profile in Figure 1, provide us with less information than the occupational scales. Nevertheless, they can be very helpful.

Your scores on the 23 basic interest scales, in effect, just report back to you what you reported on the SCII. That is, they simply measure the frequency with which you said you liked, disliked, or were indifferent to certain types of activities or subjects. For example, if you said you like art as a school subject (question 136 on the SCII), your score on the art scale would increase. If you said you did not like visiting art galleries (question 234), your score on the art scale would decrease. The only transformation the test makes is to set 50 as the mean score on each scale (with a standard deviation of 10) for a sample of 600 men and women, and to adjust your score accordingly. This allows you to compare your score to people in general.[5]

It is useful to recognize that because of the way these scales are constructed, it is possible for someone to score high on most of the scales, while another person scores low on most of the scales. In that case, the first person simply chose the "like" option very often on the SCII, while the second chose "indifferent" or "dislike" very often. It is also possible for a person to have a high basic interest score (65) on "mathematics," and yet have a low score (10) on the occupational scales m mathematician or f mathematician. In this case, the person has reported on the SCII a high liking for mathematical subjects and activities, but has not reported many of the somewhat unique interests that characterize the people in the mathematics profession (which may have nothing obvious to do with mathematics).

The General Occupational Themes

The third set of scores on the Strong Profile are called general occupational themes (look at the upper middle section of the profile in Figure 1). These scores are computed in a manner very similar to the basic interest scores;[6] the only major difference is that the scores are related not to fairly narrow activities or subjects, like science or nature, but to the six very broad occupational themes that are based on the research of John Holland (see Figure 3 for a definition of these themes). There is a second less significant difference for the Profile shown in Figure 1. Instead of giving you male and female averages and ranges for each theme, as the basic interest scales do with shaded and unshaded bars that are printed on the Profile, the general occupational

scales tell you how high or low your score is relative to others in your own sex (only). And it does so in English, beside each score, in the column marked "Results."

Because the type of person the R-Theme describes, for example, often has interests in agriculture, nature, adventure, military activities, and mechanical activities, those five interest areas are put together and marked "R" on the basic interest scales in Figure 1. Furthermore, it is because this type of person tends to prefer occupations such as Air Force officer, occupational therapist, army officer, cartographer, veterinarian, etc., that those occupational scales are grouped together and marked "R." This same organizing format applies to the other themes, interest scales, and occupational scales. In addition, the secondary themes that are inherent in each occupational scale are noted by the scale names. For example, in Figure 1, the occupational therapist f scale (upper left hand corner) has RIA printed next to it. This signifies that the main occupational theme inherent in that scale is realistic, and that the investigative and artistic are secondary themes.

In most profiles, scores across the three sets of scales (occupational, basic interest, and general occupational theme) will be roughly similar on the average, for those scales related to a single theme. For example, a person whose general occupational theme score for R is very low (25) will probably also score low on most of the basic interest scales associated with the R-Theme (e.g., agriculture, nature, etc.), and will probably also score low on most of the occupational scales associated with R (such as occupational therapist, air force officer). Such a pattern simply confirms Holland's thesis and the organizational format used in the latest version of the Strong Profile.

Other Scores

Across the top of the Strong Profile shown in Figure 1 you will find the final pieces of data that the instrument provides.

Beginning at the upper left, after the areas for name and the date the test was scored, is a box marked total responses. This shows how many answer marks the computer has read from the answer sheet; since there are 325 items, the score on this index should be 325 or close to it. Up to 32 items can be omitted without significantly affecting the results.

A second index, Infrequent Responses, shows the number of rare responses given. It is weighted so that almost everyone scores zero or higher here; if the score is *below zero*, the person has marked an uncommonly high number of rare responses. Usually a negative score indicates some confusion, such as skipping a number on the answer sheet or random marking. You can safely ignore numbers above zero.

The AOR (Academic Orientation) scale is a measure of probable persistence in an academic setting. Students graduating with a B.A. from a liberal arts college average 50, M.A.s about 55, Ph.D.s about 60. Students seeking advanced degrees who score low (around 40) on this scale inevitably report that they view their education as a necessary hurdle to be cleared and are not usually enchanted with the academic nature of their study. The item content is

---

[5]As well as to men and women in general. Norms for each sex in Figure 1 are indicated by the bars printed on each scale: the shaded bar gives the norm for men, the unshaded bar for women. The line in the middle of the bar represents the group mean. The thick portion of the bar represents the range of scores for 50% of the sample. The thin lines that extend from the bars show the range for 90% of the sample.

[6]That is, items were identified on the SCII that relate to each theme. Whenever you answer "like" to one of the items, your score goes up on the appropriate theme scale; whenever you answer "dislike," your score goes down. The scales were standardized so that the average person in a general sample of 600 people scored 50 on each scale, with a standard deviation of 10.

FIGURE 3   The Six Occupational Themes

R-Theme. People who score very high on this theme tend to be rugged, robust, practical individuals who are physically strong and frequently aggressive in outlook. They often have good physical skills but have trouble expressing themselves in words or communicating these feelings to others. They like to work outdoors and they like to work with tools, especially large, powerful machines. They prefer to deal with things rather than with ideas or with people. They generally have conventional political and economic opinions, and are usually cool to radical new ideas. They enjoy creating things with their hands and prefer occupations such as mechanic, construction work, fish and wildlife management, laboratory technician, some engineering specialties, some military jobs, agriculture, or the skilled trades. Although no single word can capture the broad meaning of the entire theme, the word "realistic" has been used to characterize this pattern, thus the term R-Theme.

I-Theme. This theme tends to center around science and scientific activities. Extremes of this type are task-oriented; they are not particularly interested in working around other people. They enjoy solving abstract problems and have a great need to understand the physical world. They prefer to think through problems rather than act them out. Such people enjoy ambiguous challenges and do not like highly structured situations with many rules. They frequently have unconventional values and attitudes and tend to be original and creative, especially in scientific areas. They prefer occupations such as design engineer, biologist, social scientist, research laboratory worker, physicist, technical writer, or meteorologist. The word "investigative" is used to summarize this pattern, thus I-Theme.

A-Theme. Those scoring high here are artistically oriented and like to work in artistic settings where there are many opportunities for self-expression. Such people have little interest in problems that are highly structured or that require gross physical strength and prefer problems that can be dealt with through self-expression in artistic media. They resemble I-Theme types in preferring to work alone, but have a greater need for individualistic expression, are usually less assertive about their own opinions and capabilities, and are more sensitive and emotional. They score higher on measures of originality than any of the other types. They describe themselves as independent, original, unconventional, expressive, and tense. Vocational choices include artist, author, cartoonist, composer, singer, dramatic coach, poet, actor or actress, and symphony conductor. This is the "artistic" theme, or A-Theme.

S-Theme. People scoring the highest on this theme are sociable, responsible, humanistic, and concerned with the welfare of others. They usually express themselves well and get along well with others. They like attention and seek situations that allow them to be at or near the center of the group. They prefer to solve problems by discussions with others or by arranging or rearranging relationships between others, but have little interest in situations that require physical exertion or working with machinery. Such people describe themselves as cheerful, popular, achieving, and good leaders. They prefer occupations such as school superintendent, clinical psychologist, high school teacher, marriage counselor, playground director, speech therapist, or vocational counselor. This is the "social" theme, or S-Theme.

E-Theme. Those who score high here have a great facility with words which they put to effective use in selling, dominating, and leading. These people are frequently in sales work. They see themselves as energetic, enthusiastic, adventurous, self-confident, and dominant, and they prefer social tasks where they can assume leadership. They enjoy persuading others to accept their viewpoints. They are impatient with precise work or work that involves long periods of intellectual effort. They like power, status, and material wealth, and enjoy working in expensive settings. Vocational preferences include business executive, buyer, hotel manager, industrial relations consultant, political campaigner, realtor, many kinds of sales work, sports promoter, and television producer. The word "enterprising" summarizes this pattern, thus E-Theme.

C-Theme. People who score high on this theme prefer the highly ordered activities, both verbal and numerical, that characterize office work. They fit well into large organizations but do not seek leadership since they respond to power and are comfortable working in a well-established chain of command. They dislike ambiguous situations and prefer to know precisely what is expected of them. Such people describe themselves as conventional, stable, well-controlled, and dependable. They have little interest in problems that require physical skills or intense relationships with others and are most effective at well-defined tasks. Like the E-Theme type, they value material possessions and status. Vocational preferences are mostly within the business world and include bank examiner, bank teller, bookkeeper, some accounting jobs, financial analyst, computer operator, inventory controller, tax expert, statistician, and traffic manager. Although one word cannot adequately represent the entire theme, the word "conventional" more or less summarizes the pattern, hence C-Theme.

Source: The SVIB-SCII Profile.

heavily oriented toward science and the arts (weighed positively) and business and blue-collar activities (weighed negatively).

On the IE (Introversion-Extroversion) scale, high scores (60 and above) indicate introversion and low scores (40 and below), extroversion. The item content is concerned almost entirely with working with people in social service, educational, entertainment, or business settings.

The LP/IP/DP indices show the percent of "Like," "Indifferent," and "Dislike" responses selected in each section of the SCII (Occupations, School Subjects, etc.). Although there is some variation from section to section, the average for LP, IP, and DP percentages is about 35, and the average standard deviation is about 16. Most of our students' percentages have been between 5 and 60. Scores in this range are normal and have no effect on the text. Percentages above 60, particularly if they occur in several sections and are consistently in the LP, IP, or DP category, may affect the test results and probably provide helpful information about the test taker in themselves.[7]

Using the Strong

A good assessor can usually learn a considerable amount from a Strong Profile by treating it as we have treated data from all other data generating instruments: that is, by making sure he or she understands the instrument and then by looking for patterns. The Strong Profile can and should be used both to identify new patterns or ideas, and to test themes and patterns that have emerged from other data.

To facilitate identifying new patterns you may find the following procedures helpful. First, on a separate sheet of paper list all your occupational scores above 45. If you have only one or two scores above 45, list all the scores above 40. Also list all your negative scores; again, if you have only one or two (or none), list all your scores less than 20. Then look for patterns within and across the lists.

Most of the higher and lower occupational scores from two Strongs are shown in Figure 4 (2 or 3 scores in each case are omitted so that it is easier to see the patterns). In the first profile, the high scores all seem to relate to the rela-

tively high level management of people. They do not include all the high level people management scales, but they include most of them. The lowest scores, on the other hand, are almost all "blue-collar" trades. None are managerial jobs. The latter contrasts sharply in socio-economic terms with the high score occupations. And, interestingly, none of the high score managerial occupations involve supervising the types of occupations included in the low scores. One might tentatively conclude from these scores that a theme labeled "manager of white collar and professional people" is appropriate.

FIGURE 4   High and Low Occupational Scores from Two Strong Profiles

Profile #1

High Scores		Low Scores	
Department Store Manager m	52	Skilled crafts m	10
Sales Manager m	50	Physical Education Teacher f	7
Navy Officer m	48	Vocational Agriculture Teacher m	3
Public Administrator m	48	Instrument Assembler f	−1
Personnel Director m	46	Farmer m	−3
Advertising Executive m	43		
Department Store Manager m	42		

Profile #2

High Scores		Low Scores	
Guidance Counselor m	62	Math Science Teacher f	19
Psychologist m	60	Army Officer m	8
Psychologist f	58	Police Officer m	6
Physical Therapist f	57	Department Store Manager m	4
English Teacher f	50	Army Officer f	−1
Social Worker m	48	Agribusiness Manager m	−4
Social Worker f	47		
Life Insurance Agent m	42		

In the second profile, the high scores generally seem to be in "helping" professions. That is, they all involve providing another person or persons professional help of some type. The low scores, however, seem to relate to occupations that put a person in the position of having to manage and perhaps discipline other people. In each case, the occupation gives the person formal authority, and expects him or her to use it to accomplish some institutionally set objectives. Possible themes that emerge from these scores might be labeled "helping professions" and "dislikes relations based on formal authority."

Of course, the tentative themes we have identified in these profiles should be checked out both with other Strong data, and with data from other devices.

A second way in which one can go about looking for patterns in a Strong Profile is by looking at the high and low scores within each of the theme related groupings. For example, in the scores in Profile 1 in Figure 5 all are from

[7]A high LP response style (LP above 60 in several sections) will inflate your scores in the General Occupational Themes and the Basic Interest Scales. If many (15 or more) Basic Interest Scales are high, only the top three to five scores should be considered. High LP types might be described as overly enthusiastic and vocationally unfocused particularly if they have none or very few "similar" ratings on Occupational Scales. They are often very energetic, but in a "ship without rudder" way.

If "dislike" percentages are generally high, the scores on the General Occupational Themes and Basic Interest Scales will be low, and some information may be gotten from treating the relatively highest scores as "High" regardless of their absolute value. According to Campbell ["Manual for the Strong-Campbell Interest Inventory" (Stanford University Press, 1974)], high DPs tend to fall into two categories: those with such an intense occupational focus that they mark everything "dislike" which falls outside their well-defined realm of interest; and those who have few "likes" in the world and find most of everything repugnant. Those of the first type usually experience few vocational problems, unless a sudden and massive insight or external turn of events shatters their world view, as in the case of many engineers in the late 1960s. The second type, however, can experience serious difficulties in career issues. One way to differentiate the two types is to check if there are at least a few Occupational Scales in the "Similar" range. If so, chances are this is a "Type 1" profile of someone with a highly focused sense of direction.

the I-theme occupations. Yet there is clearly a difference in the higher and lower scores within that theme category. The higher scored occupations are much more applied, pragmatic, and concrete than the lower scored ones. This suggests a theme we might label "applied and concrete: not abstract."

The scores from the second Profile in Figure 5 are all from the S-theme occupations. But the higher score occupations are obviously different from the lower ones. The higher are all jobs that require one to organize and manage others. The lower scored occupations involve giving help to others on a one on one basis. The pattern suggests a theme related to the organization and management of others.

Still a third way one can look for patterns in a Strong Profile is to look for high scores on the basic interest scales or the general occupational themes which automatically suggest and label a theme. That is, if the E-theme score is very high (67), then "enterprising" is obviously a potential theme. Likewise, if the nature scale has a very high score, then "nature" is a likely candidate for a theme, or for part of a theme.

To test themes or patterns that have emerged in other data with the Strong data, one can simply go over all of the Profile, asking questions like:

1. Is this scale or score relevant to the theme in question?
2. If yes, does it score support or not support the theme?

For example, if "artistic" is a theme that has emerged from the Written Interview and the AVL, one would want to examine *at least* the A-theme score, the Art basic interest scale, and the Artist (f, m) occupational scales for support or disconfirmation. Likewise, if "political" was a theme identified in other data, you would definitely want to look at the law/politics basic interest score and the public administrator, school superintendent, and chamber of commerce executive occupational scores.

There are, of course, still other approaches one can take using a Strong Profile. And as long as they include a basic understanding of the instrument and an orientation toward testing and developing themes, they too are appropriate.

FIGURE 5 Examples of Higher and Lower Scores Within Theme Related Grouping of Occupational Scales

Profile #1

Higher		Lower	
Engineer f	38	Chemist f	20
Medical Technician f	39	Physical Scientist m	18
Pharmacist f	30	Mathematician f	15
Dentist f	42	Mathematician m	19
Physician m	29	Physicist f	10
Dental Hygienist f	37	Biologist f	12
Physical Therapist f	35	Social Scientist m	19
Medical Technician m	32	College Professor f	18
Optometrist m	38	College Professor m	12
Computer Programmer f	30	Psychologist f	19
Optometrist f	40	Psychologist m	20

Profile #2

Higher		Lower	
Personnel Director m	36	Guidance Counselor m	13
School Superintendent m	25	Nurse f	14
Public Administrator m	41	Social Worker m	19
YWCA Staff f	32	Physical Therapist m	8

Exercise

To help you practice a Strong, obtain a Profile from a classmate (or if you are working alone, use your own) and try to do a complete analysis of it. Allow yourself enough time, since interpreting a Strong is much more complex than interpreting an AVL or a 24-hour diary.

VIII

Life-Style Representations

One hears a lot of talk about life style these days. People talk of liking or disliking their current life style, of the merits of various alternative life styles, of how Mary and Tim Jones have changed their life style.

The *American Heritage Dictionary* defines life style as "an internally consistent way of life or style of living that reflects the attitudes and values of an individual or a culture." That is, life style is someone's way of life. It is the pattern of how one relates to key parts of external reality; how one uses time; whom one relates with and how; how one uses or relates to objects and possessions; how one relates to geography and space generally; what one does. Second, one's life style, insofar as there is choice in its establishment, reflects some of the things inside the person. It is, in a sense, a mapping out of who one is into what one does, how one does it, and with whom or what.

Life style relates to our present purposes in two ways. First, career and job-related decisions are a subset of the total life-style decisions that people make, whether consciously or not. It would certainly make things easier if we could treat job and career decisions independently from other life-style decisions, but we really can't—they are very interdependent. If one chooses to live in a cabin in Maine, that choice makes the possibility of working as a loan officer in a bank in Los Angeles impractical. If one chooses to work for a consulting firm in a job that takes 60 hours a week, one-third of it out of town, one probably cannot spend 7 hours a day, every day, being with one's spouse and children. If one chooses to be surrounded by expensive art and yet has no independent source of funds, it is probably impractical to seek a job as the executive director of the local community chest.

Second, one's past and current life styles, in that they reflect one's attitudes and values, can provide us with data. No matter how constrained one is by economics or institutional requirements, one always has some choice about how to adapt to those constraints. And the form or pattern of adaptation says something about the person.

The transcripts (of audiotapes) and pictures that follow describe the life styles of three people. As you read them, ask yourself: what are these data telling us about these people?

The Life Styles of Three People

Nancy Fuare

Early Life

Born and raised in the state of Washington

Education

1963–64	Year of independent study in Paris
1966 —	B.A. in French from University of Washington
1974 —	M.B.A. at Harvard Business School with a marketing concentration

Job History

1967 —	Six months as a Junior High English teacher in Ohio
1967–69	High school French teacher in Ohio
1969–70	Junior high school teacher in Massachusetts
1974—	Asst. buyer for a major department store in Boston.

Personal

Married with one child; husband a Harvard M.B.A. Own house (about 7 miles from work).

I live in a residential suburb of Boston with my husband and five-year-old daughter Sarah. We have a nice house, not fancy, but it's nice. It's a very diverse neighborhood with a park and it has a pond and a beach and a place for children to play.

There are several things that give me satisfaction in my

life right now. What's fun and a challenge is trying to balance a career and a husband and a family, and I find a certain amount of satisfaction in seeming to be able to do that

The biggest problem in my life right now is trying to balance my work with the home life. There is not enough time in the day. My daughter goes to a school in Cambridge and I drop her off on my way to work at 8:30 in the morning. She goes home with a friend after school. My husband or I pick her up at 6:30 in the evening and we come home and then I

successfully. I also take satisfaction in the fact that I went to Harvard Business School and I managed to get in and get out. My motivations for going were twofold. On the positive side I had always wanted a career, even knowing that I was going to be married and have children. I still wanted a career. On the negative side I didn't like being a housewife. I stayed home two years with my daughter when she was born but I was not very good at it. So that was also a motivating factor of getting out of the house.

frantically try to cook dinner, short-order cook for about 20 minutes or so, and my husband is getting everything else ready, setting the table, playing with Sarah, feeding the cat.

The most important part of our day is when we eat together in our dining room. That is our family time and we always sit in the dining room and try and have dinner together and we discuss what we have done during the day.

It seems sometimes that I've never left the Business School. It's work all day and work all night. There are some nights when I can just sit and relax. I always stay up too late. I am a night owl by habit and I can never get enough sleep.

After dinner we play together, get Sarah ready for bed, and then have the fights between 8 and 8:30 of just when she'll go to bed. After she goes to bed at 8:30, I often have work to do.

On weekends we spend our time as a family. We don't really do a lot of outside things because we feel that is the time we make up for lost time with Sarah. We spend time with Sarah at the park. We go to the movies with her if it's a crummy day and we'll read stories to her and spend a lot of time with her. As much as we can.

In the evenings on the weekends we try and spend as much time as we can with friends. Friends are very important to us; each of us has our own set of friends, and they are nonbusiness friends. We don't socialize with people from work. Not deliberately. It's just that we already had our friends and we find it is much easier to be in a situation where politics are not involved. It makes it a real friendship rather than being with someone because this will help my husband's career or my husband wants to help my career.

I love my job. It's a vibrant, hectic, frustrating-at-times job, but it is very exciting. There is never enough time to do everything. My typical day—I start the day at 6 o'clock. I get Sarah up and ready and we have breakfast. I drive her to school and then I spend a bit of time with her at her school and then I drive on to Harvard Square. I park in an inexpensive all-day lot. Walk up Brattle Street to the subway. Grab the subway into Boston and come up and out and over into the store and up the escalator to my department, which is a sportswear area.

My job involves a lot of schlepping. I push racks around. I get my hands very, very dirty with hangers. I'm responsible for the look of the floor.

I decided to go into retailing because for me it is the ideal job. If anyone asked me what I'd like to do most in the world I would say I like to shop. It's fun to think that when I become a buyer I will be getting paid to shop, which is something I love to do anyway.

I have the displays. When new merchandise comes in, I get to count it to make sure it is the right size and color. Decide where to put it and then I have a lot of paper work that I have to do in the office. That isn't quite so much fun.

The biggest dissatisfaction in my life right now is I don't have enough private time. I have very little time to think and do nothing and study my navel if I want to. There is just no time for that. I also find that I am becoming progressively more limited. I can't develop new interests or even pick up old interests that I had at one time. I'd love to learn tennis and get more proficient at sailing and take time in the winter to ski and we just haven't been able to do that yet.

You know life, a career, and family are very important. I'm lucky I have a husband who is sure enough of himself to have a career-oriented wife and he doesn't feel threatened by it, which is great. He is willing to share the responsibility of home and family with me. And by that, really share them. He does the dishes every night while I get Sarah in her bath and it doesn't seem to emasculate him in any way.

One of the most important things for us is where we live. We are cocky enough to think we can choose whatever city we want to live in and find jobs there. The only three places at this point that we believe we could consider are Boston or Seattle or San Francisco.

We refuse to be under the control of a corporation and won't be corporate gypsies. And so far we have been able to work it that way.

My husband and I have kind of an arrangement that's explicit. It's not written down but we've talked about it. We both understand and agree that if one or the other of us thinks it's necessary for our career to go somewhere that is not the right time or place for the other, we don't just pick up and go. We'll talk about it. We'll discuss it, and if it comes to the point where the career becomes more important than being together, then that person who places that priority kind of has to go alone.

Les Rosen

Early Life

Born and raised near Boston

Education

1964 — Babson Institute degree in accounting

1967 — M.B.A. from Columbia

Job History

1964 — Spent two months running family business

1964 — (February–September) First National Bank of Boston—Credit Analyst

1967 — Prudential Insurance—Lender of long-term un-secured loans

1972 — Self-employed; acts as financial VP to five small firms; handles private placements also.

Personal

Unmarried

Rents an apartment (located about 10 miles from his office)

I think if I were to define my life style, it would be defined in one word: WORK. Over the last four or five or six years since I got out of business school it's been clearly in that direction. This is especially true in the last two or three or four months since I began my own business. I have be-

come the financial vice-president of five companies in Massachusetts and New Hampshire. These are not the typical venture-capital kind of companies, but going concerns with sales between $1 and $10 million. I probably spend 60 or 80 or 90 hours a week whether in actual work circumstances or just reading, which is a great necessity in my job—just trying to keep up with current events in the financial world.

I think about the concept of working a great deal, which leads to a necessity for having an outlet for frustrations.

I was planning on taking that much time off when I wanted to, not when I could fit it into somebody's else's schedule.

This leads me at least into physical kinds of activities, like skiing, squash, tennis, and other kinds of sports, which are usually very competitive and which easily lead to a lot of yelling and screaming and physical exertion. Typically, I probably play squash three or four times every two weeks. I've noticed that since I've gone into business for myself, the amount of squash and other physical kinds of activities has begun to increase. One of the reasons I left my old job was not because I didn't have a lot of flexibility in it, but because I didn't want to have to suggest to anybody else that

I have developed a lot of good friends both because I'm from the local area, and have known a lot of people since elementary school and junior high school, and also through working. I've developed a good group of friends that have not only been able to help me in my new career, but also tend to be a social group of friends. We participate together in work projects, so-called deals in the financial world, and also in the sporting aspects of things. Most of my other friends probably play squash, tennis, skiing, also.

Because of the kinds of things that are of interest to me, it has not been particularly important for me over the last three or four, really five years since business school, to have to put a lot of dollars into what we'll call physical kinds of things. I've always felt that the best thing to do

The time that I spend outside of the activities that I've mentioned so far is probably just going home at night and sitting down and relaxing and reading, when I'm dog tired, or going out and doing some dating, partying, and whatever fits my personality at that particular time.

with money is either to invest it or to spend it on restaurants or trips. My roommate and I have taken one major trip a year for the last three years. I don't put a lot of dollars into clothing and apartment fixtures. We now have finally moved into a new apartment, which is certainly a lot bigger than our old one, having three bedrooms and a full living room almost as big as our old living room/dining room together. The other apartment that I had moved into after graduating from business school was a great value. My cost of maintaining myself in that way was under $150 a month.

flexibility that I needed, and as it turns out it's worked extremely well for me. I say this is more luck than anything else, in terms of the way I live, which is probably exactly the way I'd like to live.

In terms of planning my career, I planned it out generally but not with great specifics of the kind of job function and

---

Jorgen Hedrich

Early Life

Born and raised in Denmark

Education

1964 — Graduated from the School of Business and Economics in Copenhagen

1969 — S.M. from Sloan School of Management (MIT) with specialty in management information systems and O.D.

Job History

1955–1957 — Apprentice in import-export business

1957–1959 — Danish army

1959–1960 — Odd jobs in Canada

1964–1967 — International Nickel in Canada

1969–1972 — Federal Reserve Bank in Chicago. Hired as an operations analyst, now a VP for Program Planning & Budgeting

Personal

Married (1964) with 2 children

Own house (located 30 miles from work)

My life now is separated basically into my job and my private life. I don't like particularly to mix my job with my home life, and I don't like to have to feel that I have to perform for customers or for the corporation when I'm really not there. So, although it's getting occasionally difficult to do that—there is a certain amount of pleasure sometimes to be derived from having a work associate over—I like to keep that to a minimum. We are separated from the work by distance, we live in the country, and that makes the break quite easy to accomplish. I have a 30-mile drive back and forth every day, and when I'm off work I'm really out in the sticks.

Our family life tends to be very informal. I like to associate with a few close friends. We don't particularly like cocktail parties or large gatherings like that. We like to go with one or two couples that we like to a show, to a concert, or something like that. We spend a lot of time with our children. We have two small children three and four years old and they require a fair amount of our attention.

The job itself is, has been, a very challenging one. The Federal Reserve System is an important institution and I feel working here is very worthwhile. I'm vice-president in

charge of planning, programming, and budgeting. What that means is that I'm in charge of long-range planning, computer operations and computer programming, operations research, and other staff specialties. All told it's about 120 people that report to me directly and indirectly. At the present time, the Federal Reserve is in a state of very rapid change and this means that I keep myself busy as well as the people that work with me. It's an exciting time to be here and I quite enjoy that.

On my typical working day I get up and have breakfast with the family, the kids are there, and I leave for work at about 7:30. It takes me about an hour in a car pool, which is

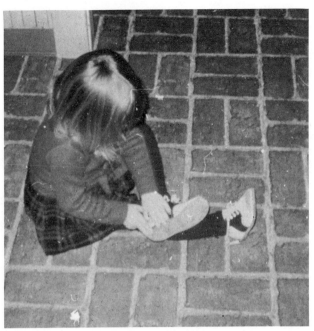

sort of a social hour before work. I leave work again around 5:30 and get back around 6:30. I spend the first hour or so

When I'm off on the weekends, whenever the weather permits, I like to be outside. I like to work around the house. We have a large wooded lot, and I have a garden. I like to do gardening, and I like to cut wood and do physical things. We like to take the kids out on weekends. We might go for a hike in the mountains or take them to a zoo or take them for a walk in the country some place, but we spend the weekends together usually. We have a foreign student from Northwestern who comes out and joins us on the weekend occasionally, sort of an additional member of the family whom the kids like very much. But we tend to keep the weekends fairly low-key and outdoors as much as we can.

playing with the kids, have a meal, and then play with them a little bit again. I make a point of putting them to bed. The contact with the kids is fairly limited because of the commute time. I do a lot of traveling, and occasionally won't be back for a couple of days or so.

My wife grew up in Canada and I worked in Canada myself and I got very fond of the Canadian north country, so whenever we have vacations in the summertime we like to go north, and we will go up and spend a couple or three weeks at a lake; it's sort of really away from it all, and

Other than that, we like to spend our vacations alone. Usually we rent a cottage someplace. Last fall we went to the lake after Labor Day when it's reasonably peaceful and quiet down there. We like walking along the beach. We like bicycle trips and that sort of thing, and that's how we spend our vacations.

no roads, there's no electricity. So you rough it when you're there. And I have no neighbors to speak of. But the country is beautiful. It's a nice clear lake. Good fishing. Unfortunately we don't get up there too often, but there is pretty nice hunting in the fall.

If I had to make any changes in our present arrangement, if the sky was the limit, so to speak, so far as money is concerned, I don't know that I would do things all that much differently. I'm really quite content with the current situation. We don't spend much time amassing material posses-

sions. I would like to run a household so that we can take a considerable cut in income without that affecting us. As far as I'm concerned, this is the sort of thing that gives me a sense of independence. If I don't like what I'm doing, I can go away and I don't have to get hung up on whether or not the job that I'm going to walk into is going to give me exactly the same income as I'm used to. If we had more money, we might expand the house slightly. The one thing that we would like to do, if our family situation were somewhat different, is to get away on the odd weekend without the kids, but since both my wife and I are immigrants, we don't have any relatives nearby that we can ask to take the kids. It has been impossible to do this sort of thing, but we think we would like to do that. Other than that I don't think we would make any drastic changes in our life style.

Creating and Analyzing Life Style Representations

The life style representations of Fuare, Rosen, and Hedrich were created by the people themselves (in conjunction with a researcher who took the pictures, and taped their verbal descriptions). With that one fact in mind, you can analyze the three representations in the same general way that you have analyzed Written Interviews and 24-hour diaries. That is, you can look for patterns in the visual and written data that might tell you something important about the individuals.

For example, one potential theme in Hedrich's data might be simply labeled "likes a sense of independence." Hedrich says he prefers to keep his job and his home life separate (i.e., independent). He lives 30 miles from work in what appears to be a sparsely populated area. He likes to spend vacations, he says, where there are "no roads" and "no electricity." And he tells us of an economic philosophy of running "a household so that we can take a considerable cut in income without that affecting us." He even uses the phrase "sense of independence."

One potential theme in Rosen's data might be called "the centrality of work." He puts in long work hours (60–90 per week), relative to most people. His friends, he tells us, are mostly his work associates. He describes his major non-work activity, sports, as an "outlet for frustrations" built up from "working a great deal." He even summarizes his overall life style as "one word: WORK."

In Fuare's data, one potential theme might be labeled "a relatively high level of diverse activity." Fuare's description of her days has her constantly on the run, doing a variety of things with family, friends, and her work. Her background is more diverse than most people's: French and

Business, teaching and buying. She describes her residential area as "diverse," and her job as "hectic." And her complaints are often directed at not being able to have a relatively high level of diverse activity (e.g., didn't like staying at home as a housewife, doesn't like the fact that the interests she has time to pursue are "becoming progressively more limited").

There are, of course, other possible themes in all three sets of life style data. Which do you see?

This method of describing a life style in words and pictures is, of course, only one of a number of ways that one could try to represent a current, a past, or a desired life style. Our students have also used diagrams (see Figure 1), drawn pictures, created collages, and written short essays.

No matter how one goes about trying to represent his or her life style, the product can be treated as data for self-assessment purposes. It is more potentially useful information that can help support or redefine emerging themes. It is another data source from which to draw inferences.

Furthermore, the very process of creating these representations can also be a useful exercise, because it gets you to think about the totality of your life, and the ways in which the various parts are interdependent. This subject of interdependence is very important, and will be explicitly discussed in the second part of the book.

Exercise

Try creating at least one life-style representation for yourself in any form you prefer. You may want to focus on a past life-style, your current one, a future one, or all three. When you are done, put the product with your other personal documents in your workbook.

FIGURE 1 A Sample Life-Style Diagram

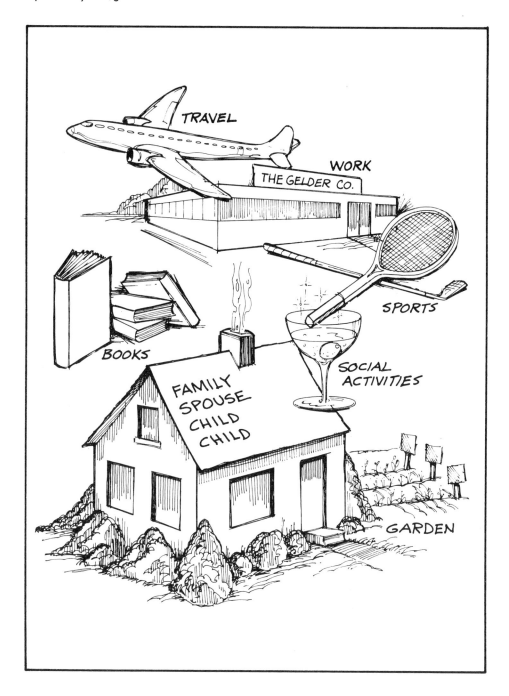

IX

Other Data-Generating Devices

NOTE:
MAKE SURE THAT YOUR FEELINGS RECORD IS UP TO
DATE AND YOUR BACKGROUND FACTS SHEET IS COMPLETED
BEFORE READING THIS CHAPTER

The only data-generating devices in the book and workbook that we have not yet talked about are the Background Facts sheet and the Feelings Record. Both can be treated just like the others; no further explanation is really necessary. They offer two more sets of potentially useful data about yourself. Although as information sources they are seldom as rich as the Written Interview or the Strong-Campbell, both should be used in your analysis such as you use the Diary, AVL, and Life-Style Representations.

The seven data-generating devices contained in the workbook should provide you with enough information to do your self-assessment. Many other possible sources of data, however, might be useful to you. You may wish to use such data to supplement those that you now have. In this chapter we shall briefly describe some of those other sources.

We would offer two caveats, however, neither of which should surprise you. First, be sure you understand the nature of other data-generating sources so that you can understand the information they produce. Second, be sure you treat the supplementary data as you have treated those from the seven devices in this book. Remember that a single datum from a single source proves nothing; look for patterns.

Other Psychological Tests

Various students of ours have at one time or another used the following instruments in their self-assessments:

1. Edwards Personal Preference Schedule.

2. Thematic Apperception Test.
3. Rorschach Inkblot Test.
4. Myers-Briggs Type Indicator.

There are numerous other instruments like these.

You may find that you cannot gain access to these tests—especially ones like the Rorschach—except from a properly trained psychologist. And this is probably how it should be. Be sure, however, if a psychologist administers a test to you and interprets its output, that YOU understand the basis of his or her interpretation.

I.Q. and Other "Aptitude" Tests

A number of I.Q. and so-called aptitude tests exist today. No doubt you have taken at least one of these tests (such as the S.A.T. or G.R.E. tests you took as a part of applying to undergraduate or graduate school). A few of the more popular are:

1. Wechsler Adult Intelligence Scale.
2. Harvard Speed Alphas.
3. Skills Inventories.
4. Miller Analogies.

Be sure to treat these devices as carefully as you do all your data-generating instruments. Sophisticated "tests" such as these look more authoritative to many people than a simple device like a 24-hour diary, and so people may be more passive, less critical, and less demanding in dealing with the output of these tests. Don't be!

Experiential Exercises and Games

In the past decade a number of exercises and games have been created that simulate some type of real-world activity and can provide interesting data to the participant. An example is the "In-Basket" test, developed by Educational Testing Service and AT&T, and today available in a variety of versions. In a typical version, an individual is given the role of a manager who has 25 items in his or her in-basket (letters, memos, phone messages, etc.), must catch a plane in three hours, and can reach no one on the phone or in person (it is Sunday). The individual is given three hours to go through the in-basket and take any actions that seem necessary (schedule meetings, write notes, etc.); his or her behavior and decisions become the output of the exercise.

Experiential exercises and games can provide useful data for people of all ages, but we've found them particularly helpful to young people—especially those with no work experience.

The output from these exercises, which can be rather rich, should be treated the same way as the output of other devices. Again, it is important to understand the data-generating device to avoid misusing its output. The most common misuse of game output is to make huge inferential leaps to grand conclusions, based on the assumption that the game experience was *exactly* like the real experience it was simulating. (For example, Joe seems to do a much better job than other participants playing a "plant manager" in the in-basket exercise. Joe therefore would probably be a good plant manager.)

The In-Basket exercise can be obtained through Educational Testing Service, Princeton, N.J. 08540. Other exercises of this type can be found in *Organizational Psychol-*ogy: An Experiential Approach by Kolb, Rubin, and McIntyre (Englewood Cliffs, N.J.: Prentice-Hall, Inc., 1974) and in *Management: An Experiential Approach* by Knudson, Woodworth, and Bell (New York: McGraw-Hill Book Company, 1973).

Other Personal/Historical Documents

Our students have occasionally used a variety of documents from their pasts as data in their self-assessments. For example, we have asked them to include their graduate school application form, since it requires them to answer a number of interesting essay questions. Some students have also used old diaries, and photographs, letters of recommendation, performance appraisals, newspaper clippings, and essays that they wrote. As long as you are sensitive to the circumstances under which these personal/historical documents were generated, they can occasionally be useful additions to your data.

Perceptual Feedback from Others

One could also use perceptual feedback from others in a self-assessment. For example, you could ask a dozen or so people who have seen you extensively in work (school or job) situations each to list anonymously what they think your five greatests strengths and five biggest weaknesses are.

Perceptual feedback can be useful as long as you are sensitive to what the data are based on. Where and under what conditions have the people you polled seen you behave? You must also get data from a fairly large number of people (not three or four). Otherwise you would have to try to take into account what is inside each of their idiosyncratic "black boxes," and that is an impossible task.

X

Finalizing Themes and Identifying Their Implications

After you have completed data generation and made a thorough initial analysis, it is time to move on to the last steps in the self-assessment process. These steps involve developing a final set of themes and identifying their job and career implications. The output of this stage in the process is a completed self-assessment.

The Number of Themes

After you have analyzed all available data and found all the themes you can, you may wonder whether the number of themes identified is typical or appropriate—"Or am I still missing something?"

Our experience suggests that the number of themes that can be generated depends, to some extent, on the number and type of data-generating instruments used. Using the devices in this book, one normally will find about 15 to 25 themes in a good analysis. Initial analyses based on data from only three or four devices may yield as many as a dozen "tentative" themes that, while not yet convincing, look promising. Good analyses based on more than our devices will generally not produce more than 30 well-supported themes.

Sometimes people are not able to locate more than a dozen convincing themes in their data. Usually they simply haven't looked hard or long enough, but that is not the only reason. Sometimes a person, either consciously or unconsciously, tries to find themes that are completely "independent"—that do not, in a sense, overlap. Similarly, one sometimes looks for themes that fit into a limited number of categories, such as "skills," "values," and "goals." In both cases the underlying problem is the same: The person is imposing a model or a set of constraints on the data, thereby limiting what the data can say. As we have

said before, it is essential to effective thematic development that one let the data speak for themselves.

A different set of factors is often associated with an analysis containing 30 to 40 themes. Often many of these themes say almost the same thing; the degree of overlap is extreme. Or many of the themes may be supported by very few data. In either instance, many similar themes can usually be collapsed into more general and better-supported themes without the loss of any important information.

A good self-assessment does not have to contain a certain quota of themes. But our experience strongly suggests that if you end up with less than 15 or more than 30 themes, it is wise to carefully reexamine them.

Assessing the Accuracy and Importance of Themes

Before you accept a set of themes as final, you have to judge the importance and accuracy of each theme that has been located and labeled. Judgment is required, because no rules, outside of one's own common sense, are available for determining whether the evidence supporting some theme is "enough" to ensure its accuracy, or whether the amount of evidence suggests that a theme is of great importance, moderate importance, or minor importance.

The questions one needs to raise in making this judgment are fairly obvious ones:

1. How many data seem to support the theme? A theme supported by ten data certainly has a greater chance of being accurate and important than one supported by only three.
2. Where do these data come from? Do they all come from just one of the data-generating devices, or do they come from more than one? A theme supported by data

from four different instruments seems more likely to be accurate and important than one supported by data from only one source.

3. How many, if any, data contradict the theme? Any contradictory datum raises the question of a theme's validity. But a theme with 10 data supporting it and one contradicting it would quite reasonably be handled differently from a theme with four data supporting it and two contradicting it.

One might suppose that, because precise decision rules are lacking, judgments about themes tend to be highly idiosyncratic. However, we have not found this to be the case. Most people, when looking at the same set of themes, tend to make similar judgments regarding the accuracy and importance of each one.

For an example of a final set of themes in a self-assessment, see Appendix A.

Drawing Implications from Themes

The final step in the self-assessment process involves identifying the career and job implications inherent in a set of themes. The ultimate purpose here is to translate the basic assessment into a more useful form.

It is often possible to identify some job and career implications directly from each theme. If the theme is "short attention span," then one might reasonably conclude that "a job requiring concentrated attention on one task for long periods might prove unpleasant." One could approach this final step in the self-assessment process in just this manner—by taking each theme, one at a time, and looking for what it implies regarding job or career. Such an approach, however, is inadequate for our purposes.

In "Identifying Themes" (Chapter VI), we suggested you avoid imposing constraints or structures or models on their form or type, but as much as possible just let the data "talk to you." This is a way to avoid excluding or distorting relevant information. As a result, however, the themes you end up with may overlap to some degree, and may not speak directly to all the issues that might be relevant. (That is, they probably won't be mutually exclusive or exhaustive.) Job and career implications drawn directly from such themes will themselves overlap and fail to address some issues; they will probably be cumbersome to use and even misleading.

To translate themes into a sound and useful set of job and career implications, first group together all the themes that overlap or are strongly related to one another. For example, suppose one had three themes that related to one's way of thinking and approaching problems and tasks: "Doesn't like detail," "Very systematic," and "Future oriented." These themes would be grouped together. So would the two themes, "Needs to be number 1" and "Needs people contact," which speak to what one wants from life. And so should the three themes, "Dislikes crowded living," "Nature very important," and "Strong affiliation with family (who live in Oregon)," which all relate to one's life-style preferences.

Some themes, of course, because they overlap a number

of other themes in a number of different ways, will end up in more than one grouping. Some themes may not fit into any groups—they seem to be quite independent of the others. The overall grouping shown in Figure 1 is a typical result of this process.

FIGURE 1 Typical First Grouping of Themes

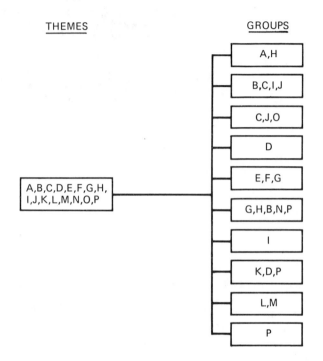

You can translate each grouping into an initial set of implications by writing a phrase, sentence, or sentences that seem to capture what is being expressed in the themes. For example:

THEMES	IMPLICATION
1. Likes immediate feedback.	This person dislikes ambiguity.
2. Prefers planning ahead.	He or she has a "no-surprise"
3. Pragmatic.	attitude toward change.
4. Has disciplined responses to uncertainty.	

Examples of some other implications, taken from self-assessment papers, are shown in Figure 2. You will note that these statements are written in a number of formats. We have not found one "best" form for expressing implications. As long as they are as precise as possible, take into account all the themes and their interdependencies, and speak to the basic aspects of a person that have job and career relevance, then any form is acceptable.

Some people find the process of grouping themes together and identifying their implications difficult. A step-by-step method that may help such people is the following:

1. Generate an initial set of implications, even if the process seems awkward and uncomfortable.

2. Evaluate your results in light of three criteria: (a) Do the implications overlap to a minimum and yet take into account the overlap inherent in the themes? (b) Do

Paper 1

1. *Prefer people with whom I can be sincere and whom I can respect.* The sincerity aspect of this implication is drawn from the theme "Outgoing, Friendly, But Not Socially Aggressive." The letter from Dillon's Beach (in Question III of the Interview) is also exemplary of an inclination to level with people: "Among friends . . . personal sincerity enhances sensitivity to individual preferences, and cooperation, therefore, is more easily realized." "A sincere expression of differences, then, should not be grounds for dissolving the friendship." Being able to respect associates is important both as fulfilling a need for this good feeling and the avoidance of fake smiles and back slapping.

2. *Prefer people who are more concerned about doing something than being somebody.* Here the emphasis is on being constructive, contributing something to the organizational effort, as opposed to emphasizing how to get ahead in terms of position or status. Data from three themes support this conclusion: "Positive Orientation/Doing Something Constructive," "Attracted to People Who Are Perceived as Strivers," and "Striving/ A Hard Worker." In addition, those who stress their being somebody tend, in my mind, to be more snobbish and politically guarded. This, in turn, mitigates against friendliness, helping others, and sincerity, personal values that surface in themes.

Paper 2

1. If daily routine isolates from people, boredom will result. (Based on themes C, D)
2. If not involved in Latin America's development, I will feel I cheated my country and sold out for dollars alone. (Themes L, M)

3. If technical ability and M.B.A. training not utilized, I will feel I have wasted the past six years. (Themes F, G, H)
4. If the people above me don't live up to my expectations, I will not work to my capacity. (Themes C, E)
5. If the person above me has different values, the work provided and rewards returned will not meet anyone's expectations. This will result in frustration. (Themes E, L, F)

Paper 3

1. *Will greatly enjoy position offering much contact with people, especially sharp people who can stimulate me to both grow as a person and become well rounded.* (Themes 10, 11, 17, and 23) If my colleagues are rather bookish or greatly hung up on minutiae, my gregarious nature will meet with frustration. I love to be with people who are both fun-loving and perceptive. This latter atmosphere would cause me to get up in the morning with a smile from knowing my day would be enjoyable.

2. *Would enjoy the posture of being the organizer of people—the person with authority over and responsibility for them—as this would result in the feeling of importance.* (Themes 1, 3, 19) I would feel my talents were really going to waste if I didn't have the opportunity to motivate and direct people toward achieving greater success for the company. Plus, if I were not to receive a visible position, a feeling of unfulfillment would arise due to lack of importance. If I were given the responsibility to start or manage a group I'd probably put my heart and soul into it and love it.

---

the implications speak about all the characteristics and behavior that are obviously relevant to job and career questions? (c) Do the implications take into account all the information in the themes? If your implications satisfy these criteria, your task is over. More often than not, they won't, and you will have to continue in an iterative process of making modifications until they do.

3. If your implications have ignored a theme, or themes, correcting this is easy. Take the theme and see if it fits into any of the groupings. If it does, change the implication based on this new addition. If it doesn't fit into any existing grouping, identify and add a new implication directly from the theme itself.

4. If some implications still seem to overlap significantly, the problem probably lies in a poor grouping of themes. By going back and trying different theme groupings, you can eliminate the problem by trial and error.

5. If the implications don't seem to speak to some career and job issues, clearly identify what those issues are and then go back to see if any of the themes speak to them. If you can find one or more relevant themes, group them together and add a new implication.

To aid in assessing whether an initial set of implications speaks to all the basic job and career issues, we have found questions of the following type to be useful:

1. Does this set of implications tell us anything about what types of people (if any) this person likes to be with and work with?
2. Does it say how he or she likes to relate to people?
3. Does it tell us what types of tasks this person prefers to work on?
4. Does it suggest what types of intrinsic and extrinsic rewards he or she prefers?
5. Does it say what types of environments this person strongly likes or dislikes?

Sometimes one will identify an issue that an initial set of implications does not address, and upon checking find that none of the themes addresses it either. If the themes have been developed properly, then one can do nothing except leave this void in the set of implications. It is very important that one not go back to raw data and try unsystematically to create an implication to fill some void.

You will find a good set of implications, along with the rest of the self-assessment paper, in Appendix A. Other examples of implications can be found in the cases at the end of this chapter and the end of Chapter XII. Looking over these examples will probably help you in writing your own paper.

Finalizing a Set of Implications

One final task should be completed before you stop working on your implications. Insofar as possible, you want to try to differentiate the implications in terms of their importance. In a typical self-assessment, some implications are more important than others, and the more clearly this is specified, the more the assessment will help you to choose among different "good" job and career options.

To differentiate implication statements by importance, you need only work backward to trace the information that each is based on. For example, an implication statement derived from three themes, each based on 15 data from five different data-generating devices, probably is speaking to a more central and important issue than one derived from a single theme based on eight data from three devices. Your own judgment is crucial here, of course, and it cannot be replaced by merely mechanical rules.

The best test of whether you are finished writing your self-assessment, or whether it still needs some finishing work, is your own opinion of it. If you feel that your set of implications is sound, accurate, and useful—then your task is done. If you don't feel that way, you need to keep working until you do. YOU ARE THE ONE WHO WILL HAVE TO USE YOUR SELF-ASSESSMENT, AND IF YOU DON'T BELIEVE IN IT, YOU WON'T USE IT. We have found that when people really believe in their self-assessment, not only do they use it, but their belief heightens their energy and motivation to overcome job and career obstacles that frustrate and stop many others. Accurate self-knowledge, in which one has confidence, can be a tremendous source of power for an individual.

Exercise

On the following pages you will find seven sources of data on one person, as well as that person's self-assessment paper. Do a thorough critique of that self-assessment paper.

Betsy Drake (A)

Written Interview

Answer Number One. Saturday afternoon, time to put all those random jottings and scattered thoughts of the past week down on paper—or at least to start. A few background facts may help keep things in order, and probably will shed some light on my later whys and wherefores. I'm the second child of five, four girls and a boy. Since Daddy is in the Navy, a dentist, we have a variety of birthplaces: Marilyn—Augusta, Me., me—Bangor, Me. (my "home" in spite of the fact that only my first six months were lived there), Sally and Jill—both in San Diego, and Dale in Pensacola. We're a close family, although each of us has different interests and ideas as adults. Maybe the ages have something to do with it, all just two years apart. Mom and Dad are both from the Midwest, and in spite of the many moves we have all grown up as Midwesterners in outlook, except maybe Dale, who spent most of his growing years in the East.

The first vivid memory I have is of my third birthday party. We lived in San Diego at the time, and the party was outside in the evening. I seem to remember that most of the guests were adults, and all of them made much of me. Someone gave me a flowered nightie, which I got to model before Daddy took me off to bed.

My only other memory of that house was stepping on a bee, going barefoot in the front yard. (It has since developed that both Daddy and some of my sisters have a serious allergy to bees; maybe the memory is clear because my physiological reaction was so strong.)

The days in Pensacola were generally happy ones, relaxed and peaceful. (Recently I wondered if this feeling about those days was due to my age—four or five—and asked Mother about it. She said that those were in fact relaxed times for the family.) The only upset of this time, for me, was starting kindergarten. Every day about an hour before time to set off, I would tell Mom of all the playing I still had to do that day. It was inevitable that she would call me to get ready, braid my hair in those tedious French braids, and tell me that I didn't have to go if I didn't want to. I'd always say that I did want to go, and then proceed to cry from the minute I got in the car to go until the carpool mother of the day picked us up in the afternoon. The only enjoyable part of the whole procedure was sitting in the front seat with my father, who took a whole group of us kindergarteners to school each day during his lunch hour.

I survived that, and first and second grades, although for years I was excessively anxious over the first day of school. Sometime during the first few years of school it came to me that other kids weren't as smart as I, and I found the work no problem. My real achievement of those years, however, was learning to "run in" in jumping rope.

After that, we moved to Port Arthur for a short while, just long enough for me to get enrolled in a third grade which I hated. We had a long ride to an overcrowded school (the new one was being built down the street, but had been delayed in construction). Even the buses ran in two shifts; in order to get the early bus home right after school, my sister and I had to take the early morning bus, and wait in the cafeteria with the rest of the early crowd for an hour before school started. The miseries of the year all stemmed from my teacher's habit of keeping us late (not as punishment, merely because she was disorganized) which meant that I continually missed the first bus, and kept Marilyn waiting. One day it was just too much; after getting out of class I asked one of the older kids to take me to the principal's office. I cried and complained to him, and from then on got released on time. Come to think of it, this was the same teacher who called all of us eight-year-olds by our last names.

That was soon over, however, and in the middle of the term we moved to Jefferson City, Mo., a tiny little town not far from Joplin. We had a good time in this little place, voted an All-American City not long before because of petunias planted all through the town square. We had good times in school and outside activities, and I developed a "best friend" friendship with a classmate who lived outside of town, and our families often picnicked together out at their farm.

This was the first time we kids got to stay alone, too, one summer when Mom volunteered to drive somewhere with a nondriving neighbor whose husband was fatally ill. I don't remember the circumstances of her trip, but I do remember that we got to "babysit" each other all day, with the help of another fifth-grade friend of my older sisters, and fix dinner for Dad at night.

The next move took us back to San Diego, the beginning of my junior high. My memories of those days include the thrill of being chosen to model in a schoolwide fashion show, winning first place in the Christmas art fair with an elaborate paper sculpture of the 12 Days of Christmas, still playing with dolls with my new best friend Cheryl (the sophisticated Barby dolls, but dolls nonetheless), and when we were feeling very flush and had gotten our Moms' permission, stopping at Walgreen's for a cherry coke. Oh, and *hating* the saddle shoes our parents loved.

About seventh grade, we (Cheryl and I) took a long camping trip with a group from school, sponsored and led by Mr. Smolich, the geography teacher. The trip was planned as a hike into the Grand Canyon, but at the last minute the canyon got its worst snow in years and we were diverted to Carlsbad Caverns. Either was fine with me. We had a great time, although I do remember being embarrassed by the rowdiness of some of the boys on the trip. (I was a prim kid in those early days, too involved in trying to be grown up instead of relaxing and realizing it would come without any interest or effort on my part.)

My sister Marilyn had taken two or three of these trips before I did, and had in fact had many of the teachers I had. So I lived with both her example and her shadow. And since she got the coveted straight A's, I followed suit.

I hated to leave all this on our *next* move, which was to Frankfort, Germany. Once we were there, though, we never wanted to leave. I loved the beautiful town, and the freedom we kids had to get around on our own with the trains and trolleys. I was enrolled in the American high school, still too college-oriented to risk losing a year by going to a German high school. I had the good luck of having a really outstanding German teacher (her influence was so strong that I almost wrote the last in German), and learned the language quickly and somewhat thoroughly.

Of all the subjects I've taken, this one has stuck the best. In fact, I don't recall much learning activity at all, except for getting right one answer on a history quiz which we had not had in class. The question was: Which two Protestant religions had settled from Pennsylvania to the Dakotas? I knew that it was the Methodists (us) and the Baptists (them) from a rare visit to my mother's mother's. My grandmother had remarked that she had even seen a few Baptists in church that morning, our minister was so good. It was a matter of not-so-friendly rivalry between the churches to get higher turnouts and host better church suppers. The lesson I gained from the history-quiz incident was the value of logic, making connections between things. It's only after observing my sisters with their kids that I realize we were *taught* how to think by our parents. (I thought it just came naturally.)

While we were in Germany, we took a number of family trips—Holland, Italy, Switzerland, Berlin, Austria. I remember them all vividly, the colors and the smells and sounds, and I loved each place more than the last. Just for the sheer, raw *experience* of new things to see and taste it was memorable. One of our favorite local jaunts became a weeklong trip to Garmisch and Berchtesgaden, sites of both the fairytale castles of the crazy Ludwigs and Hitler's hideaway.

During the Frankfort stay, Marilyn graduated from high school (first in her class, an achievement not duplicated until my younger brother graduated 10 years later). She chose the U. of Colorado, and her selection of a big state school undoubtedly influenced my decision later on. She got on the train to go up to the port at Bremerhaven and then to get herself to school from New York, and left the whole family crying. It was far more concern over her being so alone and having to cope with so much than the more usual firstborn-leaving-home tears (of poor lonely us).

The following year we returned to the States, and again I hated to leave. The family took a farewell trip through France, which we hated (to a person!) and left a week early. Spent the extra time in England, which I loved; my two enduring impressions are of green growing things *everywhere*—flowers and gardens and parks—and of being cold even though it was mid-July. Finally we sailed again for New York, giving me another chance to become deathly (I felt—not verified by any medical evidence) seasick. The only nice moment during the trip was sailing into the harbor in New York, and hearing the cheer from the homesick GI's on the ship when the Statue of Liberty came into sight. From New York we went directly down to Washington, all seven of us, with thirteen pieces of luggage, by Greyhound bus. (It takes about six weeks for the cars to be shipped over.)

As they often had before, Mom and Dad bought a house fairly quickly and we settled in. It was about 20 miles from Washington, in the middle of a neighborhood which had been considered country a few years before and still had lots of country characteristics—old trees and winding lanes (called lanes, not streets). The beauty of it for us kids was that most of the families in the neighborhood were our age, not the subdivision toddler set. We dated a lot (a lesson learned by anyone who has moved is the attractiveness of the newcomer) and joined in the informal group activities of swimming and playing pool, that summer before school started. My junior year at the high school—a huge consolidated school turning out about 900 kids a year in those days—was fun. I liked the fast pace and diversity of the new place, and its newness. By the second year, however, I was bored with school in general and frantic with the activities which we assumed were necessary for admittance to the school of our choice: German Club President, Chairman for the Prom, this committee, and that club. I hated the activities themselves, hated coming home after dark at night, and was generally tired of the whole procedure. (That spring one of the most popular rock songs was the Lovin'

Spoonful's *Daydream;* it became my theme song for that spring, with the message that it would all be over soon and freedom was ahead.)

On the happy side of that year, I did have a good group of friends, the ''intellectual'' crowd. (It was such a big school that there were several social groups considered prestigious—ours, the ''social'' crowd of football players and cheerleaders, the ''collegiate'' crowd from monied Virginia families. Of course, these are my appellations; there was nothing rigid about the groups. My boyfriend— off and on—of the time was a football player, second-string quarterback and very sexy, who hung around largely with the football crowd, so I spent time with them too.)

Sometime this year I went through the usual trauma (not from fear of rejection—just too many papers!) of filling out college applications and making that choice. I had taken an interest in Chinese after a summer course, and decided that that would be my major. This was the first cut in eliminating schools; my choices were downtown Washington (which would have violated a strong family rule that at least the first year of college had to be spent at least 500 miles from home), the Ivy League schools (against which I had a prejudice so strong that I never considered them), the Big Ten, and California. I settled for the Big Ten; a large state school was my idea of college. After a trip out to visit three which had accepted me—U. of Chicago, U. of Wisconsin, and Indiana—I settled for Wisconsin. It was a happy coincidence that the school I loved, with its pretty campus and very helpful and friendly attitude, was the best deal. I got a substantial scholarship and didn't have to pay a bit for college. (It makes graduate school seem that much more expensive by comparison, but this time it's my money and not my father's, so I feel free to spend.) My mother advised during all the decision-making process just to make a choice that ''seemed right'' and, once chosen, the school would become mine and the others would fade fast in interest. This is just what happened.

College provided no sudden revelations for me, but when I think of who went in and who came out, I know that substantial changes took place. When I started college my political ideas were somewhere to the right of Goldwater; where I picked these up I'm not sure, since my parents are moderately Republican. Probably just part of a general rigidity, which I mostly outgrew during college. In general, the three and a half years I spent at Wisconsin were good ones; I can remember enjoyable walks in the early morning to a 7:30 class when the ground was still frozen and I seemed to be the only one up; pretentious themes written for that same class—English; lots of letters to and from last summer's boyfriend. (We had met, been immediately companionable, and spent every available minute together that summer. Toward the end of the summer, though, I fell just as quickly out of love with Jeff and when I realized it—on one of our last dates—started uncontrollably crying that I no longer felt the same way. He, luckily, interpreted it as my sadness at leaving, and the romance was allowed to die gracefully over the course of the year.)

It was also a passionate time for everything. I threw myself into my school work, studying seven days straight for 10 hours a day to ensure that I got a perfect paper on my Chinese final; once my political conversion took place (gradually, somehow; I had no godsent flash on the way to

Damascus), I *knew* that I had found the truth; I worked tirelessly as a volunteer for Planned Parenthood and had nothing but disdain for the girls in my dorm who conceived children so thoughtlessly in the middle of their college careers and had to drop out of school to marry high school boyfriends (now, of course, I can understand that not only were some of these girls following a rather well-established pattern for Wisconsin, but also they didn't like school and were glad to drop out).

The first year (sad to say, this was simultaneous with all those faithful letters to the summer boyfriend) I fell in love and came close to getting married to a man who was returning to school after several years in the Peace Corps and AID. At some point along the way that year, we started diverging and gradually broke off.

The next three years were spent, socially, with another man from my department, a Ph.D. candidate. Time spent with him, of course, fills most of my memories of that time.

I can remember only a little real learning, in spite of getting a lion's share of A's. It was not until my last semester that I ran across a really outstanding teacher on an odd course picked from a vague interest and a convenient time—something about St. Paul. It was a dynamic and exciting course, and my first (formal) exposure to learning and the development of an idea by the class as a whole during our discussions.

Because I had gone to classes two summers, I was finished with my course work in January and left Wisconsin then, pretty fatigued but very satisfied with the experience. I took away no degree, yet, because of a ''slumbering incomplete'' and didn't really graduate until I finished up three years later. It goes without saying that I did not buzz back to Madison to go through graduation ceremonies.

My second college summer I was at home, working. This was a hard summer, a sad summer. My younger sister, Sally, eloped just after she had turned 18 and graduated from high school. Because they considered her husband very immature, and they felt she had not given herself a chance to try college or other experiences after high school, my parents were heartbroken. My sisters and I attended her wedding, but Dad lost contact with Sally for several years. This was more the result of his uneasiness at not knowing how to effect a reconciliation than of continued anger or self-righteousness. (The footnote to this is that Sally herself made the first move to visit him; Daddy and his grandson—by then 4 or 5 years old—hit it off and became good friends.)

Later in the summer, I heard from friends that a classmate at Wisconsin had been hurt in the Chicago convention fracas, and had been so broken in spirit that she was not returning to school.

On the last day before I was to come back to school, I got word that a very dear high school friend had drowned. He had been studying in Taiwan and had drowned while swimming in the Pacific. I was heartsick. (Mother has said recently that she almost suggested that I stay home a semester, but didn't suggest it since I seemed set on returning to school.)

The experiences of the summer made me reflect about how my ideas of misfortune changed over time. As a youngster, I thought that only a very very few families had any sort of trouble. The only one I knew of was a first-grade friend Vicky, whose mother was always sick and away in some hospital. She and her younger brothers had their father, though, and a wonderful housekeeper to take care of them. At the time that seemed enough.

When I got a little older, I began to recognize that most other people had difficulties: Catholic daughters marrying out of the church; divorces; and three of our neighbors lost sons to Hodgkin's disease. After the summer, I finally accepted the fact that no one is immune.

Back to the story line. At this point my telling may differ slightly from the norm, since it is the story of a young woman graduating from college, rather than a man. Up to the time I left school, the idea that I would have to (or get to) work *had never entered my mind*. I had had no career goals, however vague and subject to change; college studies had been merely a pleasant intellectual exercise of a good mind. My plans for the future were very casual, to do something interesting. At some subconscious level, I had in mind the notion that I merely had to keep myself busy until I married, and that was that. (This of course is different from what most boys think as they grow up; however misguided and uncertain about *what* career to choose, most at least have entertained for years the notion that they will have to have some sort of work. Yet, this subconscious holding of the breath until marriage is very common among women. Two of my closest adult friends, both in their early thirties, have until recently refused to get "real" jobs, settling instead for secretarial stints, or to buy furniture or in any other way live in the moment.)

My plan was to get a simple job—probably as a receptionist, since at the time I couldn't type—and save money for a year in order to go to Taiwan Normal School for intensive Chinese courses. At this point, I was saved by the inability to type, greed and incipient ambition, and pure luck. The jobs I qualified for were so boring and poorly paid I never took a place as a receptionist. Instead, through a sympathetic personnel agent, I got a job as a researcher for a small consulting firm, riding the boom of the Great Society programs and other social consciousness of the time.

The job turned out to be very interesting and a great education. Our main functions were to keep clients informed of what was happening in Washington which was of interest to them, and to develop programs or research proposals to be funded by any of the numerous government agencies. (The first lesson I learned was that on those programs we made our real money by always taking a piece of the action, subcontracting for the support services or the evaluation, for instance. Only the hacks settled for a flat fee for writing the proposal.)

Two of my biggest accomplishments were developing training programs for hospitals to take advantage of the Labor Department's JOBS program—providing jobs, training, and supportive services for the disadvantaged unemployed (how easily the stock phrases come, even after all this time! I think I wrote about half a dozen programs)—and writing a report and recommendations for a client engaged in cable TV software after attending an FCC hearing. I called all the shots right on that one and got

a lot of attention from the client when the final FCC decisions came out a few months later.

The trying parts of the job involved the boss, a caricature of the entrepreneur, who I think had some personality problems beyond that. He was given to quick shifts of mood, to squandering the company's money, and to trying to manipulate his staff by tying up our time and withholding information we needed for our work. On the other hand, since the staff was very small and at times I was the only "professional" in the Washington office, I got a lot of responsibility and quite a lot of power.

After a couple of years, I was ready to leave and accepted a job with the Washington city drug abuse program as administrator and writer. Because of internal hassles, however, this job never materialized. So I had a few months off. On a visit to a good friend from college days, I heard about a job opening in New York. I applied, and in spite of having the worst interview on record, got the job. This was a position as personnel person and systems developer (we never did hit a happy and reasonable job title there) for an employment program for former drug addicts. The organization running the experimental program was a prestigious one, and the two other people I worked with were absolutely great. My main memory of the first summer at the job was one of busyness; we worked 9 and 10 hours a day just to keep the thing going. Gradually we built up the structures and systems, and the day-to-day operations became easier with practice.

Maybe because it is more recent, or harder to assess, it's hard to put down what I learned on that job. However, I enjoyed it tremendously, and stayed until I started school last fall.

Answer Number Two. Back to the beginning. . . . Since I have tried to follow a chronological account in the first question, maybe I'll use this time and space for some impressions and more random memories. One of my lasting impressions of childhood is being outdoors. We lived in various places in the Southwest and had long warm seasons for playing outside in the grass and garden. Every house we lived in had a yard, and in every one Mom put in a flower garden. It was part of our household work to pull weeds and prune bushes, although she was usually glad to trade one of her indoor jobs (like doing the wash) for one of our garden jobs. I often chose this trade to avoid being in the sun and the possibility of touching a slug. (Now how often I wish for the chance to putter around in the garden.)

Wherever we lived, we kept the same routines of work and play. Each of us was responsible for her or his own bedmaking and room cleaning (which was in most houses half a room; when Marilyn and I were at war we would draw chalk lines down the center of our room, setting our territory). We also had rotating responsibility for setting the table at night and for doing the dishes. Each of us had to set one item of the table, plates and placemats being the easiest and therefore most coveted; silverware was always left for the last table setter. And dishes were done in the same way. (The unwritten rule was that the rinser should try to get off any spots left by the washer; if it got as far as the drier or put-awayer it could be returned for rewashing.)

On Saturdays, Mom would make up a list of jobs to be done that day. Then we had our choice. The routine was to initial a job as you began it, and cross it off when it was finished. This method had the advantage of giving us our choice of jobs, and provided an incentive to hurry and complete a job so as not to be left with the unpopular dregs at the end of the list.

We also celebrated all the holidays, from G.W.'s birthday (cherry chocolate cake for dessert, and red tablecloth and napkins) to Christmas. One of my first Christmas memories was about the time I was 5 or 6; we got a little mongrel puppy which Mom brought home under her coat. The dog was named (and I can't remember why) Hashebaba. She later learned how to open the front door and was killed by a truck. We were all so upset that even the truck driver was in tears. There has been a procession of dogs in the family since, but none quite took her place.

In grade school, I spent several summers at camp. The highlights of those excursions were visiting Indian reservations and ruins, riding an infuriatingly strong-willed horse named Nip (because, obviously, he liked to turn around and nip at his rider), and building a bridge across a small stream at camp.

We also had the practice, just before summer vacation each year, of making lists of things to do. (Mom's idea—when we complained about being bored she referred us back to our ambitious lists.) My list usually included reading, drawing, learning to sew, and other current interests. I was a reader almost from the first grade, and read up our children's book club selections as soon as they came, as well as hitting the library as often as possible. Sometime during this time I also developed the worthwhile project of determining how high a human being could count in a lifetime, so I'd get up a little before the rest of the family and count. I may have gotten to several thousand before I tired of this.

For several summers, Mom assigned each of us one afternoon a week to be with her for a few hours. We could choose the project, or how to spend the time. I often wanted to help her cook, or just visit.

Answer Number Three. The key word in this question, for me, is *summers*. By college, and ever since, my summers had become more structured and more important. For two summers in college—before my second year and before my fourth—I went to Asian language institutes for intensive study. The Big Ten, and a few of the large Midwestern schools not included in the BT, cooperated every year on a joint program of language studies. The hostship (is that even a word?) rotated each year, although the faculty and students were drawn from all the schools. The idea was to provide a wider range of courses than one school could support in a summer, and to share some of the outstanding faculty members and special events (speakers, for instance).

My first summer, I went to Michigan State University for second-year Chinese. The course *was* intense, two semesters (the equivalent of a five-day-per-week course) packed into three months. Every morning we had conversation and grammar, with a 10¢ fine for every word of English spoken.

This was the first five hours, followed by an interminable time in the language lab, and then calligraphy practice. At night there was study. Both the intensity of the course and the living arrangements were designed to foster close group feeling, and I made several good friends that summer. We studied together and socialized together, although we didn't keep in touch after the summer.

The next time the institute was held, Wisconsin was the host. This was a delightful time for me—I was established in a funny little house shared with two classmates and was dating someone (Tony) also from the department who had stayed at the institute. I was taking Japanese, and spent my mornings in class dutifully repeating what I heard and answering questions thrown out by the professor. Every afternoon I would cut language lab and Tony and I would drive out to the quarries to pick berries and swim. I'd spend an hour or two sitting in the rocker on our front porch (a gift from my grandmother, which I still love, who had had it for years on *her* front porch) preparing for the following day's class, and then we'd go out again in the evening.

One of the benefits of these summer institutes was that I made money. In those days the Ford Foundation, Uncle Sam (everybody's Uncle Sam; I haven't got one), and others were avid to get more Americans acquainted with Asian languages, and so provided generous financial support. I think I saved at least half of what I got, and still lived well. Now, I understand, the institutes have been eliminated as the money isn't available, and the interest has wandered elsewhere. (I also believe that some of my classmates did get offers from the government of one sort or another, but no one ever approached me to recruit me for government service. Maybe it was clear that I was a dilettante.)

My interest in Chinese had developed from a course offered by our county school system while I was in high school. Since the community had a number of government employees, it was easy to find support and teachers for the course, originally organized by a State Department official who had worked in China. About thirty of us were chosen for the summer class, which offered language in the morning—taught by a very charming and elegant Chinese woman who had been a professor for several years at the Air Force language school—and culture in the afternoon—taught by an American man who had been in China for years and years, an old China hand. This course had all the attributes of the later summer courses—the close companionship and the intensive study—but was fun as well. We (the students) were the center of a lot of attention from both the school system and outsiders, appeared on TV and in several news stories, usually in the human interest or education sections. I was also chosen as our representative to a countywide conference on improving education in the system. (Although our panel was to talk about the special programs we had been involved in, it was my comment about abolishing phys. ed. testing which got the applause.)

It was while I was in college that I had my first three work experiences. The summer I didn't go to school I worked as a clerk at a loan company. Although I didn't have the skills of a good clerk (good handwriting and patience), I was apparently smarter than some of their other summer help had been, and this was considered by my boss to somehow increase his prestige. We were a small office, and didn't have the best cashier, so he was pretty desperate for signs from the top that his office was okay; unfortunately he got the opposite signal. During that summer he was transferred to a still smaller office and replaced by another manager.

I also spent a short and unsuccessful stint as a worker in the first New York-style deli in Madison. The work was physically taxing, but eventually it was the hours which did me in, from 4 P.M. to 2 A.M. two nights in a row. I've always needed eight or ten hours of sleep, and that schedule was the end of my ability to cope, so I quit. (Read recently that the amount of sleep one needs is related to personality type rather than physical type; the more introverted people seem to need greater amounts of sleep, perhaps to resolve the greater number of things they have on their minds. Made sense to me.)

My third business venture that time was by far the most fun. While we still lived in the dorm, two friends and I created The Occasional Store, which was just that—a dorm room converted once a week or so to a store. Our goods were all handmade, most by us and a few on consignment, and geared to our dorm-bound market: clothes, cards, Xmas gifts and plants, a few pillows and lamps. When we had enough stuff to make a nice display, we'd post signs that the store would be open. What wasn't sold that evening or weekend would be put away until the next open night. It was a tiny venture, as much for fun as for money, but was mildly profitable for all of us.

What other bits and pieces are there? Vacations, at least. Our family vacations had often coincided with moves, so they don't count in my mind as real vacations. Once in a while we'd go up to my parents' parents in Minnesota and Wisconsin. I was never close to my father's parents, who had a huge dairy farm in Wisconsin, but felt close to my mother's, who live in a small town in Minnesota. The joys of their house included being able to sleep on the screened porch (somewhere I ran across a poem which described this feeling exactly: In August we carried the old horsehair mattress out to the porch and slept with our children in a row; the wind came up over the mountain and rattled the trees against the roof . . . I was happy) and of being deliciously terrified as Granddaddy chased us around the basement den. (Reading this over, I realize that it doesn't convey the texture of those days. While we didn't take many official vacations, we had a wealth of adventures and excursions: La Jolla's Old Town for shopping and dinner; picnics; Indian reservations and dances; the Exposition in San Antonio; and so on.)

Once I started working, I began taking real vacations. I went to Europe to visit my folks, who had been reassigned there; but the day after I arrived we got word that my mother's mother had died, so I turned around and came back with her. The surprise was how at home I felt in that little Minnesota town, in spite of the small amount of time I'd spent there. My second visit was more successful—a Christmas vacation. The following Christmas I spent a month in Panama, where my older sister lives. (She is married to a Panamanian; both teach at the University of Panama.) What a marvelous place! The Panamanian people have an innate graciousness and an eye for elegance I haven't seen elsewhere. This was also my first chance to meet my youngest nephew, who was one or two at the time. I've been back to Europe again, and hope to get to Guatemala this Christmas.

One of the best vacations ever was a camping and hiking trip John (friend and lover; you'll be hearing more about him) and I took through Nova Scotia last summer just before I left for school.

A lot of my time has been spent with outside classes: modeling, swimming, crafts as a kid, and as I got older a variety of adult education courses like Japanese painting and Portuguese. The one which bears on this discussion was a course at American University taken during my time in Washington: Human Skills for Women in Management. It was a workshop for professional-level women, taught by a woman with her M.B.A. from here. What a terrific course that was! It was a combination of lecture and discussion, geared toward understanding and then influencing our own actions and others'. The last formal session was a weekend event, a semistructured group experience with two psychologists who had helped in designing the course. I was just miserable—don't know what I learned since there was no follow-up. Of course, it was from our professor that I got the idea of an M.B.A.—she suggested it as a good professional degree for someone without a specific idea of where she wanted to go next, professionally.

Last spring I also taught an adult education course at the town Center, a general introduction to business. While I did enjoy the organization and preparation of class material, I didn't particularly relish the actual classroom time. Felt that the course should have been (read, I should have been) more lively. This year it's being taught by a friend of mine; with her classroom manner and my notes it will probably be a good course.

Answer Number Four. The people who are important to me have already shown up throughout this interview, so this part should be brief.

Daddy (Allen)—is quiet, almost laconic, very frugal in spite of the fact that he makes plenty of money. Two incidents probably show his greatest influences on me. Every week, when we would get our allowances (laid out on the dresser in two stacks, one to spend and one to save), he would say, "Don't spend it all in one place." The other was one Christmas, when "Santa" had brought us a backyard gym set. At the time he said that we had toys so that other kids could come over to our place to play, and we didn't have to go to theirs.

Mother (Carol)—intelligent, though not intellectual; is both practical and creative. She spent a lot of time with us in organized activities (Scout leader, room mother) and on our own. She is also optimistic in a way that doesn't so much expect only good things to happen, but more sees the good side and makes the best of what does happen.

Marilyn—intelligent and intellectual. Has gotten her M.S. and Ph.D. in plant physiology, and is considered one of the best researchers in her field. During her grad studies she met and married a Panamanian, a biophysicist. Both teach at the University of Panama. They have two kids, and sometimes I think Marilyn would like to spend more time with them. She's a spartan in many ways, has seldom been sick because she wills herself not to be. (When I visited them one Christmas after not seeing her for two years, she and I said to one another at the same time, "You're so much like Mother." Strong influence!)

Sally—the beautiful sister, since separated from her husband. She's working and beginning work on her B.A. Raising a son who's a remarkably happy, bright, and stable kid.

Jill—in many ways the most like me, stubborn, like to get our ways, same taste in material things, and yet the most incomprehensible to me. She went to the University of New Mexico for two years, left to roam around, learned computer keypunch, made several trips back and forth across the country. She's now in Virginia, has lived there for about two years.

Dale—more like Marilyn and me in outlook, values, and tastes. Is now a senior at the school where Marilyn did her grad work, studying microbiology. He's engaged and planning to get married next summer if he and his fiance get a fellowship or teaching job somewhere so that they can continue their studies. (The rule, or style, of my family is that once married, you're on your own financially. In fact, we have traditionally been responsible for financing our own graduate study too.)

John—Here I had to stop, not because there was nothing to say, but too much. I'm so in love with you, John! (since I know that you'll read this). Let's just say that with you I feel completely at home; that sums up all the feelings I have about you. Was it Washington Irving who said that home is the rallying place of the affections?

John and I have been "arranging our lives" in a compromise way—the best available under the circumstances.

When he got out of the Coast Guard last January he got a great job with one of New York's big banks in the operating end. He's quickly made officer and is enjoying the work.

This year will probably follow the pattern of last year: visits every other weekend, or a little more often, alternating between New York and Boston. Makes me look forward to Thanksgiving, and even more to our planned vacation over Christmas.

We keep in touch with letters, phone calls, and a small file (I use a bulletin board) of ideas, articles, pictures, experiences to share. It helps a little to create the day-to-day feeling of sharing, but it's not the same. (I miss the touching, too.)

I'm happy to job-hunt in New York, since that's where he's settled; if I were on my own I might choose the Midwest instead.

Joseph—my last boss, taught me a lot about how to approach problems, how to get and keep respect and power. We often get together and compare notes.

My Women Friends (Polly, Winn, and Dina) from college and jobs. They've all been good friends in the best sense of the word: sharing their ideas and time and (varied) talents for living with me. They've influenced me in subtle ways, changing my approach and style, and have helped me appreciate the essense of feminism (the basics, of course, I got from my independent mother). I still visit and write to all three—in North Carolina, Washington, Minnesota.

Answer Number Five. Now the questions are getting tougher. This one has taken more thought and produced more meager results than any of the previous questions.

The central dilemma of my future concerns the immediate question of which branch I should follow after graduating: to go back into glorified social work in the public or quasi-public sector, or to go into the profit-making sector? While this choice will have to be made once after graduation, my first choice will undoubtedly affect my later options.

The pros of the public sector are many: I have experience there, could get a job with greater responsibility and probably more money right out of school, I have moral and ideological commitments to that sort of work, and no small thing, I enjoyed the jobs I had.

On the other hand, my best chance of getting a job in the private sector will probably be right after graduation, when the choice will be wide open. The money, and to some extent the extra responsibility I would get in the public sector, is an advantage which will rather quickly be overcome by the private sector. At higher levels the private sector certainly offers more money. And do I need to prove myself in some way in the private sector?

Another question comes up in this connection: Is there a way to combine both? (Without settling for an affirmative action officer spot?)

While the arena is not clear, with an "ideal" future possible in either, the content of my first job is. I'd like to *run* something, a supported work program like the one I worked on, an operating group in a bank, a special project. A variant of this would be a combination of planning and operations; I have one tentative offer for an administrative position which would involve development of MIS and reporting systems, overseeing compliance with government regulations, and keeping direct operating responsibilities for these systems. This has a great deal of appeal.

Within a few years, I'd like to bring this kind of experience to a broader base, not so much just running a bigger operation but taking on more kinds of responsibilities such as strategic planning. There are some kinds of jobs which I can imagine having which would fit this bill, a professional city manager, or a state-level administrator in the right place. (A former New York City administrator, at the end of the Lindsay administration, went out to take over the post of Human Services Commissioner in one of the Western states. During the interviewing process and looking over the system there, he found several ways to save substantially on the welfare budget. The governor's response to this was, "But these are our poor people—we don't want to take away from them.") I have no delusions that this kind of attitude is found anywhere else, but do hold out hope that there are many public agencies at every level which want and can accept business-minded administrators. Perhaps a way to combine these interests is to become skilled in increasing productivity, cutting costs without cutting services in public agencies and bureaucracies. How does this bear on the necessity for credentials from private industry? (FIND OUT.)

In terms of the other side of my future, the nonwork side, there are some wills and won'ts (I think):

The Wills or Would Likes

1. To change jobs every few years, or at least to substantially change responsibilities.
2. To own a house; perhaps to rehabilitate an old one.
3. To balance periods of intense work and long hours (which I enjoy) with routine, quiet periods.
4. To marry.
5. Possibly to go back to the Midwest (St. Paul, St. Louis).

The Won'ts

1. Live in a planned community.
2. Work in Finance.
3. Work in Personnel.
4. Take a job which requires being constantly on the move, or being constantly "on" (i.e., selling).

As for children, on that I don't know. I can imagine equally interesting "ideal" futures with or without; either choice means giving up something I value, but as I near 30 I'll have to make a conscious decision soon.

This year I am taking a series of courses heavily geared toward the service industries, and nonprofit and nonbusiness institutions. This serves as one indicator of my interest, although most of what I'm learning would apply to a variety of service industries (both profit-making and nonprofit).

Answer Number Six. There is a series of moves which changed my situation completely—schools, friends, houses, states—but over which I had no control. These I'll list quickly, but will try to note what choices I did make along the way.

Augusta, Me.	6 mos.
San Diego, Cal.	5
Pensacola, Fla.	7
Port Arthur, Cal.	8
Jefferson City, Mo.	8 got glasses
San Diego, Cal.	11
Frankfort, Ger.	14 got contacts

Here I made a major choice to go to the U.S. high school rather than a German school.

Norfolk, Va.	18

Went to summer class—determined later choices.

At this point I left home for college and started exerting a little more control over my moves.

Wisconsin: Choice of school

Living on own; move out from dorm
Not marrying
Michigan State for summer
Job the next summer
Wisconsin for summer
Left school early; didn't stay one more semester
Choice of job at consulting firm (choice of work vs. not working)
Human Skills course—awareness of professionalism and feminism
Left that job/choice of Washington government job
Passed up Panama trip
Found N.Y. job—not much choice but was a change!
Joined block association—met John and made friends
Graduate School application and acceptance
Return to N.Y.—old job—last summer

Answer Number Seven. The first time at which turning points started involving my decisions was when I was about 13 and we moved to Germany. Then I had the choice of attending the U.S. high school—nearly an exact replica of any high school in the States—and going to a German school for a year. We lived on the economy (in a German house in a small suburb of Frankfort) rather than on the Army base, so in many ways my going to German school would have been facilitated and I did not have the pressure of all my neighbors' going to the U.S. school. However, I chose to continue with what I was used to. The main reason for this which I articulated was not wanting to be a year behind in getting out of high school and into college; fear of the unknown and fear of language inadequacy were also powerful incentives for making the "safe" decision.

The next turning point came so casually that I didn't know at the time what the implications would be. This was my choice of taking Chinese one summer before my senior year. The county school system offered half a dozen special summer courses, most of them in the sciences and math. Those held no interest for me, but the one in Chinese sounded intriguing. Other factors pushing me toward it, or at least making it easy, were the fact that we were not expected or encouraged to work during the summers, so I had free time, and the fact that I had always enjoyed language study. This course, and the continuation of our studies over the following school year, gave me an idea for a college major. I can't remember considering any other.

The appeals of majoring in Chinese were superficial (the uniqueness, attracting attention) and substantial (genuine enjoyment of the language and desire for more). As I have mentioned earlier, the thought of a career didn't play a part in this decision. At best I may have entertained some faint picture of myself translating for important conferences at the U.N.

It was the determination of a major that limited my college choices. I've told this part before, so will rush through this. I narrowed my areas of interest down to the Big Ten, the West Coast, and the Ivy League as the only kinds of schools offering extensive Asian language programs. The West Coast was too far from home, which at this time was Virginia, the Ivy League seemed too snobbish and too expensive (I had visions of compulsory attendance at football games and massive pressure to join things); this left the Big Ten. Also in favor of this general choice was the fact that I consider myself a Midwesterner, that these state schools were generally cheaper, and that Marilyn had enjoyed a large state school. I was accepted at all of my three choices (as I guess I expected to be): Indiana, University of Wisconsin, and University of Chicago. When my father had to go out to visit his hospitalized mother, I went along and we visited the schools. At Wisconsin we got a great reception, including a personal tour of the campus and an interview with a freshman counselor; this, the beauty of the campus itself, and the good scholarship offer made up my mind. (Also, I was very unhappy with the area of the University of Chicago, in spite of its great reputation.)

Once at college, a series of unmomentous decisions. After my sophomore year I moved from the dorm into a house with two other women; this was prompted by a desire to get away from the noise and people of the dorm, to have a place of my own, and was facilitated by the finding of a place by one of my roommates, without any effort from me. The choice of remaining independent rather than joining a sorority was hardly even a choice; I felt that I had put in all the time I had to on organized activities in order to get *into* college. Once there, I wasn't about to have someone telling me how to spend my time.

Another turning point was not getting married—or at least engaged—during my freshman year. While this wasn't, strictly speaking, a decision, since it wasn't a matter of turning down a proposal, it does belong in the story. Heavily on the side of getting married was the fact that I was madly in love, and with a perfectly nice and suitable man. I believe that I didn't pursue it when we got close to the decision point; it was partly my unwillingness to give up my time to try and experience things, and also some doubts that he had because we were ten years apart in age, and 18 seemed pretty young to him.

However, before we split we had both applied and been accepted at the summer institute at Michigan State. And I went because the commitment had been made.

The next summer I felt I had to work; I had gotten used to having money of my own the previous summer. The clerical job I got that summer was not much a matter of choice; I had heard about the opening from a friend, applied, and was accepted.

The following summer my motives for signing up for the institute were common ones: love, money, and convenience. By that time I was dating another man from the department, and we both decided to stay. The convenience was that it was held that year at our school, no moving. (I've had enough moving in my life.)

Two big decisions came the following January: the choice to leave school since my course work was completed, and the decision not to break up with my current boyfriend. Rational and irrational factors went into the first decision (the second was mostly irrational). It would have been an unnecessary expense to stay; by leaving in January I would have a better chance of getting a job; and I was tired of school. My decision not to break up went against all the rational factors: we weren't going to be seeing one another; neither of us had ever considered marriage to the other, so

this wasn't a temporary separation; now was the perfect time. It boiled down to my not taking the initiative to say, "This is it."

Once home I had to do *something*. Working seemed to be the only available something; at least I don't remember thinking up any others. My idea of working for a year to finance grad school was influenced by my older sister, who had done just that; by the family policy concerning grad study (although I never asked my father if he'd send me—think I was tired of school); and by the fact that school was the only thing I knew, so work was put into that context. My job search included looking through the Sunday *Post* each week and signing up with an employment agency (the only one which took the time to really help me think about what I'd *like,* and didn't humiliate me with a typing test).

Through the agency I got my first offer—selling in southern Virginia a girls' business training program—which I rejected on the grounds of too much travel, public speaking, and also some curiosity about what better offers I could get if that one were so easy. My consulting-firm job was accepted on the grounds that it seemed to offer some intellectual activity and that I liked the owner.

During that time, I also enrolled in the course for women in management; coming across the course was easy, given my habit of taking courses at night, and it looked appealing. My boss paid for half of the course, which helped that "decision" too. This was probably the beginning of viewing myself as a professional, and meeting a group of women in similiar jobs.

The decision to leave that job was one I made often—every time a particularly exasperating boss annoyed me—after the first year. I finally did quit only after getting another job lined up, an administrative/writing position with the city drug treatment program. The job suited my experience in an administrative end of the program rather than direct dealings with the clients. (At the time, counselors were a dime a dozen, while anyone interested in *not* working with the clients was a rarity.)

When the job failed to come through on time (it took about three more months of promises before I was rejected), I canceled a planned trip to Panama for Christmas, feeling that I couldn't go with the thing not settled one way or the other. It took me a long time to start looking for another job—several weeks—after I left my job. Partly, I believed that the agency would solve its internal problems and hire me, and partly because I was reluctant to give up a job which fit my interests so well.

Taking the job in N.Y. wasn't much of a choice; well, maybe it was. At the time my parents were getting ready to go back to Germany, and had invited me to go and stay with them a year. So it was that which I rejected by accepting the N.Y. job, not another job.

While in N.Y., one small act which for me represented a major change of style—I joined our block association and got interested again in outside activities. It was the beginning of meeting a great group of people and developing some neighborhood feeling about N.Y.

The idea of getting an M.B.A. had been in the back of my mind for a couple of years (since the advice of that seminar professor), but the timing was affected by lots of small things. I decided in the fall before applying in the spring for the following fall. My boss had announced his intention of leaving sometime during the summer, and while I liked his successor, I didn't want to work for him. Then there was the fact that I'd worked for five years, and was ready for a break. And I had started to make some money; going later was going to get harder and harder. Mostly since I was taking time off from working, I wanted an excellent business school. I wanted to get the most (the reputation and prestige) out of my time. It didn't really enter my mind that I wouldn't get in. (I accepted it as a possibility intellectually, but not emotionally.)

The last example I include because it is somewhat typical of my decision-making. This summer I went back to my old organization (new job, however) rather than go through the hassles of interviewing for a three-month stint. I wanted to spend the time with John, have a reasonably interesting job, and not to go through learning a whole new system for a short time. Perhaps the most compelling reasons, though, was that we were going to Europe for Xmas, and I wanted to have it settled before then.

Answer Number Eight. As I read back over the last question I can't think of much else to add. On the N.Y. job decisions, maybe there are a few things which pushed me toward accepting the job. Since my parents were moving to Germany, there was no longer the strong incentive to stay in Washington to have them in the neighborhood (I had lived in my own apartment since I started working, but did visit mother often). Other incentives were that I had friends in N.Y., including one of my closest college friends; the prestige and reputation of the organization making the offer; the idea that I should do something difficult. (I was not sure at all that I could do the work; it later became a joke around the office that the only reason *any* of us stayed was "foolish pride," my reason for not going back to Washington after a horrible first week on the job.)

Answer Number Nine. Following the first turning point I've discussed, the decision not to go to German school, the most important thing is that there wasn't much change in my life. The school was a lot like the one I had left, and I made a fairly successful effort to reestablish my old patterns. The one change which I do remember was the beginning of dating.

Taking the Chinese course definitely added something to my life, a kind of intellectual interest and discipline which had been lacking before. Because of a close friendship with one of the class members (the one who later drowned) I also had the chance to get to know our professors and an interesting group of other adults; since this was my first chance to meet with adults outside the family context, it was also the beginning of my dealings with adults as one. (Of course, this didn't happen all at once.)

Going away to school was in large part a confirmation and test of things which I had known or suspected about my abilities. The last two years of high school and all of college were the first time I had gone to schools not preceded by Marilyn, and it was reassuring to know that I could do well

on my own. This was also the beginning of a style, if that's not too overworked a word, of living which has persisted to today, at least in its small particulars. I set aside time to read things which were of interest to me, no matter how great my workload was; in fact this was done defiantly at first, because I had so much work to do, but quickly became part of my routine as reading had been in my youth. I took an interest in my "place"—dorm room or house, surrounded myself with plants, and always found the money to buy magazines. I have since then always had a place of my own, for privacy and to be able to have things my way. (This I may be growing out of some, may be somewhat more willing to share.) I also began entertaining at small informal dinners; that hasn't changed much either.

There was a side to my life then which has not come this far: the tension, or what I called earlier the passion. In politics this passion or conviction was, ironically, a sign of a very superficial commitment; I was able to change my political leanings quite quickly under the influence of the activism of the times, and this provided one outlet for a kind of intense urgency which I felt for everything. On the other hand, my rather-liberal instead of rabidly-right persuasion has persisted.

On my first job, the work itself became the focus of my interests and in many ways took the place of any kind of social life until I got acquainted with people in Washington. My mental stance became more practical, less intellectual, and I gained a great deal of self-confidence from *doing* something, and being successful (also from making enough money to support myself; this was clearly the beginning of that feeling).

When I left that job I felt that I would hate my boss forever, a feeling from the built-up annoyances over time. But I was surprised at how quickly my anger faded once I collected the money he owed me. As for not going to Panama, I regret that even now. The decisions I made to do something I have seldom regretted (i.e., quitting that job even though my offer didn't work out), while the ones I made *not* to do something, or the decisions I didn't make, stand out more clearly.

The main change after the next turning point, aside from what I learned on the job, came slowly and was probably more a function of growing up than of the actual activity or move. I gradually relaxed, began to realize that instead of doing very well for a kid right out of school, I was now doing about right for someone 23 or 24. I've come to accept things more easily, to feel more like speaking up and getting what I want, to be somewhat less obsessed with being constantly admired.

Graduate School has added a great deal, too. There was one thing which I wanted to get out of my experience: the ability to take my skills in analysis (which were already very good) and use them to come up with creative solutions (a lack which a former boss noted on my recommendation letter as a "prosaic administrative style"). And this I have gotten. This latest decision was one I feel very happy about, one which was very right.

My move last summer is important, not because of the job, but because of living with John. This added more than a new texture of living, a new dimension. For the first time the compromises and sacrifices of living together seemed not just bearable but worthwhile, even positive.

Answer Number Ten. Wednesday night, and after a day of thought I don't feel any nearer to getting this answer. I don't remember any huge discrepancies between my expectations and the actual events. For some of the experiences (going away to school) I had my sister's experiences as suggestions of what was to come, her letters and stories, and so had a somewhat realistic picture.

For others (working) I had no thoughts or expectations, since it had never occurred to me that I would work. Most of my thinking before the fact concerned itself with little details on the arrangements rather than the substance: how would I find my way to class? would I get a parking space if I drove to work? should I call my boss Jim or Mr. M___?

The penalty of memories I have for this section seems to indicate that there were no drastic shocks nor ecstatically happy surprises, although I was always somewhat pessimistic in my expectations. (The N.Y. job, for instance, I accepted with the mental caveat "just for a year," thinking from my many visits there that I couldn't stand to live in N.Y. But of course I did stay on, learned to tolerate the city and then to like it, in spite of the lack of green space.)

It's also a reflection, I think, of my tendency to make the most of the present situation, so any greater expectations I may have had faded under a conscious effort to find the good points. Although it may make the moment happier or more tolerable, it tends to wipe out a whole side of experience.

Answer Number Eleven. Whew! . . .

Decision	Pros	Cons (or other choices)
American high school	Not get behind / Safe	Language problem
Chinese course	Easy (not working) / Parents' support / Uniqueness	None except loss of free time
Wisconsin	Money—best support / Pretty campus / Helpful people / Midwest / Marilyn's example	Other campuses not as attractive—no outdoors / High cost of U. of Chicago
Move to house	Easy (they found place) / Place of my own / More privacy / Freedom from demands of living with so many others	It would have showed no initiative to stay in dorm as an upperclassman
No marriage	Mainly Phil's decision / Independence	
Michigan State	Making money / Personal—wanting to be with Phil	
Summer job	Making money / No effort in search	
Leaving school one semester early	Better chance to get a job / Tired of school	Meant doing something I'd never done seriously—working
"	Ready for change / Felt I should do the more difficult thing—not just linger	
No breakup with Tony	Easy	Against my better judgment
Accepting consulting firm offer	Intellectual / Liked people / Location good—near the folks but not too near	Not just a temporary job per my plan
Leaving that job	Annoyance with the abuse by boss / Firm's financial problems and missed paychecks / Getting another job I liked (pros of that were administration; writing; people and informal atmosphere)	Uncertainty of future
Cancellation of trip	Save money / Job-hunt	Miss seeing Marilyn; visiting Panama / Could have stayed a longer time than when working
Taking N.Y. job	People were great / Content of work interesting / Prestigious organization / More money / Less incentive to stay in Washington without my parents living close / Uncertainty about whether I could do the job (doing something difficult)	Moving to N.Y. / Uncertainty of how well I'd like it
Business School	Specific goal of learning to go from analysis to solutions / Prestige / Uncertainty as to whether I could succeed in this kind of atmosphere, oriented to action / Potential to get ahead faster and make more money / More attractive than looking for another job and taking on another 1–2 year commitment before I could leave for graduate school	Being away from John / Costs

Several enduring themes show up as important in moving me toward a decision: (1) security (i.e., American high school, move from dorm, not going to Panama); (2) family support and proximity; (3) convenience or ease of decision (summer courses, summer jobs); (4) doing something difficult or proving something to myself (N.Y. job, grad school); (5) liking the people (Wisconsin, jobs); (6) prestige or attention (Chinese, N.Y. organization); (7) money.

Over time, I seem to be more and more willing to take personal risks, to try something hard, although there is still a tendency to make some choices because they are there (i.e., last summer's job). There is no question that making money and not being poor is important to me; however, it is a sign of progress away from money-paranoia that I could plunge into debt and come to graduate school. A few years ago I would not have been able to do that. Freedom and independence come up too.

It's not articulated in the chart above, but the security component has manifested itself in two small but telling ways: None of my choices has put me into a position of constant exposure to other people (i.e., selling, negotiating, travel for business) and I have always had my own place, my home. There is another aspect of this: that I feel I have to be *in control* of my life all the time (no trips or adventures when I wasn't sure what I'd have to come back to). These are probably enduring characteristics, although their intensity may fluctuate with other things going on in my life.

Betsy Drake (B)

AVL Profile of Values

Score	Value
60	
55	— (55) Theoretical
50	
45	— (47) Social — (44) Aesthetic — (42) Economic
40	
35	
30	— (31) Political
25	
20	— (21) Religious
15	
10	

Betsy Drake (C)

24-Hour Diaries

Sunday, 10/5/75

Dear Diary . . . this comes to you from New York.

8:15–8:30	Got up, showered.
8:30	Back to bed to read a new (to me) Nero Wolfe mystery *Death of a Dude*.
9:00	John got up for his exercises and jogging; it's still chilly out and I'm glad to be warm and lazy.
10:30–11:00	John home; got up for good this time; got dressed, put on some make-up, and visited with John (his job, school, small things, joking).
11:00	Good friends from next door, the Stevenses, called to confirm brunch date; John and Jim Stevens set noon as a good meeting time. Starving, but I made do with a cup of coffee and finished my book. John finished the *Times*; we decided it was too nice a day to do the crossword puzzle.
12:00–1:00	Met Jim and Judy downstairs; walked to O'Neals (west side bar and restaurant); had no trouble getting an outdoor table. Good talk, as always with them: the city and the chances for excellence in government; their jobs; school; people; *Lives of a Cell*.
1:00–2:00	All four of us went for a walk in Central Park; discovered a series of pools (now dry of course) and sundials none of us had seen before. Watched a dog chasing and retrieving two-by-fours its master was throwing into the water. There was some discussion about it—whether it was cruel or humane. (I think cruel.)
2:00–2:30	Stopped by the S's for coffee and to admire their new chairs.
2:30–3:30	Home; packed; made plans with John for upcoming week, when and who would call, and some ideas for the long weekend. Goodbye hugs; didn't get more than two steps out the door before I was back—sunglasses broke. Frantic search for a small safety pin was unsuccessful so I left again a couple of minutes later.
3:30–3:50	To Penn Station for train. Good timing—just enough time for checking out the magazines (nothing new) and buying a pack of gum. Always feel nostalgia going through Penn Station, since I walked through it every night to the subway while I was working. Had a desire to be settled at a job in New York.
4:00–8:00	Boarded train. Usually rough ride; didn't get as much studying done as planned, but

did finish Bauer's book for Wednesday class; made up a schedule for the week (busy time ahead); had time to sit still and think about things: jobs, Peter's offer last week; John's remark about all the ads we had seen a couple of weeks ago for Montana (enticing to both of us); Christmas shopping; had an apple I had brought and a soda for my tummy.

8:00–8:45	Train got in early; took a cab home, but since I had to share with three others got home later than if had taken a train.
8:45–9:30	Unpacked; bathed; picked out something to wear Monday; browsed through *Vogue* and *Mademoiselle;* read three excellent articles: Susanna Agnelli on being young in Italy during World War II, Durbin on street hassling, and Lebowitz on uninvited music.
9:30	Bed, feeling lonesome.

Monday, 10/6/75

7:30–8:00	Got up, washed; made coffee and oj (breakfast); stepped out on porch, nice day but it feels cool; called weather, which predicted highs in the 70s.
8:00–9:00	Dressed; make-up; puttered around picking things up and gathering school stuff; more coffee.
9:00–9:45	Left for school; beautiful day so I walked; stopped to drop off pair of shoes at the shoemaker for new heels; stopped in drugstore for *Times* and usual conversation with the woman there—Nancy.
9:45–10:00	Arrived school; to bookstore (outside reading, another mystery) and today's supply of Kleenex (I'm beginning to suspect that these sniffles are an allergy, not a cold; hasn't responded to Vitamin C; hope not!); said hello to a few people; to course materials office for this afternoon's case.
10:00–11:30	Fifteen-minute visit with Doug; read paper and did crossword; reread case for this a.m.
11:30	Class; not a very high level of preparation in the class today—everyone seems so in-

terested in the "qualitative" issues that they don't bother with the economics.

1:00–1:30	To store for cottage cheese for lunch; ran into Bobby, had a quick lunch outside with him. Stopped by health center—no appointments for two weeks. Back into library to read this afternoon's case—accounting for loan profits. Had a short conversation with Bruce on the case, the day.
1:30–4:00	Class; to my surprise, about half the class hadn't gotten the case 'til this a.m.; was not a lively class.
4:45–5:30	Home; washed face; changed clothes, put away groceries; fixed avocado and orange salad for dinner; had cup of coffee (John has suggested with my caffeine addiction I should be able to find a detoxification program).
5:30–7:00	Ate dinner and read new mystery.
7:00–7:10	Called Anna about this weekend.
7:10–8:00	Went back to book; at 8:00 aroused myself to work.
8:00–8:35	Filed today's cases; got out SACD notebook and brought it up to date; read Wednesday's assignment, since I have a big written assignment in Nonprofits also due on Wednesday. Interesting differences in styles.
8:35–9:15	Stopped for quick coffee break, did Inns case for Service Ops; think the major point is the lost restaurant revenues when we have low occupancy.
9:15–9:30	Called John and we talked for a few minutes about this coming weekend. He may have to work Saturday (damn the bank). I don't mind going to New York instead of Lake George, but hate to call Anna and cancel since we have turned down a previous invitation this summer. Shall see tomorrow.
9:30–10:00	Finished case for tomorrow p.m.; will do the figures at lunch tomorrow. Not sleepy.
10:00–11:45	Typed up analyses for SACD; jotted down some ideas about the diary subjects. Wrote letter to Gayle. To bed.

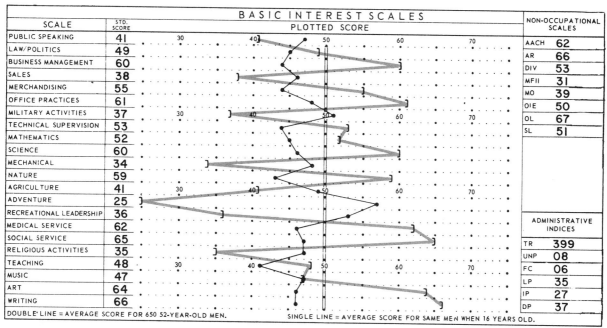

BASIC INTEREST SCALES

SCALE	STD. SCORE
PUBLIC SPEAKING	41
LAW/POLITICS	49
BUSINESS MANAGEMENT	60
SALES	38
MERCHANDISING	55
OFFICE PRACTICES	61
MILITARY ACTIVITIES	37
TECHNICAL SUPERVISION	53
MATHEMATICS	52
SCIENCE	60
MECHANICAL	34
NATURE	59
AGRICULTURE	41
ADVENTURE	25
RECREATIONAL LEADERSHIP	36
MEDICAL SERVICE	62
SOCIAL SERVICE	65
RELIGIOUS ACTIVITIES	35
TEACHING	48
MUSIC	47
ART	64
WRITING	66

DOUBLE LINE = AVERAGE SCORE FOR 650 52-YEAR-OLD MEN.

SINGLE LINE = AVERAGE SCORE FOR SAME MEN WHEN 16 YEARS OLD.

NON-OCCUPATIONAL SCALES

AACH	62
AR	66
DIV	53
MFII	31
MO	39
OIE	50
OL	67
SL	51

ADMINISTRATIVE INDICES

TR	399
UNP	08
FC	06
LP	35
IP	27
DP	37

OCCUPATIONAL SCALES

OCCUPATION	STD. SCORE
I DENTIST	20
OSTEOPATH	23
VETERINARIAN	15
PHYSICIAN	25
PSYCHIATRIST	41
PSYCHOLOGIST	53
BIOLOGIST	39
II ARCHITECT	31
MATHEMATICIAN	31
PHYSICIST	24
CHEMIST	35
ENGINEER	36
III PRODUCTION	37
ARMY OFFICER	06
AIR FORCE OFFICER	19
IV CARPENTER	14
FOREST SERVICE MAN	14
FARMER	22
MATH-SCIENCE TEACHER	25
PRINTER	23
POLICEMAN	19
V PERSONNEL DIRECTOR	48
PUBLIC ADMINISTRATOR	45
REHABILITATION COUNS.	49
YMCA STAFF MEMBER	13
SOCIAL WORKER	42
SOCIAL SCIENCE TEACHER	33
SCHOOL SUPERINTENDENT	35
MINISTER	24

OCCUPATION	STD. SCORE
VI LIBRARIAN	52
ARTIST	29
MUSICIAN PERFORMER	35
MUSIC TEACHER	22
VII C.P.A. OWNER	45
VIII SENIOR C.P.A.	20
ACCOUNTANT	40
OFFICE WORKER	39
PURCHASING AGENT	32
BANKER	29
PHARMACIST	34
FUNERAL DIRECTOR	28
IX SALES MANAGER	31
REAL ESTATE SALESMAN	31
LIFE INS. SALESMAN	26
X ADVERTISING MAN	39
LAWYER	36
AUTHOR-JOURNALIST	39
XI PRESIDENT-MFG.	35

SUPP. OCCUPATIONAL SCALES

CREDIT MANAGER	27
CHAMBER OF COM. EXEC.	30
PHYSICAL THERAPIST	25
COMPUTER PROGRAMMER	19
BUSINESS ED. TEACHER	28
COMMUNITY REC. ADMIN.	15

TESTSCOR, INC. 2309 SNELLING AVE., MINNEAPOLIS, MINNESOTA 55404 6-71

Note: Betsy used an earlier version of the Strong. The Profile is reproduced here. You should be able to interpret most of it from the explanation of the current version provided in Chapter VI.

Current. I used last summer just because it is a little more compact, a little less geographically and emotionally fragmented than my life here at school.

The fundamentals are the same, and have been for as long as I've been making my own life: a place of my own, suited to my taste; John and our shared time/place/experiences/feelings/intellects; time of my own; lots of reading; work which is satisfying and visible.

In the Next Few Years. Lots of the same elements. The only significant difference is right now a big question mark: kid or kids? If so, will I feel that I can still work?

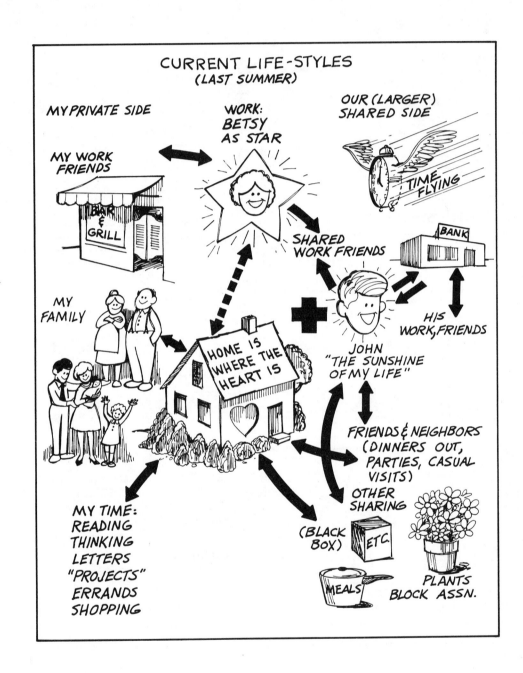

Betsy Drake (F)

Feelings Record

The Written Interview. This was a pleasure! Does it mean something that the past section was so easy and the future part so hard? Should try to give #5 some more thought before Thursday—this doesn't capture it.

A few family facts are omitted; they're very relevant but private.

The AVL. No surprises here—see interpretation.

Graduate School Application. Surprised on rereading that (1) I *wasn't* embarrassed by it; (2) my interpretation of responsibility—and giving a *negative* answer!

The 24-Hour Diary. PLAN PLAN PLAN. Knew I liked to have some idea of what was going on but didn't realize I was *obsessed* by it. However, that's clearly how I am.

The Strong. See notes and interpretation.

Generally *very*. Upper right-hand corner—why so *old?* And 39—poor manager. And I'm so damn *ordinary*, too much like average graduate school. *BLAND!* And why was Family V so high—compounds my stupid dilemma (see Job Search Diary). Damn.

The Life-Style Diagrams. Fun.

APPLICATION FOR ADMISSION TO THE CLASS ENTERING THE TWO YEAR
MASTER IN BUSINESS ADMINISTRATION PROGRAM IN SEPTEMBER, 1974

ALL APPLICATION MATERIALS MUST BE SUBMITTED BY THE
FINAL FILING DATE, APRIL 15, 1974

Name: ___Drake___ ___Betsy___ ___Ann___
         (Last)   (First)   (Middle)

Present address: ___250 West 65 Street, Apt 2H, NY, NY 10023___ Telephone No. __212/632-4319__
                 (include zip code)   (include area code)

Permanent address: ___420 Pleasant Drive, Norfolk, Va. 22003___ Telephone No. __703/218-3801__
                 (include zip code)   (include area code)

Citizen of: ___U.S.A.___

Age: __26__ Birth Date: __June 10, 1948__ Number of brothers and sisters: __4__
(as of Sept. 15. 1976)

Marital status: __single__ Number of children: __0__

Father's name __Allen E. Drake__ Mother's name __Carol Martin Drake__
      (if deceased, please indicate)   (if deceased, please indicate)

Father's occupation: __dentist – U.S. Navy__ Mother's occupation: __housewife__

Please list all high schools, colleges and universities attended:

SCHOOL	LOCATION	DATES (MONTH & YEAR) ATTENDED FROM	TO	DEGREE, IF ANY, MONTH AND YEAR RECEIVED
Frankfurt American H.S.	Germany	1962	1964	---
L.M. Wilson H.S.	Virginia	1964	1966	Academic 1966
University of Wisconsin	Madison	1966	1970	BA 1973
Michigan State (C.I.C.)	Lansing	June 1967	Sept 1967	---
American University (seminar – "Human Skills for Women in Mgt.")	Washington, D.C.	1971	1971	

On what date did you or are you planning to take the GMAT (or ATGSB)? __November 3, 1972__

If appropriate, date on which you took or will take the TOEFL? __not applicable__

Do you need the Special Financial Aid Request Form for Foreign Applicants? Yes _____ No __xx__

Have you filed a complete application for admission to any previous MBA class? __no__ Year _____

Or, in any previous year have you had recommendations and/or transcripts sent to the School? __no__ If yes, what year? _____

App. 1

Note: Instead of a Background Facts Sheet, Betsy Drake used her Application to Business School.

Cut Along This Line

1. Major field of study at college: Chinese language   minor: Anthropology

2. Major extracurricular collegiate and community activities (in order of importance to you). Please note whether your office was an elected or appointed position.

Activity	Year(s)	Office Held, if Any
West 65th Street Block Assn., Inc.	2	member - Brd. of Dir. (appointed) Cors. Secy (elected)

3. Distinctions, honors and awards (academic, military, extracurricular, community): Please note basis of selection.

Dean's List - 3.5 years   Grade Point Average

Phi Beta Kappa   Rank in Class

Committee for Institutional Cooperation   Grade point average and recommendation
    Scholarships for 2 summers' study   of Department Chairman, Dr. Y. R. Chiang

4. What did you get out of your academic and extracurricular life at college?

* a chance to grow, independent of parents and siblings, in a way not provided in even the most generous of families

* confidence in my own ability to make a happy and healthy life for myself

* the beginning of political understanding; relaxation from the strict, conservative political ideas I had had in high school

* three or four wonderful friendships which will, I hope, be lifelong

* a good working knowledge of Chinese

* appreciation for excellent teaching, but too little of that

5. Describe your avocations and hobbies.

My first love is for green growing things; I cultivate houseplants and an outdoor flower garden. I'm also collaborating on a guide to the native cerrada plants of Panama with my sister, who lives there. Other interests include needlework, from embroidery to quilting, and volunteer work for our local NET television station.

App. 2

6. Describe your three most substantial accomplishments and explain why you view them as such.

1. A middle aged man in Detroit now sits down at the dinner table to eat with his family, because for the first time in years it was his money which put the food on the table. This man is enrolled in a training/employment program in a Southside hospital, a program which I established. The program which provides jobs with training for approximately sixty unemployed residents of the local community, was funded by the U.S. Department of Labor.

This was the first project for which I had total responsibility. I went to Detroit to meet with the hospital administrators, the employers in this case, and developed a training program to meet their needs and the needs of their community. I wrote a budget and negotiated with the U.S. DOL for funding, and then assisted the hospital in setting up the program and beginning the training.

2. At the conclusion of a seminar for professional women given at American University, I organized an informal on-going study group. A number of students from the class were interested in maintaining contact and continuing study, so many of our sessions were devoted to discussions of outside reading and current problems and successes with our jobs.

As other women joined the study group, our activities expanded to include providing job-counseling, setting up a job bank for listing openings, and assisting clerical workers in upgrading their job skills.

It was very gratifying to me that as a group we were able not only to meet our own needs for continued contact and study, but also to make our resources available to others. I am convinced that whatever skills or talents professional people have which make them successful in their careers can be used to enrich or improve their lives in the community; this was certainly true in our case.

3. When I began my present job two years ago, I came in at the beginning of a new project, an experimental supported work project for ex-heroin addicts. We started with three staff members, seventeen participants, the work of cleaning the exterior of New York City's grimy buildings, and very little else. The entire structure of the organization - from crew structure to personnel policies - had to be built up from scratch.

It was part of my job to design a system for recording and measuring the productivity of the employees, all work performed in the field, the cost of each job. The number of variables was enormous, including such factors as height of the buildings, kinds of chemicals used, degree of dirtiness, surface materials, and location. I developed a system for tracking crew and individual performance, for measuring the work, and for identifying at any time where each man was working. The system begins with a daily production report completed by crew supervisors, and ends with a monthly cost analysis showing direct and indirect costs on all jobs, square footage performance, and a comparision of the month's work with preceeding months.

This reporting system - somewhat modified - is still in effect and has proved to be adaptable to computer format for more complete cost comparisons. This was, to me, a substantial accomplishment because it was built from nothing, and it works.

Candidate's Name ..... Betsy Ann Drake ....

App. 3

7. What factors led you to decide that graduate education in business administration would be most helpful to your career development?

The suggestion for getting an MBA here   came from a professor of mine, and an   alumna, Elaine Carter. The real decision to apply came gradually, beginning with a general desire to improve my professional skills and to expand my abilities so that I can take on increasing responsibilities. While some of these objectives might be met simply by continuing to work, graduate study seems to provide the best opportunity for making significant changes in my ways of thinking, and ability in problem solving.

I am hopeful that an MBA will provide a broad background applicable to a wide range of work situations and professional choices. I had considered - and rejected - a number of other possible fields for graduate study, including counseling and special education. The kinds of skills developed in graduate business study should be useful in areas where other skills would not be.

I plan to continue in the general area of socially-oriented programs, in industry or the non-profit sector. In these fields there is a crying need for trained adminis- trators to balance the heavy social work orientation. Of particular interest to me are training programs; I am looking forward to running one which is completely my responsibility at some point.

8. Discuss the vocations or professions, other than administration, which you may have seriously considered.

Throughout college, I gave no serious consideration to a career, or even a job. Instead, I was working under the prevalent feminine assumption that it would never be necessary for me to work.

However, as I got more interested in Chinese I also developed an interest in trans- lation as a career, either for the UN or US Government. I was interested in going to a special training program at Taiwan Normal School for additional preparation, and it was to earn money for this that I took my first job.

App. 4

9. Give a candid evaluation of yourself discussing those characteristics you feel have become your strengths and those you feel are your weaknesses.

Efficiency, thoroughness and attention to detail are among the characteristics which contribute to my ability to get things done, and done well. I have an uncommon amount of common sense; organizing activities or thoughts, seeing and correcting practical problems, simplifying or improving procedures all come easily to me. These traits are combined with a willingness to work and an eagerness to take on new responsibilities. I am not afraid to stand by what I have said or done.

Other personal qualities include an ability to listen and understand what others are really saying, an optimistic outlook, and a sense of humor.

These characteristics also lead to what I consider my greatest shortcoming: the lack of genuine creativity which comes from thinking in new ways, and results in new ideas and fresh solutions to problems. For me, the process of maturing has been largely one of learning to be more flexible, to take risks, to recognize the importance of changes in plans and ideas.

10. Describe a situation or job in which you felt you had some responsibility and tell us what you learned from that experience.

Recently one of the employees whom I supervise committed a white collar crime – the theft, forging and cashing of some checks from our office – within a few weeks of his hiring. Although there was never any question or suggestion of irresponsibility on my part, my initial reaction was one of almost overwhelming accountability.

In the following weeks I had to take care of the problems created, both in recovering the money from the insurance company and in prosecuting the person allegedly responsible. The dealings with the bank, the insurance adjustors, the police detectives, the courts, and the employee were an education in themselves; however, the real lesson in this entire incident for me was that while not all problems have good or happy solutions, they can and must all be dealt with. The next time I confront a situation like this, I am confident that I won't have the initial guilt-born immobility, but will instead be able to act at once.

Betsy Ann Drake

Candidate's Name ....

App. 5

11. Using the format outlined below, list on additional pages each full time position held (most recent job first). After you have listed full time positions, list your summer jobs or alternate activities while in college and those part time jobs which required more than 10 hours per week. This record along with those periods spent as a full time student should account for all of your time from high school to the present. If your answer to this question includes military service, please indicate your rank on entry and rank on separation. List dates in left margin.

Dates | Firm and size: | See Attachment Please

From: | Nature of business:

To: | Job location:

Job title: | Starting salary: | Ending salary:

Responsibilities:

12. If the following factors influenced your decision to make application to this school would you please rank them, assigning "1" to the most important, "2" to the second most important, etc.

☐ college classmates   ☐ employer or co-worker
☐ college department chairman   ☒ alumni (a)
☐ college professor(s)   ☐ staff visit to your college
☐ college placement office   ☐ news or media articles
☐ parents or relatives   ☐ none of these factors

13. Do you have any disability or illness at the present time which might affect your academic progress or which would necessitate special housing arrangements? No xx ...... Yes .... If yes, please explain.

14. Please provide below the names, addresses (include zip code), and titles of the persons you have requested to submit personal recommendations on your behalf. Your application will not be considered complete if we have not received recommendations from these two specific individuals. You should write the Admissions Office if it becomes necessary to change the name of one of these recommenders.

Name Joseph Raydo   Name Frank Maxon

Position Project Director   Position Prof. - Evaluator

Address 1410 Main Street, Hoboken, NJ   Address 343 West End Ave., 12I, NY, NY. 10023

15. | TO THE BEST OF MY KNOWLEDGE, THE INFORMATION CONTAINED IN THIS APPLICATION IS A TRUE AND ACCURATE ACCOUNT.

Betsy Ann Drake   4-1-74
Applicant's Signature   Date

App. 6

Betsy Ann Drake
March, 1974

Item #11

March 1972–
Present

ALON INSTITUTE OF JUSTICE (80 staff members)
A private, nonprofit foundation conducting research and demonstration projects in the field of criminal justice and social programs.

15 East 41st Street, New York, New York 10016

Personnel Coordinator   Salary: $9,000 to $13,500

Responsibilities: Staff member of an experimental project employing former heroin addicts in the public sector. Personnel responsibilities included screening applicants, counseling employees on personal, legal, financial, and family problems. Maintained liaison with New York City Department of Public Works which employed project participants. Developed courses in supervisory skills and personal finance.

Research responsibilities included developing management information systems for tracking all phases of performance and production. Gathered and evaluated data serving, among other purposes, as basis for recommendations to the New York City Human Rights Commission.

Control responsibilities included preparation of budgets, supervision of bookkeeping, payroll preparation and determining of wage scales.

November 1971–
March 1972

TRAINCOR, INCORPORATED (approximately 5–15 staff members)
A private consulting firm engaged primarily in development of training programs.

1000 R Street N.W., Washington, D.C. 20037

Exec. Asst./Program Development   Salary: $6,000 to $8,000

Responsibilities: Major responsibility for research and development of manpower training programs for the disadvantaged. Determined the employer's personnel needs, wrote and budgeted a program based on these needs. Followed proposal through contract negotiations with funding agencies. Designed all components of the training program, including on-the-job training curricula, basic education and counseling.

Researched and designed program for the rehabilitation and treatment of narcotics addicts. Conducted research in such fields as financing of health care, public service employment, and cable TV.

Self-Assessment Paper

rd to summarize me, I would
contained." I structure, plan,
er myself the best judge of my
, to put it into context. I prefer
a friendly basis. I'm generally

er is all about. The body of the

o Create My Own Structure
Resist Imposed Structure
pset by Schedule Changes
rtance of Being Organized
Taking Charge
ey as . . .

III

pendent
Self-Confident
Enjoy Being Center of Attention
Importance of Commitments

Group V

Importance of Family
Importance of Home
Consider Myself Midwesterner
Interaction with Environment

paper is divided into two sections: themes and implications. The sources supporting the themes are identified in each section at the beginning of each set of quotes or references. Page or question numbers are noted in parentheses. I have often abbreviated the supporting data; I hope that what we lose in richness is more than compensated for by what we gain in usefulness and manageability.

I've grouped the themes into six major categories, each including one or more central themes and the contradicting or coloring themes.

Following are the theme groups:

Group II

Importance of Analysis and Understanding
Interest in Ideas/Intellect
Disinterest in Manual Tasks
Academic Orientation Important
Interest in Communication/Writing
Interest in Science

Group IV

Prefer Small Group of Friends
Like to Be in Helping Role (in control)
Affectionate in Relationships
Not Outgoing; Don't Like to Put Myself Out

Group VI

Place of Prestige and Reputation
Concern for Professionalism
Influence of Women

II. Themes

Group I

NEED TO CREATE MY OWN STRUCTURE

Written Interview:

A few background facts may keep things in order. (1)[1]

Wherever we lived we kept the same routines of work and play. (13)

I was *established* in a funny little house with two classmates. (15)

Every afternoon I would cut language lab (to go) swim. (15)

(At an unstructured group weekend) I was just miserable. (19)

While I did enjoy the organization and preparation of class material I didn't particularly relish the actual class-room time. (19)

I have tried to follow a chronological account. (13)

Pro and con evaluation approach. (22)

Won't . . . take a job which requires being constantly on the move. (24)

I made . . . an effort to reestablish my old patterns. This was the beginning of a style . . . of living which has persisted to today. (32)

I feel I have to be *in control* of my life. (38)

24-Hour Diary:

Made plans with John for upcoming week, who and when to call.

Good timing (to train).

Didn't get as much studying done as planned.

(Plan) Christmas shopping.

---

[1]Page references refer to the location of the data in Betsy Drake's original Self-Assessment paper and not in this typed version of the paper.

Made out schedule for the week.
Work ahead to balance workload.
Called weather.
Called Anna about this weekend.
Called John about weekend.

AVL:

Highest score is Theoretical, suggesting a need to put things into context.

Strong:

Very Low Adventure.
Low on Sales (Family IX).

BUT RESIST IMPOSED STRUCTURE

Written Interview:

(In re: kindergarten) About an hour before time to set off, I would tell Mom of all the playing I still had to do that day . . . proceeded to cry from the minute I got in the car to go. . . .(2)

Bored with school and frantic with activities . . . I hated the activities themselves, hated coming home after dark. (5)

It goes without saying that I didn't buzz back to Madison for graduation ceremonies. (9)

(Our boss) trying to manipulate his staff by tying up our time. (11)

Followed by an interminable time (trapped) in the language lab. (15)

Won't live in a planned community. (24)

I had visions of compulsory attendance at football games and massive pressure to join things. (27)

The choice of remaining independent rather than joining a sorority was hardly even a choice; I felt that I had put in all the time I had to in order to get into college. Once there I wasn't about to have someone telling me how to spend my time. (27)

BUT I joined the block association (out of character). (30)

Graduate School Application²:

Only one organization (question 2).
Honors and awards all academic rather than extracurricular. (3)

Strong:

Very low (06–19) scores on military officers and policeman.

---

²Rather than use her background information data, Betsy Drake referred to her graduate school application form as a supplementary data source.

Life Style:

Concentrates on activities which we control; only mention of organized group is the block association.

AM UPSET BY SCHEDULE CHANGES
Written Interview:

I *hated* to leave all this. (4)

Long reference to missing the early bus every day when we had made arrangements to take it. (2)

Too college-oriented to risk missing a year by going to German school. (4)

Hated to leave (Germany). (5)

Hated coming home after dark. (5)

Won't take a job which requires being constantly on the move. (24)

Choice of high schools—not wanting to be a year behind in getting into college. (26)

Rejected on the grounds of too much travel. (29)

Feel I have to be *in control* of my life all the time. (38)

Graduate School Application:

Long answer on upset and immobility when one of our employees stole and forged checks. (10)

24-Hour Diary:

Good timing in getting train.
Hate to call Anna and cancel (although more from dislike of making the call than change in plans).

BUT LOOK FORWARD TO BIG CHANGES PLANNED BY ME
Written Interview:

Bored with high school in general. (6)

After a couple of years I was ready to leave. (12)

Once I started working, I began taking real vacations. (18)

(I would like) to change jobs every few years. (23)

Once at home I had to do something. (29)

Tired of school and ready for a change. (29)

I was ready for a break (from work to HBS). (30)

In the summary for question 11, two mentions of ready for a change and three of a desire to do something difficult. (36)

Graduate School Application:

Opportunity for making significant changes in my ways of thinking. (7)

IMPORTANCE OF BEING ORGANIZED
Written Interview:

Teacher's habit of keeping us late (not as punishment, merely because she was *disorganized*). (2)

Developed training programs. (11)

This was a position as . . . systems developer. (12)

Gradually we built up the structures and systems. (12)

I've tried to follow a chronological account. (13)

Long description of our systems for jobs around the house. (13)

Mom would make up a list. (13)

We also made lists of things to do. (14)

Mom assigned each of us one afternoon a week. (14)

Long paragraphs devoted to how the institutes were organized. (16)

While I did enjoy the organization and preparation of class material, I didn't particularly relish the classroom time. (19)

We keep in touch with . . . a small file of (things) to share. (21A)

Graduate School Application:

Approach to question 4.

Organizing activities and thoughts comes easily to me. (9)

Developed MIS systems. (11)

We started with nothing . . . built organization. (6)

Strong:

In my peak Family V, heavy on the administrative component rather than face-to-face helping.

High in office practices (?).

24-Hour Diary:

Six references to planning (see Need to Structure . . .).

Organized by change in activity with times noted.

Life Style:

Note—used last summer because it's *less fragmented.*

LIKE TAKING CHARGE
Written Interview:

I got a lot of power and responsibility. (12)

I accepted a job as administrator. (12)

Most like me (stubborn, like to get our own way). (21)

Joseph . . . taught me a lot . . . about how to get and keep power. (21)

I'd like to *run* something. (22)

Tentative offer for an administrative position which would involve development of MIS . . . overseeing compliance with . . . regulations, and direct operating responsibilities for those systems. (22)

Most enjoyment of own store in three jobs. (17)

Graduate School Application:

First project for which I had total responsibility. (6)

I organized an informal, on-going study group. (6)

Running (something) which is completely my responsibility. (7)

Eagerness to take on responsibility. (9)

Strong:

In peak Family V, emphasis on administrator and director jobs.

High CPA owner vs. low Sr. CPA.

BUT only 33 average on Managers vs. 30 on Entrepreneurs (suggests less that I want purely to manage— especially manage other people—than that I want to have something which is *my own responsibility* to run and not depend on/take direction from others).

This may be supported somewhat by rather high scores on professional jobs which don't require manual skills (Psychiatrist, Psychologist, Biologist) and high O/L score for professional-level jobs—suggesting liking to be in charge of my own work.

MONEY AS A MEANS TO INDEPENDENCE/SECURITY
Written Interview:

(Getting college scholarships) makes HBS seem that much more expensive, but this time it's my money and not my father's, so I feel free to spend. (7)

(Boss) was given to squandering the company's money. (12)

One of the benefits of the summer institutes was that I made money. I saved . . . half of what I got. (16)

One of the few references to my father, "Don't spend it all in one place." (20)

Good scholarship offer made up my mind (i.e., less dependent on parents). (27)

I had gotten used to having money of my own. (28)

I had started to make some money (so it would be harder to come to HBS later when I would be making even more). (30)

I gained a great deal of self-confidence from making enough to support myself. (33)

Six references to money in analysis of decision making.

Several references to paying for own graduate school.

AVL:

Economic score is in a tight group of three values which together have second priority; may suggest valuing money somewhat highly as *means to an end.*

MONEY AS A MEANS OF GETTING THINGS I ENJOY
Written Interview:

I was saved by . . . greed. (11)

Save money for a year to go (back to school). (11)

Always found money to buy magazines. (32)

Numerous references to creating an environment I like (Interaction with Environment).

Group II

IMPORTANCE OF ANALYSIS AND UNDERSTANDING

Written Interview:

Shed some light on my later whys and wherefores. (1)

Learned the value of logic . . . it's only after observing my sisters with their kids that I realize we were *taught* to think. (4)

Read recently that the amount of sleep one needs is related to personality type rather than physical type . . . *made sense to me.* (17)

Geared toward understanding . . . our own actions and others'. (19)

Joseph . . . taught me a lot about how to approach a problem. (21)

Pro and con approach in evaluating options. (22)

I raised a question in the course of writing the interview—follow with a note to myself to FIND OUT. (23)

I'll have to make a *conscious decision* (re: kids) soon. (24)

I visited schools (getting evidence). (27)

Analysis of past decisions as rational or irrational. (28)

I have also *at least eight parenthetical references* to other information, subsequent understanding, etc. For example, I went back and checked with Mother about my impressions of the Pensacola period; devoted two paragraphs to the development of my ideas about misfortunes; analyzed why I would remember a bee sting. (1, 2, 3, 5, 6, 8, 10, 35)

My skills in analysis were . . . very good. (34)

AVL:

Highest score is theoretical—55 as compared to 47 for the next score.

My comment "always been interested in why."

24-Hour Diary:

Discussion of whether excellence in government is possible; discussion about dog.

Query about whether sniffles were cold or allergy—and made MD appointment.

Strong:

Very high Psychologist, quite high Biologist and Psychiatrist, although above average on Family II, with Mathematician and Chemist above people-in-general.

Quite high on BIS for math, science, nature (?).

INTEREST IN IDEAS/INTELLECT

Written Interview:

Can remember only a little real learning. (8)

My first exposure to . . . development of an idea . . . by the class as a whole. (9)

I was a reader almost from the first grade. (14)

Quote from poem. (18)

Quote from Washington Irving. (18)

Job accepted on the grounds that it seemed to offer some intellectual activity. (29)

Added intellectual interest and discipline. (32)

Intellectual crowd at high school. (9)

Numerous references to enjoyment of language study *per se.*

24-Hour Diary:

Three references to ideas in articles.

Six references to books.

Two references to crossword puzzle.

Ideas discussed.

Strong:

High librarian, suggests high interest in books and ideas.

High Psychologist.

BIS high in art, writing.

Very high AACH (?).

AVL:

Highest in theoretical, ideas or scientific investigation for its own sake.

Life Style:

Thinking.

DISINTEREST IN MANUAL TASKS

Written Interview:

Complete absence of references to anything done with my hands; one reference to sports—swimming.

Strong:

Family IV very low; professions in I which require manual dexterity also eliminated.

BIS low on mechanical.

ACADEMIC ORIENTATION IMPORTANT

Written Interview:

Long description of summer study. (15)

A lot of my time has been spent with outside classes. (19)

My idea of working for a year to finance grad school . . . work was put in that context. (29)

Went to school two summers while in college.

Took course which led to recommendation that I come to HBS.

Marilyn's degrees. (20)
Reference to both Sally and Jill in terms of college. (21)
BUT didn't enjoy teaching.
Tired of school.

Strong:

High librarian.
BUT generally very low on teaching.
High AACH (?)

Graduate School Application:

All awards academic. (3)
Set up *training* program. (6)
Set up sessions for on-going *study*. (6)
Considered more training (in response to question re: careers). (8)
Developed courses, training programs. (11)
Two summers' study. (11)

24-Hour Diary:

Equal attention given to rest and study (school) times.
Letter to Gayle.

Life Style:

Letters.

INTEREST IN COMMUNICATION/WRITING

Written Interview:

Accepted job as administrator and writer. (12)
Long section on language study. (15)
Enjoyed language study . . . genuine enjoyment of the language. (26)
Writing job with the city. (29)
One of two listed accomplishments on first job was good written report.
Claim to have enjoyed writing WI in feelings record.

Strong:

Highest BIS score is writing.
BUT low on public speaking.
Moderately high on Family X.

Life Style:

Letters.

24-Hour Diary:

Letter to Gayle.

INTEREST IN SCIENCE, ESPECIALLY BIOLOGY AND PSYCHOLOGY

Written Interview:

It's since developed that Daddy and some of my sisters have a serious allergy. (1)
Read recently that the amount of sleep one needs is related to personality type. (17)
Mention that Marilyn, her husband Ruy, and my brother Dale all are in biology.

AVL:

Theoretical score results in part from interest in natural sciences.

Strong:

BIS high on nature, science, medical service.
Psychologist is highest score.
I think that others in family were consciously dampened by my visualizing the manual tasks required.

Group III

INDEPENDENT

Written Interview:

First time we kids got to stay alone. (3)
I loved . . . the freedom we had to get around on our own. (4)
This time it's my money, not my father's, so I feel free to spend. (7)
The basics, *of course,* I got from my independent mother. (21)
Desire to have a place of my own. (27)
The choice of remaining independent rather than joining a sorority was hardly even a choice. (27)
My unwillingness to give up my time. (28)
Took N.Y. job rather than go to Germany with Mother and Daddy. (30)
Took an interest in *my* place. (30)
Gained self-confidence from making enough money to support myself. (33)
Always had my own place, my own home. (38)
Like to get my own way. (12)
I could do well on my own. (32)
In the WI (and also in the application) it is notable that everything listed as an accomplishment is something which I did largely by myself: developing training programs, writing reports, setting up MIS. And these were considered accomplishments by me; they met my own standards. From the *absence* of data about superiors' or peers' reaction I infer that these other people's responses were less important than my own evaluation, further reinforcement for the independent theme.

Graduate School Application:

Chance to grow, independent. (4)

Confidence in my own ability to make a life for myself. (4)

All accomplishments were individual (total responsibility, I organized, my job). (6)

Not afraid to stand by what I have done. (9)

Life Style:

One whole side devoted to my life separate from John.

AVL:

Very low Political score—next to the bottom and 11 points below its predecessor—might indicate that I have no interest in working through other people, that I would rather do the work than influence others to do it. In combination with a rather high Economic score (42 vs. 31 for Political), this makes even more sense: I want to see tangible results, but not to get them through selling.

SELF-CONFIDENT, ESPECIALLY IN INTELLECTUAL AREA

Written Interview:

Other kids not as smart as I. (2)

Found the work no problem. (2)

She got coveted straight A's; I followed suit. (4)

The trauma (not from fear of rejection, just too much paper) of filling out applications for college. (7)

I got a substantial scholarship. (8)

Studied seven days straight *to ensure* a perfect exam. (8)

Got a lion's share of A's. (8)

I was smarter than some of their other summer help. (17)

I was accepted at all three schools, as I had expected. (27)

I believed that the agency would solve its internal problems and hire me. (30)

It didn't enter my mind that I wouldn't get in here (HBS). (34)

This last decision (HBS) was very right . . . feel happy about it. (34)

My skills in analysis were already very good. (34)

24-Hour Diary:

Not nervous about leaving case to do over lunch hour for that day's class.

Graduate School Application:

Suggestion of knowing exactly what I wanted in (7)—I plan to continue . . . training programs . . . one which is completely my responsibility.

BUT NEED TO PROVE MYSELF IN MORE ACTIVE, NONINTELLECTUAL AREAS

Written Interview:

Do I need to prove myself in the private sector? (22)

Case method was important as a test of whether I could handle problems—do something difficult—instead of merely reading and responding. (30)

I was not at all sure that I could do the work. (31)

The idea that I should do something difficult (i.e. go to work). (31)

Going away to school was a confirmation and test of things which I had known or suspected about my abilities (to create own life). (32)

Gained self-confidence from *doing* something and being successful . . . from making money to support myself. (33)

ENJOY BEING CENTER OF ATTENTION

Written Interview:

First memory . . . adults made much of me . . . modeled nightie. (1)

Only enjoyable part was sitting in the front seat with Dad. (2)

Thrill of being chosen to model . . . winning first place in the Christmas Art Fair. (3)

My telling may differ slightly from the norm. (10)

I called all the shots right on that one . . . got a lot of attention from the client. (11)

I was the only professional in the . . . office. (12)

We . . . were the center of . . . attention . . . on TV and in the newspapers. (12)

I was chosen . . . and my remark . . . got the applause. (17)

The (superficial) appeals were uniqueness, attracting attention. (26)

Faint picture of myself translating at *important* UN conferences. (26)

Counselors were a dime a dozen, while anyone (like me) not interested in working with clients was a rarity. (29)

Somewhat less obsessed with being constantly admired. (33)

Life Style:

"Betsy as Star" at work.

I interpret this as enjoying attention, liking to be unique, but expecting it rather than seeking it. A revealing sentence from my WI says that I called the shots right in predicting how the FCC would rule on cable TV, and thus got a lot of attention from the client.

IMPORTANCE OF COMMITMENTS

Written Interview:

I was set on returning to school. (9)

I went because the commitment had been made. (28)

"Foolish pride"—my reason for staying at N.Y. job after a terrible first week. (31)

Didn't want to commit myself to another job for one to two years before HBS. (37)

24-Hour Diary:

Didn't want to break commitment to Anna.

Group IV

PREFER SMALL GROUP OF FRIENDS

Written Interview:

Pattern of finding a "best friend" at each new location while growing up. (3)

I did have a good group of friends. (6)

Joined in the informal group activities of playing pool and swimming. (7)

I made several good friends that summer . . . although we didn't keep in touch. (15)

My women friends . . . still visit and write to all three. (21)

Meeting a great group of people. (30)

Life Style:

Compartmentalization of different groups of friends: John's work friends, mine, shared, and friends and neighbors.

LIKE TO BE IN HELPING ROLE

Written Interview:

Volunteer for Planned Parenthood. (8)

Develop training programs. (11)

Taught an adult education course. (19)

Human Services Association story. (23)

BUT numerous mentions of not enjoying the immediate, face-to-face "helping" activities; for example, in teaching I didn't relish the classroom time. And there is no reference to the fact that about half my time at the Traincor job was spent in face-to-face counseling with employees.

Graduate School Application:

Two major accomplishments were setting up training programs and study groups which made our resources available to others. (6)

Counseling. (11)

Strong:

BIS very high in Medical Service and Social Service.

Peak in Family V BUT low in many of the face-to-face occupations in V, such as teacher, minister.

AVL:

Social is second score.

Taken as a group, this evidence seems to fit closely with the Independent theme, and that of Like to Take Charge; it suggests that while I like to help people, the motivation is, at least in part, to be in charge, in a giving rather than taking relationship with others. Also fits with some of my ideas about money—better to be in control, not dependent on others, although I don't mind sharing what I have.

AFFECTIONATE IN RELATIONSHIPS/VALUE INDIVIDUALS

Written Interview:

Use of people's names prevalent.

As kids, babysitting each other. (3)

Concern for Marilyn's being alone and far from home. (5)

Concern for Jeff when we broke up. (8)

Crying. (8)

Concern for friend who was hurt in Chicago. (9)

Mention of two close adult friends "holding their breath" before marriage. (10)

My women friends, Polly, Winn, and Dina. (21)

Miss the touching (John). (21A)

24-Hour Diary:

Goodbye hugs.

AVL:

Social second highest.

Graduate School Application:

Told story in terms of one known individual (6).

NOT OUTGOING—DON'T LIKE TO PUT MYSELF OUT

Written Interview:

More introverted people (like me) seem to need more sleep. (17)

I didn't relish the classroom time (teaching). Felt I should have been more lively. (19)

One of the few mentions of Daddy. (20)

We had a gym set so that other kids could come over to our house and we didn't have to go to theirs. (20)

Won't take a job that requires being constantly "on" (i.e., selling). (24)

Get away from the noise and the people of the dorm. (27)

Rejected on the grounds of public speaking. (29)

I've come to feel . . . more like speaking up. (33)

None of my choices has put me in a position of constant exposure to other people. (38)

24-Hour Diary:

Other people in the cab intruded on my schedule—would have preferred not to be with them.

Strong:

As noted before, not high in teaching or selling.

AVL:

It's interesting to examine Social (second—47), Economic (close fourth—44), and Political (low—31) together. Their placement suggests that while I like people as individuals, and like getting tangible results (Economics), I do not like working through or influencing others.

Group V

IMPORTANCE OF FAMILY

Written Interview:

Close family. (1)
Asked Mother. (1)
Relaxed time for the family. (1)
Only enjoyable part was sitting in the front seat with Daddy. (2)
Only after observing my *sisters* with their *kids* that I realized that we were taught to think by our *parents*. (4)
Marilyn's leaving for school. (5)
A strong family rule. (7)
My mother advised during the decision making. . . . (7)
Impact on the family when Sally eloped. (9)
My rocker, gift from my grandmother. (16)
I was never close to my father's parents but felt close to my mother's. (18)
"You're so much like Mother." (30)
Response to #4—in first response all immediate family. (20)
Since my parents were moving to Germany there was no longer a strong incentive to stay (near them) in Washington . . . did visit Mother often. (31)
Parents' support. (36)
I had my sister's experiences . . . her letters and stories. (35)
Detailed descriptions of family arrangements of jobs, buying house and settling in, trips and celebrations.
Spent vacations with folks after starting work—three in Europe with Mom and Dad, one in Panama with Marilyn.

Life Style:

Inclusion of each member of my family.

Graduate School Application:

A chance to grow . . . independent . . . in a way not provided in even the most generous of families.
Mention of Marilyn. (5)
BUT took N.Y. job rather than go with folks to Germany. (WI)

IMPORTANCE OF HOME

Written Interview:

In love with John because I feel at home with him. (21)
"Home is the rallying place of affections." (21)
West Coast was too far from home. (27)
Desire to have a place of my own. (27)
Took an interest in my place. (30)
Always had my own place, my own home. (30)
Own a house. (23)

Life Style:

Large picture of house and heart—"Home is where the heart is."
Shown as focal point.

CONSIDER MYSELF MIDWESTERNER

Written Interview:

Mom and Dad are both from the Midwest and in spite of the many moves we have all grown up as Midwesterners in outlook. (1)
Story of two sects settling the MW. (4)
Quote from Poem. (18)
The surprise was how at home I felt in that little Minnesota town in spite of the small amount of time I had spent there. (18)
Might job-hunt in the MW if not for John. (21A)
Possibly go *back* (although looking over the list of places I've lived, I've never really been there) to MW. (23)
I consider myself a Midwesterner. (27)
Went to WU—big state school was my idea of college.
Mention of birthplace—my "home." (1)

24-Hour Diary:

Montana—enticing to both of us.

INTERACTION WITH ENVIRONMENT
Written Interview:

The party was outside in the evening. (1)
Wait in the cafeteria with the rest of the early crowd. (2)
A tiny little town, an All-American City . . . with petunias planted all through the town square. (3)
I loved the beautiful town. (4)

Remember vividly . . . the colors and smells and sounds. (5)

Lots of country characteristics, old trees and lanes. (6)

Drive out to the quarries . . . pick berries and swim. (15)

The hours of the deli did me in. (17)

Panama—marvelous place. (18)

Beauty of the campus itself . . . made up my mind. I was very unahppy with the area of the U of C, in spite of its great reputation. (27)

Learned to tolerate N.Y.C. and then to like it, in spite of the lack of green space. (35)

England which I loved, green growing things everywhere. (5)

Every house we lived in had a garden. (13)

Surrounded myself with plants. (32)

Numerous references to my own place, suited to my tastes.

Graduate School Application:

Hobbies—green growing things.

Life Style:

(In color) mention and picture of plants.

AVL:

Aesthetic score a high third.

24-Hour Diary:

Chilly outside; glad to be warm and lazy.
Beautiful day so I walked.

Group VI

This group is made up of three minor themes which, while they're not supported by many data, seem important to me.

PLACE OF PRESTIGE AND REPUTATION
Written Interview:

Organization was a prestigious one. (12)

John quickly made officer. (21A)

I wanted to get the most reputation and prestige out of my time. HBS was the only school I really wanted. (30)

Prestige of the organization as a reason to take the job. (31)

But Ivy League was snobbish. (30)

I was very unhappy with the U of C, in spite of its great reputation. (30)

CONCERN FOR PROFESSIONALISM
Written Interview:

I was the only professional in the Washington office. (12)

Workshop for professional-level women. (19)

Awareness of professionalism. (25)

View myself as a professional. (29)

Graduate School Application:

Improve my professional skills.

Strong:

High scores in professional-type jobs.

INFLUENCE OF WOMEN/INTEREST IN FEMINISM
Written Interview:

Numerous references to my Mother; few to Daddy.

Influence of Mom, Grandmother, sisters, women friends, two female teachers, and one female professor.

Organized women's seminar.

III. Implications

1. It emerges clearly (from the themes: Need to Create Structure; but Resist Imposed Structure; Am Upset by Schedule Changes; and Importance of Being Organized) that I'm happiest in situations which I can structure, ones in which I can plan and control my own time and activities.

This implies an organization which provides infrastructure like a phone, a desk, and freedom from sudden and frequent interruptions, but does not impose a rigid hierarchy or highly structured requirements on me. I prefer working in one location, with local excursions or out-of-town trips held to a minimum, and even those carefully planned in advance by me. An ideal task would be one in which I was given a loosely defined problem or need and could set up my own inquiry leading to a solution.

Two kinds of organizations, and some kinds of jobs within organizations, would seem to be eliminated in light of this implication: those which are crisis-oriented, always requiring responses to uncontrollable external events, and those which are already rigidly set out. Not for me to spend exactly 2.5 years on audits before moving up to supervision for another precise 3.5 years.

2. If I understand and agree with the goals and importance of my work, I will work hard, confidently, and successfully. I don't work well in response to other kinds of motivation (i.e., competition with peers or direction from supervisor).

(Supporting themes are: Need to Create My Own Structure, Importance of Analysis, Like Taking Charge, Independent, Self-Confident, Enjoy Being Center of Attention with comments, and Commitment.)

The most compelling supporting data for this is what

isn't there—any indication of what others thought of what I did. The implication is that I need to work somewhere where it is possible to understand the scope of my job, and where my own judgment of what is adequate or good performance is either the only standard or is the same as the standard by which I'll be judged. I also need to understand the whole context (why, when, my work is needed and what use will be made of it), as I'm only comfortable when I can analyze something and fit it into the big picture.

3. My preferred tasks are those which involve intellectual and analytical work and implementation of my ideas—those which I am responsible for from start to finish.

(Supporting themes are: Importance of Analysis and Understanding, Interest in Ideas, Disinterest in Manual Tasks, Communication, Independent and Self-Confident in Intellectual Areas, and Like Big Changes.)

This implies that the content of the job should be largely idea-oriented, rather than technical or manual or even purely operational, and that I prefer to do one complete job from analysis to implementation. At that point, however, I lose interest and am ready to move on to a new analyze-solve-implement job.

4. I am most comfortable dealing with people on my own terms in informal peer relationships. Once the terms of the relationship are established, I like warm, affectionate relationships.

(Supporting themes are: Prefer Small Groups of Friends, Like to Help, Not Outgoing, Affectionate in Relationships, and Like Taking Charge.)

This makes an effort to capture contradictions apparent in the data: I like people and want to help them, but don't like the face-to-face dealings; want to deal with others as peers yet have a need to always be in control of the situation or relationship. These can be reconciled by recognizing that I have a reserve toward people in general, not liking to put myself out for them nor to be dependent on them; yet I do like people as individuals, as friends, once I get past my reserved feelings and can develop warm and equal friendships.

The implication is that I'd like to work where superior/subordinate relationships can be friendly and informal (both up and down the ladder from me); where I work with a stable group, or where I am stable (in control) and others come and go. I'll look for a first-name, informal atmosphere where I'll be working with a stable group of people.

5. I prefer responsibilities and rewards based on individual merit rather than personal relationships.

(Supporting themes are: Like Taking Charge, Independent, Self-Confident, Not Outgoing, Professionalism, and comments, Enjoy Being Center of Attention.)

An organization which is intensely political (internally) is not for me.

6. Intense periods of work should be balanced with more quiet periods for me to be happy.

(Supporting themes are: Importance of Family, Home, Commitments.)

The implication of this need to have time at home to balance time at work is that a project-oriented job would suit me: intense work times followed by relaxed times, or any other job with variety in the workload.

A POSTSCRIPT TO PART ONE

You have reached the point now where you have been introduced to all the essentials of self-assessment. The next step is to practice actually doing a self-assessment (the Dyad Assignment), and then to do your own. Detailed instructions are included in the Workbook for both the Dyad Assignment and the actual self-assessment paper.

The Dyad exercise will both give you additional practice in self-assessment and provide you with an assessment of your own data by another person. Both the practice and the other person's assessment will be very useful in helping you get started with your own self-assessment paper.

This concludes the first part of this book. Our attention shifts in Part Two from the creation of a self-assessment to its use in the career development process.

Part Two

CAREER DEVELOPMENT

XI

The Career Development Process

Over the past 30 years a fairly large number of people have studied various aspects of career development. One recent review of this literature references well over 500 books and articles.[1] Because many of these writers approached the subject with very different backgrounds and for very different purposes, the literature tends to be split into a number of camps with little cross-referencing or building. Although there have been several attempts to synthesize these divergent approaches, as yet there is no one generally accepted theory of career development.

The different camps may be characterized as having a sociological or a psychological perspective. The sociological approach tends to look at society as a social structure consisting of various occupations. Careers are viewed as movement from one occupational level to another in a social structure stratified by status and by the occupational role expectations of a person in a given status. The occupational level achieved in career development is seen in terms of a process of social causation. Membership in a social class (indicated normally by father's occupational status) and socialization—the process by which individuals are trained, their expectations developed, and their values internalized—are seen as the prime determinants of occupational level. In addition, environmental factors (e.g., personal contacts, available financial backing, and socioeconomic conditions in society) are also relevant. Any one of these factors may attain major importance as an independent or explanatory variable, depending on the interests of the researcher in question.

The psychological perspective is taken by those who support an individual theory of career causation. Some take an intrapsychic approach, seeing unconscious forces as influencing conscious decision making. The shape of these unconscious needs or drives is often postulated to stem from early childhood experiences. Satisfying them then becomes a major determinant in job choice. Others take a rational decision-making approach to career development. Individuals are seen as testing themselves through interaction with their environment, weighing the factors and alternatives, then making conscious career choices. According to some scholars, this all occurs in a developmental process consisting of various stages through which the individual passes.

Scholars in these various camps disagree particularly with respect to the relative importance of different variables. Some claim that environmental factors are most important in career development; others make the same claim for intrapsychic factors. Some believe that most career and job decisions are made consciously by individuals, while others feel they are made unconsciously. Some believe that a person's experiences during the first few years of life are most central to career development; others do not. And so on.

For our purposes, these disagreements need not distract us. The basic points upon which most of the experts agree are strong enough to provide us with a solid base from which to proceed. Specifically, there is general agreement that a person's career development is determined by the following factors:

1. Who the individual is now, especially with regard to the most central and least changing aspects of the person (i.e., the "core personality").
2. The natural internal physiological and psychological development patterns (e.g., aging) that are common to all people and that have an impact on the individual (factor 1) over time.

---

[1]S. H. Osipow, *Theories of Career Development* (New York: Appleton-Century-Crofts, 1973).

3. The interaction between the person and his or her environment, which can change the person (factor 1) over time. For most people (i.e., in a typical life style) the two most important environmental factors are job and family.
4. The job opportunities available in the person's environment at specific points in time.
5. The career paths associated with those job opportunities.
6. Broad social, economic, and political forces that change the structure of available jobs (factor 4) and careers (factor 5) over time.
7. The individual's desire or ability to gain access to available opportunities.
8. The job and career decisions a person makes consciously or unconsciously over time (which determine a key aspect of his or her environment, factor 3).

This elementary model of career development, although not very detailed, nevertheless implies a course of action for people who wish to control job and career decisions more consciously. That course of action could briefly be described as follows:

Do the best you can, using information from the present and past, to understand who you are, how people tend naturally to change as they grow older, what job and career opportunities exist, how these opportunities have changed in the recent past, and how people more and less effectively gain access to those opportunities. For each possibility you successfully gain access to, use your knowledge of yourself, the opportunity, and how both might change over time and make future projections about what would happen if you accepted that possibility. Finally, choose among the sets of potential future events.

In the first half of this book we dealt with what tends to be the hardest single part of this process: self-assessment. In the remaining chapters we will focus on other issues of career development: identifying job and career opportunities, gaining access to those opportunities, selecting an option given several opportunities, managing the issues and problems at various stages of one's career, and making career plans. More specifically, Chapters XII through XVI deal with various aspects of getting a job—or, if you're currently employed, a better job. That includes focusing your job campaign, obtaining job offers, assessing job offers (or potential offers), and accepting a job offer. Chapter XVII focuses on the career-related problems and issues that face the recent graduate. Chapter XVIII introduces the notion of stages in a career, while Chapters XIX and XX focus on the typical problems and opportunities associated with specific stages. Finally, Chapter XXI integrates the discussion in the previous four chapters around the issue of managing a career over time.

XII

Focusing a Job Campaign

Most people find themselves in the job market, either by choice or necessity, a number of times in their career. At such times, skills in the various aspects of job hunting can play a leading role in career management. In this and the next four chapters we shall focus on job hunting and the more effective ways people have found to engage in it.

The Importance of Focus

Considerable evidence suggests that one of the primary reasons some people are much more successful at job hunting than others is that they approach the job market with a clearly defined and reasonably narrow focus.[1] That is, they look not for "opportunities" but for a reasonably specific type of job and career opportunity. Instead of looking for "something exciting" or "a good-paying job," for example, they look for "an entry-level position in a large retailing organization with prospects for promotion to a general management position within seven years" or "a general management consulting job within a moderate to large established firm in the United States."

With a moment's reflection, it is not difficult to understand why a focused approach to job hunting is important. There are over 100 different identifiable major "industries" in the United States (see Figure 1 for a partial listing[2]). Each has a large number of different kinds of career opportunities and jobs within it. Indeed, one government publication covering all industries lists 21,741 different types of jobs.[3] And that listing, of course, does not take into account that two jobs with the same title can differ significantly in two different organizations. In the United States alone there are well over 100,000 different organizations that regularly hire people. Operationally this means the number of career and job opportunities that exist at any single point in time, even in a depressed economy, is very large—so large, in fact, that no job hunter could ever hope to pursue more than a mere fraction of the total opportunities. There just aren't enough hours in the day.

A little bit of arithmetic will help clarify this very important point. Let's assume for a moment that you wish to get a job within the next four months. Let's further assume that you can spend four hours per day, on the average, for six days a week engaged in job hunting activities. This adds up to a total of 24 hours per week, and about 400 hours over the four-month period. To identify a specific job opportunity, to go through a set of employment interviews, and to get to the point where you might get a job offer will require, at a bare minimum, about 10 hours of your time. It will usually require considerably more than 10 hours. Therefore, at the very most, you can actively pursue about 40 opportunities and stay within your budgeted 400 hours. Now, if we restrict ourselves to the United States, at any point in time the 100,000 or so organizations that actively hire people will probably have well over a million different job openings (possibly many more). If we take the conservative

---

[1]For example, in a survey of a sample of the 1974 M.B.A. class at Harvard, we found that those people who reported the highest level of job satisfaction seven months after graduation interviewed fewer employers on campus, wrote fewer unsolicited letters, and pursued a smaller number of different types of organizations while job hunting.

[2]For a more detailed listing see the *Standard Industrial Classification Manual*, U.S. Office of Management and Budget (Washington, D.C.: U.S. Government Printing Office, 1972).

[3]*Dictionary of Occupational Titles*, Vol. I, *Definitions of Titles*, U.S. Department of Labor (Washington, D.C.: U.S. Government Printing Office, 1965).

FIGURE 1 A Partial Listing of Industries

Advertising

Aerospace (airframes, general aircraft, and parts)

Airlines

Appliances

Auditing and consulting

Automotive (autos, trucks, equipment, and parts)

Banks and bank holding companies

Beverages (brewers, distillers, soft drinks)

Building materials (cement, wood, paint, heating and plumbing, roofing, etc.)

Chemicals

Conglomerates

Containers

Drugs (and hospital supplies)

Education

Electrical and electronic

Food processing (baked goods, canned and packaged foods, dairy products, meat, etc.)

Food and lodging

General machinery (machine tools, industrial machinery, metal fabricators, etc.)

Government

Health and medical services

Instruments (controls, measuring devices, photo and optical)

Insurance

Leisure-time industries

Legal services

Metals and mining (nonferrous metals, iron ore, etc.)

Natural resources fuel (crude, oil, coal)

Nonbank financial (brokers, investment bankers, etc.)

Office equipment and computers

Oil service and supply

Paper

Personal care products (cosmetics, soap, etc.)

Publishing (periodicals, books, magazines)

Radio and TV broadcasting

Railroads

Real estate and housing

Retailing—food

Retailing—nonfood (department, discount, mail order, variety, specialty stores)

Savings and loan

Service industries (leasing, vending machines, wholesaling, etc.)

Specialty machinery (farm, construction, materials handling)

Steel

Textiles and apparel

Tire and rubber

Tobacco

Trucking

Utilities (telephone, electric, gas)

figure of one million, that means that you will have at most time to pursue about 40 out of one million, or one out of 25,000 job opportunities. Without a clear focus to help identify which one of 25,000 job opportunities to pursue, it is inevitable that a job hunter will waste a great deal of time and energy, and experience considerable frustration. Job hunting without a clear focus is not unlike trying to hit a target the size of a quarter from 50 yards, using a shotgun, while blindfolded.

Without clear criteria to use in screening possibilities, students often find the process of selecting companies to interview on campus frustrating and time consuming. In their efforts to leave "no rock unturned," they waste time and experience anxiety trying to choose whom to interview, then waste still more time going through two or three times as many interviews as their friends who have a focused job campaign. It is not unusual for job hunters who have a focused campaign to send out 20 letters to a carefully chosen group of potential employers and to receive in return invitations from 10 of them to have an interview. People with an unfocused job campaign sometimes "shotgun" out 100 or 200 standardized letters to a poorly screened group of potential employers and receive in return no favorable replies at all. We've seen people waste hours aimlessly reading help wanted ads or talking to employment agencies because they didn't have a clear idea what they were looking for. People who tell their friends and acquaintances that they are looking for a job are more likely to get useful job leads in return if they specify in some detail exactly what they want.[4] By giving reasonably clear and tight screening criteria to professional friends and acquaintances, for example, you not only increase the chances that they will indeed "keep their eyes open" for you, but you also save yourself the time and effort of following up inappropriate leads that might otherwise be passed on to you.

In job hunting, knowing in advance what you want significantly increases the chances that you will get what you want and significantly reduces the costs associated with the process itself.

Creating an Appropriate Focus

The key to creating a useful focus for job hunting is self-knowledge. Without a clear understanding of who you are, you cannot rationally decide what kind of job and career opportunities you should pursue. A good self-assessment can be *enormously* helpful in this regard.

By carefully examining your self-assessment, in light of what you currently know about job and career opportunities, you can identify a number of areas that look promising and a number that don't. For example, if one implication in a self-assessment paper is "hates to travel more than two days a month except for vacations," and if one has reliable knowledge that almost all management consultants spend 20 to 75 percent of their time traveling,

---

[4]Imagine yourself in the position of friend or acquaintance. How would you react if someone said he or she was in the market for a new apartment or home, but didn't specify what kind? You would probably ask for more information. What would you do if the only reply was, "I want something very nice"?

then management consulting should be given a very low priority if not tentatively eliminated. By systematically going through all the implications in a self-assessment in this manner, one can usually identify two or three career areas that seem very promising (e.g., banking, financial analyst work for money management firms), a number of other areas that might be promising (e.g. corporate financial work in large manufacturing firms, auditing for a C.P.A. firm), and a large number of areas that can be tentatively eliminated (such as all production work, all public and nonprofit work, etc.). Of course, the more information you have on what job and career opportunities are like, the more focused the output of this exercise will be.

With both your tentative conclusions from this analysis of your self-assessment, and the questions you raised while doing the exercise you can next take one step further in the focusing process by gathering information from written library sources and from people.

Most large public libraries and university-associated libraries have considerable information about job and career opportunities. In Appendix C at the end of this book, we have listed the best library sources we know of for information on topics our students have typically researched.

People, although often less accessible than books, can be enormously useful sources of information on specific job and career issues.[5] Our students have found that by using whatever personal contacts they have to set up meetings (often at lunch) with people who actually work in the industries, companies, types of jobs, or geographic areas in which they think they might be interested, they can get a large amount of useful information very quickly. Armed with specific questions created in conjunction with a self-assessment paper, a person can sometimes learn more in 30 to 60 minutes from a well-informed source than from six hours in a library.

For example, Jerry Jones knows from his self-assessment, among other things, that he does not tend to work well under pressure and that he is very ambitious. In an initial analysis of his self-assessment, he decides he should look more deeply into professional auditing work. So on Tuesday he sets up a lunch with Jim Smith, a partner in a large C.P.A. firm who also graduated from Jerry's college. (Jerry got Smith's name from his accounting professor.) Among the questions Jerry asks Smith are the following:

1. Do people in the C.P.A. profession have to work with tight time and/or cost constraints? Or does it vary from firm to firm or job to job?
2. Do you feel much pressure in your job? What about most new employees you have observed—do they feel a lot of pressure?
3. How much does the average employee in your firm make after 5, 10, or 15 years?

---

[5]We've noticed that some of our students resist this strategy of identifying and using people because they feel they don't know any such people or because they think it would just be too cumbersome to try to find such people and to convince them to talk. Once prodded into action, however, virtually all of our students have found that: (a) they do know someone who in turn knows the type of person they are looking for; and (b) when contacted, people are usually more than willing to talk.

4. Is your firm growing? How fast? Is the industry growing? How fast?
5. Out of every 20 people hired each year, how many will probably become partners? How long will that take most people?

Contrast that scenario with this one. Phil Roy has a "gut feel" he may enjoy being a C.P.A. He spends his lunch hour on Tuesday asking the people who are sitting at his table in one of the university's cafeterias whether they think being an auditor is a good job. He gets two unqualified yeses, two qualified yeses, three maybes, one noncommital response, two qualified nos, and a piece of paper thrown at him (possibly an unqualified no).

It is very easy, while job hunting, to end up in Phil Roy's position—wasting his own and other people's time in endless dialogs about careers and job opportunities which do not help him focus on a limited number of rational opportunities out of the many possibilities. And the reason it is easy is because most people do not begin job hunting with a good, accurate, up-to-date assessment of themselves.

The Key: Self Assessment

By systematically going back and forth from analyzing one's self-assessment, to gathering some more information, to reanalyzing the self-assessment, one can create in a practical amount of time a rational focus for a job campaign (see Figure 2). Hundreds of students have done just that.

FIGURE 2 The Process of Creating a Focus for a Job Campaign Based on a Self-Assessment

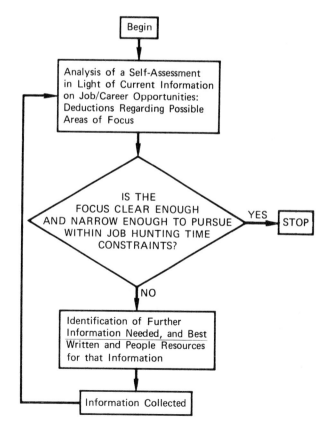

And the competitive advantage this has given them over those classmates who behave more like Phil Roy while job hunting is very significant.

Exercise

To gain some practice in creating such a focus, read the following excerpts from three self-assessment papers. With the information you currently have about jobs and careers, try to answer three questions for each:

1. What job and career areas seem promising for this person? Why?
2. What areas can be eliminated? Why?
3. What areas might be promising, although you're not sure because you don't have enough information? What extra information would you like to have?

Jerry, Suzanne, and Brad
Excerpts from Three Self-Assessment Papers

A. Jerry

(The following are pages 18–23 of his Self-Assessment paper.)

These implications are not mutually exclusive; rather, they were derived by starting with a general topic (e.g., task preference), locating the relevant themes, and summarizing them. Some of the statements are not directly translatable into job characteristics or life-style preferences; rather, they are simply groupings (such as "strengths and weaknesses") that provide convenient summaries for me of the analysis underlying this paper.

The source themes used to derive each general statement are listed parenthetically after each subtitle. In summary, those themes are:

1. Importance of family
2. Competition
3. Winning
4. Insecurity
5. Knowing the score
6. Theoretical man
7. Blacks and whites
8. Goal-oriented
9. Planning ahead
10. Tension
11. Sports
12. Independence
13. Pragmatism
14. Activity
15. Fairness
16. Power
17. Fear of failure
18. Determination
19. Status
20. Discipline
21. Disciplined response to uncertainty
22. Money
23. Quantitative
24. Need to belong to an organization
25. Poor relations with nonauthoritarian superiors
26. Big-city life
27. Mediator
28. No large groups
29. Like authoritarian bosses

Task preference (5, 6, 7, 8, 9, 13, 14, 20, 21, 23)

I prefer to undertake tasks that involve the application of theoretical principles to a concrete situation in a rational, systematic way. I enjoy the discipline of a quantitative approach. The ideal task for me would involve evaluating a relatively small number of clear alternatives where the analysis could be quantified (e.g., alternative A has a 30% better ROI than alternative B). I am equally at home in both planning and action-oriented situations, and prefer to be charged with responsibility for both conceiving and executing my recommendations. It is important that I understand the purpose, the goals, of my analysis so that at any point in time I am able to measure my progress against them. I am capable of devoting a great deal of time and energy to completing my analysis. If, however, I am placed in a situation where the goals, techniques, or any other segment of the process is unclear, I will resort to some sort of disciplined, structured approach—and it may not always be the appropriate one for the situation.

Goals (3, 8, 15, 16, 19, 22, 24, 25)

I place a tremendous emphasis on winning, on being the best at what I do. I like to compete with others in honest, disciplined ways for recognition and the appropriate rewards, which for me include money, status, authority, and respect. I feel that I can accomplish these goals most effectively in an organization that allows me a degree of independence in my work.

Relationships with others in work situations (2, 12, 16, 19, 27, 28, 15)

I prefer to be a member of small, closely knit groups that are charged with a common task and that may or may not be affiliated with a larger organization. It is important that the lines of authority in the groups be clearly drawn, especially as regards my relationships to superiors. My ideal boss would tell me what to do, and perhaps suggest an approach, but would then leave me free to work in my own preferred style (see "approach to tasks" below). I would then be able to compare my progress to that of others in my groups working in similar capacities, in order to have a feel for my standing at all times. I prefer to work with a small number of people in situations where the evaluation procedures, rules, and rewards for good performance are known by me and where all of us abide by them scrupulously. Although I want to be the best at what I do, and expect to be rewarded for working hard and well, I don't want to antagonize others who may be competing with me. I prefer friendly rivalry where I would not be hesitant to work with my colleagues, thus gaining respect and status not only as a "winner" but also as a "nice guy." I am capable of great commitment to organizations offering me these opportunities.

Approach to tasks (6, 7, 9, 13, 14, 18, 20, 21, 23)

I prefer to analyze situations in terms of their quantifiable aspects. I tend to start with a broad overview of the situation, attempting to discern general trends in order to facilitate more detailed (quantitative) analyses later on. I tend to view things in terms of a limited number of alternatives—my approaches, analyses, and conclusions are rarely what might be considered overly radical or creative departures from tradition. I *always* plan out my analysis before proceeding, attempting to lump uncertainties into smaller, more manageable categories that I can separate and deal with one at a time, in a much more pragmatic manner. Again, I am capable of devoting a great deal of energy and enthusiasm to such tasks.

Life style
(1, 8, 11, 12, 14, 15, 16, 18, 19, 22, 24, 26, 27, 28, 10)

I would prefer a life style in which I could balance my energy and time, enjoying both the warmth and love of my family and the challenges confronting me at work. This at present is a major problem for me—how to decide when to stop working and take it easy, especially when I am at home. I would like a job that I could "leave in the office" at the end of each day, so that I could go home to my family and enjoy our time together. Right now the conflict between work and family is causing me a lot of worry—it is an uncertain situation that I *can't* really respond to by organizing it, as is my wont. I do want a life full of activities—I want to work hard and play hard, and not just let life pass me by. I envision myself living in the suburbs of a large city, probably Cleveland, being wealthy and enjoying the respect of others in our community.

Attitude toward changes (5, 9, 13, 20, 21)

I hate ambiguity in whatever I do. It makes me extremely uncomfortable not to know where I'll be, what I'll be doing, who I'll be with tomorrow, next week, or next year. I prefer situations where I can plan ahead toward known goals (be they either materialistic goals or simply events in

time—e.g., graduating from the Business School). I like to stay *put*—once I am familiar with a particular place, activity, person, or whatever, it is hard for me to leave it for something that is uncertain.

My leadership style (3, 18, 15, 16, 19, 20, 27, 28)

I seek positions of authority and status. I prefer to gain them through hard work, accomplishment, and dedication to the organization of which I am a part (as opposed to playing corporate politics or inheriting a firm from Dad). I would be happiest in a situation where I could lead by example, rather than by the exercise of raw power. In other words, I would rather persuade people to work with me by dint of the results of my own hard work, vigor, and dedication to the task, rather than forcing them to do things by threats, coercion, or other forceful measures. I guess I want to be liked as a person as well as respected as a competent manager.

My perceived strengths and weaknesses

My strengths:

1. Organizaton and discipline.
2. Ability to apply theoretical principles in a pragmatic way.
3. Enthusiasm, vigor, and ambition to win.
4. Quantitative analysis.
5. Ability to serve as a mediator among people.

My weaknesses:

1. Tendency to view situations in terms of a limited number of alternatives.
2. Discomfort with large groups of people.
3. Insecurity and fear of failure.
4. Nervousness, tension.
5. Inability to get along with nonauthoritarian superiors.
6. Tendency to compete in almost any situation, overemphasis on winning.
7. Extreme discomfort with uncertain, ambiguous situations.
8. Tendency to force generalizations from limited data.
9. Tendency to panic in crisis situations (or situations that are really not crises but that I perceive to be as such).

B. Suzanne

(The following are pages 20–24 of her Self-Assessment paper.)

I can relate best to situations that are flexible enough to:

1. Accept me as a distinct individual as opposed to "someone to fill the slot."
2. Provide the "room" to let me have my own overall concept as to how things should get done (for my own task).
3. Give me enough freedom to execute the details in following through with my plan.

4. Allow some means for eventual progress toward more difficult tasks.

These implications are based on the following themes:

1. Need for progress, development, and achievement that is visible to self and others.
2. Preference for integrative situations; pulling things together, organizing, creating own "structure."
3. Doubt of/need to prove intellectual capability.
4. Need for pleasant, productive relationships.
5. Need for emotional independence; for being a "distinct" person.
6. Need to plan; to be in control of a situation.

Comments. Several items of data had particular impact on me. I was startled to see the extent to which I *had to* operate in my own total conceptual framework of a situation . . . and to which I was *unable* to operate within someone else's framework. It is even true of my experience in graduate school: I am not accepting a "channelized" view of what I "should take" in order to be accepted by the investment banking people or the corporate planning people, etc. My view of the school, and the program I have made for myself (even in first year, where I "made" my own program by emphasizing and deemphasizing things), is that I am making it fit my own notion of "what I might want to be."

I can best relate to people when:

1. I can view *them* as distinct individuals and as equals.
2. I am neither being imposed upon from above *nor* imposing upon below.
3. There is an atmosphere of congeniality.
4. I have won their favor and support.

These implications draw on the following themes:

1. Need for . . . achievement visible to self and others.
2. Need for pleasant, productive relationships with people.
3. Need for emotional independence; for being a "distinct" person.

Comments. Nothing came out in the data that really surprised me at all. There is something that I would like to explain further, however, relating to the conflict that might emerge over my wanting to impose structure and control while still viewing people as equals. In viewing people as equals, I am really saying that people, whatever their abilities and talents and proclivities, should be all that they can and want to be. When I meet and deal with people, I try to find out what they are about and who they are and to let them know that I perceive them in such and such a way. People often respond positively to this and counter by wanting to know who I am and what I am about, and eventually a "pleasant, productive relationship" comes about, in which each other's way of ticking is known, appreciated, and left to tick. If I were given a chance to have my own "structure" and it needed people, I have a strong feeling that I would go a long way in trying to find just the right people for the structure, who would be happy and

productive there without the need for my constant imposition on them. I expect to be viewed in the same way by my superiors; I want to be "just the right person" for their structure, and sent to my corner to be happy and productive without being constantly imposed on.

I think of or approach just about any problem by:

1. trying to figure out *if* I can do it at all, and if so
2. conceptualizing it as a whole as best I can (trying to get a "feel" for it),
3. and *then* formulating a "master plan" for getting it done,
4. and *then* taking care of all the details and seeing it happen.

These implications are based on the following themes:

1. Need for progress . . . achievement visible to self and others.
2. Preference for integrative situations, organizing, creating a structure.
3. Doubt of/need to prove (intellectual capability).
4. Need to be a distinct person.
5. Need to plan; to be in control of a situation.

Comments. I was aware that this was going on, but didn't realize the *extent* to which I thought out *everything in my life* . . . including complex emotional situations . . . in these terms. There is also a trend toward tackling larger and larger concepts; and, as the concepts get bigger and bigger, the tendency is to want to work through the material thoroughly (into a system) and then leave it to be operated by someone else. In other words, I am content to establish "it" and "see it happen" but not to maintain "it" forever myself.

The thing that I can best relate to in terms of content is visual harmony or visual aesthetics.

These implications are based on the following themes:

1. Preference for integrative situations . . . pulling things together . . . creating structure.
2. Aesthetics; need for visual harmony.

Comments. This has simply been a pervasive need that has existed over a very long period of time (18 years since interest in architecture began to emerge).

C. Brad

(The following are pages 13–16 of his Self-Assessment paper.)

A number of implications about myself can be drawn from the themes and data discussed in the preceding analysis. These implications fall into two basic categories—people and my preferences for certain tasks.

People

1. I prefer to deal with people who are a good deal like myself—practical, easygoing, down-to-earth, unpretenti-

ous, and with a broad range of interests. They should be intelligent, but not really intellectual. Most important, they should be active people—interested in having a good time. This would preclude overly ambitious, money-conscious Wall Street hot-shots and stiff, pompous, serious business types. It would also preclude pseudointellectuals, such as many of the so-called professionals who live on New York's East Side. I do not like dull people, who have done nothing exciting and live "typical" dreary existences—the stereotyped accountant, who has his life planned out for twenty years ahead. I do not like people whom I see as a threat to my own position or image. Plain, honest "middle-American" types fit many of the criteria that I like in people, although often these people do not have the wide range of interests and experiences I look for. Active young professionals, easygoing management types, and honest people who enjoy life are the types of people I get along well with. Young people, i.e., kids, satisfy many of the criteria I have set down, and perhaps that is why I like working with good-natured, intelligent children.

This implication is supported by several themes and pieces of data—people-oriented, tough-minded, practical, active, and variety themes all support this generalization. The Strong Test showed that I think mostly like people-oriented professionals (teachers, counsellors, personnel directors) and lower-key managers (Chamber of Commerce executives, salesmen, recreation administrators), rather than scientists, theoreticians, and business-detail types.

2. I prefer to deal with people in a situation where I can be influential, give advice and direction. I like to be directive and play the "Big Brother" role. I should have high status relative to the group I am dealing with, and people should look to me for advice and information. This is based upon my people orientation, "Big Brother syndrome," desire for status, desire to be influential, and desire for "communication." High teacher/counsellor scores on Strong support these data, as does a tendency to be authoritarian.

3. I prefer to deal with a stable group of people with whom I can develop close, easygoing relationships. I should be able to engage freely in verbal communication and get a certain amount of recognition and approval from those people. At the same time, I should be able to perform well enough in relation to these others so that I do not feel under undue pressure to regard any of them as a competitive threat. This implication about my relationship with others is based upon my desire to be number one, dislike of competition, desire for contact and camaraderie and a sense of community, and my preference for verbal communications and exhibition. My constant references to wanting a "community" and liking to be in groups where I am the center of attention further support the implication.

Tasks

1. I prefer tasks that involve activity and offer the opportunity to move around, talk with others, and get things done. A quiet, paper-producing staff-type job, involving a myriad of details, would be most unfitting.

2. I prefer tasks that are practical, important to an operation, and where I can affect the results directly by my actions. This is a product of my practical nature and my desire to be influential and important. Part of the reason I disliked my first job was that I felt that personnel was too removed from the main line of the business, and I could not significantly affect profits by my work. In addition to my practical nature, the idea of being "out of the mainstream" affects my sense of security, since in a downturn, nonessential people are the first to go. Thus, a practical, important job is usually a secure one.

3. I prefer tasks that provide constant feedback and results, so that good performance can be recognized and approved. Feedback could be either quantitative or qualitative, but it should be visible and present. This implication is supported by my desire for recognition and approval and my desire to be "the best." (It is difficult to be "the best" at something if there is no way to measure it.) Being practical and tough-minded also indicates a desire for measurable results. Feedback can build one's ego (assuming it is good), bolster confidence, and enhance a feeling of security.

4. The tasks I prefer would allow day-to-day autonomy and flexibility and allow for free time when I need it. Day-to-day autonomy implies that someone will not be standing over my shoulder telling me what to do, and that I will be free to come and go as I please providing I am getting my job done. This would imply a relatively informal, easygoing work situation, where pressure is largely self-induced. This implication is strongly supported by my desire to engage in a wide variety of activities, which necessitates a flexible schedule, my dislike for being "bossed," as discussed in the themes section, and my desire for independence. It should also be noted that one of the things I liked most about working in Tanzania was that I was completely free to work when and as I pleased. My low-key personnel job also allowed sufficient autonomy and free time to pursue my outside interests. I like leaving my job at the office.

5. The ideal job should provide for variety and challenge in its day-to-day tasks, and yet should not involve constant pressure. Although the situations I must deal with should be varied and challenging, I should be able to control most of the factors that affect the outcome and thus be able to "feel on top" of my job and have control over every situation. This is supported by my desire for variety and activity, as well as my desire to feel "on top" of every situation. I do not mind dealing with different crises, so long as I feel I have some control over how things will work out in the end. A "dislike for pressure" refers to constant, insecure feelings about a situation, and *not* necessarily to challenge or the need to perform. I should be able to control most of my own "destiny." I do not like being dependent on others.

6. A job must provide status within the community in which I exist, and should provide enough money to enable me to maintain the active life style I desire. I have to be able to "keep up with the Joneses," whoever the Joneses happen to be in the community where I spend my time. My interests in travel, skiing, etc., cost money. If I have a family, I want to be able to support them in an upper-middle-class manner, but don't need to make millions. This implication is amply supported by my "status" theme, independence theme, security theme, and life-style papers. It is worth noting that I define status in a *relative* manner—it depends on where I am and who I consider the relevant group for comparison at any given time.

XIII

Getting Job Offers

The process of obtaining job offers typically includes a number of key activities: getting job leads, getting interviews, interviewing, and follow-up. In this chapter we'll explore each of these activities, along with the more effective ways in which people engage in them.

Sources of Job Leads

There are five primary sources of job leads: college-associated placement offices, unsolicited direct-mail campaigns, friends and acquaintances, ads in newspapers and journals, and profit-making placement firms (such as personnel agencies and executive search firms). A typical successful job hunter relies on one, two, or three of these sources, depending on his or her particular needs.

The placement offices of colleges and universities are generally designed to help graduating students get together with moderate to large prospective employers from the local area. (The more prestigious the school, the larger the area.) Most placement offices are very good at that limited objective. They are generally not particularly helpful if one is looking for a job in a small company, or in another part of the world, or in any type of organization that hires few of the school's graduates (e.g., few hospitals interview at business schools). In addition, most placement offices are not organized to help their alumni or students seeking summer jobs.

Virtually all undergraduates and most graduate students use their placement office as a source of job leads. From our own observations, we suspect that few people who should use the placement office as their primary source fail to do so, while a considerable number who should be relying primarily on other sources instead rely exclusively on placement offices, simply because it's easier that way.

To decide how much to rely on a placement office for job leads (or whether to rely on it at all), a student needs to learn, well in advance of the recruiting season, which organizations with what types of job tend to recruit on campus. (Lists of organizations, along with job descriptions from the previous year's recruitment activities, are usually available at placement offices.) If the types of companies and jobs on which you are focusing don't usually recruit on your campus, you will need to rely on other sources for job leads. We have known many graduate students who obtained very satisfying jobs without ever using their placement offices.

Most of our students who have not relied primarily on our placement office have gotten their job leads through direct personal solicitation.[1] That is, they have written unsolicited letters to potential employers asking if they have any job openings. In a typical case, a student will send out 10, 20, or 30 one- or two-page letters to carefully chosen targets.[2] The letter, in one way or another, asks that the writer be considered for a job, and encloses a resumé. If the letter and resumé are well written, and if the targets are well chosen, the person may expect to receive from 10 to 50 percent "positive responses" (usually an invitation for an interview). Poorly written letters and resumes sent out to inadequately screened targets often net no positive responses. We've seen people send out 100 letters and receive mimeographed rejection letters from 20 organizations, per-

---

[1] In a 1973 survey, 45 percent of the entire graduating class at Harvard Business School said they learned of the job they eventually accepted through placement-office activities. Twenty-seven percent learned of their job through personal solicitation. Fourteen percent learned of it through summer or previous employment.

[2] Chapter XIV will have more to say on exactly how one "carefully chooses" such targets.

sonal rejection letters from another 3, and no response from the remaining 77.

Personal solicitation can be time consuming and very frustrating. It takes a reasonably strong ego to withstand getting rejections in the mail day after day after day. It's both easier and less ego deflating to look over ads in the newspaper or lists of employers at the placement office—a process in which *you* reject (screen) *them*. As a result, most job hunters probably underutilize personal solicitation as a source of leads.

The single most important source of job leads for nonstudent professional, technical, and managerial workers is their own personal contacts. In a study of such people who had changed jobs in the past five years in one geographical area, Mark Granovetter found that about 55 to 60 percent of them had identified their new job using a personal contact source. (The percentage was even higher for managers and people earning over $25,000 per year.) Furthermore, these people expressed a higher level of satisfaction with the jobs they obtained that way than people who relied on other sources.[3]

The most useful personal sources of leads include people who are looking for a similar job, former work associates, and professional acquaintances made through professional organizations.[4] People inside an organization often know of, or can easily find out about, job possibilities that are never advertised externally. Professional associations often actively solicit job-possibility information from all their members and then make that information available to their members or to anyone who requests it. The tactic of trading leads with another similar job hunter often can net one a large number of previously unknown possibilities.

Some successful job hunters spend virtually all their effort in the first month of job hunting setting up a network of contacts who are aware of their new job-hunting status as well as the exact focus of their job campaign. They then use that network as a radar screen to identify job leads.

A fourth source of leads that job hunters often use is advertisements. Newspapers carry job ads on a daily basis for the area they serve. Professional journals and magazines sometimes include a help wanted section. Access to these sources is relatively easy, by subscription or through a library.

Almost all job seekers who are out of school use this source of leads to some degree, probably because it is easy and doesn't require much personal initiative. And ads are the most visible source of job leads. However, very few students seem to actually find jobs through this source, and a relatively small percentage of nonstudent professionals (managerial or technical) actually gain their jobs through ads.

However, job advertisements may serve a useful function beyond being a source of job leads. For the same reason that advertising in general is often useful to people who are not currently looking for a specific product, job advertisements probably help some people get a useful "feel" for the job market. That is, they can sometimes supply infor-

mation to a job hunter regarding what types of jobs, at what salaries, exist in what numbers, and where. Particularly at the start of a job hunt, such information could be very useful.

A final source of leads commonly used by job hunters is profit-making organizations such as executive search firms and personnel agencies. We know of no student at all who has found a job as a result of a lead from these sources. And although we have known many nonstudents who have used this source of leads, very few have actually found jobs that way.

We have personally heard many more bad stories than good about people's interactions with personnel agencies. One gets the sense that they can be helpful to nonstudents, but that there are plenty of risks involved, due to the large number of marginally competent people in those agencies.

Many of the established and larger executive search firms have a reputation of doing a competent job for their market. But that market is fairly small—managers in the $30,000-and-up bracket.[5]

Figure 1 summarizes this discussion. The number-one job-lead source for students is the placement office. For nonstudents, the number-one source is personal contacts. Unsolicited letter campaigns and other forms of direct application are the second most-used source for both groups.

FIGURE 1 Summary Chart: Sources of Job Leads

Sources	Comments
1. College placement office	By far the most widely used source for students. Probably overused.
2. Unsolicited direct-mail campaigns	Number-two source for all job hunters.
3. Personal contacts	By far the most widely used source for nonstudents.
4. Advertisements	Useful for job-market data. Not terribly useful for specific leads.
5. Personnel agencies and executive search firms	Best for people earning $30,000 a year or more.

Getting an Interview

When using most job-lead sources—the placement office is the key exception—one does not automatically have a right to an interview. One must usually earn that right by passing an initial employer screen. Most employers have no more desire to waste their time in the labor market than you do. So they too set up some type of more or less thought-out screening process.

Getting a first interview sometimes involves sending someone a resumé, or a resumé and a letter, or talking to someone briefly on the phone, or getting someone to recommend you. In any case, the key to success is to differen-

---

[3]Mark Granovetter, *Getting a Job* (Cambridge, Mass.: Harvard University Press, 1974).

[4]Granovetter found that most of the contacts people successfully used were work and educational acquaintances, not social friends.

[5]For an interesting discussion of executive search firms see Jacquelin A. Thompson, ''The MBA Guide to Executive Recruiters: Who They Are and How They Work,'' *MBA*, May 1976.

tiate yourself from the masses and convince the decision maker that the time taken to interview you probably isn't going to be wasted.

It is not altogether unusual for an organization to receive 20 to 50 inquiries for a job opening. Some jobs will attract hundreds of inquiries. Since hiring a single managerial or professional person can cost an organization as much as $20,000,[6] employers have a strong financial incentive to try to keep costs down. Interviewing everyone who inquires about a job opening can significantly increase one's costs.

Convincing some decision maker to take the time to interview you is not an exercise, as many people seem to think, in making yourself look "impressive" in some ill-defined, abstract sense. What is "impressive," like beauty, is determined in the eyes of the beholder. The beholder is an employer with particular goals, values, problems, and needs. And here lies the key not just to getting an initial interview, but to getting job offers.

The more you can put yourself in the position of the potential employer and understand that person's (or those people's) point of view, the more successful you will be in getting job offers. With respect to getting an initial interview, this means that it helps enormously to know something about the potential employer before you make your initial contact. If you can somehow communicate to the persons making the screening decision that you may have the potential of meeting *their needs*, you will certainly get the interview.

Let's take a specific example. Most people, even those with no full-time job experience, could write a 30-page resumé if asked. They could elaborate at length on their schooling, their part-time jobs, their hobbies, their health, their job objective, etc. Most people don't, of course. Instead, they ask someone what a resumé is supposed to look like, or for a sample resumé, and then semiconsciously select things to put into that format. The end result is seldom a great resumé.

A good resumé is nothing more than a tool that can convince an employer that you may well be able to meet their particular needs, help with their problems, and share enough in common with them to "fit in." Creating a good resumé therefore depends upon your understanding of what an employer's needs are, what their problems are, what their values are, and what you can contribute. Any person who has gone through the process of creating a rational focus for a job campaign, and who has done the little additional research necessary to screen leads, has probably learned enough about potential employers to make the type of initial contact that gets one an interview. It doesn't require hours and hours of additional effort. Since so many job hunters do almost no research, doing just a little can be a real competitive advantage.

Finally, regardless of your source of initial contact (letter, resumé,[7] phone call), it should look polished and pro-

fessional. A resumé that looks as if it were typed on a cheap typewriter by a nontypist communicates a number of things about you. It says that you are just always a sloppy person (and who wants to hire a sloppy person?) or you really don't care much about getting a job (and who wants to hire someone who doesn't want to work?) or you don't really care much about the person you sent the resumé to (etc.?). It's worth the time and money to look professional and interested.

Interviewing

A professional person will virtually always be asked to interview with from 1 to 25 or more different members of a hiring organization. Many people look forward to these interviews, especially initial "screening" interviews, with the same ambivalence that precedes an operation. And with good reason. Interviewing, for many people, is an anxiety-arousing, painful experience in which they display little skill or common sense.[8]

The archetype of the poor interviewee is the young student. Such a person goes into an interview, especially at the beginning of the recruiting season, with an awkward feeling that is usually reinforced by his or her friends ("Hey, Jerry, is that really you underneath that suit and without any hair?!"). Sometimes people have a gnawing feeling, which they know is silly, that they are basically unemployable (born in the wrong century). At some level, these young people often see the interviewer as someone with life-or-death power over them (which frightens some and enrages others). The fright, anger, and awkwardness are made even worse in the interview when the interviewer doesn't behave as the interviewee somehow expects. Trembling or hostile, interviewees exhibit defensive behaviors that even they usually recognize are not in their own best interests. As a result, some people have real difficulty getting job offers—even people who eventually go on to have splendid careers.

Much of the anxiety that accompanies a person into an interview can be reduced or eliminated by following the procedures outlined previously in this book. People who are confident in knowing who they are and what they want invariably feel more relaxed going into interviews than people who don't. Even people who spend just a half-hour or so before an interview (or a set of interviews) doing some research on the employer tend to be more confident and relaxed.

In addition, we have found that anxiety can be significantly reduced if you have a realistic understanding of the context of the job interview, the different types of job interviews, and the situation the interviewer is in. A surprisingly large number of people go into interviewing situations with very unrealistic assumptions.

For example, most job interviews are 30 to 60 minutes long. As any successful salesman knows, it's extremely difficult to sell an expensive and complex product (and let's face it, you are an expensive and complex product) under a

---

[6]Including costs associated with placing ads, bringing out-of-town applicants to visit them, interviewing and selecting, training, paying a salary while the person trains, and turnover.

[7]So much has been written about resumés that we've decided not to repeat it all again here. For a good treatment of the subject, see Chapter 8 in Benedetto Greco, *How to Get the Job That's Right for You* (Homewood, Ill.: Dow Jones-Irwin, 1975).

[8]If you feel uncomfortable with the prospect of interviewing, the interviewing exercise in the workbook on p. 305 may be of considerable help.

short time constraint without excellent preparation. Yet many interviewees don't adequately prepare.

Being prepared in a job interview has two elements: (a) anticipating what the interviewer will want from you and being ready to supply it; (b) knowing what you want from the interviewer and being ready to ask for it. (We'll explore the latter in the next chapter.)

Figures 2 and 3 supply data on what interviewers want from an interview. When 236 recruiters were asked recently what behavior on the part of interviewees led to the "best" interviews, they responded as shown in Figure 2. Interviewers seem generally to like interviewees who have "done their homework"—who know what they want, and who know something about the organization they are interviewing. In another survey of well-known business and industrial concerns, college recruiters were asked what types of questions they typically ask in an interview (see Figure 3). Some students take the time to create short (1- to 5-minute) articulate answers to these kinds of questions before they begin interviewing prospective employers. These students seem to be much more successful at interviewing.

When preparing for interviews and while interviewing, it is important to take into account that there are a number of different kinds of job interviews.

The primary purpose of the "screening" interview is to save an organization and its managers time and money by limiting the number of job applications they will have to closely examine. The interviewer has a very limited number of more or less specific criteria that constitute the rough screen. The question he or she is addressing is simply: does the interviewee make it through the screen or not? The campus interview is typically a screening interview. So are many of the interviews in large companies with a person from "personnel."

The most common mistake made by job applicants in screening interviews is to try to get into too much depth. In many cases, especially with larger corporations, the responsibility of the individual doing the screening stops at selecting from among the interviewees the most appropriate candidates to be invited for a second interview, usually on the company's premises. The interviewer in such cases is seldom the final decision maker regarding a job offer and may not even know the specific requirements of the jobs to be filled. Consequently an interviewee who attempts to tell an interviewer everything about him or herself, and who tries to learn everything about the company and job, as if both parties had to make a final decision regarding employment on the spot, seriously undermines a screening interview.

A second type of interview is with the person (or one of the persons) whose responsibility it is to actually make the hiring decision. These interviews sometimes conclude with the interviewer making a job offer. The question that guides the interviewer's behavior is: do I want to hire this person? In this type of interview one wants to make one's entire "sales presentation." Forgetting or not having time to tell all the major messages you have—about what you want in a job and career, why you want that, and why you think that you can help them with their needs and problems—can

FIGURE 2 What Made the Best Interviews?*

1. *Interviewee knew about company* ("had done homework," "knows the field") 66% (174)

2. *Interviewee had specific career goals* ("knew what he/she wanted," "good fit between our needs and his/hers," "well-thought-out career interests") 41% (108)

3. *Interviewee knowledgeable* ("asked good questions," "knew what to ask") 29% (76)

4. *Interviewee socially adept* ("rapport," "in tune with me," "outgoing and expressive") 28% (74)

5. *Interviewee articulate* ("able to express ideas," "spoke well," "good with tricky questions") 19% (50)

*Based on questionnaire responses from 236 people who recruited at Harvard Business School in 1973; more than one response allowed.

FIGURE 3 The Most Commonly Asked Questions*: General Classification

1. Goals and purposes—Life purposes—Career objectives
2. Type of work desired—Kind of Job—Job expectations
3. Reasons for selection of company—Knowledge of company
4. Personal qualifications—Strengths and weaknesses
5. Career choice—Reasons for decisions
6. Qualifications for the job—How college education has prepared the candidate
7. Educational choices and plans—Choice of college—Choice of major
8. Geographical preferences—Willingness to relocate
9. Major achievements and accomplishments

*From the 29th Annual Endicott Report, by Frank S. Endicott, Director of Placement Emeritus, Northwestern University, Copyright 1974 by Northwestern University.

diminish your possibilities of getting a job offer. At this stage it is important to get into details.

A third type of interview is with people who will have only an input into the hiring decision, and who often will end up working with the person who is hired. Because they have less at stake in the hiring decision, they often are more casual and less prepared for the interview. The key question that tends to go through their minds is: what's it going to be like around here if this person is hired?

Interviewees often treat this third type of interview just like the second one; this is a mistake that can create problems. It's important in this third type of interview just to establish some rapport with the person, and not to try to make the big sale. Coming on too strong with potential peers might hurt an interviewee (few people like the idea of too much competition around them). Because the stakes are somewhat lower in this type of interview than in the second type, one can also safely allocate more time to gathering information from the interviewer (more on that in the next chapter).

Although the objectives of these three types of interviews are different, they are seldom in direct conflict with the objectives of the interviewee. Both parties want very much to find someone who can meet their needs. A job decision never works out really well unless both sets of needs are met. (If only one set is met, the employee will typically quit or be fired before too long.) For these reasons it is in the best interests of both parties to see if they have compatible resources and needs. Yet interviewees sometimes assume an adversary relationship, taking the interviewer's objectives to be in conflict with their own. They behave in a somewhat guarded and competitive way. Not only does that behavior undermine the interview, but it usually gives the interviewer a poor impression of the interviewee.[9]

Still other problems job hunters have with interviewing can be traced to a lack of appreciation of the interviewer's situation. The following candid remarks from two people who have done a lot of job interviewing for their organizations are very instructive in this regard. Although all interviewers are not like these two people, virtually all share at least some of their attitudes and perspectives:

I spend nearly all of my time between January and March interviewing at universities. It's a tough three months. I'm almost always on the road and away from home. The pace can be very hectic.

Yesterday is a beautiful example of the difficulties involved in this job. I got in late two nights ago. Yesterday morning during breakfast I briefly looked over the resumés of the 15 people I was supposed to see that day. Three of them looked like a mistake; I couldn't imagine why they wanted an interview with us. Because I was running late I walked three blocks in the rain to flag down a cab. I managed to get to the campus a few minutes before my first interview—who didn't show up. I got some coffee and then had a good interview at 9:30. When I asked the 10:00 interviewee, shortly after we started talking, if he had worked full time before coming to school, he gave this annoyed look and said, "I sent you my resumé two months ago—haven't you read it yet?" The interview went downhill from there. My schedule had no break in it until 12:30, and for that last half-hour I thought more about my bladder than about the student I was interviewing. I think my 2:00 interviewee was just trying to kill a half-hour between the naps he takes in his classes. He didn't even know what business we were in and had no conception of what he wanted to do. What a waste of time. My 4:00 interviewee was a very impressive young man, but I can't get over the feeling that I was conned. Some of these kids are more skilled at interviewing than I am. When I got back to

my hotel at 5:45, I immediately started reviewing the day and my notes. Already the interviews were beginning to blur together. You know, you end up thinking, now which one was the guy who said such and such.

Last week I came up against one of the parts of the job that really annoys me. I interviewed a young woman that I think could turn out to be a very important addition to one of our divisions. But I decided against recommending her because it was too risky. You see, in evaluating my contribution it can take years and years to determine whether the people I recommended (who eventually join the company) are a real success. But it only takes 12 months or less to determine if they are a disaster. So I tend to be evaluated more on not producing disasters. And that, of course, discourages risk taking. And hiring that woman would, I'm afraid, be risky.

I hired seven people for my department last year. I must have interviewed around 50 people. Of all the parts of my job, I feel in many ways least sure about this one. I keep thinking, there must be a better way.

Interviewing is often an intrusion on other parts of my job. As a result, I'm sure that at least some of the time when I'm interviewing someone my mind and heart are elsewhere. And I can't believe I do an effective job under those circumstances. I often wish I could spend a lot more time with interviewees, but that's just not possible.

I've read a few things on the subject of how to interview, but they haven't been terribly useful. I still wonder if I'm asking the right questions or correctly interpreting the interviewee's remarks.

I just don't know what to do with the person who doesn't really know much about us or our industry, or the one who isn't sure what he or she wants. You could spend hours talking to that kind of person trying to sort things out.

On some days when I'm tired and hassled, I wish the interviewee would run the interview. I've actually seen a few who did just that.

Some of the most common mistakes interviewees make stem from their own inaccurate assumptions regarding the interviewer and the position such a person is in. Job hunters, for example, often behave as if the responsibility for the success or failure of the interview were solely the interviewer's. They themselves assume no responsibility. They further behave as if expecting the interviewer to be extremely competent and working under ideal conditions. When the interviewer subsequently doesn't behave as he or she "should," these people get angry or annoyed, and that feeling further undermines the interview. Less-than-ideal conditions, a less-than-perfect interviewer, and an interviewee who is prepared to tolerate neither, systematically produce bad interviews.

The best interviewees not only have realistic expectations regarding the interviewer, they even try to empathize with him or her. Such activity helps them develop a rapport that leaves a favorable impression, as well as helping the kind of information exchange that is needed to meet the objectives of the interview.

---

[9]Interviewers usually react negatively if they think the interviewee isn't being honest. This happens surprisingly often. In a 1973 survey of interviewers at Harvard Business School, 60 percent said they felt they were being more honest than the interviewees, while only 9 percent said they felt less honest than the interviewees. An interviewee who assumes an adversary stance often comes across as being not very honest.

Follow-Up

After interviewing for a job, and before a job offer is made (or not made), an interviewee often feels left in a helpless position, where there is nothing to do but wait, and hope. While it's easy to understand why people feel this way—the ball, so to speak, is in the employer's court—passive behavior nonetheless is not in an interviewee's best interests.

Systematic follow-up after interviewing can be an important part of successful job hunting. Three aspects of such follow-up seem particularly helpful.

Getting a Commitment from the Employer

Always get a commitment from the employer before leaving an interview (or a set of interviews) regarding what they will be doing next, and when you will hear from them next.

Some of the uncertainty that accompanies this period in job hunting can be eliminated simply by asking the employer to clarify the process. When will you make a decision as to whether a job offer will be made? How is that decision reached? When will I hear from you next? Most employers will expect better, more confident job applicants to ask these questions.

In addition, by getting a specific date when you can expect to hear from them next, you put yourself in a less dependent position. The knowledge of that date allows you to plan more accurately the other aspects of your own job campaign so that you don't suddenly find yourself caught in a timing conflict. If you find that date is too far away—after, for example, you are expected to accept or decline someone else's offer—you can tell the employer so and often get it changed. And when you interview with other employers and are asked when you can reply to their offer, you can respond knowing that it will be after you hear from the places you have already interviewed.

Getting a commitment regarding the time of an employer's reply also reduces the chances that you will be strung along. Without a date, some job hunters wait for weeks or months, often afraid to call or write the employer because it will make them look impatient or desperate. The job applicant who has got a commitment to a specific date can legitimately call at once if the employer doesn't respond as promised.

Keeping in Contact

Keep in contact with potential employers during the waiting period(s). After an initial screening interview, and after a final set of interviews, many successful job hunters will write a letter (or letters) to those with whom they spoke. The letter can communicate your appreciation of the way in which you were treated, your interest, your initiative, and the reasons why you think there may be a good match between your abilities and desires and the job. It can also help keep you visible, even though you're not there.

When visiting a potential employer, if you find that you share some professional interests with someone you meet, you may wish to follow up on that after leaving. Successful job hunters will sometimes stay in contact by letter or in person (if the employer is geographically close by) with a few of the people they met at a particularly interesting potential employer. Such contacts can help produce job offers.

Persisting and Persevering

Recognize that the key to getting what you really want—not your second, or third, or tenth choice—often depends upon your own perseverance. Some people would argue that the key to the whole process of getting job offers is persistence. The following story, while not at all typical, is instructive in this regard.

Jim Howard began job hunting with a major focus on consumer product management jobs and a minor focus on advertising jobs. Primarily because he had a good understanding of product management jobs, of himself, and of why he would probably make a good product manager, he was enormously successful in his initial interviews with consumer product companies. He contacted 10 such companies, got initial interviews with each, and was invited for a second set of interviews at all but one place. His understanding of advertising jobs and how he might fit in, as well as his commitment to an advertising career, was much lower. He contacted six ad agencies, was invited to interview with two, and was invited back to only one. All this occurred in January and February.

During March, while Jim was going through the second round of on-site interviews, he began to learn more about advertising through a course and his own research, and as he did he grew more and more excited about it. It became clearer and clearer to him that he could be really good at account management and derive a lot of satisfaction from it.

In April Jim found himself in a rather unusual position. He was the envy of all of his friends—for he had seven attractive job offers. Unfortunately, all seven offers were in product management, which he was no longer convinced that he wanted. Worse yet, he had fallen in love with the ad firm in which he had a set of second interviews. And the attraction was not just emotional infatuation. The job and company sounded almost perfect in light of his self-assessment paper.

On April 15, five days before he had promised some employers that he would respond to their job offers, Jim tentatively decided to accept a particular product management job. But it didn't feel right to him. He kept thinking to himself—if you know what you want, why take anything else unless you have to.

The next day he called the one person at the ad firm who had seemed to respond the most favorably toward him when he had visited them six weeks earlier. He invited that person to lunch, saying he needed some advice. At lunch he presented his dilemma, including his detailed analysis of why he would probably do a very good job at that ad firm. He effectively ended by saying that unless he heard very convincing evidence to the contrary, he was going to turn down his other offers and pursue the ad firm until it offered him a job. The man he spoke with was visibly impressed.

At 8:30 the next morning his luncheon partner from the previous day called and invited him to come down to the agency that afternoon. Jim spent the afternoon talking to other employees of the firm, much as he did with the first person the day before.

On April 19, one day before he was to respond to his other offers, the ad firm called and offered him a job. He accepted, and when last heard from was doing very well and was extremely pleased with his job and company.

Exercise

Jim Lydon, a second-year M.B.A. student, sent the accompanying letter [Jim Lydon (A)] to 12 prospective real estate employers. What is your evaluation of the letter? Why do you evaluate it as you have?

Jim Lydon (A)

Dear Mr. _____:

I shall receive an M.B.A. in June 1978 and plan a career in the real estate field with a leading properties firm. My survey of the industry indicates that your firm has established an outstanding record and, therefore, it would be advantageous for me to learn more about the specific opportunities it offers and to discuss with you my objectives and capabilities.

My highest priority is to find a challenging, fulfilling environment in which to learn and work. Pursuant to this objective, I seek a firm which: (1) recognizes the need for professional management of M.B.A. caliber in this rapidly growing field, (2) gives a broad exposure to real estate and discourages overspecialization, (3) operates in an informal structure with close personal relationships among employees, (4) allows new M.B.A.'s to contribute immediately and to assume early responsibilities, and (5) measures performance and allocates compensation and advancement accordingly without regard for senority. I would like to know more about your firm with respect to these criteria.

The enclosed resume gives you a brief outline of my background but does not deal with relevant personal qualities. I have an entrepreneurial spirit, the ability to coordinate several projects simultaneously with proven results, and a "knack" for working successfully with diverse groups of people eliciting their trust and confidence. I am performance-oriented, mature, willing to travel, able to communicate effectively, and confident that the pattern of success that has characterized my past will lead me to greater achievements in the near future.

Mr. _____, if you feel that my objectives and qualifications may be compatible with your firm's opportunities and needs, please contact me to arrange a meeting that could be to our mutual benefit. I shall hope to hear from you soon.

Sincerely,

James L. Lydon

JLL/lmm

Enclosure

XIV

Assessing a Job Offer

To rationally assess job offers, a job hunter needs a considerable amount of information (see Figure 1). Although some people would argue that you can't know much about a company or job until you have actually worked in it for six months, evidence from our students suggests otherwise. Clearly, there is a limit to what you can "know" about a job without directly experiencing it, but many people stop far short of that limit during job hunting. Often, because they are either so worried about being rejected by potential employers or so flattered by all the attention and offers they are getting, some job hunters neglect to seriously and rationally assess their job offers and potential offers. By neglecting to use all available sources of information, by failing to understand how properly to utilize their sources, and by relying on inappropriate methods to analyze the data they obtain, they consistently make poorly informed decisions on which potential offers to pursue, which to eliminate, and finally which offer to accept.

FIGURE 1 Information That Is Often Useful in Assessing a Job Offer or Potential Offer

---

Regarding the Job Itself

1. What major tasks are involved and what are their key characteristics?
2. What skills are needed to perform each task?
3. Approximately what percent of the time will the job holder spend on each task? How does this vary (if at all) over time?
4. What time and resource constraints does the job holder have to work within?
5. How many hours per week do people holding similar jobs work?
6. What percent of the time will the job holder be working alone?
7. Who else will the job holder interact with? What are these people like? What percent of the time will the job holder be with them?
8. How much discretion will the job holder have in deciding how to perform the job?
9. How many people and how much money or equipment will the job holder be responsible for?
10. How many people will report to the job holder?

11. Who will be the job holder's boss? What is this person like? How good a coach is he or she?
12. How is performance measured in this job?
13. What type of salary and other rewards are available given what level of performance?
14. Specifically what type of advancement opportunities are available to the job holder?
15. Who makes decisions and how regarding promotions?

Regarding the Organization

16. How large is the organization's industry (employment, number of competitors) and what are its prospects for future growth?
17. Specifically what parts of the industry will probably grow (or decline) at what rates over the next few decades?
18. What are the industry's most important characteristics? (Is business seasonal? What type of organizations do well or poorly?)
19. How is the industry changing now?
20. How old is the organization? What are the big events in its history?

FIGURE 1 (cont.)

21. How large is the organization (people, assets, sales volume, net income)?
22. What goods and services does it produce?
23. How does it produce these goods and services?
24. Where does it have plants or offices?
25. Does the organization have any particularly important suppliers, customers, or regulators? If yes, who are they, what are they like, and what is their relationship to the organization?
26. What important technologies does the organization use?
27. What are the major parts of the organization and how are they structured?
28. What are the organization's compensation policies? Performance appraisal practices? Training and development practices? Other important personnel policies?
29. What type of people work for the organization?
30. What do they generally like about the organization? Dislike about it?
31. Does the organization have any important traditions?
32. How are the people and the way in which they interact different from people in other organizations you have known?
33. What are the company's plans for the future?

Effective assessment of job offers and potential offers, much like effective self-assessment, requires that one understand what data sources are available, what the nature of each source is, how to analyze and integrate the data from the various sources, and for what purpose (under what constraints) you are working. In this chapter we will examine each of these elements of job assessment.

Sources of Information

There are three basic sources of information on potential jobs and on the organizations in which the jobs are located: published documents, people, and direct observation. Each is different in the information it can supply and the cost of obtaining that information, but all three can be very useful.

Written sources, such as those listed in Figure 2, can be especially useful in supplying information on an organization's past financial performance, its current demographic characteristics (size, products/services offered, assets, etc.), its industry, and its major actions (bringing out a new product line, bringing in a new president, etc.). Published sources have the advantage of relative ease of access. All major libraries will have most of the sources in Figure 2. You can look over such information at your convenience, as often as you wish; you only need to allocate enough time to this task.

FIGURE 2 Where to Find Written Information about Companies

A. Directories

There are many published directories of companies. A few are general lists of larger companies, others are specialized, either by location (country, state or city) or by industry or trade. Some give as much information as the first three below, others merely give address or industry. These first three directories are probably used most often as a starting point for brief information on larger U.S. companies.

Poor's Register of Corporations, Directors and Executives.
Alphabetical list of approximately 33,000 U.S. and Canadian corporations, giving officers, products (if manufacturer), standard industrial classification (SIC), sales range, and number of employees. The latter half consists of brief information on about 75,000 executives and directors. Index of companies by SIC is at front. See also its *Geographical Index.*

Dun & Bradstreet. *Million Dollar Directory.*
Lists approximately 31,000 U.S. companies with an indicated worth of $1 million or over. Gives officers, products (if manufacturer), standard industrial classification, approximate sales, and number of employees. The yellow pages list companies geographically and the blue pages by SIC industries. The white pages at the end are an alphabetical listing of officers and directors.

Dun & Bradstreet. *Middle Market Directory.*
Lists approximately 33,000 U.S. companies with an indicated worth of $500,000 to $999,999. Coverage and information given are similar to that of the directory above except that officers and directors are not listed.

If your company is a manufacturer, you may find it listed in the following comprehensive directory:

Thomas Register of American Manufacturers. 10 vols., annual.
Volumes 1–6 list manufacturers by specific product. Volume 7 is an alphabetical list of companies and includes address, branch offices, subsidiaries, products, estimated capitalization. Volume 8 is an "Index" to produce categories and it also contains a list of leading trade names (pink sheets). Volumes 9–10 are a "Catalog of Companies."

1. Regional and State Manufacturers Directories

If your manufacturing company is not in *Thomas* and you know in which state it is located, try looking for it in a state directory. Several examples are:

California Manufacturers Register.
Directory of New England Manufacturers.
Greater Boston Directory of Manufacturers.
Massachusetts Dept. of Commerce and Development. *Industrial Directory of Massachusetts Manufacturers.*
New York State Industrial Directory.

2. Directories of Companies in Foreign Countries

Several examples are:

Japan Directory. 2 vols.

Schweizerische Zentrale für Handelsforderung. *Directory of Swiss Manufacturers and Producers.*

3. Directories for Specific Industries or Trades

Several examples are:

American Management Association. *Directory of Consultant Members.*

Directory of Department Stores.

Davison's Textile Blue Book.

Franchise Guide: An Encyclopedia of Franchise Opportunities.

Lockwood's Directory of the Paper and Allied Trades.

Rubber Red Book.

American Marketing Association, New York Chapter. *International Directory of Marketing Research Houses and Services.*

Money Management Directories Inc., *Money Market Directory.* 1977. A directory of institutional investors and their portfolio managers.

Investment Bankers Association of America. *The Blue Book.* 1971.

National Association of Real Estate Investment Funds. *NAREIF Handbook of Member Trusts.*

Rand McNally International Bankers Directory.

Security Dealers of North America.

Standard Directory of Advertising Agencies.

Venture Capital. Monthly publication.

World Space Directory Including Oceanology.

4. Directories of American Firms with Foreign Subsidiaries

Directory of American Firms Operating in Foreign Countries. 8th Edition, 1975.

Finance Magazine, *International Almanac of Business and Finance.*

Who Owns Whom: International Subsidiaries of U.S. Companies.

5. Guides to Directories

If you still do not find a directory for the industry or geographic area you want, look for a bibliography of directories that may list a trade directory that your library does not have or a directory issue of a trade journal. One of the best bibliographies is:

Guide to American Directories.

B. Financial Information about Companies

The following documents for New York and American Stock Exchange companies can be very useful:

Annual Reports to Stockholders

10-K Reports to the Securities and Exchange Commission

Listing Statements

Proxy Statements

Registration Statements

C. Articles about Companies

F & S Index of Corporations & Industries (weekly, cumulated monthly and annually).

Indexes articles on companies and industries that have appeared in selected business and financial publications, and also brokerage house reports.

F & S International (monthly, cumulated annually). An index similar to the one above, for foreign companies.

Wall Street Journal Index (monthly, with annual cumulation).

Each issue has two parts: Corporate News and General News. Indexing is based on the final Eastern Edition.

Wall Street Transcript (weekly).

A compilation of brokerage house reports on companies and industries. Each issue is indexed, and there is also a periodic cumulated index.

People we have observed who have not been very successful at job hunting almost always seem to underutilize published information sources. Their time and their energy get absorbed elsewhere, in less productive activities.

There are two types of human information sources about potential jobs: current employees of the organizations with the job openings, and others. These others might be former employees, consultants who have worked with the organization, financial analysts who have studied the organization for their own money management firms, and so on. A job hunter automatically gains access to some of the organization's employees while interviewing. For moderate-sized to large organizations, our students have almost always been able to find a few people who fall into that ''other'' category. It is a rare case, for example, in which no faculty

member has ever had dealings with such an organization and no fellow student has worked for it (if only for a summer).

In brief conversations with informed nonemployees, one can usually get reasonably candid and unbiased information of a type that doesn't tend to appear in print and that is awkward to obtain from the organization's current employees. What kind of problems does the organization have? How do they treat their employees? Are they really going to be able to grow as fast as they say? If you previously worked for this organization, did you enjoy it? Why?

Inside sources can supply slightly different types of data. They can give you first-hand information on what it is currently like to work for that organization, what the potential job is really like, what the career path associated with it is really like, and what the people you would be working with are like. And possibly the easiest way to get that information is to ask these people about themselves. How long have you been working here? Why did you join up? What job did you start in? Specifically what did you do? Who did you work with? What did you like and dislike about that job? What job did you move to next? When did that move occur? Why did it occur? Describe what you did in your next job? And so on. People generally enjoy talking about themselves. When describing their own careers and jobs, they also generally give much more accurate and useful information than when they try to generalize about careers or jobs in their organization.

It's useful to distinguish between two types of inside information sources: those who would be your superiors and those who would be peers. The former are better equipped to give you data on careers in the company and the company itself. The latter are usually the best sources of information about the job itself.

Do not underestimate the helpfulness of talking to someone who is in a job exactly like, or similar to, the one you have been (or might be) offered. Talking to such a person about what he or she actually does on a daily basis can be enormously useful. We have seen people actually accept job offers based on an image they have developed that unfortunately has nothing to do with what the job actually demands. At the extreme this produces mild tragedies. One young man we knew took a job, as he put it, as a "California banker," no doubt with great images of sun, surf, and doling out money behind a large mahogany desk. When he arrived in L.A. he discovered that being a California banker in his case meant spending 2½ hours a day driving to and from work, and 8 hours a day in a small branch many miles from the ocean performing clerical functions as a part of a 12-month "training program."

We have also learned from our students that one should not underestimate the importance of meeting and talking to the person you will be reporting to (your boss) if you accept the job. We have seen a number of people accept what seemed to be excellent jobs, only to discover after starting work that they could not get along with the boss they hadn't met while job hunting.

And finally, don't underestimate the usefulness of talking to more than just two or three insiders. In a sample of M.B.A. students from the Harvard Business School class of 1974, those who reported high job satisfaction seven months after graduation had spent more time talking to more people at their future employer's during job hunting than had those people who reported lower job satisfaction. By talking to a number of employees while interviewing, most people can begin to get a "feel" for an organization that is difficult to develop from other sources.

If an employer does not take the initiative in scheduling interviews for you with your potential boss, with a person occupying a job similar to the one that is open, and with a number of peers and superiors, then the job applicant must do so. Most employers will respond favorably to that kind of initiative. And even if they don't respond positively, you learn something very important about them in the process.

A third source of information on jobs is direct observation. Most professionals are invited to visit the organization itself before any job offer is extended, even if that means a long trip (at the organization's expense). The four to 20 hours that are spent in the organization itself can provide an enormous amount of information beyond that obtained in interviews. All you have to do is keep your eyes and ears open.

Job hunters tend to underuse direct observation for a number of reasons (chief among them is that most well-educated people do not seem to be very visually oriented). Yet this information source is very attractive in two ways. First, it doesn't require the use of the job hunter's most precious resource—time. If you visit a company for a day, you get eight hours of visual data at no extra cost. Second, it can be an incredibly rich source of impressionistic data, which you can use in checking out your conclusions about the company and its people that you derived primarily from what people were saying.

Ignoring visual data, or not being alert to cues provided by direct observation, can get a job hunter into trouble. The following story, related by a very bright and capable young man, illustrates this point rather clearly:

While job hunting, I found this small firm that built the most beautiful modern lighting that money can buy. I spent a full day there and yet I just didn't pay attention to all the visual clues that suggested I might not get along with the boss. I was so enchanted by the job, and by what he said, that I didn't see the obvious signs.

You see, I recognize that I have a fairly large need for autonomy, and a fairly large need for an aesthetic environment. The job opening was for a director of marketing (reporting to the president), which was exactly what I wanted. When I talked to the company president, he assured me that I would be able to run my own show without interference. Since he did not have a background in marketing, nor any great interest in it, I believed him.

Most of the time I spent visiting the company was with him at his home and at a restaurant, but we did meet for about two hours in his office. His office is quite large—about 40 by 40 feet. It has very functional furniture in it, and it's usually a mess. Outside his office is a smaller office area, 20 by 20 feet, that has five desks in it (yes, five people share that office!). It has the same functional furniture and it's slightly less messy. Off of that area are three other small offices, 9 by 9 feet, each with a functional desk, chair, and grey filing cabinet.

So here we have a setup where his space is clearly dominant, and where his tastes (he has an engineering/manufacturing background) dominate also. I sat in the middle of that for two hours and yet didn't really see it.

When I came on board, I was given one of the 9 by 9 offices, and for the first month everything was OK. Then the dreary office area began to bug me and when I asked my boss about getting some nice office furniture, he just effectively ignored the request. Each month thereafter, especially as I started to initiate some new marketing programs, we began to clash. After five months it became clear he was not about to give me the autonomy he promised. I quit after six months.

This entire discussion of information sources and their uses is summarized in Figure 3.

Figure 3 Information Sources and Their Uses

	Information Source				
	Library	**Informed Nonemployees**	**Potential Boss and Superiors**	**Potential Peers and Others**	**Direct Observation**
Industry Characteristics	***	**	*	*	
Major organizational characteristics (what it does, where, etc.)	***	**	*	*	
How the organization functions		***	**	*	**
What it's like to work for the organization		**	*	***	***
Job characteristics			*	***	*
Career possibilities	*	*	***	*	

***best source   ** good source   *a source

An Effective Assessment Strategy

People we have known who have been very successful at job hunting tend to rely extensively on all the information sources we've mentioned. Their less successful peers, on the other hand, don't. And if asked why they didn't, they will often complain that they just didn't have the time. The management of one's time is a very real problem for the job hunter. In the case of assessing job offers, the dimensions of the problem can be understood if we consider how much time a professional (consultant or financial analyst) will typically spend just assessing a single company (not including an assessment of a specific job in it). Forty to 100 hours is typical. If job hunters tried to do a thorough professional job of assessing each job and organization they were interested in, it would require literally thousands of hours. Since that is impractical, many job hunters simply give up and do a very random and superficial job.

The keys to an effective strategy to assess potential job offers are: (1) utilizing all information sources, but systematically emphasizing different ones at different times, depending upon how many organizations and jobs are under examination at the time; (2) accurate self-knowledge.

The method we have seen successful job hunters use to assess offers and potential offers of interest to them is summarized in Figure 4. Most people start job hunting with a fairly large number of job/organizations that are potentially interesting. That number decreases steadily with time. During different phases of their screening procedure these people will emphasize different information sources. When looking at a large number of organizations, they devise simple screening criteria from their self-assessment themes and implications and use published sources to assess all the jobs and organizations. Many will be eliminated by this type of assessment. With a smaller number of jobs

FIGURE 4 A Method for Assessing Job Offers (and Potential Offers)

The Assessment Process	Number of Jobs and Organizations of Interest	Assessment Screening Method
Phase I	100+	Devise clear and simple criteria from the themes and implications in your self-assessment to screen potential employers. Rely on published data.
Phase II	50	Do the above, then devise more complex criteria from your self-assessment. Identify people who can supply you with information about the organizations of interest. Screen again based on their responses.
Phase III	20	Do both of the above. Then continue to screen based on information gained from interviewing with the employers.
Phase IV	10	Do all of the above, and extensively use information gained from visiting the employer and talking to a number of people there.
Phase V	2	Do a complete Organizational Assessment based on interviews, published data, visual data, etc. Pay special attention to issues raised by the themes and implications in your self-assessment.

FIGURE 5 One Job Hunter's "Postinterview Questionnaire"

Company Name and Address_____

Interviewer's Name and Title_____

Today's Date and Anticipated Date of Company Response_____

	WEIGHT	TOTAL

1. Will the job offer excitement and will it be fun
    in the present?   ___ x 9 = ___
         10 = tremendously
          0 = no, it will be boring and staid
    Comments:
2. Will the job require much work with small details?   ___ x 3 = ___
          10 = a minimal amount
           0 = a great amount
    Comments:
3. Will I be organizing and managing and have both the
    authority to carry it out well and the responsibility
    (reward or punishment) for its success or failure?   ___ x 7 = ___
          10 = just the right amount
           0 = not at all or much too much
    Comments:
4. Will I have a lot of contact with people, especially
    sharp ones?   ___ x 8 = ___
          10 = a great deal
           0 = none
    Comments:
5. Will I feel important?
         Status inside firm
         5 = very high; 0 = very low   ___
         Prestige outside firm
         5 = very high; 0 = very low   ___
    Subtotal   ___ x 6 = ___
    Comments:
6. Will the job entail heavy competition with peers and
    long hours?   ___ x 8 = ___
          10 = just the right balance
           0 - much too much or much too little
    Comments:
7. Will I have a chance to employ my entrepreneurial
    flair?   ___ x 6 = ___
          10 = very much so and in my own style
           0 = not at all
    Comments:
8. Will the opportunity possibly result in my making   ___ x 4 = ___
    a great deal of money?
          10 = a fair chance at seven figures
           0 = no chance
    Comments:
9. Will the job allow me sufficient chance to broaden
    myself and pursue self-improvement?   ___ x 7 = ___
          10 = yes, in fact it will encourage me
           0 = none at all, it will stifle these efforts
    Comments:
10. Will the location of the job be such that much
    beauty will be perceived and that I can pursue
    harmonious activities?   ___ x 8 = ___
         10 = very beautiful with many harmonious
              opportunities
          0 = ugly with no harmonious opportunities
    Comments:
11. Will the job be an advancement toward the
    achievement of my long-range goals?   ___ x 10 = ___
         10 = a big step directly on the path
          0 = a step backward
    Comments:

    Other observations and comments:

and organizations, people using this strategy then develop more complex criteria from their self-assessments and rely primarily on external people as sources of information. Such assessments usually reduce the number of potential jobs and organizations down to a practical number for interviewing. The next level of assessment, relying heavily on interview data, can usually cut the jobs and organizations down to a number that are practical to visit. After the visits, the job hunter uses the additional data gained from employees and direct observation for a further assessment, which can usually narrow the focus to a very few options. These can be very thoroughly examined, using data from all sources, and giving particular attention to the key issues raised in the self-assessment. This entire assessment strategy does, of course, require considerable time and effort. Having watched numerous people successfully use it, however, we know that its demands are within practical bounds.

Some of our students have devised a variety of more specific tactics and methods to aid them in this assessment process. For phase III, screening based on a first interview, some have developed short questionnaires that they fill out immediately following each interview (see Figure 5). The structure of the questionnaire is, of course, based on their self-assessment papers.

Some of our students have told us that to prevent losing the information that one gets verbally and visually from a visit to a prospective employer (phase IV), it's a good idea to sit down and write out a debriefing as soon as possible after you leave the organization. If, for example, you are flying home on a plane, spend some of that time *writing* out answers to the following types of questions:

1. To whom did you talk today?
2. What did you learn from each?
3. What do you think of each of them?

4. What did you notice about the architecture and the physical setting that might be important?
5. What did you notice about the people in general, and how they interacted with each other?
6. How do you feel right now about the possibility of working there?

It is important not only to write out your answers, but to do so soon after the visit. Time clouds a memory.

Tactics similar to the postinterview questionnaire and the postvisit debriefing can be devised for each stage in the process. None of these methods is likely to be useful to everyone; you will have to experiment to see what you yourself find helpful. Just keep in mind that the primary purpose of the overall assessment strategy and these particular tactics is to aid you in effectively assessing potential job offers within a practical amount of time.

Exercise

The pictures that follow simulate a company visit and will give you some practice at "direct observation." As you examine them try to answer the following questions:

1. As a job applicant visiting Goldman Sachs, what might you reasonably conclude about the company from what you see? Exactly what are those conclusions or tentative conclusions based on?
2. After looking at Goldman Sachs' annual report, what do you think it suggests about the usefulness or lack of usefulness of annual reports for a job hunter? Is the company attempting to project an image the same as, or substantially different from, the one you have acquired through "direct observation"?

The accompanying pictures were taken by a visitor to Goldman Sachs' main offices (55 Broad Street in New York City) in December of 1972. The visitor was given a quick (unannounced) tour of the type a job applicant might receive.

55 Broad Street

The ground floor

The reception area on the fourth (main) floor

The Board Room, also on the fourth (main) floor

Goldman Sachs International (fourth floor)

The Order Room (fourth floor)   Convertible Bond and Listed Block Trading (fourth floor)

Sales Administration (fourth floor)

A salesman who sells to individuals (fourth floor)

Stairway between the fourth and fifth floors

Commercial Paper Sales (fifth floor)

Fixed Income Trading (fifth floor)

Sales and Trading of Short Run Instruments (fifth floor)

Sixth-floor reception area

Library (sixth floor)

Research Department (sixth floor)

An analyst—specializes in the broadcasting industry (sixth floor)

The Research Department (sixth floor)

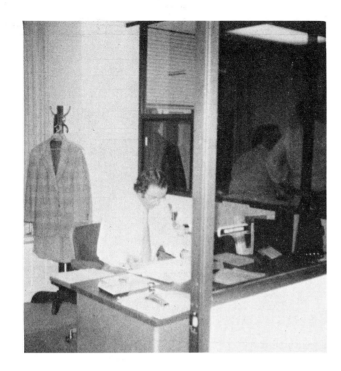

Tenth-floor reception area

Goldman Sachs (B)

The Pictures in the 1971 Annual Report

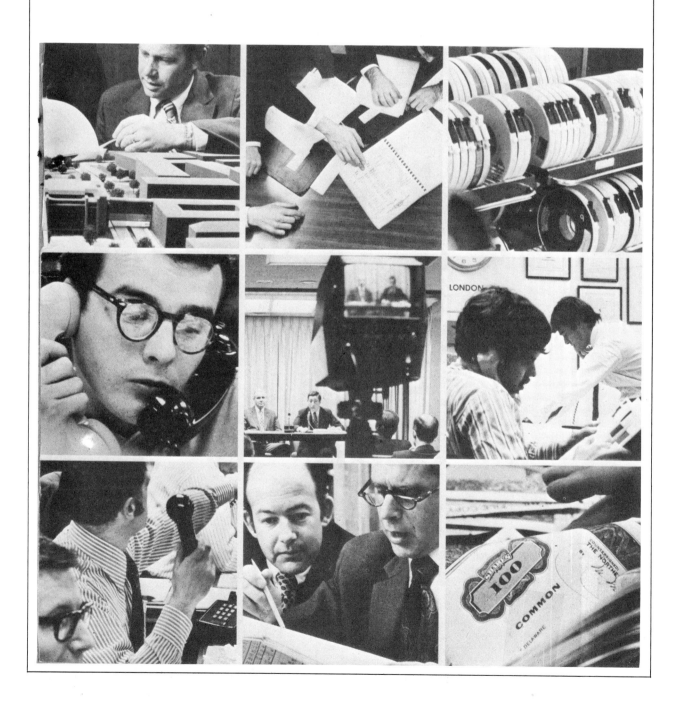

Goldman Sachs

Goldman, Sachs & Co.
Annual Review 1971

Left Goldman Sachs has arranged dozens of lease financings for projects ranging from headquarters buildings to power generators.
Right Private placement specialists, in constant contact with major institutional lenders, help tailor terms to best meet client needs.

Top Left Corporate finance personnel keep skills up-to-date with frequent meetings and seminars.
Top Right Careful structuring of underwriting and selling groups aids the success of managed offerings.
Bottom Corporate clients receive in-depth counsel on managed public financings.

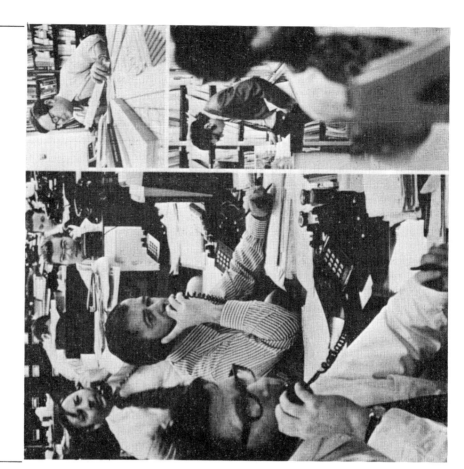

Left Emphasis on constant service and "best realized prices" helped Goldman Sachs set another institutional sales record in 1971.
Top Right Our economists provide important perspective to research and investing departments of the firm.
Bottom Right Investment research analysts have access to one of the most extensive business libraries in the financial community.

Top As the country's largest commercial paper dealer, Goldman Sachs registered approximately $50 billion in sales in 1971.
Bottom Corporate merger specialists have completed more than 130 transactions for clients in the past five years.

Top Left Portfolio managers give close, personalized attention to each investment management account.
Top Right In-house and external computer facilities provide service to virtually every department of the firm.
Bottom Highly skilled operations personnel readily handled record brokerage volume in 1971.

Top Left Investing opportunities for clients are reviewed daily in conference calls connecting all regional offices.
Bottom Left Traders provide day-in, day-out liquidity to securities markets by making bids and offers on blocks of all sizes.

Top Right Goldman Sachs securities salesmen often operate in teams to better serve individual investors.
Middle Right Continual dialogue between research and sales personnel helps speed the flow of investing ideas.
Bottom Right Specialists in domestic and international securities arbitrage help maintain Goldman Sachs' leading position in this field.

Top Securities sales for international clients have increased substantially, aided by new direct communications between London and New York.
Bottom Goldman Sachs International Corp. personnel discuss financing strategy for one of many corporate clients served during the year.

Top Left Municipal department traders maintain active markets in many tax-exempt securities, including issues managed by the firm.
Top Right Municipal finance experts structured 19 pollution control and industrial revenue issues for clients in 1971.

Bottom The Goldman Sachs Management Committee—Ray Young, Ed Schrader, Gustave Levy (Chairman), John Weinberg, John Whitehead and George Doty—constantly review firm plans and performance.

XV

Accepting a Job Offer

The final phase of job hunting involves a decision-making process. The job hunter typically examines a number of options—to accept job A or job B, or (rarely) to accept no job at all—and makes a decision. Representing, as it does, the culmination of considerable time and effort, this decision-making process is obviously important.

Job-offer decision making can usefully be thought of as made up of two parts: (1) analysis and (2) choice. To understand this type of decision making, one needs to understand both of these very different parts of the overall process. By avoiding or doing a poor job at either part, job hunters can create serious problems for themselves.

Analysis

The analytical part of decision-making processes is characterized by words such as cognitive, conscious, rational, and objective. With regard to job selection, it involves the systematic assessment of an individual, the systematic assessment of a number of job options, and the deduction of a set of most probable future events for each option if that option were selected by that individual. Virtually the entire book, up to this point, has been directed at helping you become more aware of this process and more skilled at using it.

Engaging effectively in analysis helps a job hunter more accurately predict the future consequences of accepting each of the available options. It provides a more realistic understanding of the rewards one might receive, and the problems one might encounter, with different options.

For a number of reasons, job hunters sometimes engage in analysis in a superficial and ineffective manner. Many people simply do not have the information, the expertise, or the training to analyze job offers effectively. Others are just

not analytically oriented; they neglect serious analysis in almost all of their decision making. Still others avoid analysis in this particular case because, at some level, they don't want to have to face the objective reality of their own personal limitations, or the limited future possibilities that their current options offer them.

The person who fails to engage effectively in the analysis of a job decision may end up in a situation where he or she simply cannot do what is being demanded and expected, and is constantly and unpleasantly surprised by obstacles and problems. Typically, the individual who does a poor job of analysis while selecting a job offer will either quit or be asked to leave the job in four to twelve months. The employer will often be disappointed in the person's performance, and the employee will often be disappointed in his or her lack of satisfaction in the job.

Most job hunters we have observed do a fair or good job of analysis before selecting a job offer. A small number do an excellent job of analysis, and an equally small number do a very poor job.

Choice

Unlike analysis, the process of choice is nonrational, emotional, subjective, and largely unconscious. We don't know a great deal about its actual dynamics, but we do know the function it seems to serve and the consequences of not engaging in it.

In the only systematic examination of the job-offer decision-making process that we are aware of, Peer Soelberg studied 32 graduate students at the Sloan School of Management (MIT) while they were job hunting.[1] He was

[1]See Peer Soelberg, *A Study of Decision Making: Job Choice* (Dissertation, Sloan School, 1967) and "Conclusion From a Study of Decision Making" (M.I.T. Working Paper 173–66).

surprised to find that the process these students engaged in, especially near the end, was much less rational and analytic than he expected. Among other things, he found that:

1. The students tended to reduce their options down to two (*precisely* two in almost every case) using a pragmatic, although not very elegant, analytical process.
2. They would then often agonize while deciding which of the two options to take.
3. Significantly before the average student would announce that he had reached a decision, Soelberg found he could predict which option would eventually be chosen.
4. Upon announcing a decision, the average student could then provide an elaborate "justification" for his choice, the details of which sometimes clashed with what he had said earlier.

These findings are entirely consistent with what we have observed less systematically over the past few years. Even people who have done an excellent job at analytically assessing themselves and their options typically go through an emotional phase of varying lengths and intensities during which they seem to unconsciously: (1) create a situation of choice (usually between two options); (2) emotionally try to come to grips with the implications of each option; (3) choose one of the options; and (4) find some rationale for rejecting the option not chosen.

No matter what the exact dynamic of this process is, it seems to be important, or needed, because it serves two important functions. It helps the decision maker develop an *emotional* commitment to one of the options. It also helps the decision maker cope with feelings of loss associated with cutting off the other option.

To follow through on a major life decision with the energy and vigor needed to ensure its successful implementation, people seem to need some emotional commitment to the direction the decision will take them. Among other things, that commitment seems to help them overcome obstacles when they encounter them. But the very process of choosing, and emotionally committing oneself to one option, means that another must be cut off. The *feeling* of loss associated with such cutting off can be very powerful and troublesome to people. To help cope with these feelings, people tend to find some "rational" reason that minimizes the loss.

People sometimes avoid choosing or engage in it only minimally. They allow others, or "fate," to choose for

them. Or they simply deny that they have a choice. (How often have you heard someone say, "I had no choice."?) Some people always behave this way in their decision making, just as some others always avoid serious analysis. Sometimes it seems they just can't accept the responsibility of cutting off what might be a "good" option. The loss of what "could be" is too painful for them.

The consequences of not engaging in choice can be as serious as the consequences of not engaging in analysis. Without the emotional commitment to a particular direction, it is often very difficult to mobilize one's energies and overcome the inevitable obstacles. Without effectively dismissing the other options, and suffering the loss, one can often be plagued by thoughts of their continuing availability. These thoughts can paralyze a person.

One student we observed, a very bright and highly analytic young man, devised an elaborate mathematical formula to help him select one among four job offers. He announced that he did so to help him make a rational decision, "not an emotional one like so many people seem to." The formula gave option 1, 110 points; option 2, 85 points; option 3, 118 points; and option 4, 96 points. He aggressively defended his formula against occasional jokes from friends. ("What does an eight-point difference mean, Larry? One less ulcer every 8.0 years?") He accepted option 3, even though he didn't feel entirely sure it was right. After eight months on the job, a downturn in his company's sales and a layoff of personnel put everyone in Larry's division under some pressure. He thought there must be better opportunities elsewhere and quit. Five months later he started to work in another job. When his boss was promoted six months after that, and the person who replaced his boss was not "as easy to work with," Larry quit again. He was also to get still another job within three months. When we talked to him last, he expressed concern that his career did not seem to be progressing as well as those of some of his less able classmates. We are left wondering whether his seeming inability to really choose some option, and to commit himself to it, might not underlie his lack of career progress.

Exercise

To help you get additional insight into the choice process for job hunters, the following case describes in some detail the events that lead up to one person's selection of a job offer. As you read this case, ask yourself: What is actually happening here? What does this imply for other people when they are making a job decision?

Choosing

Well, I guess the best way to tell you about this is sort of chronologically. Of course I went through all the interviews here, and it was kind of funny because I always had the feeling that when something went well, those were the places I got invited back, and whenever I thought, I don't know about this place, I didn't get invited for the second interview. So I had four or five second interviews, basically with consumer products companies and they happened relatively quickly. United Foods was the first—they invited me, in a week, back to Chicago. So it was two weeks from

the time I had the interview here to the time I had the interview there. When it was done I knew I had done a good job of interviewing and I expected an offer, which they gave me—an offer for 16, which was lower than I wanted. But you know it was the only one I had, so I said, "Well, that sounds reasonable," and kind of hedged over the phone, and told them I'd let them know by April 1. And you know at the time I felt kind of ambivalent about the whole thing, because it was good up to the point of dollar salary and that's where it kind of fell down. I could use the dough. I have a lot of bills to pay back. But more than that, hell if everyone else is getting $17,500 that's what I want. (Laughs) Because I'm every bit as good. That was quite a while ago, the beginning of March or end of February—something like that. It was a long while ago.

Just before getting the offer from United, I interviewed with Belton-Carter. When I got done with that at the end of the day I sat down and wrote up my notes and I decided that unless they offered me substantially more money I wouldn't take the job there for a number of reasons. United is in Chicago and that's my home and I didn't really want to commute from New York City, which is where I would want to live, for 30 miles to get to Belton-Carter. And that life-style kind of a thing is important to me. So I decided they would have to offer quite a few more dollars for me to live in N.Y. and commute up. But other than that I thought the interview went very well and I expected an offer. So it did surprise me when I got turned down. So there must be something there that can sort of sense that you won't take the job, or there's some sort of linkage that has to be there, and if it's not on both sides, it doesn't happen at all.

I interviewed Robinson and Crandel Products and there was no doubt in my mind as soon as I left the place and I started writing them up, that there's no way I could work for that place. I just didn't like it at all. Although I thought I did a very good job of interviewing, I got turned down by them. (Laughs)

One thing that happened was really crazy. When I was at United it seemed important to my boss and to my boss's boss (both of whom I interviewed with) for them to help the people who were beneath them. In other words, they'd say something like, "In order for this company to progress in the future, we're growing rapidly, we need bright people coming up through the ranks. And so it's very important for me as a manager to develop my people. Of course that's not my only job, but it's very important." And everybody said that all day long. And all of a sudden you start realizing either they're putting out memos saying tell your people to tell the interviewees that this is what we do around here or else it's really something in the institution. Well, I would tend to believe the latter, because if they lie to you, they're just going to lose you after a year anyway. So at this other place it was just the opposite. I almost came out screaming at the guys, "Well what about your people?" I'd ask concealed questions, like to the person who would be my boss's boss: "What do you view as some of your main responsibilities?" And he never once talked in terms of his people. It was always, "Well, I'm trying to bring on new products and develop better products and raise market share and of course there's a lot of internal competition here—friendly—but it gets pretty good. And everybody here is pretty competitive and I'm trying to do better than my boss and trying to do better than the guy next door," and all that type of thing. And I asked him another question, a very similar question. "Well, what are your personal goals here, what do you want to do?" And I kept after the guy. All I wanted him to say was: "And I also like to help out my people and see to it that they become the best people they can." And he never said it. And I asked a couple of people

that, and they didn't say anything about people. So I figured, the hell with this. I need that like I need a hole in the head: "Here's your job kid and I'll see you in three years if you make it." That's not what I consider to be a good job. And so as soon as I left there I decided, no way.

There was very little, if any, sense of loss with either one, Belton-Carter or this other firm. It was just more of a logical kind of thing. I looked at the facts. I compared them—I took the self-assessment course—with some of the things that I knew just offhand I needed, and I just decided there was no comparison. Even United at 16 was much better than they would be unless they went to tremendous sums of money. So those two were out.

I got to talk to Mason Brothers. One thing—all the marketing people there came from [a large well-known corporation], and that's got to tell something about how progressive they are. They have a corporate philosophy that they don't do anything first. They have never been the leader in anything. They're the biggest and they probably do it the best, but they will not introduce a new product first. They will wait until somebody else introduces it, and then they'll not necessarily copy it, but they'll wait for the market to test it, and then they'll introduce a better one. I couldn't dig waiting around with a bunch of 90-year-old people over my head. They tried to contact me for a second interview and those were the only people I turned down as far as the second interview goes.

So anyway here I am with an offer from United, and then I interviewed with Kenton Scientific here on campus. And I was reasonably impressed. They sent down the number-four man in the organization, so they take this very seriously. I wanted something different from them. I wanted to work on the sales force if I worked for them. And they were kind of surprised at that—you know, here's a Harvard M.B.A. who's willing to sell—and I think I'd be a damned good salesman, but that's beside the point. I had tried to get a summer job with Kenton the year before, and I was unsuccessful at that because they just don't—or what they said was they don't—hire anybody for the summer. I don't know. So I had been corresponding with their personnel department for a while, although John Phelps (he's the exec. V.P.) didn't know about that. I told him fast enough: "Well, I've been trying to get a job with Kenton for over a year now." "Oh really?" So that shows that you're interested. But I was. So I had a good interview with him and he said at the end of the interview, "We'd like to have you into Chicago sometime," so I thought, you know, that would be good. Also I realized that spring vacation was coming up, so I thought I could kill two birds, kill three birds with one stone (Laughs): you know, get an interview, get a vacation at home, and also pay for a trip to Miami by taking the triangle route. They paid for most of it anyway. So sure enough, they called me up, like two weeks before spring break—perfect timing—and they wanted to schedule me in for the week before. I said, "Oh, I can't make it that day," and so I ended up scheduling it for the first Monday of vacation.

Got to back up. Over Christmas vacation I had a couple of spare days, so I called up Kenton Scientific. I just talked to one of the Harvard M.B.A. recent grads there, and I said, "Listen, have you got a spare day here. I'd like to come in and talk to you.'' So he said fine. Well, as it turned out, we missed connections anyway, so I was there all day talking to various people. And I did get a chance to talk to this guy Jack Baxter, who was in charge of their executive placement or whatever. So we rapped for an hour or so and basically he was telling me about Kenton and a couple of things he said raised questions as far as I'm concerned. Like he said, ''We don't sacrifice people here, but. . . .'' They are so rapidly moving, so fast changing, and so much of this up or out, that it's not a very secure well-defined position there. They say we want you to come to work for Kenton and not care too much about what job you have, because your job will change almost daily as the growth creates a need for change. So I thought, well, that's something to think about, because one of the things on my self-assessment paper says ''secure and well-defined position.'' So anyway, that was one thing I had in mind. I talked it over with John Phelps when he was here and he didn't seem to think it was that much of a problem. I didn't put it out as that much of a problem, because I figured I didn't want to turn him off. I wanted to at least get the second interview and see for myself. I think at that point I was looking more for assurance than I was looking for fact. (Laughs)

But anyway I had the offer from United and I had to let them know by April 1, and so by the time I talked to Kenton I was already starting to push on that. That was the second to last week of March. So I had the interview with them, and everything went very well, I thought. The third or fourth person I talked to was the Director of Sales for one of Kenton's divisions, and I talked to him very specifically about this structure, definition, job definition, and stuff like that. And he said, ''Well, in sales we have a very rigid training program. It's really tough. It's eight weeks long, which is pretty long, and it's really good. You'll never have to worry about lack of structure in the sales force because that's the only place where we are reasonably structured.'' I thought, OK, that's good. And then I asked him a bunch of questions like what does a salesman do, and about life style and all that type of thing. And he started explaining it, and he stops for a minute, and he says, ''Well, why don't you travel with a salesman?'' So I thought, that sounds good. So I said sure. Then we went on from there.

I always had on the tip of my tongue what I considered the ten most important things from the self-assessment paper. As a matter of fact, that's how I originally arrived at some of the companies I would interview, because you know you can get certain ideas of what the place is about just looking at corporate records and talking to people. I was reasonably selective coming into the first interview situations. So I guess I had things pretty well down pat before I even started all this.

So anyway, it went on for the rest of the day and the only questions that arose that I was uncertain of were: we don't sacrifice people, but . . . thing, and a life-style thing. United Foods is downtown. I went through all this in self-assessment. Everybody in the course knew where I wanted to live and all that kind of stuff because I made this statement one day. We were talking about people who look for jobs for location, and I said, ''Well I know within four blocks of where I want to live.'' And that's really true. I know exactly where I want to live in Chicago. Not necessarily the building, but I have a couple in mind. So that's

important to me, and the nice part about United Foods is that I could just about walk to work from there. And that appeals to me. I mean, that sounds crazy, but that just appeals to me—a nice day, well I won't take the bus I'll walk to work. So Kenton Scientific is kind of out in the sticks. So I'd still want to live in the city, but that would mean some kind of a commute, which I consider to be a hassle. So that was a minor criterion. Other than that, the place was pretty good. I'm looking for a very dynamic kind of a situation, because I think I can move very rapidly. I like independence and a sales job has that. Most of the variables were there, except for these two question marks.

Back to United. That provided me with, I thought, the same. I thought that United filled all my needs. The problems there, of course, were the lack of dough for one thing, and it's not quite as fast-moving a situation as is Kenton.

I kind of expected a call from this guy Jack Baxter, but it never did come. Two days later I got a call from a Kenton salesmen and the whole thing was set up for me to travel with him. So the next day I showed up at his apartment, which is two blocks from the center of my circle of four blocks. Real nice to know this. Nice place too. I thought it would be just a little bit out of my first budget for apartments, but that it would be my second apartment. And he dresses about like how I dress. You know, he's an ex-football player, went to high school at the high school next to mine. You know we played each other in football and all that. So we just started rappin' and stuff, and I traveled with him all that day. And I noticed how he has to shift gears—shift personalities back and forth, you know—depending on who he's dealing with and what he's trying to do. Well, that's one of my fortes. You know I can shift personalities faster than Mario Andretti can go through the gears. So I thought I could do a great job. You know I'm a very outgoing, garrulous kind of person and that's how he was too. And I thought, I could do a real job. And not only that, but he had a life style very similar to what I would like to have. Kind of outgoing. And his social life and business life kind of go together with a lot of entertaining and stuff like that. He'll come in early one day and leave late or take a break in the middle of the day and play tennis with one of the doctors that he's working with or something like that. Just in general, I thought I could really dig doing this. Not only that but he said, ''I've been in this position for two years now and I'm expecting a promotion. You might even get my territory.'' And I thought: that sounds real good.

I left for vacation (I was in Miami for a week). I was expecting a call down there. I got a cable, or a cable was sent to my parents' home and here in Boston, and my roommate and my mother called, and they both got me at the Golds' house. It turns out that the guy from United called up and he's trying to get in touch with me. So I called him up and I thought, either he wants to give me a raise or he's telling me I'm sorry but we can't use you. I thought it had to be the first one because there's no way they ever take back offers around here. And it was! He increased the offer to $17,500, making some explanation like ''We've compared our things with every . . . ,'' which really means that two people turned them down for not enough dough. They gave me the exact amount of money I had originally thought I should get—so that's a definitely good offer now.

I still waited for Kenton, and waited for Kenton, and

nothing happened while I was there. I got home Sunday night or early Monday morning April first, and realized I had to make the decision that day. Well, I didn't show up for class on the first because I called Jack Baxter at Kenton in the morning and he wasn't in the office and so I tried to get in touch with him all day long. I was just waiting around for his call, so that as soon as I got his call I could sit down and analyze the whole thing and make the decision. Little did I know. (Laughs) Well, anyway, it didn't happen all day long and so finally I called him about 4:00—no about 5:00 Boston time, which is 4:00 their time. I called up (it wasn't a collect call) person-to-person and asked for Jack Baxter. And they said, "I'm sorry but he's home for the night." I thought, home for the night? 4:00? Kenton people usually work late. And I said, "Well, could I speak to his secretary?" just to get a little bit of feedback on what's going on. And they said, "She's gone home for the day too." And I thought, that's the runaround. What's really happening here is that they want to turn me down and he chickened out and he doesn't want to tell me over the phone—always a difficult thing. So he's writing me a letter and tomorrow I'm going to get a letter in the mail saying, "Sorry but we've looked over the thing and your abilities and background do not exactly (laughs) . . . ," you know, the typical letter. I thought, oh well, there goes Kenton.

And suddenly I felt kind of relieved (laughs), because I didn't have a decision to make now. I felt the sense of loss on one hand because they didn't need me, and I thought I should get an offer. But on the other hand, I thought, I've got an easy job now. (Laughs) Because I have this theory that I have a very easy life—things just happen to fall in place for me. So I thought, here it goes again. I fall right into it. And I'm going around saying, well, it looks like I'm going to be working for United.

So I decided, OK, I'm going to go out and have a drink tonight. So I was going to go to Jack's, my favorite place in Cambridge, but first I had to go to school to read something, an assignment, I didn't have a copy of. So I read that, and I came home in about 10 minutes because it was very short. And I sit down, and I'm just getting ready to go to Jack's, and the phone rings. "Hello, it's Jack Baxter. Well, Fred, we'd like to offer you a job." And so I thought, well, that's kind of late. He's calling me from home. "I finally got in touch with so-and-so-and and they'd like to offer you a job." It turned out to be precisely the same amount of money. It was a $12,000 base plus a guaranteed $4,000-a-year commission, which is $16,000, plus a car which I considered as $1,500. So that's $17,500, exactly what I would have made at United. Hmmm. And he says, "We're never sure about sales territories. We can guarantee you either Peoria or Champaign." Peoria is out as far as I'm concerned because I couldn't even conceive of myself living in Peoria, Illinois—even if they do make Caterpillars there. Champaign is kind of a funny thing. I went to school there for four years, so I just really know the place and I kind of dig it, but it also brings back a few bad memories.

Like it's really strange, but the last thing that happened to me in Champaign, Illinois, was that my heart was torn from my body and spread all over the place. So it's kind of a funny thing, but that will be there for a while yet. I don't even feel comfortable thinking about it. I haven't been

down there since. And I don't think I'd feel comfortable visiting either of my sisters, both of whom go to school there. And another thing, I didn't think I wanted to get stuck in that old "college grind" thing again because you know I've gotta do some things differently now. I'm leading a different type of life. I'm changing and moving more into a mature-member-of-society kind of a thing, and the undergraduate days are gone. I'm a different person now than I was then, and I thought that by being back there it would be like living nostalgia and every place I went would remind me of something in the past. It's not even the sadness, because there were more good times than there were bad. It's just that the bad one was pretty bad. And you know, like I said, that's out of my four blocks too. And I felt, hmmm. So anyway, I thought, well, United is sounding better.

And he said, "Well, how do you feel about this?" And I said, "Well, I wanted Chicago, but I'll have to give some serious consideration to it because after all I did go to school in Champaign, that wouldn't be all that bad." And so anyway I hedged on the phone for a while and I was thinking, hmmm, United sounded better.

Earlier in the day I had to call United and say, "Look, would it hang you guys up too much if I don't tell you today. I know I promised you I would, but you know I just haven't heard from Kenton yet. It's almost like a cruel April Fool's day joke, but the guy's not at work and I can't get in touch with him." "Well, we appreciate it, and as soon as you can let us know, let us know."

OK, so here I am, Monday night, and I have an offer from both people, so I decide I'm not going to think about it tonight, I'm going out to Jack's. So I went out to Jack's and didn't think about it. And then of course when I came home my roommate said, "Well, I hear you had a good offer from Kenton. What are you going to do?" And I go, "Well, I don't know man. They offered me Peoria, which is out, or Champaign, which I don't really want to do." And he's very pro-Kenton. So I go, "Well, I think I'm going to United." And then he goes, "Well, I think you should go to Kenton," blah blah blah. Well, I was still thinking in terms of United. But I was very confused, you know, because now I had a choice to make.

It was sort of going around in my mind for a while, very equal kinds of choices. And the closer and closer I got to it, you know, I had to make up my mind by Friday, the harder and harder and harder it got to do. So I decided, you know, to look over my self-assessment paper: equal, equal, Kenton, Kenton, United, equal, United, going right down the list. And you know I kept iterating and iterating and iterating (laughing), looking for the things. And then, uhh, you know, it kept coming down to, well Kenton might offer me a chance for a little bit faster movement, but then again I don't know if I want to hassle with Champaign for two years, which is how long I'd be selling for.

Then I made what might have been a mistake, and I called up a friend of mine who's also interviewing Kenton. I think this is a guy who could live a spartan life till the day he's 45, when he wants to retire. So I called him up. What I wanted him, what I wanted everybody to say, was, "Well I think you should go to United." (Laughs) That would have made it a lot easier. Well, he didn't. He was very pro-Kenton too. I called him up and he goes, "Well, why do you want to go to United?" And I explained to him the whole life-style thing, which is what I had it down to. I had Champaign vs. life style in Chicago, which I preferred. Chicago and United. He goes, ''Well, for Pete's sake if you're going to let something like livin' in Chicago—after all how old are you?'' I go, ''Twenty-three.'' ''Well, for Chr . . . , you'll only be there for two years . . . you'll be young when you get out. I mean I can't see you making up your mind on the basis of not living in Chicago for two years, and I think this medical field has got such a lot of growth to it and Kenton's such a good company and I can't see, I mean (and this is my roommate from last year), I can't see you doing this. I think the product line is so much better there.'' So then I go, ''Well, you son of a . . . ,'' and he goes, ''Why, what's the matter with you? (Laughs) Were you leaning the other way?'' (Laughs) ''Yeah, I was, as a matter of fact,'' and he says, ''Well, I don't know. I prefer Kenton.''

So anyway there I was. (Laughs) Now I'm in bad shape, cause I got a couple more things that are leaning toward Kenton. Well, after all I am only 23 and I could stand, I'm sure I could stand Champaign for two years. And how important is Chicago to me for only two years and this kind of stuff. And after all he has opinions which I respect, so that went against what my gut reactions were originally. So that was like Tuesday night or maybe it was still Monday night. So anyway, I kept thinking and thinking, and talking to people.

You know, its really incredible the reactions I got from people. This one guy I know is kind of, well he's young and I consider him very immature, and he just says he's looking for a classy place to work and he's having a very difficult time. I don't think he's a very good judge for himself, much less for me. So he says, ''I think you should go to Kenton,'' but that's basically because his father's a doctor and he would prefer to see me at Kenton because that way he could say his friend works for Kenton Scientific as opposed to his friend works for Colonel Chocolate.[2] At one point I called my folks. I was saying, ''The two possibilities are the job in Chicago with United and the sales job with Kenton.'' And they thought, ''Sales job? What's this? You know my son's been going to school and now he says he's going to be a salesman?'' And I said, ''Yeah, and the pay is partially commission.'' And they thought, ''Oh man, you don't want to get into commission because they can screw you on that kind of a thing,'' that was my mother. There it is, that very much risk-averse person. ''Don't want to put yourself up for the possibility of not getting paid commission.'' I talked to a couple of my neighbors about it too. They were coming back from school or something, and I was walking around and they're giving me all this heat lately about my suntan. They go, ''Who's this bronze boy walking at us now?'' So I go, ''Hi, how're you doin'.'' My head was up in the sky someplace. And they go, ''Well, have you decided anything about jobs?'' And I said, ''well, that's what I'm thinkin about right now.'' So I gave them a quick rap about the thing, and the first one of them said, ''Oh, I think you should go to United Foods cause I just love Colonel Chocolate.'' I get that so often. Either that or ''I don't think

you should go to work for them because I hate Colonel Chocolate.''

Anyway, the next day, Wednesday, like during classes, I called up Pops—that's Lou Johnson, my 40-year-old roommate from last year, father image in my life at school, right? So I called him up. ''Hey, Pops, what are you doing, man?'' ''Oh nothin','' which he always answered. And then he goes, ''Well, what do you want.'' He sees through me like I was a glass and it ticks me off so much, it's just impossible. So anyway I go, ''Well, I figured I'd stop over and talk to you.'' So he goes, ''Uh huh.'' Well, he knows it already. So I walk into his room, you know, 15 minutes later, and my roomie was coming in, so he gave me a lift over here. So I walk in there, and he goes, ''Well, what do you want?'' and gives me that sly look. And I go ''Well, Pops,'' and immediately he thought it was women problems, so he starts throwing a couple things at me. And I go, ''No, no, no, I'm just thinking about jobs.'' And he goes, ''Uh huh,'' and already he knows the problems. So there I am, and we go over to the Pub and have a beer and stuff. And then I said, ''You know I got this and that and I'm thinking about this and that,'' and he goes, ''Well, if you had to answer me in the next 10 seconds which one would you pick?'' And I go, ''United.'' And he goes, ''That's it, you go to United.'' So I go, ''WHAT ARE YOU TALKING ABOUT? YOU CAN'T. . . . (Laughs) What's this 10-second garbage? There's arguments on both sides.'' And he goes, ''No, you're going to go to United.'' So anyway we talked about it for a while and he said that basically the fact that I'd brought it down to Champaign vs. Chicago and that I could see that otherwise the two were just identical, completely equal, that I should go with that emotional kind of decision and go for Chicago. So I said OK, that sounds good. But I still had my other roommate's comments, you know, spinning around in my head.

So anyway, Jack Baxter had said if you start feeling yourself slipping in the other direction, I'd appreciate your giving me a call before you make up your mind one way or the other so we could talk about it. So I guess Wednesday I called him up and rapped about it for a while, and he threw in a couple more pieces of information—namely that Kenton is switching into a divisionalized structure. And the first thing I thought of was General Manager, which is something I want. I started asking him a number of questions about that, about the possibility of me getting into that position, and it looked reasonably good. So now I'm not only talking Chicago vs. Champaign, I'm talking about the possibility of getting to a position I want quicker. So that tends to weigh a little bit more toward Kenton now. Now they're back equal again. And then he put in another thing, ''Well, look, the main difference between the two companies is that United is much bigger and it's lot more structured environment and that type of thing and if you like that unstructured kind of free-wheeling sort of style, you'll like it better here I think. And if you need structure, if you're a person who can't stand the unstructured environment here, I think you'd do a better job at United. And after all, you know I appreciate your concerns and your problems with making up your mind. I think what's actually best for us is for you to make up your mind with what's best for you. We don't want you if you'll be unhappy here,'' and that

---

kind of stuff. So anyway I thought, OK, I'll give it some thought. And he said, "Well if you want to, you can call me up tonight at home." So I said, "OK, I might do that."

So I sat and thought about that for a while and I whipped out my self-assessment paper. And I'm tracing down the list again, and I'm reading down and reading down and finally it said—secure, well-defined position. And then I went back and read the blurb on that and I read through it and I flipped back through some other things—secure, well-defined position, secure, well-defined position. How do I balance that with what he just said: "If you like an unstructured kind of a thing you'll dig Kenton, otherwise you won't"?

At this point, the two companies look identical and you know I want them both and I can't have them both and I feel terrible. You know, like I want to even be oscillating faster than I am because I feel uncomfortable wanting one for a longer period of time than the other. So there I am, and I keep looking for it, and I go, this must be wrong because I'm thinking United too long a period of time. So I'm flipping through there and that kept coming out at me. I need structure.

And I'm thinking, all right now why do I need structure? You know I got this German upbringing. My mother especially is a very risk-averse person, and I'm very compulsive and orderly and all that type of thing. And then I thought, all right, let me put myself into some situations where I had structure, and where I didn't have structure, and try to think about that. And then I thought, wait a minute. Phil (the guy who was talking pro-Kenton) is more structured than I am by far. So I called him up and he goes, "Hello," and I go, "Hello, Phil, how can you stand to go to Kenton if you're such a structured person?" And then he goes, "Well, I didn't really, uh, uh, well, I suppose it is, well, of course in production (he's going into production) things are a lot more structured than they would be in sales." And then another guy who was in his room, and who was also very pro-Kenton, talked to me for a while. And he goes, "Well, yes, but what do you expect from a company that's growing at 20 percent a year." Well, I don't know. I don't care about excuses. I have to make up my mind. And he goes, "Yes, it's very unstructured," and all that kind of stuff. And so I decided, yeah, it is very unstructured.

And then I talked to Phil (he knew a little bit about what was on my self-assessment paper), and he goes, "Well, you know, if you're looking for structure I could see how that might hurt you with Kenton. And, y'know, Lou told me last night that you'd probably go with United anyway, and, uh, that's probably best for you," and that kind of stuff. And I thought, yeah, maybe now at least things are starting to come together. People are starting to agree here. And then finally I talked again with the second guy who's saying, "Yeah, really unstructured, and you should give that a lot of consideration." And I said, "OK, thanks a lot," and we shot the breeze for a while and finally I hung up the phone.

And I started to think again. And I tried to put myself in the position of structured vs. nonstructured. I thought of last year's business game, and in my subprogram we did a thing on the MBTA. And I was the president of my team, my group, and well I was primarily interested in the business game. You know, here's a thing where the rules are

very well defined. And I made my corporation and we broke down functionally and everybody had certain duties and responsibilities. We moved like hell. I mean we were just clicking like crazy and the decisions had to be made almost instantaneously but there was a definite structure and I had really dug it. I had more fun in that than I had had in anything here probably. And then I thought about the MBTA thing, which is totally unstructured and we had to make up our own structure—what there was of it. And it never did get exactly down pat. It was just kind of a free-wheeling sort of a thing and I hated it. I really detested the whole project. And I thought, umm. Then I looked back at all my jobs, and everything I liked and everything I didn't like doing. And I started noticing that not only is structure a positive thing, but lack of structure is very detrimental to me.

And right then, that was five minutes after I hung up the phone with Phil, I just sat there in my chair and I said, "United," and I felt like something was like torn from me. I physically exhaled and my head went down and I went (loud sigh). I sort of sat there. And it reminded me to a lesser extent of when I sat in Champaign, Illinois, two or three years ago and the girl I had been going with for three years said, well, I'm in love with somebody else. And it was the same kind of a loss, not as terrific this time, and I was in the same kind of a mood to sit back and think for a minute—head down and like not ready to do anything or move or anything. And I thought, huh, which is exactly what I thought two years before in Champaign. (Laughs) Huh, United. And from then on it was kind of uphill. Kenton was gone then, you know. I had made up my mind then, as opposed to vacillating back and forth. The decision was made and already I had gone through this tremendous low, and this sort of depression. And then I started thinking of all the things—let's see, four blocks from here, and that's kind of a nice building over there, and Jerry Randell who's my boss's boss, he's a pretty nice guy you know, and we'd better start working a little bit harder on advertising cause that's going to be pretty important, and all this type of thing. So then I started looking forward to United.

Last night as I hit the sack I started thinking, they've been pretty good to me at Kenton. I'm going to have to write a few people letters and say, "Well, look, I really appreciate it, but these are the reasons I don't think I could come to work for you. And I really appreciate all the time you spent with me and maybe I'll see you sometime"—something like that. I composed three or four letters and then I sort of tossed and turned for quite a little while thinking in terms of United and what I'd be doing there. The decision was made. I'm high now. I feel good about it. But that's how it went and it was really amazing. Just that sudden PHEW, when I made the decision.

I haven't spoken to Jack Baxter yet. I have to tell him no. I tried to call him this afternoon but he wasn't there. I was almost considering saying something along the lines of, "Well, you know, maybe something will happen in the future." And I thought, huh uh, it won't, because this is the choice point. I'm virtually cutting myself off from the possibility of that path. I'm going into consumer marketing, and so there's no sense in me trying to kid myself that maybe if this doesn't work out I can turn around and take the path that I passed up. It's an unrealistic possibility. So I thought, well you might as well not kid yourself on that. It's sort of a total decision at this point and so now I can run with it.

It's funny, I came out of the self-assessment course with a very detailed plan for the next four months. "In the end I'm going to make my decision and that's going to be it. In the last couple of days I'm not going to talk to anybody. I'm going to make the decision on my own. I'm just going to rely on my own internal kinds of things. I'm not going to go through this fluctuation stuff like everybody else does. I'm just going to look at my self-assessment paper and go over this stuff that I saw at the places and make my decision." And that's exactly what I didn't do. (Laughs) I was totally unable to do that kind of thing, because the two things were so equal.

Decision Making For Couples

In a situation where a job hunter is not a relatively independent individual, but is highly interdependent with another person—such as a spouse or a fiance—any decisions made will directly affect not just one, but two people. As such, the job selection decision-making process, which we have already seen is complex for an individual, becomes even more complex when the decision maker is a part of a couple. But exactly how much more complex it becomes, and in what ways, will vary depending upon the nature of the couple's relationship.

Figure 1 presents a spectrum of relationships for couples. At the extreme left of the spectrum is the traditional relationship: The husband is the breadwinner and the wife is the homemaker and child-raiser. As one moves from left to right across the spectrum, male and female roles change toward more equal participation in family and career. At the right extreme, both people in the couple essentially assume the same role, in terms of their careers and homes.

In the case of the traditional couple, the job selection decision-making process usually comes the closest to what we have already seen for individuals. The only additional complication is that the decision maker typically adds to his selection criteria a few constraints that are related to his perception of his spouse's needs (e.g., "she will never move outside the United States, so I won't bother to pursue non-U.S. jobs").

As we move to the right on the spectrum in Figure 1, the job selection decision-making process tends to become more complex. The further right we are, the more we are likely to find not one, but two decision makers, both involved in analysis and choice. The additional complexity derives from the need to somehow coordinate two different cognitive *and* emotional processes—which may be very difficult and time-consuming.

Today, most couple relationships are still traditional, or semi-traditional. But the trend over the past decade has been movement from left to right in Figure 1. And for our purposes, that means movement toward additional complexity in job related decision making. One might reasonably wonder how well prepared most people are for the increased complexity.

Exercise

The case that follows is of a young couple involved in a job decision. Consider these questions when you study the case:

1. How is the decision being reached?
2. What are the key forces that affected the manner in which they went about reaching a decision?

FIGURE 1 A Spectrum of Relationships for Couples

THE TRADITIONAL COUPLE	THE SEMI-TRADITIONAL COUPLE	THE TYPICAL DUAL CAREER COUPLE	THE EGALITARIAN COUPLE
HE is the breadwinner SHE is the homemaker and child-raiser HE competes and succeeds for both SHE provides child care, social, and maintenance for both	HE is the breadwinner (with some involvement in family and home) SHE is the homemaker and child-raiser but she also works, usually for a specific purpose (such as better vacations for the family, college tuition, braces for someone's teeth, her own personal satisfaction) HE has the dominant career but acknowledges her contribution to their quality of life, and her need for some kind of outside activity SHE works, but neither of them thinks of her as having a "career"	HE is committed to a professional career SHE is committed to a professional career The couple think of themselves as being a dual career family BUT, one of them (almost always the woman) takes on more than 50 percent of the responsibility for housekeeping and child-raising, and provides less than 50 percent of the income	HIS and HER roles vis-à-vis career and home are essentially the same. BOTH work; they have an equal commitment to their jobs. BOTH do 50 percent of the housework. BOTH do 50 percent of the child-raising.

Note: Couples can change their relationships on the continuum. Perhaps the most typical example we see of this today is the couple who in their twenties assume a traditional couple role. In their thirties, after their children are in school, they shift to the semi-traditional role. And in their forties, after the children have left home, they become a dual career couple.

3. What job do you think Jim accepted? Why?
4. How well do you think subsequent events will work out for the Bradshaws?
5. What generalizations, if any, might you draw from this case regarding job decision making for couples?

The Bradshaws

Jim and Helen Bradshaw, both in their late twenties, looked tired and somewhat tense as they sat down in the apartment of a close friend on the afternoon of April thirtieth. They had felt the need to talk over their current problems with someone whom they knew to be a good listener. Jim, a second-year M.B.A. student, had promised one company that he would let them know by May first whether he would accept their offer for full-time employment. He and Helen had spent the last few nights talking nonstop about the merits and drawbacks of the two offers they were considering. After lighting a cigarette, Jim launched into the subject.

Jim: A lot of things have been happening lately and it seems like it is happening a little bit too quickly. We have been on the merry-go-round here the last two years with Helen out working and me totally involved in school work. Now all of a sudden we're being confronted with issues that we didn't really spend enough time thinking about or discussing.

The way I see it, there are really two dilemmas. One is the personal dilemma I have regarding job choice, and that can't really be separated from the other dilemma, which is my relationship with Helen.

Helen: I think it would be helpful if we explained to Doug what the two jobs are and the difference between them, since he doesn't really know.

Jim: Well, there are two companies. One is Davidson Manufacturing Company, which is located in St. Joseph, Missouri, and . . .

Helen: Small town—30,000 people.

Jim: . . . on a continuum that would be at one extreme according to my viewpoint, as far as its being the typical M.B.A. opportunity. It has a lot of responsibility and a lot of exposure to top-level management. They have a lot of Harvard M.B.A.s and they push them ahead and give them many opportunities to move around. The big negative is the location. St. Joseph, Missouri, is just out in farm country and it's a small town.

Helen: It's not near a big city and it doesn't have in its immediate vicinity all the nice things about a city that we very much like; theatre, museums, galleries, restaurants, etc.

Jim: On a rational level I can say that as an M.B.A. going to work for them I would be on the fast track and it would just be very stimulating professionally, but socially it would leave just an awful lot to

be desired. Everyone we talked to who's from that area or works for the company says it's a great place to raise a family.

Helen: Which *we* have no interest in doing and everybody there does!

Jim: The other extreme is working for Browning Corporation in San Francisco. I would start out as an auditor—an internal consultant type. I would be on my own or working with another person—which really appeals to me—but I would have to travel at least 50 percent of the time. I would be going to all their subsidiaries and operations to find out what their problems are and to make some recommendations. There would be a lot of, I guess what people would term, mechanical work to that as well. A lot of number crunching.

And yet that's a location we both like. We lived there before we came here. We enjoyed the life style out west. Our friends are out west. If we ever wanted to settle in a place, that would be it.

The reason I've said this option is toward the other end of the spectrum is that there aren't many M.B.A.s in the company. There is some uncertainty at this point concerning what I might be doing in the future. It's not clear that in one and a half years I would get this or that type of job. The potential is certainly there, because they are growing at the same rate Davidson is. They are a larger company to begin with, which means that it might be a little faster moving, but it is so difficult to tell based on one visit. The reason Davidson is so attractive is that I worked for them last summer, or rather for one of their distributors (which is an independent business). Anyway I got to meet a lot of the people, and they got to know me and I performed very well and I guess they all liked me.

Helen: Jim's got a couple of friends here at the school who worked with them, and so when we are with them it is very easy to get carried away and become very excited about the possibilities of working for that company.

Jim: There are so many little minor pluses and minuses. You can live very well in St. Joseph, Missouri. It is very inexpensive. You can get a house comparable to something in Boston at half the price. Yet the wages there are higher or equal to Boston and New York. On the other hand, this offer on the west coast is substantially lower in salary. Now money is not my top priority. I don't think money is that important in the short run or even in the long run. There has to be enough so we can live comfortably, but I don't think I would make a job decision based solely on that. I would make a decision based on the elements of the job.

Helen: If you were just making a decision on money, then the decision would very easily be made.

Jim: Right. I have talked to two firms in New York and one in Boston that I'll probably get offers from at higher salaries. (Turning to Helen) Perhaps this is a good time for you to get into the aspect of what you'd like to be doing, and I can talk about those

Helen: My problem is I don't know what I want to do. I want to work and I feel a very urgent need to work but I don't have any professional expertise. I don't have any credentials. I went to college and was then married and I have worked as a secretary ever since.

Jim: And part of the reason that took place is we were moving every two years.

Helen: We were never in one place long enough for me to get into anything.

Jim: And there's always been that certainty. We knew when we got to a location that we would only be there as short as six months or as long as two years. That's been part of the problem, I guess.

Helen: But I do want to work. I don't know what I want to do, as I said. In St. Joseph, Missouri, I don't see very many alternatives. I see none in the town itself. It's all unionized and there have been layoffs left and right, and it is not a good time for someone from outside the area to come in and expect to be able to get a job. It is located about 30 miles from Greensville, which is where the University is. I suppose if I wanted to commute, I would look there for either employment at the University or consider going back to school. Neither of those options has an enormous amount of appeal to me right now. In San Francisco there are lots of options. I know several people who are in various businesses that I have some interest in. I see a couple of choices for myself out there. Some things I would like to try. I don't see any in Missouri.

Jim: Another thing about Davidson is that if you survive and do very well with the company, opportunities are pretty much in St. Joseph, Missouri. Certainly there are field operations and international operations, which would be a sidelight for a few years, but if you thought in terms of the long term, that's where we would be. The thought of that kind of scares me, because the things we like to do socially and even athleticwise just don't happen to be in the midwest. They happen to be on the coasts. The life style itself is something we have always taken for granted because we have always lived in good places. In Georgia we lived not too far from Atlanta. We lived overseas for a couple of years in Japan, when I was in the Navy, and then the west coast, and then Washington, D.C. These are all places we were very comfortable with—big cities, metropolitan areas, lots of activity. Of course Boston has a lot more to offer also.

Helen: I think that the closest I have ever come to living in what I would call a small-town environment is when we were in the military overseas. The American community was very close-knit and I didn't particularly like that. My idea of living in a foreign country is not spending your life on the base. So I had very few American friends over there and I had many Japanese friends. The thing I disliked about the ugly-American syndrome which went on over there was that U.S. people had nothing better to do than talk about other U.S. people, and I don't like—I am not comfortable in—an environment where everybody knows me, everybody knows when I come and go. I like the city. I have a need for that kind of privacy.

Jim: Because we have always had a lot of the good things that a big city has to offer, it's hard to decide what it is exactly that really attracts us. I did receive what I considered good professional offers in New York City, but the jungle aspect of the city just sort of overwhelmed me.

There's another company which I guess would be a compromise between the two companies we talked about earlier, and that was Johnson Company. It's in Chicago, which is a big city and not a bad place. The company happens to be located in the suburbs. It's not San Francisco, certainly, but it takes away the disadvantages that Davidson has, being in a small town in Missouri, because it has the restaurants, the museums, and what have you. I was really expecting to get an offer from them, and had I received an offer from them, that would have been the best of both worlds. It would have been a professional challenge on one hand, and also it wouldn't have been such a bad place to live. We have never lived in Chicago before, so it would be an adventure for us, and we probably would have really enjoyed it. The program that they had for M.B.A.s was very flexible. You could almost name the area you wanted to start in, and they would guarantee that you have a different job after about 6 to 12 months. There was a lot of mobility, top-management exposure, and good salaries. It just really seemed to be sort of an ideal situation. Unfortunately, I didn't quite make the final cut, and I know why—I had a good set of interviews with the exception of one person and he happened to be the person that they were looking for an M.B.A. to work with. He was a little bit older than everyone else, and I knew he wasn't totally impressed with me. I wasn't totally impressed with him either. I have one trait which sometimes turns out to be a weakness. I am honest. After the day was over, someone asked me what my impression was, and I told them exactly what my impression was. I felt that at that point in the job search I fool myself when I try to fool anyone else, because it can come back and bite me in the ass. I also value very highly a person's honesty and straightforwardness, and that's why I discuss everything the way I see it. I think that's probably the way I cut my throat, although they waited until the very end until they rejected me. I suspect that I wasn't unacceptable, but there were other people that were more acceptable, so they had to wait until they had everything in.

There was another factor that added to the confusion of the job search. The company I worked for last summer was in Los Angeles and, as I said, was an independent distributor for Davidson Manufacturing. They have on the order of $15 million in sales. When the summer was over I was told by my employer, who was an H.B.S. alumni, that he would be in a position to offer me a job. He was president of a company by the age of 36 or something like that. He was 32 when he got out of the B-School, so he didn't waste much time in going through the hierarchy. He went in as a divisional manager and a year later he was a vice-president and two years later he had his own business. He was in Boston last week, and unfortunately I didn't get to see him. I just talked to him on the phone. He saw Helen before he saw me.

Helen: And so he told me that he couldn't offer Jim a job. . . .

Jim: . . . because of the economy. He said the last nine months had been slow. So he told Helen. I was on an interview trip out in Denver. She called me up on the phone the night before I had my interview with Browning (that's where their headquarters is). . . .

Helen: I thought you'd like to know.

Jim: I'm glad you told me, because prior to that I wasn't too serious about Browning. I got rejected from Johnson at the beginning of the same week, which was last week. Johnson rejected me on Monday morning and on Thursday afternoon I found out that I wouldn't have an offer from the place in L.A. Then—this is the same day—I called Davidson because I hadn't heard from them in a month, and they told me the job I was being considered for initially at Davidson, which was assistant to this Executive Vice-President, and which I was really excited about, was being filled by someone else. So now they had something else in mind for me but they didn't know exactly what it was. I found out just last night when this other vice-president called that essentially it would be a sales rep. I would do that for six months just to learn the product, and that appeals to me. I think that would be the best way to find out about the nature of the business and their customers and deal with the people.

Helen: Well, it's almost a kick in the teeth from them, isn't it?

Jim: Well, in a sense. But then again, when I asked them last night on the phone if they didn't hire me for this job would they hire someone else, they said no, they wouldn't hire anyone. So that sort of rebuilt my ego a little bit by saying that they are interested in me as a long-term investment as a person. The fact that I got rejected from Johnson and the guy I worked for last summer in the same week and I didn't know what my status was has sort of weighed a little bit heavy on me. Now I am getting a little concerned that while the job in San Francisco has so many pluses, there are a lot of question marks.

Helen: Long-term question marks you mean.

Jim: Right. I must admit that the organization and the people I have met in Davidson by and large really impressed me. I got along with them, and it's just a great working environment. But then there is St. Joseph. There would always be other options—I could take no job and just pack up and go out to the west coast or any other place.

Helen: I don't really see that as beyond the realm of possibility.

Jim: At the same time it is not something that one would like to do.

Helen: It's the riskiest option.

Jim: Right. There's enough uncertainty in our lives already. It costs a lot of money to move, so financially it would be a hardship in the short run. Of course in the long run I am sure we are talking about nickels and dimes. On the other hand, if we did go out to San Francisco, say, no matter what company I would go with, unless it was a small business, chances are that I wouldn't stay in one place.

Helen: To get ahead and have the kind of professional future that we would like, we must move. That's always been our assumption.

Jim: I think I've always enjoyed moving. I love being on the go, and adventure, and new experiences, and new challenges and not doing the same thing year after year. That's been in my blood, but needless to say, that might change. I try to keep an open mind even now.

Helen: In me that is starting to change now. The idea of settling down and staying in one place has more appeal to me today than it used to. Maybe that's because I'm tired out—I'm moved out.

Jim: But the reason that appeals to you is that you were in a place, the San Francisco Bay area, that you really enjoyed. Since you're a little more uncertain about your professional future than I am, you feel that you have to be in a location for longer than just a year so that you can get into a job and get some experience and maybe find out some of the things you'd like to do. I don't think you could say with certainty that a profession you might get into would require that you would stay in one place forever and ever.

Helen: It might not, I'm just saying that, professional considerations aside, I think what I want to do more and more is settle down, have a house, live in a neighborhood.

Jim: That definitely has appeal, but one of my problems is that I'm not ready to say that's what I want to do. (Pause)

Going to San Francisco if nothing else has some very good short-term considerations from our point of view, and it could or could not have some good long-term possibilities. But when you look at Missouri, you think that it wouldn't be so bad for a couple of years. Professionally I could do very well, and yet the thought of spending 20 or 30 years in a place like that just leaves us both very cold.

Helen: I keep thinking, well you know it might only be for

a year and a half and then we would move someplace else, but the fear that keeps jumping into my head is that someday I am going to wake up 40 and be in the same damn spot that I am right now and I really don't want that to happen.

Jim: I could always say, well a company like Davidson would be a great challenge and give me much more than I could handle, which would push me along and help me. Then after a couple of years if I found I didn't really like St. Joseph, Missouri, I could go somewhere else. It's a good place for corporate headhunters, so there is a lot of visibility there. Yet making a decision to do that scares me a little bit, too, because I have never done anything like that.

When I was in the military for four years, I always got my first choice and I had independent jobs so that people were not pressing their thumbs down on me all the time. I had a lot of flexibility and latitude. I was allowed to become an expert in some areas that nobody else had any detailed knowledge of. It was very rewarding and satisfying. Yet at the B-School here it has been a very painful experience. Certainly there's more work here than any place I have been before, although I am not averse to work. Most of my classmates say they view it the same way. I must admit, it's a real chore to get up in the morning at times.

Two years is a short amount of time, however. I certainly don't regret the decision, and it will be worth it to me. I probably won't realize the benefits fully until I have been gone for several years, because many of the things we acquire at the B-School are intangible. After having been here, I say maybe I'm ready to quit postponing my pleasure.

I don't mind paying my dues. I realize that whatever company I go to work for will have services I'm not totally knowledgeable about, and it will take a little bit of effort in burning some midnight oil to come up to speed and learn the politics of the organization and learn how everything flows. I think that is normal wherever one goes. I think I can be very happy in a place if I have an unpalatable job or if there are some painful things to do for a few months like working late or working on weekends. But when you put together a bad environment with bad working conditions, well, I'd rather dig ditches, I really would.

Helen: You just answered the question then.

Jim: I say that now, but my gut will be gnawing away at me when I go home tonight. I'll be thinking, now wait a minute, am I giving up an opportunity. . . . If I say no I don't want to go to Missouri, am I giving up an opportunity that I might have had otherwise?

Helen: If it were such a great opportunity, it wouldn't be this hard to make a decision, would it?

Jim: Well, probably not.

Helen: (Looking at Doug and shaking her head) We seem to be going back and forth just day in and day out.

Jim: We're very happy about Davidson and that offer, and then not so happy about the other. Then the next day we'll think of San Francisco and some of the possibilities with Browning, and I guess when we do this we rationalize whichever decision we seem to be leaning toward. For instance, the other day we were looking through the St. Joseph local newspaper and looking at the houses. There were some fantastic prices and just really far-out things. We were, I don't know, trying to come up with some good things we could do there that we couldn't do elsewhere. You could play golf cheaply and play it every weekend, for example.

Helen: Somehow all of those very nice little things don't add up to having enough weight to really swing us that way.

Jim: And yet the anxiety about going the other way is that. . . .

Helen: Maybe part of the problem with the Browning job is that you don't have a clear enough picture in your mind as to where you could go with that company, whereas you do have somewhat of a clearer idea of where you would go in Davidson.

Jim: Well, that's part of it. But I'm not averse to that kind of uncertainty—that's what life's all about.

Helen: It's not just a question of uncertainty. You don't even know what options there are.

Jim: Well, I know a little bit about the options. They have a computer subsidiary and they have a leasing subsidiary which leases anything. It is a financial institution. They have many service operations like food service, catering, transportation, and things along that line. While their total sales aren't growing at the same rate that some companies' sales are going, some of their businesses are growing quite a bit. I'm certain that at some point in the future, if I decided I liked the company, I'd be given the advantage of these vacant slots. But there aren't a lot of M.B.A.s in the company and so they look upon this institution as, you know, one of those Ivy League schools which turns out arrogant people. It demands exorbitant salaries for people who don't like to get their hands dirty. Some of it's true. They do hire M.B.A.s, though; in fact what they call an internal audit staff is composed of 26 people evenly divided between career people and M.B.A.s—young guys like myself who come in and go out and see all the businesses and give them a lot of ideas and yet rely on experience that the older guys have. So there is a constant turnover and the average guy maybe takes three years before he goes into a line job. The best guy probably gets out in about 18 months. Now I would consider myself as good as the rest of the competition. I could get out of some of the mundane tasks within two years. That doesn't bother me. I think I could learn an awful lot about their business and a lot about just going in and evaluating businesses.

Helen: Now you see, my impression all along has been

that that was the part of the offer that you found most unpalatable. I have been thinking all along that you would just be unhappy for the first 18 months and wouldn't like what you were doing. (Directed to Doug) I don't want to ask him to do that.

Jim: Well, if I was with Davidson, my dues-paying period would be shorter, probably about six months. As long as I was learning, that Browning deal wouldn't bother me at all. There is travel involved in the Browning job which would involve a month or two months in one location, where I'd be by myself. That's a little bit of a headache. On the other hand, I don't mind personally at this point in my life traveling around. I think the M.B.A. program really prepares one to adjust to situations like that very rapdily.

We're still not addressing the problem that we as a couple, as a married couple, face. We've avoided the issue very conveniently in the past—realizing that what Helen wants to do and what is best for her growth and what is best for me might not be in the same place. We don't have any children, so that's not a factor, and we don't have aspirations of starting a family now. I still suspect that in a couple of years from now, at most, when I do well, I will be offered an opportunity and it probably won't be in San Francisco. It will probably be somewhere else. It could be in Denver, could be Boston, could be anywhere. Someone will come to me or I will go to them and say, "Hey, I want to get my teeth into a little bigger responsibility," and there will be an offer made. We have no idea what Helen will be into at that point.

Helen: And that's a problem. I don't know how to find answers short of trying a bunch of things, but I have to be in an environment where the possibilities are open so I can try them.

Jim: I realize that it would be unfair for me to expect Helen just to pack up and move wherever the company says they want to send me.

Helen: That's what we call the tag-along syndrome.

Jim: Well, we have been married six years and Helen has had to move along wherever I have gone up until now. I guess there was some hesitancy in the past. You didn't really want to come to Boston because you liked San Francisco. You even applied to Stanford, and in fact I didn't apply to Stanford, even though it probably would have been the easy way out. I probably could have found it a bit easier to get a job on the west coast when I graduated had I been there. Harvard was unquestionably the best opportunity for me as far as graduate education, and it was really Helen who pushed me toward it.

Helen: That's what I've done all along, encouraged Jim to go after the *best* opportunity available.

Jim: And yet, up to now I haven't pushed her into anything. That is the basic difference in our personalities.

Helen: It's a big difference. It's just the whole way I was raised. I wasn't taught to think. I was always pushed—told I would do this and I would do that. I would go to college. It didn't matter where I went. Nothing mattered but that after a certain number of years the sheepskin. My parents expected that I would then get married and be a housewife just like my mother, and I didn't really quite question that or start thinking about it until the last few years. Now I'm really in a fix because I don't know what to do or how to go about finding out what I'm good at.

Jim: Well, there are two problems in that regard. The first being that I don't have that much confidence in my ability to be objective and to help Helen find out what she wants to do. I certainly don't have any training or experience. By nature, I just don't like to impose my standards or my ideals consciously on someone else, and my perception is that's what I'd be doing if I tried to suggest what Helen should do and. . . .

Helen: And I don't quite see it the same way.

Jim: In fact you see it very differently.

Helen: In fact, I would like to think that Jim would say, you know, well here's the way I see you, here's what I think you are good at, why not check out these possibilities. I want to hear something from him. I want some advice.

Jim: Based on our conversation the other day, I suspect you would also like a little bit of firmness from me, like saying, "Hey, get off your ass and go do this."

Helen: That wouldn't hurt. But that's not what I need. I know full well that nobody can make any decisions for me; I just feel that I'm not aware enough of what sorts of jobs are out there. It sounds incredibly naive, but I don't feel that I have the knowledge of what sorts of positions I could go after and I want some help in trying to find out what they are.

Jim: And since I don't go ahead and fulfill the expectations that she has for help, she looks upon me as being unconcerned, or less concerned, which isn't true.

Helen: Well yes, but you see that's the biggest difference between Jim and me. He's an extremely analytical person and I operate intuitively, almost exclusively. So you can see how he's trying at this level and I'm at another level—and it gets in the way.

Jim: In the past when I have tried to explain things to Helen, it has become very frustrating for me because on my terms she won't understand it. If I can be aware that I should relate to her on her level then perhaps I can be persuasive, but that takes a lot of awareness and a lot of energy as well.

Helen: See, because I am such an intuitive person, I am greatly affected by my environment. If I'm not going to feel happy there, I'm not going to be happy there. I'm not going to feel comfortable or at ease. I'm not going to like it. I mean that's the only way to say it.

Jim: Why, Helen?

Helen: Well, you know when one is talking about intuitive feelings it is very difficult to say why I am not going to like it.

Jim: Since we both make decisions at a very different level, one of the things we know that happens between us is that Helen often has a tendency to overreact or to imagine bad situations as being worse than they really turn out to be, and I on the other hand tend to underestimate the badness. Many times unconsciously and unknowingly we can both make totally different assumptions in a situation. I'm trying to think of a good example that has happened recently. Well, we made a different assumption the other day and we both got upset and started arguing and there was no cause for that.

Helen: We had a conversation and I came away perfectly satisfied that I knew what was supposed to take place. Jim came away satisfied that he knew exactly what was going to take place, but we were thinking different things.

Jim: So in the case of this job decision I made a lot of assumptions about Helen that are just very far off base compared to her assumptions, especially with respect to this job search for her and this uncertainty she has about what she might be doing. So I guess Helen doesn't want to feel that her needs are being imposed on me by saying, "Well, we have to go to San Francisco because that's where I can do my thing." She doesn't want to feel guilty or responsible if I take a job that I don't consider to be the best job for me just to make her happy. Yet I don't want to say, "Hey, Helen you have to go to St. Joseph, Missouri, and live there for a while," because that would be forcing my structure on her.

So I guess there's another option. She can go to San Francisco, and I can go to St. Joseph, Missouri, which probably creates more problems in the long run than it would solve. Although we certainly have an element of independence. Last summer I spent three months on the west coast and she stayed here most of the time because that was the best job opportunity. Now I could have stayed here and had a job that I didn't enjoy. After spending nine months at H.B.S. doing work I didn't enjoy I wasn't about to do that. She really couldn't have quit her job because part of the condition of her employment was that she would stay here during the summer.

Helen: Well, I accepted that job and I felt I didn't want to give it up for what was in my mind a ridiculous reason. I have a sense of responsibility about wherever I work even though it might not be the most glamorous job in the world. It was my choice to stay at work.

Jim: In that case, it was a simple decision for both of us. While I was in the Navy I was always away, so it was not a new experience to be separated. Living under the same roof 365 days a year tends to make one nonobjective at times. We all need a rest and a change of pace.

The way we come out is we don't mind sacrificing for the other person, but if you're in that other person's role the knowledge that the other one is giving up something just for you is just not acceptable. That's why if we had another job offer. . . .

Helen: Well, we don't, so that's not another possibility—two jobs or none.

Jim: Well, we can just pack up and start driving around and I can extend my job search for a while longer. (He pauses and stares at the floor, and then lifts his head suddenly) The other thing that is frustrating from my point of view is that I haven't fully thought this out and it's sort of catching up to me. The circumstances are sort of forcing me to think about it. Yet to compare all our awareness of this dilemma we're in now versus what it was two months ago—is just a totally different situation. We've really sort of been complacent, I guess for too long. We can't undo that, of course, so we won't sit here and be anxious about it, but . . .

Helen: I have no doubt that I will eventually find some work which is meaningful to me and satisfying to me and that's not my real problem. My real problem. . . . Six months ago if anyone had said, "What are you going to do in June?" my answer would have been, "Well, we'll go where Jim gets a job." But I took an Interpersonal Behavior course this spring and I began to really think about me and Jim, and now I don't like the implications of simply following Jim around. But now we get down to what's more important. . . . Is it more important for me to be Jim's wife or for me to be an employed member of the work force? Since I'm only just beginning to think about the implications of both, I don't know which direction I am going in. (Long pause) Work is not so important to me that I would do that at the risk of our relationship, however . . . . (Long pause)

Jim: Well, you've already said that you don't want to go to Missouri. So if I said I want to take that job because that's the best job for me, we have a problem?

Helen: Right.

Jim: Whereas if I take the other job, which I may be a little more anxious about myself because there is not quite as much certainty as to how or where I'll progress, then I'm giving in a little bit to you. But, I. . . . (Pause)

Helen: Well, I can't make the decision for you.

Jim: (Pause) I realize that . . .

On the following day, Doug stopped by Helen's office at noontime to find out what they had decided to do.

Doug: Well?

Helen: Jim is supposed to phone both companies at 1:00.

Doug: And . . . ?

Helen: (Long pause) I don't know for sure. . . .

XVI

The Dynamics of the Job-Hunting Process

In the past five chapters we have discussed better and worse ways to approach the various parts of job hunting—from creating a focus for one's job campaign to choosing among offers. The whole process, however, is more than just the sum of its parts. This chapter will help you better understand the job-hunting process as a whole, including the four major problems typically encountered by job hunters, and some of the better ways that individuals have found to deal with those problems.

Managing One's Time

It should be apparent from our discussion in the past few chapters that job hunting can be a very time-consuming activity. People who have not recently had to search for a job seem invariably to underestimate the time involved. It is not at all unusual for a nonstudent to spend half to all of his or her time for three or four months looking for a job. Even students will often spend about a quarter of their time for four months. Some individuals, in both cases, spend up to five times as long.

Because job hunting is time consuming, it seldom fits very neatly into someone's already busy life. It causes conflicts with school, work, family, and one's leisure time. Unless one is prepared for these conflicts and prepared to manage them, they can create a continuing sense of crisis.

Individuals who normally have a busy schedule, and who normally manage it well, tend to be quite successful at managing their time while job hunting. People who do not typically have a busy schedule, or who do not usually manage their time well, often run into problems while job hunting.

For the person who has problems managing time or who normally has an unbusy schedule, we offer two specific recommendations that can help you manage your time while job hunting. First, get an appointment book (if you don't already have one). By recording in it all of your time commitments (not just appointments) while job hunting, you can make it serve as an effective time-management tool. Second, every time you undertake a task, stop and ask yourself a few questions. Do I really need to do this? Can someone else do it instead? Do I have to do this now? Or is something else a higher priority? What is the most efficient way to get this done? And so on.

Effectively managing one's time can make job hunting much less of a burden.

Managing the Scope of One's Search

As we mentioned in Chapter XII, people who are more successful in finding a very satisfying job tend to keep a narrower focus during job hunting. Among other things, a clearer and more structured focus helps one keep one's time demands within reasonable bounds.

Despite its importance and usefulness, however, maintaining a restricted scope while job hunting can be very difficult. Forces exist that push toward a widening of one's focus. For a variety of reasons people sometimes do succumb to these forces, and they end up facing all the problems associated with an unfocused job search.

For example, most job hunters, at one point or another, begin to worry that maybe they just won't get any job offers. Some try to reduce that possibility by broadening the scope of their search. We've seen students who, after receiving their first rejection letter, panic and discard any and all focus in their job campaign. Many people, once they have spread the word that they are looking for a job, receive a few unsolicited leads that are not even close to what they are looking for. But, if they are attractive in some way, some job hunters will take the bait. We've seen companies send telegrams to students telling them what wonderful things the company has heard about them and asking them to please sign up to interview with the company when it is on campus. Students who have no interest whatsoever in the firm or its jobs will often sign up for an interview. Maintaining a rational focus in a job search is also difficult when one is around other job hunters, whose enthusiasm for a different kind of job can be infectious. Some students seem to change the focus of their search almost daily to whatever the last excited friend they talked to was describing. The "grass-is-greener" phenomenon is very much at work here. Finally, some people expand the scope of their job search after they receive their first job offer. They seem to find their first "valentine" very exciting, want more, and so they go out and collect lots and lots of job offers.

If you feel yourself wanting to broaden your focus while job hunting, don't do it immediately. Examine the idea carefully over a period of time. You will probably decide it is not a good idea.

Managing Anxiety

There are many reasons why people find job hunting anxiety producing. Serious young students, in particular, often overestimate the stakes involved and then worry about making errors. Many people, who find rejection in any kind of social situation unpleasant, live in daily fear of being rejected by some employer they are beginning to like. The stream of ambiguous information a job hunter receives from potential employers drives some people to despair. The relative success experienced by other job hunters leave some people feeling like the "ugly child at the orphanage." And the stream of first positive (an invitation to a second set of interviews), then negative (a rejection), then positive (a job offer) stimuli can turn one's life into an emotional roller coaster.

It has been our observation that many of the poor judgments people make while job hunting are due to their own anxiety, or more broadly, to an emotional state that is increasingly out of control. An individual's success at managing his or her own emotional state can be a very important factor while job hunting.

Just knowing that it is not unusual to feel anxious, and knowing the typical events that create anxiety, can help you to reduce and manage your anxiety while job hunting. People become "out of control" when they are surprised by and frightened by their own anxiety. When typical human anxiety becomes predictable, it becomes manageable.

A technique our students have found useful in putting the hectic events of job hunting in a rational perspective is to keep a diary. By spending just a few minutes almost every day to summarize job-hunting events, your own thoughts and strategies, and your current feelings, you create a "monitoring system" that can be very useful in keeping things under control. By periodically rereading the entries for the last few weeks or months, one is able to make current decisions based on a more accurate understanding of what has really been happening. Rereading the diary helps put things in perspective. An example of such a diary can be found at the end of this chapter. Further instructions regarding its creation and use are in the workbook on p. 270.

Managing Pressure

Most job hunters get more than enough advice regarding what they "should" do: from friends, professors, parents, spouses—even from a little voice inside them. While this advice is sometimes helpful, many times it is not. One of the challenges of job hunting is to not succumb to well-intentioned but inappropriate advice and pressure.

When Fran Kelly's parents learned that he was not looking for a job in banking, they let him know (almost on a daily basis) how terribly disappointed they were that he wasn't following in the family tradition. When John Allen decided he would not interview anyone on campus or even look for a job until after he graduated and moved to the city he wanted to make his home, his peers gave him blank stares and an occasional "Boy, does that sound like a dumb idea." When Frank Lenaro decided to change his career field after working for 10 years, his friends made it a habit of saying (while Frank was present), "Frank's decided to throw out everything he has built up over the past 10 years." When Kim Evans decided that she wanted to look for a job in an area seldom entered by graduates from her school, she was greeted constantly with puzzled looks and questions such as, "Why don't you want any of the *good* jobs?"

The more highly one is integrated into a network of friends, relatives, and acquaintances, the more pressure one is likely to feel from others while job hunting. This short-run pressure can, and sometimes does, push people away from a rational course of action.

Differentiating between inappropriate pressure and good advice can be difficult, especially if you are already out of control, letting events and feelings direct your behavior. Periodically reviewing your themes and their implications from your self-assessment can be invaluable at this point. So can keeping a job-search diary. Both can help you keep on the right rack.

Exercise

The case that follows is one person's job-hunting diary. It is followed by a report of a study made of M.B.A. job hunting. For anyone who is interested in what job hunting can be like for someone over 50, we strongly recommend an article by Anne Chamberlain that appeared in *Fortune* (November 1974), "An Executive Odyssey: Looking for a Job at 55." As you read the case, consider the following questions:

1. How does Sandra manage her time, the scope of her search, her anxiety, and the pressures on her?
2. How successful is Sandra in her job search?

Sandra Evans

Job-Search Diary

Fall 1974. During the first semester I formulated the strategy for my impending job campaign, both in terms of my initial job and in terms of where I wanted to be over the longer term. I wanted to join a small real estate development company where I could gain a partial ownership interest. I was looking for a position with a fairly general viewpoint dealing with legal, finance, construction, marketing, and development kinds of tasks rather than being locked into something fairly specialized. I wanted to be able to work on a project basis and gain exposure to different types of developments in areas where I currently don't have expertise. I wanted to deal as much as possible with people outside the firm and make as many contacts as I could for any future deals that I would want to put together for my own account.

Geographically, I wanted to be someplace warm, preferably on a coast. My three target states were Texas, California, and Florida (where I had grown up). They all have a growth rate that I thought would be conducive to the kinds of activities I wanted to be involved in and they have not been hit by the recession to the same extent as other parts of the country. So, when I started out I had an idea of the kind of job I wanted and of where geographically I wanted to be. I wanted to find a springboard kind of a job, establish a track record, make contacts, and then go into a partnership in real estate (or some other project-oriented kind of business) to deal on my own account within five years. By then I hope to have paid down a considerable portion of my outstanding (in both senses of the word) school loans. These loans are of concern to me and I feel that I would not want to take a job where there would be some risk that my paycheck would not be forthcoming.

For the longer term, I would like to be in a position to start up these ventures and then delegate day-to-day management. Within 10 to 15 years of graduating I want to be able to live off the income from these investments, get a doctorate, and go into teaching and travel, etc. I've always felt that I would like to teach at the college level later on—sort of a second career, if you will.

My strategy for this particular job market is sort of two-pronged. The economic situation is so uncertain that I feel my chances of going into a small real estate business with equity participation are quite limited and, given the "consolidation" in the industry, it would be sort of a risky strategy to pursue. So I have decided to interview on campus with sort of port-in-the-storm kinds of companies—get some useful experience, meet people, and, when the economy turns up, jump back out into real estate. I also feel that, should the economy improve dramatically by, let's say, February or March, I can then launch a direct-mail campaign aimed at real estate companies. It would be dysfunctional now for me to send out a barrage of letters and just be disappointed by the lack of response. (Last year I had started making up a list of these companies because I was looking for a small real estate company for the summer. So, I have a partial list, which I am adding to.)

December 1974. The placement office released a list of companies which will be interviewing this year, and I chose a couple of real estate companies. I fear these companies will end up canceling because the economy has definitely gotten worse. I've also decided to do some research and make a list of insurance companies and banks, because some of them in the past have had job descriptions having to do with real estate lending. So, I intend to look up past job descriptions in real estate and put those companies on my priority card.

Over Christmas I'm going down to Florida to see my family, and while there talk with a few people in real estate and get some names to add to my mailing list.

January 1975. Every other day or so I go to the placement office and look at job descriptions and correspondence opportunities. I have started receiving letters from C.P.A. firms inviting me to interview before they come on campus. I'm really not interested in auditing, but I've decided to look at those Big Eight firms that would allow me to go into consulting immediately.

January 17. Today I signed up for Concord Mortgage and Midwest Mortgage Real Estate Lending. So far a couple of the firms on my list that had real estate jobs last year do not have them this year. This week and next week I'm going to the career resources library to look up Concord and Midwest and read everything that they have in the folder. Then I'm going to read the industry files on banking and a file of my own on mortgage banking technical notes from the Management of Lending course. I've also been watching The *Wall Street Journal* very carefully, because they've been having the annual report results for the REIT's. I've started clipping those out of the paper to get a better feel for what's going on with the bank REIT's.

January 28. Today I had my first interview with Concord. I signed up for a 9:00 A.M. interview because I thought it would be a good idea to be the first on the list. (I think that they remember the first person and the last person pretty well but are somewhat fuzzy about the people in the middle.) The interview was really fantastic. The interviewer was the kind of person that I relate very well with. He's very open and enthusiastic about the company; a low-pressure kind of guy—he didn't act like, "Well, this is a buyer's market, so tough." And I really respected the way he treated me in the interview. There is one thing that sort of concerns me about that interview—it took a half hour for him to get warmed up and get into an interviewing mode. Fortunately, there was no one signed up for the next slot, so I did spend over an hour with him. I ran into him again and had lunch with him and another Concord Mortgage interviewer. From the way they talked, there is no question that I'll be invited back. So, I think it's really fantastic that my first interview turned out so well. There is some ambiguity about the jobs they have available. I'm interested in going out there and deal-making immediately and he was talking about the sort of a job where you stay at corporate headquarters in Detroit for a year and then move into line management. While you are in corporate headquarters you perform some sort of projects for the president or one of the vice-presidents. I kept trying to maneuver myself into position where I will get into deal-making in the income loan division right away. I want to be physically located in the Texas or Florida regions. I don't want to go to Detroit; I don't think I can stand much longer another of these depressing winters.

January 29. I signed up for two Big Eight C.P.A. firms, because it seems that I can go into consulting immediately with them; and I'm going to tell them I'm interested in Texas, California, and Florida and see what happens.

January 31. I had my interview with Transnational Realty this afternoon and superficially my interviewer and I were getting along, but we didn't mesh in style *at all*. I was really disappointed that this real estate guy acted like a banker—he really did; he acted like he wanted me to be passive, and I was trying to pin him down on how long it takes to have responsibilities, have the authority to say yes or no on a large loan. But the thing that really blew my mind was the extent to which courtesy is situational, depending upon one's environmental cues. The sun was shining in today in the alcove, so I removed the jacket that goes with the suit I was wearing, and he looked at me and said, "You may remove your jacket." And I thought, why does he think he has the right to tell me whether I may or may not remove my jacket—I couldn't believe it—what formality! I really didn't like the interview much; I didn't like his style very much either. I brought in a clipping showing how the REIT had lost quite a bit of money (this was the clipping from The *Wall Street Journal*), and he got very defensive about it. Now, I didn't bring the clipping in to say, "Look how poorly you've done," because everyone's doing poorly. What I wanted to know was, what is the bank's relationship and his relationship to the REIT—what are my chances of going to Los Angeles and helping the REIT, since I don't want to be in Chicago, and how is their equity REIT doing. But he got very defensive about that and more or less indicated that my chances of going to L.A. to work with the REIT were quite limited and I think we were both happy when this interview terminated half an hour later. I guess I should just say that this interview definitely was a screening device, because I'm really not interested in them now.

I keep receiving letters from corporations like AMOCO, etc., telling me about great positions in their corporate treasurer's office and in their finance department, and it's just too bad I'm not interested in going with a big corporation. Most of these corporations are located in cold, miserable weather. So I tell myself, "Don't be tempted."

February 5. Today Western Union called with a message from Concord Mortgage. Would I be interested in coming in for a company visit? YES!!! I called Detroit and talked with the personnel representative and arranged to go on the 17th (Washington's Birthday) rather than waiting until spring vacation or even later. I really would like to go as soon as possible so I can get an experience base for company visits. Also I won't be so pressured at the end of this process by not having gone on any visits, not having any offers, and therefore having my desperation index go up.

So I've decided to go now and I'm really looking forward to it. If everyone else is as nice as the two interviewers I met and the person I talked to on the phone, I think things are going to be fantastic. I'm feeling really happy about it.

February 6. I had my interview this afternoon with Big Eight firm A. What an experience! After receiving a letter saying, "We are so happy to see that you are still interested in consulting," we went around and around with him saying that I should go into auditing first and me saying I could be better utilized in consulting. Finally I said, "It's not that I don't like accounting, after all, I majored in it undergrad, it's just that I feel I could be better utilized in consulting. But, if you think that I really should, from the firm's viewpoint and for my own good, go into auditing first, I'll consider it." I really blew that one! I would not acquiesce until the last five minutes of the interview. I told him I wanted to be in Texas, and he said he'd check it out for me, but I think he was somewhat unhappy that I was so intransigent about consulting. I was amazed that he kept pushing auditing when he specifically wrote telling me how glad he was that I was interested in consulting. Well, maybe I'll have a chance of hearing something good from them. Other than that, the interview went well. But I really don't want to get snowed into going into auditing. I guess I could pursue two strategies here; I could say to the national recruiting partner, "Well, I'll go into auditing," and hope that when I get to the local office I can convince them to let me go into consulting. Or I can fight for consulting now.

That was not an entirely satisfactory interview and in sort of a postmortem I can see that I really should have been a little more flexible and then hoped to change their minds at a local office. But I don't think I'll have the chance to do that after the battle we just had. So, it's a good thing I've already heard from Concord and set up an interview, otherwise I might be getting discouraged with these past two interviews.

February 12. Today I had my interview with Big Eight firm B, and things went exceptionally well. I think I learned my lesson last week with Big Eight firm A, because today I pushed for consulting but I wasn't totally inflexible. As it turned out, I had been signed up with the wrong person. (I was signed up with the Boston recruiter.) So I talked with him for a half-hour and then he sent me down to talk with the national recruiter who took referrals from the recruiters. I had to wait about 15 minutes to talk with him. I was feeling pretty good; I felt like my interview was over because I had already spent a half hour with the Boston guy, who more or less came right out and told me consulting is peripheral to their business, especially in a recession, when consultants are the first ones to go anyway. The national partner and I got along famously. I don't know what it was—we just hit it off; he was very open; he was just very nice. I told him very frankly that I'm ambitious; that if I go with them I want to go to the top, that I'm looking for opportunities to move along as quickly as I can. We got along so well that we were interrupting each other—there was no formality in it at all—there was quite a bit of excitement. At the end he asked me if I would be interested in the New York office. I explained to him that although I was interested in California, Florida, and Texas, I had not ruled New York out entirely—it certainly wasn't a priority. He felt I could handle New York. He told me he had been in this business a long time and I've got what it takes to go to the top with them. We then discussed the pros and cons of the small versus large office. He did concede that in a smaller office I would have a broader viewpoint and I would get involved in a broader range of activities. When I told him, "Look, I'm probably not interested in New York," he said that he would hate me to rule it out without seeing it. If I am interested in coming down to New York they would love to fly me down and acquaint me with New York City and the office. So I'm supposed to call him back next week and tell him whether I'm interested in New York or whether I would just prefer to have him check out offices in California and Florida. (He told me that Texas is already filled.) So, I'm feeling pretty good about this interview. I will probably not go to New York. I'll probably tell him on the phone that I've thought about it and decided not to because I really don't want to get tempted and then end up there when I know that's not really my kind of place. The office is just too big—about 500 professionals. I would just see some little tiny bit of a very big company. But I will ask him what the story is for California and Florida. He was exceptionally positive in his feedback, so I have a feeling that he'll be pushing me for a company visit. I guess I have a 50–50 batting average now—two companies that I really like, and two that I didn't get along with too well at all.

February 13. As I expected, one of my real estate priorities has canceled. They all seem to be canceling and it's a good thing I added some other companies to my priority list beside real estate companies. A couple of priorities came up—a couple of insurance companies and a bank—and unfortunately they had nothing in real estate. So, it looks like priorities are turning out to be an essentially meaningless exercise.

February 17. Today I had my company visit with Concord in Detroit and things went exceptionally well. I felt very comfortable there from the first moment that I arrived—late, because of foggy weather—and I really enjoyed the people there very much. They were stressing over and over again that they are looking for good people, that there is no implicit seniority requirement, that you will progress as fast as you produce and prove yourself. They are very open and friendly—I don't know if this is sort of a midwestern kind of thing or what it is, but everyone was just very, very unpretentious and I really enjoyed that.

The thing that concerned me during my all-day visit, which ended up lasting from 11:00 A.M. 'til 8:00 P.M., plus dinner until midnight or one, was that I kept talking about deal-making and they kept pushing this project management job where you stay in headquarters for a year and work on a project and then you become a line manager for another region. I came to the conclusion that there is very little chance that I could get into deal-making right away, and despite the opportunities that I see here at Concord, I don't know if I could tolerate living in Detroit for a minimum of a year. I knew I was doing pretty well because I ended up in the executive vice-president's office. After my interview, he took me into the president's office and I figured if I made it to the president's office at the end of the day I must be

doing all right. And then, the personnel person said that they would like to make me an offer. So that really took the pressure off me.

The president stressed again that it's a high-pressure environment, etc. He asked me how I felt I could do as a woman in this business, for there are very few women. I told him I didn't think there'd be any problem at all. I also told him that I believe in people's lib, not just women's lib. I believe in equal opportunity, not better-than-equal opportunity. I wouldn't say I want as much pay as male M.B.A.s and the same job title and then say, "But I can't travel," or I can't do this or that, I think he was really happy to hear what my attitude is. The other thing that was kind of interesting was that he asked about my divorce. He said, "I see here that you're divorced." I said, "That's right." He said, "Well, what seemed to be the problem?" And I said, "We had a lack of goal congruence; my goals and objectives in life and my ex-husband's were not the same; we had changed over time." And then he asked if I think I made the right decision, and I told him that I couldn't say whether any other decision was right or wrong, but that the one I did make—i.e., to get divorced—was the right one. He said, "So you do feel that you're good at making decisions and you can make decisions," and I said, "Most definitely."

The only thing that bothered me was that I got the impression I would have little or no choice about the region, the division, or the projects to which I would be assigned. I ended up asking the personnel manager how job assignments with project managers are made. He said that the president and the vice-presidents bid on the person. I'm really not comfortable with that. The president asked me if I'd be willing to get their computer system squared away. I might be willing to do it, but I certainly didn't want to spend my whole first year working on that. So I will want to resolve exactly what I would be doing before I would accept their offer. The other disappointment is that there seems to be little chance that I could go into the region immediately and get into deal-making. I'm not certain the advantage of going with Concord immediately would be enough to compensate for staying in headquarters for a year and doing some staff type of work. I really do feel there are real opportunities, because they have been growing extremely fast. So I really feel it is a real place to go.

I have mixed feelings at this point. I'm very happy they thought enough of me to make an offer the very same day I interviewed, but I'm rather unhappy at what the job is going to be and over the lack of choice I'll have. So, I'll see how things go with my other interviews before I make any decision (they want to know by March 31st, which is a little unreasonable, I think). Before I let them know I would have to really tie down what my job would be and exactly how long I would probably remain in headquarters.

Before I went into this interview I had done a considerable amount of homework, going over everything I could find on mortgage banking; talking with people who had been in banking; talking with people who knew people who had worked for Concord; talking with anybody I could find; reading everything I could find; going to the career resources library; reading The *Wall Street Journal*; looking things up in my real estate books. I really wanted to be on top of the technical aspects of this business. None of that ever came out, but I felt more secure knowing I had prepared. I have a tendency to do as much homework as I can within a certain time limit. I set a number of hours to devote to this, given my schedule, and then try to home in on what the key issues are for that company and for the industry and be conversant in these issues so that they will realize when they talk to me that I am interested enough to know what's important to them. I felt I had a good handle on what Concord's strategy is and on what the important tasks are for them to achieve their growth goals. I am really happy that I decided to have this visit before spring vacation, and that my first visit went so well—and ended with an offer!

February 18. Today, as I predicted, I received my ding from Midwest Mortgage. I don't know if this is the standard kind of ding or not. But the man wrote me and said they don't have the kind of opportunities I *expect* and *deserve*. I got kind of a kick out of the letter—it sounded a little tongue-in-cheek to me.

February 19. Today I had an interview with Big Eight firm C's consulting group. This had to be a classic interview; they tried to pull the high-pressure routine on me, and it just didn't work!!! I guess I'm feeling pretty cocky after the company visit I had in Detroit, and pretty good knowing that on Friday of this week I will call Big Eight firm B's national recruiting partner back to tell him I'm not interested in New York and to hear if my company visit will be to California or Florida. So I'm feeling like I don't have to take garbage from anybody!!!

I walked into my interview with a cup of coffee—I'd run from my last class and didn't have time for lunch. A young man was seated across the table, and he said, "May I remove my jacket?" And I said, "Certainly; may I drink my coffee?" and he said, "Certainly." We started off with fantastic rapport—then in walks this other man. My interviewer looked surprised to see him, stood up, put his jacket back on, and sat back down again. I knew things were headed downhill. The other man walked across the room and said, "I'll just sit in the corner and be quiet." Now, I must admit that at times I talk when I should be listening. So, just to let him know I didn't mind that he was there and that I didn't sort of crumble at the prospect of being observed or having two people interview me at once, I said, "Oh, it's all right if you even ask me some questions, as long as I have the same privilege!" I have a feeling he didn't like that much. He said, "Of course, you may ask me some questions," but I could tell that he didn't like it. In that interview, again, I told them I was interested in California, Florida, and Texas. I asked them how important consulting was to them and they indicated they thought it was a key part of their strategy in terms of remaining in the Big Eight. I didn't like the attitude of the second man who had come in and he, I could tell, had some qualms about my being a woman. He asked how would I feel working with men, as they have very few women. I patiently explained to him that I've always been in situations where men have been the majority. I explained to him that my only concern about women would be why they had so few—was it because they were having recruiting problems, or was it because. . . . They were uncomfortable with this and I

didn't pursue it. They also seemed to be rather upset by my limited geographical preference.

I was not altogether surprised by their attitude, though. I talked with a couple of people who told me they had had very unsatisfactory interviews with Big Eight firm C; that they were very cold interviews; and basically I was expecting sort of a bad interview. I am just sorry I couldn't or didn't have the opportunity to speak only with the initial guy—I think he and I would have hit it off and I think it would have been a very constructive interview. The way it turned out, it was just sort of a power play—the one man seeing if he could intimidate me, and me showing, perhaps too much, that I'm not about to be intimidated by anybody.

February 20. I've been taking Labor Relations this semester, and I've decided that I would make a dynamite arbitrator. It's quite fascinating and it is also something I could do on sort of a part-time basis that would add variety to my life (although, to be an arbitrator, you have to be seen as a neutral party)! Anyhow, I decided to go talk to my professor about it, and I gave him a couple of resumés in the event something really interesting comes up in labor relations. By now it's obvious to me that the economy is not going to turn up in time for me to launch a direct-mail campaign and, further, that I will probably be better off accepting a job with a company that will still be around by the summer. So I've more or less decided to focus on the companies I'm interviewing with on campus. I have become risk averse in the sense that I'm not interested in interviewing with a small real estate company that may go bankrupt and leave me high and dry with a lot of loans to repay.

February 25. At 9:00 this morning I had an interview with a major west coast bank. My purpose in interviewing them was to get to California. I thought if I could get a second visit to California and see what that's like (because I've never been there before)—and maybe it would not be a bad idea to get a job with the biggest bank in the United States in real estate or one of its real estate subsidiaries. The interview lasted half an hour and the guy never woke up until 9:25. He came in looking somewhat confused and I introduced myself. He didn't tell me what his name was, he didn't tell me what division he worked for, he didn't tell me anything about himself and I had to ask him who he was. This shows you the condition this poor man was in; apparently he had just arrived that morning and was basically dragging. He and I never did get to talk about banking; he talked about Florida and how his mother-in-law has a place there. It was a very unsatisfactory interview and I was quite disappointed. I didn't want to totally lead the interview, but if I hadn't taken some initiative I would have never found out what his name was. So, I may as well write them off.

I had my interview before class and I ran into a guy who had a 9:00 A.M. interview with the bank, and he was just as disgusted as I was. So apparently it isn't a good idea to have a 9:00 interview if it can last only until 9:30, because the interviewer never sort of wakes up and gets into an interviewing frame of mind. I'm coming to the conclusion that I don't belong in a bank at all. I just don't seem to relate well to these people. Although I kept thinking that the real estate people in a bank were different than the typical banker, they're too much like bankers for me to get along with them. I do want to get along with bankers, though, when it comes to asking for money for my own projects, ho, ho!

February 28. I called Big Eight firm B's national recruiting partner last week and told him I was not interested in New York, and he told me he would check the situation out for California and Florida. So today I called him back and he told me that the Miami office is interested in talking to me and that I should call collect down there to set up an appropriate interview date. So, since this is so close to spring vacation, and since I would like to go to Florida for spring vacation, that's when I'm going to schedule it. And I'm feeling good about that. The Miami office is small enough it would fit into my small-business concept and it is in one of my target states, so I'm quite pleased about going down there.

March 5. Today I had an interview with the trust division of a major Florida bank. It was quite a good interview. They had several positions open and I'm vying for the trust administration job because I feel that I will be meeting people who are good to know. I would learn an awful lot about investments, trust administration, etc. This would probably be useful to me later on when I'm trying to put some ventures together. My interviewer told me that, while she can't tell if they want to see me again today, I should look forward to hearing from them. (Apparently she isn't supposed to tell you at the end of the half-hour interview.) One thing does concern me—she handed me an application at the end and asked that I fill it out and mail it to her so that she and the president can go over it. I do not feel that it is appropriate to fill out an application before you accept an offer. And when I looked at this application today I decided I will not fill it out. It requests a personal financial statement. The conditions of employment listed on the back are absurd. I'm disappointed that the application looks the way it does because this tells me something about the organization that was not at all apparent in the interview. Although it looks like there are an awful lot of opportunities with them, I don't like this application. I've decided to write her a letter saying that if filling out the application is optional, then I am interested in pursuing opportunities with them. See what she says!

March 12. Today I received the expected ding from Big Eight firm A—sure took them a long time. I had an interview with Cyphernetics, who wrote me and had some sort of account exec. position where you go in as a consultant and help them computerize some business problems. I'm really not interested in getting back into computer work, but I decided that just for fun I would talk with them and let them convince me (!!!) to consider them. Going in there with that attitude was not a good idea. . . . I really didn't have a good interview. I'm really not interested in doing that sort of work, but since I've only had, let's see, seven interviews, I was beginning to feel that I may be limiting myself quite a bit. It is somewhat distressing that there are so few companies interviewing on campus that appeal to me in any way whatsoever. So I decided, oh well, go in and

interview. He said, "You probably aren't interested in this work." Apparently that was the attitude that M.B.A.s conveyed. And I said, "Well, I'm not really interested in this work—it depends on what the opportunities are." I guess it just proves that a person shouldn't go into an interview with a company they aren't interested in.

March 14. I received a phone call today from the personnel manager of the Florida bank. She told me the president will be interviewing at a big hotel downtown on the 20th (the day before spring vacation) and that he would be interested in talking with me. So I set up an interview. She hadn't received my letter yet about the application, so she asked me if the application was on the way, and I explained that the letter was on the way. She told me I could fill out the parts I wanted to and leave the other ones blank for now and that she would send me another application. This application is becoming a thorn in my side, because I know darn well I don't want to fill it out. First of all, I would never sign conditions of employment before I accept employment, and I certainly would never agree to these conditions of employment, which are absurd. One of them is that they require any medical or nonmedical examination they may deem necessary to continue employment, and this looks like they could make you have psychological counseling, or any number of things. So I'm not going to fill the application out—I'll interview with the president and see what happens. But if the president only wants to talk with me if I have the application, then he's not going to be talking with me for long, because I do refuse to fill it out.

March 14. Today I received a letter asking me if I would be interested in the doctoral program. That letter was a blow to me. I got, sort of, angry at having to even address the subject. I had talked during self-assessment about the fact that I do want to teach later on, but that I want to go out and get some real-world experience and build up some capital before I do it. I just don't want to get tempted now to stay on. For one thing, I really do want to get out of this climate for a while; and second, I really don't know if now is the time for me to go on. So I read the letter, and, to make matters worse, they indicated there might be a research assistant position available to help pay my way through. I hadn't been on the emotional roller coaster too much during this interviewing process, but that letter did it. I made an appointment to talk about it on the 17th. I plan to go by and see what's going on. I'll also get a copy of the brochure from the Doctoral House and take a look at what's involved.

I feel very uncertain, almost depressed, at contemplating the thought of having to make a decision, of having a decision essentially thrust upon me about going on for my doctorate right now. I received the letter and I had to go to a class after that and the whole time my mind wandered and I started thinking about the things I had written in my self-assessment paper; wanting to do the academic thing, and sort of reviewing in my own mind my themes and implications. I just sat there in sort of a daze through the whole class. It must have been pretty apparent that something had gotten me down, because I'm usually pretty happy and fairly high-spirited. I walked into the class and one of the guys that sits behind me said, "How are you today?" And I said, "Don't ask!" He said, "Is something wrong?" I said, "I'm not sure!" After I got out of class I came back to my room and I reread my whole self-assessment paper, and I was getting more and more depressed. Damn!

March 14. I went in and talked to a professor and batted the idea around and said I wanted more real-world experience; that I have $16,000 in debts; education loans to repay, etc., etc. I walked out of that conversation feeling even more depressed because I knew that part of what I was saying was me setting up a smokescreen to avoid the issue.

Today I talked with a person from the Federal Home Loan Bank board on the telephone. I had given my resumé to a professor two weeks ago when he indicated there was an opening, and I was hoping it had something to do with real estate. It turned out to have to do with investments and the man said he was interested in talking with me and that he would be coming to Boston after spring vacation. I said I may be interested in talking with him.

I have also written away on two correspondence opportunities; one was as a real estate manager in an oil corporation (I could tell by the way the job description was worked that it wasn't going to be any good); the other, the Texas division of a major food processor, has a tremendous reputation for design (but I had talked with a few people and found out that there are no women in that organization in any position of responsibility). Today I received a note from Texas telling me that they were not interested in interviewing me. I didn't feel very good after that. On the other hand, I would not want to go there if I wouldn't fit in.

Monday, March 17. Today I talked about the doctoral program at some length. They are not interested in people who are 40 or 45 years old who come in for the program. They're looking for people who are relatively young and who plan to devote their whole career, essentially, to academics. I just don't want to make that decision now. I left it that I would let them know after spring vacation, because I wanted to have some time to think about it, some time to talk with Big Eight firm B in Miami and time to talk with some professors I had at the University of Miami. I was still feeling rather down about the whole thing. When I found out I was going to interview with firm B in Miami on or about the third of March, I wrote all the other Big Eight firms and said, "I will be in Miami. Enclosed is my resumé; if you're interested in interviewing me, let me know." I had gotten a letter from Big Eight firm D indicating they would be interested in talking to me when I was down there. I haven't heard anything from the others so far.

March 20. I had my interview downtown with the president of the Florida bank. He did not ask me for the application and I was quite relieved. The interview went well and I feel very certain that they will be interested in talking with me again. I explained to him that I would be in Miami over spring vacation and I gave him my number there. He is a rather interesting person. He considers himself a maverick in the trust business, and I think he would be an interesting person to work for. However, I have this nagging feeling that the application does indicate something about the holding company and I just have sort of a bad feeling about the whole thing, even though he didn't ask me for the applica-

tion. There are certain things I won't do, no job is worth it; and one of the little things I won't do is give up my freedom entirely. That's what those job conditions indicate. Anyway, I'm going down to Miami tonight and really looking forward to it.

March 21. Today I had my interview with Big Eight firm B's Miami office. It went quite well and lasted from 11:00 A.M. to 8:00 P.M. I liked the people. I also successfully positioned myself into consulting. Originally I had been told that there were no consulting openings, but after I had talked with them today I sort of convinced them that I would like to spend at least part of the time in consulting. I also found out that as long as I'm working for them, my experience counts toward the C.P.A. experience requirement. So, I do plan, if I go with them, to sit for the C.P.A. exam within a year.

The other thing that really excited me was the chance to work in business development with a partner in charge of consulting. He and I had quite a long discussion about this, and they really are interested in increasing the consulting business. He's a fairly new partner; he's only been there a little over a year and so I guess he wants to establish some sort of performance record for himself. I was really impressed with him because of a couple of things having to do with his managerial style. He has a round desk; I'm not sure exactly what that means, but it is possibly useful data. The other thing I noticed was that all the managers and staff-level people have pictures of little kids on the wall—no wives, just little kids. Granted they are at the age where that would be normal or predictable, but I still thought that it might mean something in terms of the homogeneity of the group. As it turns out, there is only one bachelor with an office there. Some of the lower-level staff persons are bachelors, too, but most of those who have achieved a manager or partner level are married and have a family. I'm not certain how that will impact, how they will treat me in terms of being a woman and a professional and how they will view my lack of interest in getting married at least in the formal way they're accustomed to and my decision not to have children. Even though I had been there all day I didn't have a chance to talk with a staff-level person, so the personnel manager told me that if I would like to come back in a couple of days he would be more than happy to arrange it. They asked me what my salary requirements were, and I didn't handle that question very well. I indicated that I was aware that the market rate for M.B.A.s at public accounting firms was $16,000, and they indicated that that was a high figure for the Miami office. And that's sort of how we left it.

When I got home I found out that the personnel manager at the bank had called. I was quite impressed that they had called right away. I had had my interview with the president just last Thursday. So, I guess that's a pretty good sign.

March 25. Today I had an interview with Big Eight firm D's Miami office. I was somewhat concerned by the fact that I didn't get to talk with anyone today other than personnel people and the partner, except during lunch when I spoke with a senior and a staff-level auditing person. The interview went quite well in terms of my getting along with the partner, but I didn't get a good feel for what they're looking for, nor did I get a feel for whether I could go into consulting right away, especially since I hadn't talked to anyone in consulting or even any of the audit managers.

The personnel manager of the bank was on the phone when I returned home that evening. The first thing she asked me about was the application, and said that they would like to have me come in for an all-day interview. I tentatively scheduled that for Thursday, the 27th. I'm still feeling very uncomfortable about the whole thing. I sort of went round and round again about the application. Again she asked that I fill out the parts I feel OK about and bring it in for the interview on Thursday. I tried to reiterate my position, which was that it's unreasonable to expect someone to fill out a detailed application of this kind before they've accepted employment, and further, that the conditions of employment were unacceptable. I'm feeling less and less comfortable about the whole thing as I go along, even though the job itself sounds interesting. I plan to call the president tomorrow and get this clarified before I go in on Thursday. If they are going to adhere to the policy of requiring the application, then I don't plan to even bother to have another interview with them; I'm just simply not interested.

Wednesday, March 26. Today I went back to Big Eight firm B to meet a staff-level person. I talked with him a while. He has his M.B.A. from a Florida school and seemed to be quite happy. He was a little uncertain how to answer some of my tough questions, such as, "What do you wish you had known before you accepted a job with them?" After I had finished talking with him I was called back in to talk with the consulting partner and they made me an offer. They ended up offering me $16,000 to start off in consulting, but I had to go through the audit training program first. I feel sort of sorry now that I had answered the salary question in a market-based way by saying what I heard the market was rather than telling them what I really want in salary (which is more than that). I will be eligible for overtime, however.

I had a chance to talk more with the partner today; he explained that he doesn't like people who hide behind big massive desks, that's why his is round; that he believes in sort of equal power when people are discussing things; that he generally talks with people on the chairs and couch at the other side of his office. We talked awhile about our philosophies of life, I guess you would call it. We both believe in a progressive career—not getting locked into one thing and at the point when you don't receive the satisfaction you want, having the mobility (by that I mean psychological mobility) to do something else. He did say that there is only one thing that concerns him about me, and that is whether I will remain challenged enough while working for them. I responded that I plan to take responsibility for keeping myself challenged, by influencing my job assignments and by looking for things to keep me challenged. I think he does have a point, though—I think many of us become disillusioned once we get out into the real world and find out it isn't all grand strategic work. Part of it is working with detailed, not terribly exciting things. He reiterated that he hopes I will join them. The personnel manager more or less said the same thing. He also asked me

if I felt that women in business are discriminated against. I asked him if he meant women in accounting, women in business, myself in business, or myself in accounting, because I thought there were different answers to those questions. He asked me if I though that women in business were discriminated against, and I said I feared that there were some impasses that women run into, given the sort of stereotyped impressions that some businessmen have. I feel that conditioning, that is, getting used to dealing with women who are in responsible positions, will mitigate against this. And in terms of myself being discriminated against, I made it clear that I will behave in such a way that this will not become an issue. He reaffirmed that there certainly wouldn't be any discrimination against me at firm B. This was the first time the question of women or discrimination came up and I was a little surprised that he even felt compelled to say it. At one point he said, "As a matter of curiosity, not in my role as personnel director, but, do you want to get married again—what about kids?" I told him I was serious about a career, which is how I saw my life. I didn't feel the need to rush into a formal marriage again but maybe I'll adopt kids much later on. He is a bachelor and I guess he was pointing out what might be a problem being single. Perhaps this is something that he has been told to do when interviewing. It made me feel a little suspicious, because I think that if I felt there would be a discriminatory attitude I would have ascertained that at some earlier point in the interviews. The only thing that does bother me is that in Miami they called the staff women "staff girls." I plan to change that if I accept that job!!

I left the office feeling good about the offer and some of the kinds of tasks they indicated I would have and about the people there.

Later on I called the president of the bank. He and I had a fairly lengthy conversation about the application. I put him on the spot by more or less indicating that I wouldn't fill it out. He told me he wants me to fill out the application, come in for an all-day visit, and he wants to make me an offer, in that order. He then asked me if I want the job, and I told him that depends upon the conditions under which I'm accepting it. He more or less implied that if I want the job I will fill out the application, period. I went though the application page by page and through each job condition specifically with him early in the conversation, making him explain to me exactly what these things mean. And, as I suspected, the prohibitions in the job conditions are great. I would be prohibited from pursuing any outside form of business I might want, due to possible conflict of interests. He told me they do require psychological exams for promotion to an officer level. I find this intolerable, and I would not work for a company that has that kind of policy. He told me he doesn't even own common stock in anything due to a possible conflict of interest. There was no way I could work in an environment where my hands were tied in that way in terms of my own investment strategy. He started getting angry and seemed to be losing his control. Finally I told him, "Thank you very much, but I am not interested in coming back for an all-day intereview." He told me that out of the 300 people or so they interviewed this fall they had five job openings and they pursued five people to the point of wanting them to come back to headquarters. He was making it very clear that should I decide to fill out the application I would be given an offer. I'm no longer interested. First of all, I think enough animosity has arisen over this—at one point in the conversation he told me he didn't like my attitude about this application, and I explained I'm sorry he felt that way, but that I felt I didn't like their unreasonable attitude. I didn't use exactly those words. I was tactful, but the meaning came across quite clearly. So, even if I decided I could operate in that kind of restrictive environment, I feel enough damage has been done that I would be precluded for some time from establishing a good working relationship.

Tomorrow I plan to call a couple of my old accounting professors, a management professor and a marketing professor, and see what they have to say. Also I plan to talk to my old boss and the Dean of the University of Miami Business School.

March 27. Talking with these people (who have all taught me or know me) was a somewhat discomforting experience—they all encouraged me to go on for my doctorate. I would start out the conversation asking them about the job market in Miami and what they perceived the opportunities to be down here right now. It seems that the accounting majors aren't having much trouble, but that some of the other students are. But when I mentioned the opportunity of going on for my doctorate, they all recommended that I take this opportunity while I have it, pointing out that the likelihood of returning later is low, and that they think that I would enjoy being a professor. I feel somewhat uncomfortable because one of them started talking about what it's like and almost repeated things from *my* self-assessment paper; independence; spending your time the way you see fit; having a chance to consult; having a chance to learn constantly and satisfy one's thirst for knowledge.

Oh, sigh! It's pretty upsetting because it makes my decision even more difficult. I kept trying to say I agree, that it's the right thing some day, but I'm just not sure that right now is the time. A couple of them told me that being a woman and having my degree would give me a ticket to go anywhere and teach anywhere, that I would be very much in demand. That'd sure be nice!!, but I still don't know if this is the right time.

I got so influenced by all this that I tried to call the doctoral office a couple of times today to get an application to the program. I hadn't wanted to look at one yet; I've read the handbook, but I didn't ask for an application. No one was there and so I won't be able to look at an application 'til Monday, and by then maybe I can make a decision. Sort of hard to weigh some of these things now. I really wish I hadn't been confronted by this decision at this time.

I got another interesting phone call today. One of the Big Eight firms that had received my resumé called and said a client of theirs might be interested in talking to me. The guy asked how the job hunt was going and I said, "Just fine." He didn't seem too happy about that. I guess they were looking for someone desperate. I got the impression that they weren't going to be willing to pay the kind of salary I'm interested in. It was sort of interesting to receive that phone call, though.

Friday, March 28. I leave today to go back and I'm still very much uncertain about what to do regarding the doctorate. I had a long talk with my parents. They seem surprised that I'm even hesitating in going on; they fully expected me to. I guess that's because they know I've always planned to some day. I told them that I'm going to list out the pros and cons, and try to come up with some decision about it within the next week so that I can get it squared away in terms of replying to my offers.

April 1. I've done a lot of thinking about this and I've decided not to go for the doctorate. I feel that I was right in my initial assessment of the situation, which was to get out there in the real world and after I'm financially secure come back and continue with the doctorate. I guess in terms of being in the priority age group for a doctorate I can still be out in the real world for three or four years. Otherwise I'll be in the nonprime age group and things might be a little more difficult. So I want to reassess the situation in the next couple of years and rethink whether I want to go back sooner or whether I want to wait five or ten years. I decided that if I did go on now I would be precluded from doing some of the entrepreneurial things I would like to do, because I'm afraid I would be in a position where I wouldn't want to make a mistake. I knew a guy who taught at the University of Miami who went straight through for his degree and he seemed to be trapped by his own credentials. It just seemed he was precluded from doing some of the things he wanted to do. He seemed to regret not having had the opportunity to go out there and make some of the mistakes he might need to make in order to succeed. He felt being a professor meant he was pretty much restricted in the kinds of activities he could pursue.

This has not been an easy decision for me to make. I guess I feel the frustration of realizing I can't do everything and have everything all at once—tradeoffs *do* have to be made.

I've made another decision too: given the ambiguity concerning the job offered at Concord; the relative advantages of visibility with real estate clients; getting my C.P.A.; and being in the climate I like, I've decided to call up and let Concord know I will not be accepting their offer.

April 7. I received an offer from Big Eight firm D today and it was for less than I had requested. They said they had wanted to offer me a job when I was in Miami but the salary thing held them up. I really feel there would be advantages for me to choose firm B over firm D and I've decided to do so. For one thing, firm D's office is larger and I would be less visible. Second, I'm not that certain that I could get into consulting. And third, overall, I think firm B has one of the best names in the business. So I plan to call them today and accept. I'm pretty certain now about what I want to do. I feel like I am at the end of the decision tree on this and would prefer to accept and sort of complete the process. I received a call from the Federal Home Loan Bank board, wanting to interview me, and I explained that I will no longer be available for interviewing. They seemed somewhat disappointed, but I think it would be a waste of my time and theirs for me to talk to them, since they have a job that I really don't want.

I called firm B today and they seemed quite pleased that I have decided to accept their offer. I also asked to be placed on their mailing list (one of my postacceptance activities so I can try to get some orientation or feel for the office). I will be reporting for work on July 7th and will take a one-month training program in auditing.

April 9. I went in to the doctoral office and told them of my decision. They said that it was perfectly reasonable that I would want to get some real-world experience first, but that I should definitely reassess the situation and keep in touch and perhaps in a year or two I would be interested in joining the program. I feel good about the place where I will be working. I also feel that from a larger perspective it was good that I was confronted with this doctoral decision now, because otherwise I would have avoided it. It made me go back over my goals and objectives, over my strategy in terms of my career and my career path and basically made me rethink some of the things I had decided upon before. I think it was a beneficial thing for me to do, because it made me realize how easy it might be to get locked in to doing one thing or another and lose the kind of psychological mobility and flexibility which are so important in my particular scheme of things.

If I were to summarize my recruiting experiences in the whole interviewing process, I guess I would say that all in all it didn't take up too much of my time. I was able to schedule my interviews so that I didn't miss many classes. I would also say that it is true that you can learn a great deal about an office from a one-day visit. As a small example, at one place the people I talked to at lunch kept talking about sports teams, and I got the idea of sports as a socializing center or focus for their lives. I got the impression that if one is working for them, one also spends time socializing with the people and participating on teams. I'm not particularly interested in spending all my time with my colleagues from work, so that sort of pointed out to me that I may not get along too well with some of the people there. My personal mode is to have a social relationship with many diverse kinds of people and not just with people of the same occupation.

I also learned a little bit about companies' fears regarding recruiting and hiring M.B.A.s. I think it's pretty clear that companies do want to talk to someone who has a sincere interest, who will listen to them and respect their viewpoint, even though they may or may not have an M.B.A. I viewed all my interviews as nonadversary relationships, where both sides were trying to determine if there was a mutuality of interests and a fit. And I think with that attitude I was able to avoid feeling personally rejected when there was not fit—it was just clearly a case of lack of fit and not a rejection of me as a person.

The Job-Hunting Process as Experienced By M.B.A. Students

On January 1, 1975, a questionnaire was sent to 142 Harvard M.B.A.s who had graduated the previous June. The group was selected to be representative of the entire class. After follow-up, 83 percent of the sample responded. The conclusions that follow are based on an analysis of the first section of that questionnaire.

The average second-year M.B.A. spends about 175 hours between September and May looking for a job. This activity peaks in February and March.

Job hunting is a time-consuming activity for M.B.A.s. On the average, people spend one-half hour per week in September, one hour per week in October, three hours per week in November, five in December, eight in January, ten and one-third in February, ten and one-half in March, four and one-third in April, and one in May. Over all it absorbs almost as much total time as two semester-long courses. At the extreme, some people spend as much as 50 or 60 hours per week on job hunting in February, March, and April.

Comparing people who report high vs. low job satisfaction[1] seven months after graduation, we find the highs spent more

time on job-hunting activities in September through January and less time in February through June than the lows.

People who subsequently report high job satisfaction say they spend about 77 hours engaged in job hunting between September and January, compared with 64 hours for the lows. Between February and June the highs spend 88 hours while the lows spend 109 hours.

Most people reported that in September of the second year they really didn't have a clear picture of what kind of job they wanted after school. That picture, however, gets clearer each month right up to April, when most people report that they knew what they wanted.

On a scale of 1 (confused, not at all clear) to 5 (know exactly what I want), the mean report for September was 2.39, January 3.27, February 3.64, March 4.03, and April 4.25. Only 17 percent of the M.B.A.s knew what they wanted in September (reported a 4 or 5). Fifty-three percent of the group began their job interviews with less than a clear picture of what they wanted (reported a 1, 2, or 3). In April, 20 percent of the M.B.A.s reported they still weren't sure what they wanted (1, 2, or 3).

People reporting high job satisfaction seven months after graduation say they were less confused about what they wanted (than those reporting low) throughout the job-hunting process.

Twenty-one percent of highs vs. 33 percent of the lows reported that they were totally confused in September (re-

---

[1]People who reported they were "very" or "extraordinarily" satisfied with their job were included in the "high" group. People who reported they felt "neutral" or were "somewhat dissatisfied," "dissatisfied," or "very dissatisfied" were included in the "low" group. People who reported they were "satisfied" or "somewhat satisfied" were excluded in this comparison.

ported a 1). Six percent of the highs vs. 33 percent of the lows reported being still fairly confused in April (1, 2, or 3).

Placement Office activities and personal solicitation (on the part of the student) account for 92 percent of the contacts students make with potential employers.

The average student writes about 10 letters to companies, directly approaches two or three others, is contacted by seven companies because of the Resumé Book, and signs up for about nine interviews on campus. The faculty, ads in The *Wall Street Journal*, third-party recruiters, etc., tend to be unimportant in bringing students and employers together.

People who report low job satisfaction seven months after graduation report that they contacted (or were contacted by) more potential employers than did the high-job-satisfaction group.

In particular, the low group wrote more letters to potential employers, averaging 16 per person (vs. 12 for the high group).

The average M.B.A. focused in on about four types of organizations while job hunting. Those who subsequently reported high job satisfaction focused in on fewer types than those who subsequently reported low job satisfaction.

A typical person might, for example, seriously consider jobs with a few large diversified manufacturers, a number of medium-sized consulting companies, two government agencies, and some small electronics manufacturers. Some people focus in on just one type of organization, while a few look at nine or ten different types. Those reporting high job satisfaction say they focused on an average of 3.6 types vs. 4.1 for the lows.

The average M.B.A. actually interviews with about 11 different potential employers. Those who subsequently report high job satisfaction interview less than those who report low job satisfaction.

The high group has one or more interviews with 9.7 organizations vs. 11.5 for the low group.

The average M.B.A. got four job offers. Those subsequently reporting high job satisfaction got more job offers than those reporting low job satisfaction.

Thirteen percent of the sample received only one job offer, while one person was given 15 offers. The high-job-satisfaction group averaged 4.6 offers, while the low group averaged 3.8.

The average M.B.A. spent a total of 13 hours talking to seven people at his or her future employers before accepting the job. The high-job-satisfaction group talked to slightly more people for a longer time than did the low group.

"Average" is not terribly informative here because of the broad range. Some people talked to no one except a recruiter, while some talked to 25 people. Some spent up to 96 hours talking to people.

Forty-seven percent of the M.B.A.s took their highest-paying job offer, 35 percent took their second highest-paying offer, while the rest accepted a lower offer still.

Because 13 percent of the sample had only one job offer, this means that 34 percent of the group actually *chose* their highest offer.

Thirty-one percent of all respondents said job hunting was either quite or extremely emotionally difficult. The high-job-satisfaction group reported that it was less emotionally difficult than the lows.

Twenty-four percent of the total sample said job hunting was not emotionally difficult, while 45 percent said it was somewhat emotionally difficult, 24 percent said it was quite difficult, and 7 percent said it was extremely difficult. Forty-two percent of the low-job-satisfaction group reported it was quite or extremely difficult, while 28 percent of the high group reported it that way.

Comparing the types of organizations students seriously look at in December, January, and February to the types of organizations in which they eventually accept jobs, we find no great differences except in two "glamour" fields.

More students appear to have wanted jobs in real estate and investment banking than actually got such jobs. Generally, however, there were no obvious supply/demand mismatches. Even in the area of "small business," 14 percent of the class seriously went after such jobs and 12 percent found them.

Summary and Discussion

During the second year of the M.B.A. program, students spend a considerable amount of time job hunting. On top of regular course demands, one would suspect that this puts many students under considerable pressure. They rely almost entirely on the Placement Office and personal solicitation to meet potential employers. Most begin interviewing in January without a clear idea of what type of job they eventually want. Apparently a combination of interview-

ing, discussions with peers and advisors, and soul searching helps most of the confused people to decide fairly clearly what they want by April. For most of the students, the process of interviewing, visiting employers, and choosing is emotionally difficult, although in varying degrees. When the dust has settled in May, almost everyone has a job, and there seem to be no large mismatches between what students as a whole were looking for and what they got.

The job-hunting pattern for the person who subsequently reports low job satisfaction is one of confused passivity during the fall semester and a frenzy of ineffective activity during the spring. Writing more letters, looking at more types of organizations, interviewing more, this type of person ends up emotionally exhausted, with fewer job offers than most, and often still confused. The opposite can generally be said for those who subsequently report high job satisfaction.

XVII

The First Year Out

For many people the first year of work after graduating from school is a period of great challenge and excitement. It is a time characterized by considerable changes—a new job, new work associates, a new dwelling, a new city.

The first year out can also be a difficult period. In a recent survey of M.B.A.s six months after graduation, 62 percent reported that they were less than happy with either job, employer, career progress, or life style. Only 5 percent of those sampled reported no real problems since graduation.

Those who have studied the experiences of recent graduates have concluded that people who have a relatively trouble-free first year out tend to be systemically different from those who experience some difficulty. Specifically, those students who make more personally appropriate job choices, who start work with realistic expectations concerning what will follow, and who take an active role in managing their own "joining-up" process, seem to experience significantly fewer problems during their first year out than those students who don't. In this chapter we explore the nature and consequences of each of these patterns of differences.

The Impact of Job Choice (and Related Decisions)

As one might expect, many of the problems reported by people during their first year out can be traced directly to an inappropriate job selection. For a variety of reasons, some people make job decisions based on an incomplete or inaccurate understanding of themselves, the job, or both. These kinds of decisions invariably lead to problems and often to a change of jobs within a year of graduation. The experiences of Phillip Murray (reported in Chapter VII) are a good example of how even a bright and talented person can fall into this trap.

The same underlying causes that lead people to poor job decisions often lead them to poor decisions in other important areas of their lives. Recent graduates sometimes make inappropriate decisions regarding how to approach a new job, where to live, how to allocate their income, and so on. Again, an incomplete or inaccurate understanding of themselves, the option they are choosing, or both, creates first-year-out problems for them.

Underestimating how much he depends on the proximity of friends for relaxation and support, Bill Jones takes an apartment by himself in an area where he knows no one. Within three months his loneliness seriously affects his work. Helen Johnson, who never commuted more than a few miles to work or school before, finds exactly what she wants in a house about 25 miles from work. After moving in, she finds that it takes one hour to drive to or from work. The 10-hours-a-week commute eats into both her work and nonwork activities, creating a variety of problems for her. Herb Palmer is not really aware of how slowly he gets up to speed in a new situation, so he bases his decision to "not even think about work" after accepting the job offer on other considerations. The same is the case with his decision to take a six-week vacation and start work on August 1. When October 1 comes, all of Herb's contemporaries are well settled in their jobs and Herb's continuing awkwardness stands out like a sore thumb to him and others, including his boss.

As the above examples suggest, virtually none of the important individual decisions made just before or during one's first year of work are independent of the other decisions. Each decision tends to affect other parts of one's life in small and large ways, now and in the future. Insensitivity to the interdependence among decisions and their consequences inevitably leads to problems for many recent graduates.

Pete and Pam Marsh, for example, really wanted to return to a less urban part of the Midwest after graduation. Their families and many of their old friends were still there. Pete carefully looked for jobs in that area but found nothing really appealing. Bit by bit, he began to search in a wider area and he eventually landed a job, enviously considered by his friends to be "a find." The starting salary was good and the company would allow a long vacation period and pay moving expenses—to New York City! After a tense and anxiety-producing process, the Marshes agreed to accept the job. They found a decent apartment and put their six-year-old in school. Pam made some friends and so did their four-year-old. Pete threw himself into the job. Next came another "find"—a great house, close to the apartment, and at a good price. They moved. But after eight months Pete became increasingly frustrated. The job was not developing, and the company seemed less than supportive as time wore on. After 10 months he left. He wanted once again to look for jobs in the less urban part of the Midwest. But what of the child in school, the other child's friends, Pam's attempts to dig in, and the house? He ended up taking another job in the city. Their big-city life style in a short time quite subtly had become the constraint affecting Pete's job choice. It didn't start out that way.

Operationally, this means that in making important job and nonjob decisions one needs to take into account *all* aspects of one's life. The relevant system to analyze when making a job decision or a life-style decision is one's entire life system (see Figure 1).

FIGURE 1 A "Life System"

People occasionally like to deny that these decisions are interdependent. They want to believe that what they do at work and what they do out of work can be totally separated. They want that "freedom." As they soon learn, the world as we experience it today is one big interdependent mass, and the interdependencies are growing, not shrinking. And those who do not understand that, or who refuse to accept it, are in for a tough time.

Unrealistic Expectations

The change from student to employee is, in most instances, a very large change. Many people, especially those with little or no full-time work experience, tend to underestimate the size and nature of this change. They enter their job with very unrealistic expectations, based mostly on their student experiences. This leads to inappropriate behavior, which sometimes alienates others or is just ineffective at accomplishing given tasks. The end result for the individual is frustration and disappointment.

Consider for a moment a few of the major ways in which the environment of a student and that of a full-time employee differ:

1. *Bosses.* A student at any one point in time will have four, five, or six "bosses" (teachers), who usually change every four months, and who are often selected by the student. An employee usually has one boss, sometimes for years, with little if any influence over the choice of that superior. These different situations make for very different superior/subordinate dynamics. New workers sometimes continue to behave as if their boss were a professor whom they could ignore, or at worst, get rid of in a few months. Such behavior causes obvious problems.

2. *Feedback from Superiors.* A student learns to expect brief, quantitative performance evaluations (grades) on numerous specific occasions throughout the year. Such a person will often get written feedback on his or her work also. An employee, on the other hand, may *never* get any concrete feedback from superiors outside of pay raises or promotions. It is not unusual for new workers to feel that they are working in a vacuum and that the organization is at fault for not giving them more feedback.

3. *Time Span.* A student learns to think in terms of time cycles of one or two hours (a class), one week (after which a sequence of classes repeats itself), and four months (a semester, when classes change). The time span of an employee can be as short as a few hours (in some production/operating jobs) or as long as many years (in some planning jobs). More importantly, the time cycle can change on the job, often leaving the new employee confused and disoriented.

4. *Magnitude of Decisions.* A business student often gets used to making a number of major decisions (hypothetically) every day. At least at first, the new employee will rarely make any major decisions in his or her job. This often leads to feelings of being underused or ignored.

5. *Speed of Change.* Because of the pace of academic life and the number of major innovations and changes students are encouraged to consider, they often develop highly unrealistic expectations concerning the ease and quickness of making changes in the real world. Discovery of the realities is often quite frustrating and depressing.

6. *Promotion.* A student with a master's degree and no full-time work experience has lived in an environment where promotion occurred once every 12 months—

nineteen promotions in 19 years. It is no wonder that when a student takes a job five levels below the president, others often complain that "the young hot-shot seems to want to be president in just a few years."

7. *The Nature of Problems.* Schools often carefully select problems that can be solved in a short period of time using some method or theory that is being taught. Such a process is "efficient" by many educational standards. New workers often find it incredibly frustrating when the problems they are given aren't as neat and solvable and the information needed for a decision isn't available.

And we could go on, but the point should be clear by now.

Individuals also create a slightly different kind of unrealistic expectation through a poor assessment of themselves and the job while job hunting. The benefits of the self-assessment, opportunity-assessment, and job-assessment processes, described earlier in the book, go far beyond the job-offer decision. The very process of systematically assessing yourself, your future organization, and your job helps create more realistic expectations about what your initial experiences will be like in that job. More realistic expectations lead to fewer disappointing surprises and to more intelligent, adaptive, problem-solving decisions on your part.

Phil Hammer, for example, learned through his self-assessment how much he tended to overlook detail. He learned through his job assessment that his new job would require some (not a lot of) attention to certain types of detail. When he started work in his new job, he took specific actions to avoid a potential problem. First, he managed to rearrange his secretarial assignment so that he was assigned a person who was very detail oriented. Second, he explained his "problem" to his secretary, whom he requested as a major aspect of secretarial responsibility to keep track of details for him. Finally, he made it a habit to carry a note pad with him at all times and forced himself to make himself notes so that he wouldn't overlook things. After 12 months on the job, Phil had not created one single significant problem because of his personal "weakness."

Regardless of the source, inaccurate expectations cause problems for recent graduates. They cause poor performance, disappointment, frustration, and low morale. In some cases the organization concludes that the inappropriate behavior reflects a poor employee selection on their part, and the person is let go. In some cases, feeling "had" by the organization for not being warned about what was to come, the employee quits. In still other cases the problems are overcome, but seldom without leaving some bad feelings all around.

Managing One's Own "Joining Up"

Perhaps one of the most lethal expectations of recent graduates is that, in effect, "It is the organization's responsibility to make sure that the new employee gets the orientation and training needed to be able to do his or her job." Some organizations do try to systematically and quickly help all new employees get "up to speed." They have "orientation programs," "training programs," and "special first assignments." But very few companies do even a fair job of making sure that all new people get the specific orientation, training, and help they need to get "up to speed" quickly and efficiently.

Most people who have an effective, relatively trouble-free year after leaving school, explicitly or implicitly take responsibility for their own "joining up." Regardless of whether their organization has "programs" for new people, these people systematically take actions to help themselves get "on board." They recognize that if they don't take the initiative, and something goes wrong, they will probably have to suffer the consequences.

In assuming responsibility for their own joining up, people typically take a variety of actions both before they start work and immediately afterward (see Figure 2). While

FIGURE 2 Examples of Actions That Can Help a Person Get Up to Speed in a New Job

Before Starting Work

1. Get on the organization's mailing list.
2. Get your new boss's secretary to send you copies of memos, etc., that you would receive if you had already started work.
3. Request an organization chart and a book of pictures of employees (if one exists) and start learning names and faces.
4. Subscribe to the local paper in the town or city where you will be working.
5. Write to the Chamber of Commerce and real estate agents for information on housing, schools, etc.
6. Open a local bank account.

After Starting Work

1. Invite people to lunch to get to know them.
2. Get to know the secretaries (great sources of information).
3. If athletically inclined, join some of the organization's teams (a good way to form relationships informally).
4. Sit down and have a long talk with your boss regarding what he or she expects of you.

most students do virtually nothing between the day they accept a job offer and the day they show up for work to help their period of adjustment from school to work, others do a number of useful and practical things. By requesting an organization chart and a book of employee pictures (if available), for example, you can start to learn the names and faces of people you will be working with on your new job. Knowing who's who, of course, can be enormously helpful to a new employee. It's much easier for most people to do this in a leisurely way over a two- or three-month period instead of trying to intensely learn names and faces the first few weeks of work, when you are trying to learn so many other things too. As a general rule, the more that you can do before starting work to relieve the burden of your first few weeks on the job, the fewer problems you will face in your first year out.

A variety of actions that people sometimes take once they start work are designed primarily to assist their joining up. By sitting down and having a fairly long and detailed talk with one's boss, for example, regarding what he or she expects, you can help minimize the probability that you will inadvertently violate those expectations. Disappointing, surprising, or annoying your new boss during your first few months on the job can prove to be a major impediment to your joining up, since your boss is usually the key person who can help you during that period, or block your way.

Different people will no doubt prefer different specific tactics to help them once they have started work. However, two general rules of thumb seem to be universally applicable to aid the recent graduate. We'll end this discussion of the first year out by passing this sage advice on to you: (1) A modicum of humility usually helps. (2) So does listening very carefully.

Exercise

The case that follows describes one person's job hunt and first year out. As you read the case, ask yourself how successful a first year out will Bill Edwards have? What (in detail) is your conclusion based on?

Bill Edwards (A)

Bill Edwards was only two months away from graduation when he interviewed for a job at ATOC—an agency within the Atomic Energy Commission (AEC). Bill had majored in management at Bradly and had done very well. He had carefully chosen eight companies to interview, based on the data the Placement Office had posted concerning the interviewing companies and their openings. ATOC was the seventh organization that Bill had interviewed. The notice on the Placement Office's bulletin board said that ATOC needed people to work in their project management office. The projects involved were large, expensive, and important, the notice said. Compared to most of the other notices, Bill felt that this one sounded more exciting and offered a job with more responsibility.

ATOC had sent Jon Hollins to interview candidates at Bradly. Jon was a senior manager at ATOC, although only 34 years old. He was a very intelligent and affable man who had been handpicked by the agency head to interview at some key schools. Mal Davis, the ATOC Director, felt that someone like Jon made a much better impression at important campuses than "some hack from Personnel."

On March 28th, Jon and Bill sat down in one of the cubicles at the Placement Office to talk. They obviously hit it off very well and spent nearly an hour discussing a wide variety of topics. Specifically with regard to a job, Bill tried to make it clear that he was interested in a "challenging, important job." In trying to give Bill some feeling for the agency, Jon described his own job in some detail.

Basically, it's my job to manage a staff of about 80 people who in turn monitor and manage about 30 million dollars worth of projects yearly. This includes making sure that these projects, which employ a work force in the thousands, proceed on time and within their budget, and that they accomplish their objectives. One of the projects we monitored last year provided a breakthrough in solar energy concepts which could revolutionize the entire energy production system within 15 years.

Although Bill went through the motions of following up the other interviews, he was clearly sold on ATOC after talking to Hollins. Hollins too was impressed by Bill's school record and his conversations with him. In April, Bill was given an offer to work at ATOC, and he accepted it. Hollins sent Bill a letter in May with advice concerning getting a place to live (ATOC was located nearly 1000 miles away from the Bradly campus), and explaining when and where he should report to work. He pointed out that he would immediately begin a 1½-month training program before actually being given his first assignment.

Bill arrived at ATOC on June 6th. On the first day he spent most of his time filling out forms and talking to people in the Personnel Office. He briefly met Mal Davis. In the afternoon he was given materials for his training course and was shown where to come the following day.

The training course had one instructor, 10 students, and a format much like a good college course. Frank Belman, an instructor from a central training agency, was a very personable, intelligent man. He had designed the course himself two years before on the assumption that new hires would learn fastest if put in a learning environment similar to what they were accustomed to.

The course turned out to be very popular among the new hires. Frank was particularly good at getting them to work hard and to learn quickly. He was a warm and supportive person and found it natural and easy to encourage and reward students who got the right answers quickly, and who worked hard.

The subject matter of the course fell into roughly three categories: PERT charting and scheduling, budgeting and financial control, and project evaluation. Belman had located and was using the latest programmed learning texts for all three areas. The course was very intensive, since it covered the equivalent of three term-long college courses in a little over one month.

Bill Edwards did very well in this training program and reported to work on July 18th with a great deal of enthusiasm. He was escorted to the office of Frank Williams, who, he was told, would be his supervisor.

Williams had been with ATOC for six years. He was one of the supervisors in the Environmental Impact Group (see Organization Chart, Figure 3). He supervised nine people whose general job title was "Project Management Personnel." The typical PMP job is outlined in Figure 4.

Frank had been informed on July 2nd that Bill would be put into his section. However, Williams's section was to get no new projects for at least two months. Frank decided that it was too costly to really get Bill Edwards into an ongoing project in a complete way, and too risky to involve him peripherally. Frank had heard from Jon Hollins that Bill was a "good man." He was afraid that peripheral involvement would mean that Bill would end up doing all of

FIGURE 3 ATOC Organization

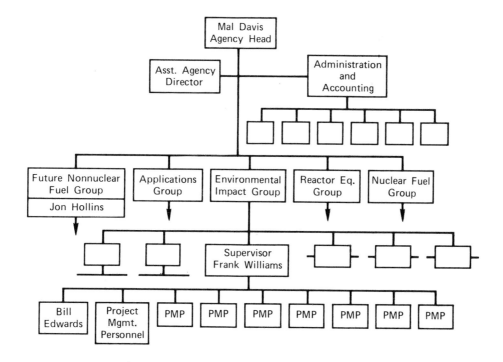

FIGURE 4 Typical PMP Job

Activity	Percent of Total Job
1. Talking with members of some project group, getting information from them, and trying to influence them in some way—watch money, speed up, don't overlook the objective, etc.	40%
2. Record keeping—recording, ordering, and filing data on time, money, etc.	35%
3. Technical—creating schedules and budgets, doing evaluations, etc.	15%
4. Other— wide variety of activities.	10%

the ''dog'' work, surely turning him off. Williams decided that his only practical alternative was to take one or two of his own ''back-burner'' problems and let Bill take a crack at them until a new project came in.

On the morning of the 18th, Edwards and Williams sat in Frank's office for nearly an hour chatting. Frank told Bill that he had heard good things about him and looked forward to his working at ATOC. He related a number of ''inside'' stories to Bill, including one about a man two years ago who had become a supervisor after being at ATOC only a little more than a year. Frank concluded the conversation by explaining that Bill would be given a temporary assignment that was, nevertheless, an important one to the agency.

In the next month or two I want you to find us a significantly better method for handling our internal personnel evaluations. The agency has never really taken a good look at this process. I know damn well that other organizations do a better job than

this. I've already thought of three or four places that you might visit besides doing some library work and general thinking.

Edwards took on the assignment with enthusiasm. It sounded important and challenging and gave him a lot of responsibility. For the next two months he spent nearly 80 percent of his time running around outside of ATOC talking to people, gathering information, thinking, and writing. He tried to make a habit of checking in with Frank twice weekly to let him know of his progress. Although Frank was a very busy person, he enjoyed talking to Bill. Frank was more casual about the frequency of their visits, however: ''It's not important that it be done at a certain time, it's important that it be done well.''

After nearly a month and a half, Bill was quite happy with his job. He was also pleased with Frank, although some things did annoy him. Frank had a habit of not being very helpful when Bill had questions. Being very busy himself, Frank tended to brush questions aside and do things for Bill instead of taking the time to show Bill how to do them himself. However, this complaint seemed small when compared to Frank's better aspects. He had given Bill an important and challenging job and was really very tolerant. The third day Bill was on the job he came in for just a few minutes to get something and bumped into Frank. Bill was terribly embarrassed, since he was dressed in levis and a sweatshirt. Frank had slapped him on the back and said that ''he didn't give a damn how he dressed as long as he did good work.''

On September 12th, Frank realized that he had a problem and went to his boss to discuss it. He had just learned that, due to three or four factors, his section would be getting no new contracts for another two months. Adding this information to the fact that Bill Edwards was just about to complete his first project, and that he was about to embark on a three-week vacation himself, Frank decided something had to be done. His boss reached the conclusion that Frank really didn't want to hear: "Bill's going to have to move out of your section into one that is getting a new project or two."

Before leaving on his vacation, Frank explained what had happened to Bill and expressed his delight over the work he had done for him. Frank also talked briefly to Ron Peters, the supervisor who was to be responsible for Bill now. He told Ron that Bill was "top notch." Ron, the second most senior supervisor in the agency, was delighted to get Bill.

On September 18th Bill went to work for Ron and was assigned to help handle a new project.

XVIII

Career Stages

Stages in Life

It was Sigmund Freud who first convincingly suggested that children go through fairly predictable stages as they grow up. These stages are primarily a function of natural physiological changes and (to a lesser degree, he believed) of the environments in which they are raised. Variations on and extensions of his ideas are now used by most modern parents in anticipating typical childhood problems, and in helping them manage their children's upbringing.

Erik Erikson was the first of a number of psychologists

and psychiatrists to suggest that adults, as well as children, displayed patterns as they grew older that were a function of both their psychological/physiological development and their social environment. In the past two decades a number of people have begun serious study of this subject, including Dan Levinson, Roger Gould, George Vaillant, Charles McArthur, and Gail Sheehy. Their work, to date, seems to confirm Erikson's basic idea. That is, they have found that many people within broad age groups face the same types of problems, opportunities, and issues. A summary of some of this initial research is shown in Figures 1, 2, and 3.

FIGURE 1   Erik Erikson

Age

Late adolescence–early middle age

Young Adulthood. Key issues: Intimacy vs. Isolation. Intimacy: The ability to share with and care about another person without fear of losing oneself in the process; need not involve sexuality. If a sense of intimacy is not established with friends or with a marriage partner, the result is a sense of isolation—of being alone without anyone to share with or care for.

Middle age

Adulthood. Key issues: Generativity vs. Self-Absorption. Generativity: Person begins to be concerned with others beyond the immediate family; with future generations and the nature of the world in which these generations will live. Active concern

with the welfare of young people. Failure to establish a sense of generativity leads to a state of self-absorption, stagnation, and often bitterness in which personal needs and comforts are of predominant concern.

Old age

Old Age. Key issues: Integrity vs. Despair. Major efforts are nearing completion. There is time for reflection, and the enjoyment of grandchildren, if any. The ability to look back on one's life with satisfaction gives rise to a sense of integrity. If one looks back at one's life as a series of missed opportunities and directions, realizing that now it is too late to start again, there is despair over what might have been.

FIGURE 2   Roger Gould

Age

16–18   Need to break away from parents. Still part of family of origin; think of selves more as members of family than as individuals. Autonomy is precarious, often fortified by negativism.

18–22   Feels halfway out of family; unsure about being pulled back in. Peer support important to break out of family, but demands price of subscription to group norms. Autonomy felt to be established but in jeopardy. Open to new ideas re the world.

23–28   Established, autonomous; feels "adult." Doesn't waste energy considering correctness of commitments made. Most of energy spent mastering what they are supposed to be. Still proving adult competence to parents. Self-reliance more important than peer or parental support. Commitment to spouse to make a good marriage. Living for "now"; growing and building for the future. Learning the proper emotional tone for adult life.

29–34   "What is this life all about now that I am doing what I'm supposed to?" "Is what I am the only way for me to be?" Marriage and career lives are established. Children are growing. Weary of being what one is supposed to; desire to be what one is. No longer need to prove oneself to parents. Spouse often acts as witness to former self, is seen as not willing to accept emerging "new" self. (Marriage absorbs and reflects stresses and strains.) Focus shifts from parents to children. Children become companions and love objects. Feeling of not making enough money to do what one wants. Increasing feeling that parents are cause of many unsolved, stubborn personality problems now being faced.

35–43   Continued questioning of self, values, life itself. Increasing awareness of a "time squeeze." Increasing tone of quiet desperation. "Have I done the right thing?" "Is there time to change?" Children seen as emerging end products of one's parenting and reflections of one's own worth. Conflict with parents muffled because they are aging. The finitude of time is felt; there is an equal eye to the past, present, and future. Spouse looked to for support. Work may offer "one last chance to make it big." An active social life seems less important. Personal comfort decreases; marital comfort remains at a low level. Early 40s are unstable, uncomfortable.

44–50   Finite time is resigned to as reality; one feels "the die is cast." Personality set. Eagerness, for friends and social activities, but often on a superficial basis. Active involvement with young adult children. Dependency on spouse for sympathy and affection. May regret "mistakes" in raising one's children. Money becomes less important. Feeling that it's too late to make major career changes. A reconciliation of what is with what might have been. Life settles down, becomes even. An acceptance of the new ordering of things.

50+   A mellowing; a warming up. Children seen as potential sources of comfort and satisfaction. Value spouse more. Greater self-acceptance. Little concern for past or future; the present is emphasized. Concern for time. Renewed questioning of the meaningfulness of life. One's work contributions to the world are renewed. A hunger for personal relationships. Concerns about health. An increasing sense of inability to do things as well as one once did.

FIGURE 3   Daniel Levinson, et al.

Age

16/18–20/24   LF—Leaving the Family. Transition from adolescence and the family of origin into the adult world. Half in, half out of the family. Making an effort to separate oneself from the family; to reduce dependence on familial support and authority, and regard oneself as an adult making one's way in the adult world.

Early 20s–27/29   GIAW—Getting Into the Adult World. Exploration; provisional commitment to adult roles, memberships, responsibilities, relationships. Attempt to establish an occupational direction. Begin to engage in more adult friendships and sexual relationships. Attempt to fashion an initial life structure that provides a viable link between the valued self and the wider adult world. May have mentor(s).

28–32   Transitional Period between GIAW and Settling Down. May take different forms. Examples:
(a) Question, then decide to remain in, the occupation chosen in the 20s. Get married, or reaffirm the existing marriage.
(b) Question the initial occupational choice, decide it was wrong. Make a major shift in occupation and life structure, sometimes including marriage.

(c) Lead a transient, unsettled life in the 20s, then feel a desperate need at around 30 to increase order and stability in one's life.

Often an earlier Dream (or vision of one's personal future) is reactivated during this transitional period, and a sense of betrayal or compromise of the Dream energizes a major shift in life direction. The Age Thirty Transition may occasion considerable turmoil, confusion, struggle with the environment and within oneself; or it may involve a more quiet reassessment and intensification of effort. People often have mentors during this period.

30s–early 40s   SD—Settling Down. Seek order, stability, security, control. Make deeper commitments; invest more of self in work, family, valued interests. Make and pursue more long-range plans and goals. Strive, move onward and upward; have an inner timetable that contains major goals and way stations, and ages by which they must be reached. Yet a disposition to be free—not tied to any structure no matter how great its current satisfaction or future promise; open to new possibilities, ready to soar and wander as the spirit moves one—frequently reappears toward the end of SD. The SD period often contains illusions—of autonomy, for example, or about the importance and meaning of achieving one's occupational goals—that are not totally realistic. People often have mentors during SD.

35–39   Becoming One's Own Man. A time of peaking. The high point of early adulthood and the beginning of what lies beyond. A feeling that, no matter what one has accomplished to date, he is not sufficiently his own man. Feeling of overdependence upon and constraints from those in positions of authority or influence. Sense of constraint and oppression may also occur in marriage and other relationships. Final giving up of all mentors by those who have had them. A desperate desire to be affirmed by society in the roles one values most. Try for that crucial promotion or other recognition. A fixation (between ages 39–42) on some key event in one's career as the ultimate affirmation or devaluation by society. Because the outcome of this key event takes several (3–6) years to unfold, the years around 40 are often ones of "suspended animation."

38–mid 40s   Midlife Transition. A turning point or boundary between two periods of greater stability. The Midlife

Transition occurs whether one succeeds or fails in the search for affirmation by society; it is only the form that varies. The sense of disparity between "What I've gotten to this point" and "What it is I really want" instigates a soul-searching for what one really wants. One may find his not inconsiderable success hollow or bittersweet. There is a sense of bodily decline, and more vivid recognition of one's mortality. A sense of aging; of being old rather than young. For men, an emergence and integration of the more feminine aspects of self, and changing relationships to women. The crucial issue at midlife is the changing relation to the self.

mid 40s   The Beginning of Middle Adulthood. A period of re-stabilization. A new life structure begins to take shape, to provide a basis for living in middle adulthood. A time both of possibility for developmental advance and of great threat to the self. Many men who don't have a crisis at 40 become terribly weighted down and lose the vitality needed to continue developing through adulthood. Others make large developmental gains through their crises. Levinson continues to study this and later developmental stages of adult life.

Patterns in a Career

A major part of the lives of working professionals is, of course, their career. The research on adult life stages, as well as the research on specific professions, suggests that careers can be usefully thought of as occurring in stages. For example, based primarily on studies of engineers, Paul Thompson, Gene Dalton, and Ray Price have suggested that professional careers occur in four stages:[1]

Stage I: Apprentice. "When an individual first enters his career, there are three main concepts he needs to learn: (1) how to make the transition from theoretical learning to applied technical work; (2) how to be an effective subordinate; and (3) how the informal social system and the political system work. This learning can occur most effectively under the tutelage of a more senior mentor. The junior person learns by helping the mentor with his work; quite often he is assigned the detailed tasks. To be effective in the first stage an individual must understand the goals of the mentor and help him achieve those goals, perform detailed work promptly and efficiently, be observant and willing to learn, and finally be aggressive and take some initiative. This is an important developmental stage because the junior person learns many important concepts, gains confidence in his ability, but most of all has the power of an established mentor to help and guide him."

Stage II: Independent Specialist. "The individual then begins to move out on his own, to have his own ideas and the ability to pursue them. The primary goal of this stage is to establish oneself as a competent individual and to be able to

work independently without constant supervision. To develop credibility and a reputation it is almost mandatory to specialize either in a content area or a specialized set of skills. Finally he needs to begin dealing with people outside his own little work group in order to gain what Jennings terms visiposure; that is, visibility to see what the organization or system around is like and how it operates; and exposure so people with power both above and lateral to the individual will recognize his work and ability.

"The basis of power at this stage is the individual's specialty. To exercise that power he must be able to ask questions intelligently, bring something original to the problem or project, develop a reputation, and understand how his technical problem will interface with the entire system."

Stage III: Mentor. "The overriding characteristics of the mentor stage is the broadening into new areas of technical application and involvement in other aspects of the organization. As he generates new ideas and projects, he recognizes the need to involve other people in the development of those ideas. Now, instead of doing all the detailed work himself, he can delegate much of it to other people, while still maintaining control. Thus his power is increased because of new, more encompassing ideas but probably more through the relationships he begins to cultivate.

"The individual's power and influence are additionally increased if he performs all of the functions of this stage in a competent manner. Some of those functions are: (1) being the driving force in the system, (2) taking the initiative for his own work and that of other people, (3) setting objectives and dividing the work effectively, (4) seeing how the talents of others can best be directed toward a particular problem or goal, and (5) focusing on communications both written and oral."

Stage IV: Developer. "As the individual begins to assess the outside environment and assists the organization in adapting to it, his credibility and influence are strengthened even further.

---

[1]From Raymond Price and Thomas Harrell, "Management Development: A Conceptual Model," Technical Report No. 11, NR 170-755. For more information on this model see Paul Thompson and Gene Dalton, "Are R&D Organizations Obsolete?" *Harvard Business Review.* November-December, 1976.

People both above and below him have greater confidence in his judgment both in terms of the direction the organization should go and guidance for their own careers. His power is based on an increase in his perspective, scope, and responsibility, in general his conceptual skills. In this manner his influence is extended beyond just a small group.

"The other major task of this stage, in addition to developing a direction for the organization, is the development of future key people. To perform this task well, he must be able to assess people accurately in the organizational environment."

This, of course, is rather early and tentative research. Nevertheless it is important, because for people who wish to actively manage their careers, the ability to correctly anticipate what the next set of opportunities and pitfalls will be is almost priceless. Although current research on career development is far from being able to provide people with a clear map of their future development challenges, it can, when combined with typical case studies, provide one with some very useful insights.

Exercise

Some of the recent literature on career and adult life stages is listed below. You may find it valuable to read some of this literature, to gain a greater familiarization with the subject matter of this chapter. What implications are there for your own career development?

DAVID ELKIND, "Erik Erikson's Eight Ages of Man," *New York Times Magazine*, 1970.

ROGER GOULD, "The Phases of Adult Life: A Study in Developmental Psychology," *American Journal of Psychiatry*, November 1972.

DANIEL J. LEVINSON, CHARLOTTE M. DARROW, EDWARD B. KLEIN, MARIE LEVINSON, BRAXTON MCKEE, "The Psychosocial Development of Man in Early Adulthood and the Midlife Transition," *Life History Research in Psychopathology*, Vol. 3, D. F. RICKS, A. THOMAS, and M. ROFF (eds.), University of Minnesota Press, 1974.

GAIL SHEEHY, *Passages: Predictable Crises of Adult Life*, New York: E.P. Dutton, 1976.

GEORGE E. VAILLANT, "The Climb to Maturity: How the Best and the Brightest Came of Age," *Psychology Today*, Vol. 11(4), September 1977, pp. 34–49, 107–10.

XIX

The Early Career

In the early phase of a career, usually between ages 20 and 35, people make and deepen initial commitments to a type of work, an organization, and a nonwork life style. Professionals, in particular, expend considerable energy to become competent (and recognized as such by others) in their chosen trade. It is usually an exciting period, in which one begins to try to fulfill expectations about the "professional me" that have been developing (through education) for two decades.

Four general sets of issues seem to be particularly important if one is to try to understand this early phase, the obstacles encountered, and the methods typically used to deal with them. One set of issues relates to adapting to being an employee in a complex human organization. A second has to do with getting established in one's work or organization and achieving some initial success. A third has to do with establishing some type of a workable relationship between one's career and the nonwork aspects of life. The fourth relates to a period of questioning of initial career and noncareer choices, which most people go through around age 30.

Adapting to the Realities of Complex Organizations

Most professionals start their careers within an established organization. Having been students in an educational setting for anywhere from 16 to 22 years, they suddenly become employees inside what are usually noneducational organizations. As we discussed in Chapter XVII, this change can create some serious problems for people in their first year of work. Beyond that, the ability to grasp quickly the more subtle realities associated with human organizations often makes the difference between a very

successful and an ordinary early career. Some of the more important of these realities are discussed below.

Distribution of Rewards

Simply doing what you think is a good job, or even a very good job, is no guarantee that you will receive the rewards you desire.

For a number of complex reasons, most established organizations do not have performance evaluation systems that (1) completely define what "good performance" is for each job, (2) make sure that employees are aware of those performance criteria, (3) systematically collect data on employees' performances, (4) feed those data back to employees so they can monitor how they are doing, and (5) use those data as the basis for distributing rewards (such as interesting assignments, promotions, money, discretion, etc.). Considerable evidence exists that such a system would be very beneficial for employees, especially during the early career. But because "good" performance is often difficult and expensive to define and measure, and because creating such systems where they don't exist is expensive and time consuming, good performance appraisal systems are very seldom found in organizations.

Instead, rewards are distributed in most organizations based on the "judgments" of a number of people (a person's immediate superior is usually the key judge), some of whom may have only secondhand information on many of the people they are asked to judge. People who are successful in their initial careers are those who perform well on the criteria used by the judges, and whose performance record is known by the judges. It is for these reasons that the better "how to" books on building a successful career stress (a) learning what your bosses' expectations are concerning your work and (b) getting involved in some highly visible projects.

Development of Potential

Most organizations have no coherent system to make sure that people, in their early careers, get the experience, training, and human contacts needed to really develop their potential for their own benefit and the organization's.

Although the development of people is an important goal for most organizations, it is a *long-range goal*. In most organizations, long-run objectives receive a priority lower than short-run concerns. For this and other reasons (e.g., expense) employee development is seldom given anything close to the resources needed to do a uniformly good job. Even in companies where resources have been allocated to employee development, and where training programs and job rotation systems have been created, numerous individuals seem to end up coping with short-run demands at the expense of their future development.

We have seen many former students who seem to learn more in their first five years of work than others learn in 15 years or more. The fast-learning group appear to be different from others in that they proactively take responsibility for their own learning. They seek out role models and mentors, recognizing that one relationship with a highly talented and successful senior person can be enormously instructive. They don't stay in any one job for more than a few years, taking advantage of the fact that almost all the learning associated with most jobs comes in the first two years. They don't wait to be assigned to new projects and jobs by others; they nominate themselves. In this and other ways they actively manage their own careers.

Dependency on Others

Most professional jobs in organizations, especially managerial jobs, make an individual dependent on numerous others, who often have different or conflicting objectives. Complex interdependencies and conflict are facts of life in most organizations. Individuals who cannot (or will not) find a way to effectively manage their own dependencies are in for a hard time.

Younger people in particular often feel their dependence on others who know more than they do about the job, the organization, the people, and how to get things done. Young managers will often find themselves dependent on the cooperation of subordinates, a boss, other senior officials, various service departments, and possibly even outside suppliers, customers, and regulators. All of these individuals and groups have limited time and talent, and their objectives sometimes clash with cooperation. Students are seldom if ever trained in how to manage this type of dependence network.

Managers use a wide variety of techniques to cope with their complex dependencies. Their techniques are sometimes aimed at reducing dependence, sometimes at influencing those on whom they are dependent to cooperate in certain ways, and sometimes at gaining power over the dependencies (which makes influencing them much easier). The faster a young employee learns to use these techniques effectively, the more successful he or she will generally be in the early career.

The larger and more complex the organization, the more time people end up having to spend managing interdependencies. For example, the following is excerpted from a 29-year-old manager's description of what he does in a typical day at a moderately large manufacturing company:

When I arrive in the morning I normally read the paper for 15 minutes or a half hour to catch up on the latest news. Randomly throughout the month I will call my boss before working hours actually begin, to let him know that I'm there and on the job, and he can reach me whenever he wants me. This is an important game to play in my situation, because he is located in a different building eight miles away, and sometimes he feels a little insecure as to whether all of his people are working full time and are doing the kinds of things he would like to have done.

I spend about one-fourth of the day actually here in my office. The table in the center of the office is the major working area, and it's round. I don't have a standard desk. This was something that I designed when I was promoted six months ago. The average age of my direct reports was about 47–48 years old, and I felt that it would be very difficult for me, being only 28 at the time, to sit behind a big desk and give these guys orders. They had 20 years of experience and knew the company backward and forward. There wasn't any way I could effectively tell them what to do. So I decided to get in a round table and to make sure that all the chairs around the table were of the same type and description so there wouldn't be any overt status difference between anyone in the office, so that we could build a teamwork relationship among all members of the group.

After reading the morning paper I would normally attend several meetings. I spend almost 70 percent of my normal day in meetings. By the way, that drives a lot of people nuts, and it bothers me too, but most of our meetings really are necessary. My peers and I have got to know what each other and top management are doing or we trip all over each other. Meetings are often the best way to get the information across. Meetings are also useful when I need the commitment from other divisions for some action, and when we have a problem but not all the expertise to solve it.

This would take me normally till about 10:30 or 10:45, at which point I would come back to the office and handle the mail. The mail comes in a stack of about 4 to 6 inches each day. I would quickly sort it and deliver messages to my staff to work on the projects and various assignments that came through the mail. I would delegate all the assignments with the exception of *politically* sensitive issues. Those I would discuss with the appropriate manager and handle then together with him. Normally it would take me 10 or 15 minutes to sort the mail and another 15 to 20 discussing the various sensitive issues.

This would bring me to around 11:30–11:45, where I would work on my personal mail, which includes salary and merit reviews, expense accounts, purchase requisitions, etc. This would take me right up to lunch.

After lunch, the schedule of activities changes, depending on what part of the year it is. During the first half of the year the work load is not as heavy as during the last half. During the first half of the year I would spend most of the afternoon in meetings of the type described earlier. In the latter part of the year I spend a great deal of time working on the annual long-range plan. This is a very extensive effort and requires hundreds and hundreds of man-hours of work to put together the details, schedules, and plans that support the strategies of this division. One of the reasons that this effort takes such a great deal of my personal time is that my boss' incentive salary depends on the achievement of many specific goals.

Parenthetically, this young man has had a very successful and satisfying early career.

Achieving

For most professionals, the early career is a period directed toward personal achievement. Considerable time and energy are invested in work and in establishing themselves as credible professionals with proven "track records."

In most of the cases we have observed personally, or heard others report, those people who achieved the most profesionally in their early careers were people who were able to generate what Doug Hall has called a "success syndrome."[1] As we have observed it, this process can be described as follows:

1. The new employee does not usually have a traumatic first year and is able to adjust rather quickly to organizational realities. As a result of careful selection or luck, the individual fits well with the organization and its work.
2. The individual gets some challenging initial assignments which, because of the lack of adjustment problem and the generally good fit, he or she performs well on.
3. This initial success bolsters the individual's self-confidence and helps him or her get challenging, more important (and visible) assignments.
4. The person's self-confidence, on top of everything else, helps him or her to do well in these next assignments.
5. These successes continue to bolster the individual's self-confidence and provide access to additional human and technical resources that are needed to continue to quickly grow and handle more important work.
6. The cycle continues, more or less dramatically, throughout the early career period. Success continues to breed success.

The "high flyers"—those who achieve more success in less time than 95 percent of their peers—seem to be people who position themselves to have opportunities come their way, and then take advantage of most of these opportunities. Eugene Jennings had studied this process in managerial careers,[2] which he calls developing mobility, and has identified the types of underlying rules associated with it. Those rules are:

1. Never become overspecialized. Get broad experience in a number of areas and always maintain your options.
2. Become a "crucial" subordinate to a very mobile and successful boss. If you find yourself working for an immobile superior, move.
3. Make yourself highly visible. Make sure your superiors know about your accomplishments and your ambitions.
4. If you are blocked and can't find a way out, leave the organization, but do it in a way that allows you to part as friends. Never allow a showdown to occur, and don't quit work with an emotional parting shot.

Both moderately and very successful people seem to reach a point late in the early career period where continued growth in their achievements requires that they be put "in charge." It is not unusual for professionals around age 35 to abandon their mentors and begin to feel frustrated because they don't have the power to continue producing even larger achievements. For many, this period doesn't last long, because they are soon put "in charge."

Establishing a Workable Relationship Between a Job and Other Aspects of One's Life

Most professionals develop two key commitments during their twenties—a commitment to get a job (or organization) and a commitment to an off-the-job life style (with or without a spouse, with or without children). The demands made on an individual by these two commitments periodically change in ways that conflict and put strain on the individual.

The following example, reported by a 28-year-old man who had established a successful initial career at a bank, is not atypical:

I usually get home by 6:00 P.M. My wife and I have got until at least 7:30 P.M. before we really have any time to exchange more than a "Hi, how are you?" By 7:30 we get the kids to bed. Sometimes we eat with Bobby, sometimes we don't. After dinner we do get some time together, even though we're both a little bit tired. Alice complains, with some reason, that I read magazines and newspapers during the little free time that we have together. We find that time is more precious than it was before. Ever since the baby came, we haven't been able to go to bed before 11 P.M. because that's when Alice completes her last nursing. Normally, we would try to get to bed earlier than that. We hope to resume our normal schedule as soon as the baby starts sleeping through the night.

We're thinking of moving out to the suburbs soon. There's not much for kids to do in the city. There are a lot of other reasons, though. One of our biggest problems is that it is just too damn expensive to live in the city. So we might buy a house—we're really looking into it now—but with a lot of mixed feelings.

Kids, I don't know, we didn't realize until after we had them how much time they require of you. They are just so damn dependent upon you. There's so much work involved with younger children that you've just got to reorder your life a bit. We found the change from being young marrieds without kids

[1]Douglas T. Hall, *Careers in Organizations* (Pacific Palisades, Calif.: Goodyear Publishing Co., 1976).

[2]Eugene Jennings, *The Mobile Manager* (New York: McGraw-Hill Book Company, 1967).

to being young marrieds with kids to be something more than we expected.

We have no real desire to go to the suburbs. It's just that it costs so much less to live in the suburbs than in the city. We can own a house, save money, and build up equity at the same time. But in the suburbs I would have a 45-minute commute. I don't like the thought of that very much. On the other hand, I should get to play a little more tennis out there. I have let myself go; I've gotten a little soft. The extra commuting will make time even more precious than it was before though. It's a rough choice . . .

Young professionals whose spouses also are pursuing careers often find it even more difficult to establish and maintain a workable relationship between their two jobs and an off-the-job life style. "Dual-career" couples who also have children usually find that their time and energy are very scarce resources (recall the case of Nancy Fuare in Chapter VIII).[3]

The work vs. off-the-job strains that develop during the early part of a career are not confined to married couples or couples with children. Single people often run into difficulties, too. Witness the comments of these two young men:

We're having a meeting next week out at St. Georges. This is the fifth week out of the last eight that I have been at one of these conventions. Many of these conventions are executive oriented, and many of the executives bring their wives. This creates an interesting situation for a bachelor like myself, particularly when most of the women are middle-aged and older. You see, they don't appreciate seeing me show up at each convention with a different attractive young woman.

I'm in a rather tough situation right now, and I don't see any relief in sight. I was given a promotion six months ago, and at 31 I am now the company's youngest plant manager—which, of course, is terrific. But, the promotion moved me from Chicago to Panto Flats, Texas, which has a population of about 6000. I would like very much to establish a permanent relationship with a woman, but unlike in Chicago, there just aren't many unmarried women around here. My nonwork life style, at this point, is very unsatisfactory.

There are three ways in which people generally deal with a work/nonwork conflict. Some people make changes in their nonwork lives that, in effect, reduce their commitment there. Many successful young executives take this option. One *New Yorker* cartoon captures this response well. A 30- to 35-year-old manager in a posh office holds a phone in his hand and displays a very annoyed expression. The caption reads: "Martha, how many times have I told you not to bother me while I'm on the way up?"

A second option some people choose is to take actions that reduce their commitment to work. Individuals who receive a great deal of satisfaction from their nonwork lives, and individuals who are disappointed in the amount of satisfaction they are getting from their work, both often select this option.

A third option people sometimes choose attempts not to

reduce the commitment to either work or other activities, but simply to allow the conflict to exist and to personally absorb the strain. The young plant manager from Panto Flats "solved" his problem by jetting to Houston and back an average of two to three nights per week, where he eventually did meet a young woman and got engaged. In the interim, he lived with less sleep and a special variety of jet lag.

Not everyone, of course, experiences the same amount of work/nonwork conflict during the early career. The people we have observed who have experienced the most conflict, and who tend to "solve" this problem in ways that eventually create even more conflicts and problems, make decisions in one aspect of their lives without considering the implications for the other parts. That is, they ignore, to some degree, the interdependence that exists between the various aspects of a life. We have even seen people who tend to be planning oriented create problems for themselves by planning only *within* their careers. People who behave this way are often able to survive during their early career, but the lack of total-life planning and decision making eventually catches up with most of them—often in the midlife period between 35 and 45.

Questioning Initial Choices

Most professionals seem to go through a period of questioning their initial work, organization, family, and life-style choices after about five to ten years. For some this is a mild period, while for others it can be fairly difficult and traumatic. As a result, some people abandon their initial commitments and make new ones; they sometimes change organizations, go back to school, start over in a new line of work in a new city, or get married or divorced.

People who make poor initial decisions—who start work with very unrealistic expectations, or who have serious problems adapting to their new environments, or who have trouble creating a workable arrangement between their work and nonwork lives—often find around age 30 that the satisfaction they are getting from the various aspects of their lives is less than they expected or desired. This leads them to a period of reexamination. A few are forced into reexamination and change. Some are fired. Others lose a key promotion they expected. The spouses of a few walk out on them. Even people who are fundamentally satisfied with their lives seem at least to pause and ponder their life situation around age 30. Is this what life is really all about? Have I really made the right choices? Am I responding too much to what I think I "should" do?

Those who actually make major changes as a result of this period of questioning are a minority, no doubt partly because of the difficulties associated with change. Unless one is in a highly unsatisfying position, change usually increases the pain one feels in the short run. Finding a new job, or breaking off a marriage relationship, can be a traumatic experience.

After the period of questioning is over, or after a change has been made, people generally plunge back into their careers with increased dedication and energy. For five to ten years they focus again on achievement in their chosen profession.

_____

[3]In Appendix D you will find a number of references specifically on the topic of dual-career families.

The case that follows describes one person's career and life between the ages of 27 and 34. Hardly typical, it is nevertheless very interesting for a number of reasons. As you read the case, consider these questions: (1) Why is Ben in the situation he is in? (2) What, if anything, should he do about it?

Ben Jerrow (A)

At age 34, Ben Jerrow was the youngest full partner in C. B. Kline and Company, one of the world's most prestigious management consulting firms. Jerrow, his wife, and three children led a very comfortable life on his $65,000 salary.

Except for a slight cold, May 12 (1974) was in many ways a very typical day for Jerrow. He left his Westchester home at 6:30 A.M. and arrived at his office in Manhattan at 8:00. At 3:00 in the afternoon he took a cab to LaGuardia, then flew to Pittsburg for what was scheduled to be a short planning meeting with one of his clients. Instead of ending at 8:00, however, the discussion dragged on until 12:30, at which point Jerrow headed back toward the airport in his rented car. At 1:15 A.M., about three miles from the airport, Jerrow fell asleep at the wheel and drove his car at 50 miles per hour into the back of a truck parked on the side of the road. At 2:12 A.M. Nancy Jerrow received a call from the Woodlands Community Hospital informing her that her husband was in critical condition in their emergency room.

* * *

Benjamin Jerrow was born and raised in Chicago, the second son of a behavioral science professor at a local college. His father served as a consultant to a number of organizations in the Chicago area, and Ben actually worked with him during his summers while going to school at Northwestern. After getting his B.S. in economics, Ben attended a Midwestern business school, getting both an M.B.A. and a doctorate. While in graduate school he married Nancy McKenzie. They had their first child soon after he began work at Kline in their Chicago office.

"I started work at Kline," Ben had said to others, "thinking I'd transform the place in a couple of years into something more competent and exciting. I suppose almost everyone who is attracted to Kline is that way: the five-letter men, the superstars, who just look at a problem and it gets solved. Which is to say, they are all very egocentric."

I remember my first assignment well. The old Buttersworth College was taken over by the Board of Regents for higher education in Illinois. They were going to transform a 3500-student technical school into a 30,000-student university in the course of five years, and ours was the mission to figure out how the hell to do it; how should you organize, how should you staff, and on and on and on. I remember thinking, well that looks easy enough.

What I didn't know at the time was that the study was badly negotiated, and even more poorly managed. Jim Welch was the study manager. He's about 5 foot 6 and had a mind that went about 400 miles an hour and a mouth that went about 500. Unfortunately they weren't quite in sync. Jim was very bright, but he could tick off the Good Humor Man. He was just unbelievable. We'd go up to Jim and say, "Here are the five

different organizational alternatives we've got," all laid out on charts. He'd say, "Where's the date?" "What do you mean, where's the date?" "Well, there's no date on the organization chart." Half an hour later after a lecture as to why dates are important, you grab the thing and say, "All right Jim, I'll put a bloody date on it." It was just interchange after interchange like that. In all fairness, every time he'd come up with things like that, there would be a message in it. You just had to pull the skin over your head to make sure it didn't absolutely destroy you.

About halfway through the study, or what we thought was halfway through it, Jim ended up crossing irons with the head of the Board of Regents commissioned by the Governor to get this college going. We had laid out the economic analyses and what the organizational and staffing alternatives were, etc. In that meeting, the chairman said, "No, no, that isn't what I really want. I want to know what the University of Illinois, the University of Chicago, Northwestern, and half a dozen other universities are organized like and I'll decide which type of organization we want." That isn't the way Kline operates. To make a long story short, it ended up with Jim ticking off the chairman and we got pulled off the study. It just ended right there. An absolute disaster.

Jerrow's second assignment at Kline was not a disaster, but his performance, as rated by the project manager, was close to being unsatisfactory.

I didn't know what the hell I was doing and I wasn't thinking very clearly. That was a phenomenal ego blow. It isn't that it hadn't happened previously in sports or whatever. Part of my game has always been that of the street fighter—I may not start out winning but by the time the thing is over I will. And it was clear at that point in time that I not only wasn't winning but it wasn't all that clear that I ever would. I had serious doubts about whether I was smart enough to be able to do it. I knew I worked hard enough to be able to get it done. I began to wonder whether I fit with them from a personal chemistry point of view, and so forth. In fact, I started looking a little for a job. I figured, forget this, I just gotta do something else. I got a couple of offers, none of which really seemed very exciting, but they did help my wounded feelings at that point in time.

Six months after joining Kline, Jerrow began his third assignment. He ended up traveling five days a week for the next six months with almost no break. His performance, as judged by more senior employees, rose to "average" during this period.

It was then I got my first little view of political infighting. I found ideas on this or that which we trade over cocktails or dinner circling back and being presented to the engagement director and the engagement manager by some people as their own neat new idea. I found that happened two or three times and it ended up tickin' me off a little bit. So I decided at that point in time, all right, I'll set you up with one that will give you 80 percent of the answer and when you get shot out of the saddle I'll come in with the other 20 percent and make it clear who the hell's idea it was anyway. Well, one guy got cut up pretty badly on that one. It was good clean fun.

After one year with Kline, Jerrow decided he probably wasn't ever going to "make it" there. He seriously considered taking a job offered as a VP for an $80-million-a-year industrial firm. The offer, however, came from a long-standing client of his Dad, and it wasn't ever clear to Jerrow whether the offer was made because of that relationship or because of his demonstrated abilities. He turned it down. "It got to the point where I didn't really give a damn whether I stayed at Kline or not. And that really helped in a way, because I started to be a bit more bold. I decided to take a number of calculated risks."

In July, on a plane from Montreal to Chicago, John Michaels (the head of the Chicago office) asked Ben if the project teams that he had seen since joining the company were different in any ways from what he had expected. Ben said yes, that they were about one-half as effective as he would have expected. A month later, Michaels sent Ben a note asking him to take on the administrative assignment of looking into the effectiveness of their project teams. In September, Jerrow put together an effort that included a questionnaire survey of all people in the Chicago office concerning the effectiveness of project teams and the methods by which they usually operated. He analyzed the results, gave them to Michaels, along with suggestions for corrective action. Michaels agreed with Jerrow's report and told him to go ahead with his improvement program. By December, almost everyone in the office agreed that the working climate had changed considerably for the better. Michaels was clearly impressed. "By early December, while I was far from being out of trouble, the bleeding had stopped and it looked like I was at least not going to be fired. By January this was virtually assured."

In February, Jerrow was asked to come and do a similar survey in the San Francisco office. In April, he was asked by the New York office (headquarters) to work with virtually every Kline office to evaluate and improve their effectiveness. By April, Jerrow was beginning to establish a positive reputation throughout the firm.

Kline had been anxious to make headway into the market for organization, manpower planning, and compensation studies, but had been relatively unsuccessful for the previous three years. With Jerrow's new visibility and reputation, principals in New York began to solicit and then listen to his ideas about how to get into these areas. They also began to ask his advice regarding the two or three cases in that area which they did have.

On May 10, Jerrow received a call from the managing director in New York asking him to take a look at a questionnaire they had developed as a part of a large manpower planning project they were doing for one of the 10 largest industrial companies in the U.S.

A couple of weeks later, I finally got the questionnaire. I looked at it, called them back and said it's dog meat. It's just not going to work. It's poorly designed. I don't understand really what you're trying to do, and so on. To make a long story short, they asked me to come to New York to help. I went, and found the way they were trying to go about the case didn't make any sense at all. I ended up spending five days a week there for the next two months—the Monday morning special going out and Friday night or Saturday morning coming back. We ended up completely changing the thrust of the study from one in which we were going to provide answers to one where we were going to provide questions. It served as the first real personnel diagnostic I think the firm had done.

With great effort, we finished just before we were scheduled to present the findings. Our presentation wasn't going to give the chairman the answers he was looking for. In fact it was going to raise questions that would make him as well as the whole personnel function look awfully bad. And I probably was a little overly aggressive on that one. I showed the presentation to the managing partner on the case (Bob Jordan) the day before the meeting, and he turned white. He said, "Oh, hell, we're dead. The chairman isn't going to like this even a little." But he didn't have time to change the presentation and he didn't really want to cancel the meeting or postpone it, so he made one of the other guys, George Elms, give the presentation with me there. It was one of those things where you figure, "That's it, baby, I better get the resumé polished up." The chairman sat there for 45 minutes or so just stone-faced. There wasn't a word that came out of anyone in this whole entourage of his. About three-quarters of the way through the presentation there was one specific piece of data that a personnel guy picked up on and started to blast. Elms couldn't answer the question and immediately passed it to me. I came up with one quick fact that put it all back into perspective again, while the personnel guy sat there smoking. He started to interrupt one other time and the chairman told him to shut up and quit trying to cover his ass and that he wanted to hear the whole story. That was when I knew we were in pretty good shape.

I pulled one other coup on that one which was unbeknownst to either Bob or George. I suspected the question that was going to come out of it was, "All right, what do we do from here? You've pointed out that things are in total disarray, how do we fix them?" I had half a dozen slides prepared the day before showing how to proceed from there. The chairman asked the question at the end of the session; Bob turned white and George turned red. We took a five-minute break and I gave the slides to George and—bang—we were right in for another 200,000 bucks or so with a new project.

In June, Jerrow was asked to come permanently to the New York office, with a healthy increase in pay. They moved in July, to the chagrin of his wife. "Nancy was thoroughly ticked off with me for being away too much, and moving to New York didn't really help any."

Kline began getting more contracts in the areas of Jerrow's interests, and he succeeded in developing a few techniques that were considered technical breakthroughs. One of his clients offered a VP job at a 75 percent increase in pay, but he turned it down on the basis that he was having a good time and learning a lot at Kline. When the annual spring announcement of new partners at Kline came, Jerrow expected to be named one. He wasn't.

It was a legitimate decision. The catch is that I had been led to believe I was going to be made a partner that year. And one other person made it whose track record wasn't as good as mine. I was clearly disappointed, and went out looking for job offers. I got two or three attractive ones, but each had some fatal flaw. And I began to think it would be smarter to wait a year and leave after being elected partner so there would be no questions at all about whether I cut it or not.

I learned later that Jerry York, a very influential partner in the New York office, had real trouble supporting my candidacy. Jerry is a silver-spoon type of guy, very bright, very good. I managed to finagle my way into doing a project with him, which was the first study we had ever done for this fairly complex client organization. The chairman was an old school buddy of Jerry's. It turned out to be a very interesting study and the beginning of a long-standing relationship—five years now—with the firm. Jerry was directing it and I was managing it. (For all intents and purposes I was directing it, too.) I got very close with the president of their major subsidiary as a result of our compensation work. It was clear that there were sticky problems of communications, trust, and direction between New York, which is where the headquarters were, and Los Angeles, where the subheadquarters were. This subsidiary represented 60 percent of their sales and about 90 percent of their growth potential.

The chairman of the corporation, Ted Young, knew there were problems but wasn't really fully aware of the magnitude. We had an intriguing session with him. I guess I had met with him twice prior to that meeting. The last item on a four- or five-point agenda was something innocuously worded like "closing the gap between Los Angeles and New York." I went through a brief academic description of what I saw were some of their problems, communicationswise, without really suggesting what the source of the problem was. Jerry began to get a little uncomfortable. Ted has a style of listening in which he will give you his undivided attention while you're talking and won't think about the thing until you stop. Then there will be a massive pregnant pause as he considers a reply. And he has a complete poker face all the time. You'd get absolutely no response—no laughter, nod, shake of the head. I was convinced that I wasn't getting through to him, and Jerry meantime didn't know what the hell was going on. He kept confusing the issue with general management platitudes about this, that, and the other thing. About 10 minutes into it, I said, "Let me try and put it as crisply and clearly as I can in terms of this last specific event we were talking about. You blew it." Honest, I thought Jerry was going to crawl under the table. He started talking about 84 different things at 100 miles an hour. Ted is sitting there with an absolute poker face. Five minutes later Jerry stops. Ted just sat there. There had to be what felt like a 10-minute pause, although it was probably 30 seconds or so. Jerry couldn't stand it any longer so he started back into it again. When he stopped, another 30-second pause, and he started again. Ted broke in and said, "Jerry, you're covering old ground. Ben, why did you tell me I blew it?" I said, "Two reasons: one, you did, and two, I didn't know any other way to get your attention." And then we started into it. Jerry was obviously sweating armpits through the whole thing. We made some major strides in terms of helping Ted understand what the problem was and what he could be doing about it.

Jerry and I have been good friends ever since. That was the turning point in my relationship with a number of the powers that be at Kline. If it was still a bit unclear whether I was going to make it at Kline, after that it wasn't.

Within six months Jerrow was elected a partner.

* * *

The 12-room Westchester home owned by the Jerrows sits on three acres of land overlooking a small valley. Approaching it from the road, all one sees at first is a large driveway bordered by woods on one side and by grass and flower gardens on the other.

A friend of Ben's stopped by on July 2, 1974, to see how well he was recovering. He found Jerrow in very good spirits, despite still being confined to either a bed or a wheelchair. The doctors had concluded a week earlier that there would be no permanent damage, but that he still needed a few more months of rest.

Nancy's been an absolute savior the last two months—especially just after the accident. She got in touch with Kline the day after the accident and gave my secretary the 48-item agenda I had planned for the next day and worked with her to notify people, and so on. She made it VERY clear that "No conversation with him is allowed. I don't care what your problem is, he just is not available." Two or three days after the accident, when I could see that projects were going down the tubes, my reaction would have been to start calling people from the hospital and setting up shop by the bed.

Three or four days after I got home, as we were getting ready for a medical progress review, about a dozen guys from Kline showed up. And I can remember just sitting out there thinking, "Well, you S.O.B., I guess you're really going to have to die before you are going to get these guys off your back."

That started me thinking. All right, if you're going to stay with Kline for any extended period of time you're just going to have to do some things to cut down on the work load, especially the physical demands. My average workday had been 10 or 12 hours, and then I'd have a 3½-hour commute on top of that. I'd spend some time with Nancy and yet have very little time with the three kids. So it would mean I'd get four or five, or if I was lucky six, hours of sleep.

I suppose if Nancy were less effective and less strong, then this thing may well have been precipitated a lot earlier. She's doing a super job raising the kids. We've always assumed that, you know, her job is to raise the kids and my job is to go out and raise the money. Now we're beginning to realize that really wasn't the way to operate.

Anyway, in the past week I've been trying to think out what my alternatives are. So far I've identified several.

I could try to cut back my responsibilities at Kline. Right now I'm responsible for all training activities for our U.S. offices, for secretarial and support services for the New York office, for three firm research projects, as well as a full client load. And that's insane. If I could just cut off a few things, to get the 65-hour work week down to say 45–50 hours, I think I could manage.

I'm unquestionably in a good position right now to go to the people at Kline and get them to take some of these things off me. What I'm afraid of is that because of the way Kline is, they won't stay off. Other things will come up and I guess I'm afraid that in a place where (1) there is an unending amount of work to be done, and (2) the norm is for everyone, or at least all the young stars, to work until they drop, it might not be possible to work a 50-hour week.

A second obvious option is to try cutting down the commute time. There are seven of us from the New York office that live within a five-mile radius of here, so why not open an office up here? It would be a working office—not for clients. Even if we still had to go into the city two days a week, that would save 10½ hours. And it would be so nice to be able to drive home for lunch.

This idea just might not be practical. Economically it's no problem. And I talked to two of the Kline people who live nearby and they think it's a good idea. But I don't know.

Of course, I could leave Kline. The thought has crossed my mind before. I've got one offer and two potential offers floating around right now. All three are for VP jobs in very large companies. The money in all three cases is very nice, as much as double what I get now. All three of them have the major drawback of being in New York City, which brings us back to the problems of the commute. In two of these there is substantially less travel involved. In the other there is about as much travel. I think in all three cases I could cut the work week back considerably. But I'm not sure. I've always had itchy fingers to run something and all three offer that. But I'd frankly just as soon not get bogged down in a bunch of administrative trivia. It's all I can do to screw up my courage to pay our personal household bills, and the fewer administrative things I have to worry about, the better I feel about it. In terms of types of people to interact with, it's one of the real negatives in leaving Kline. They are very bright, talented, creative kinds of people. You look at any of the corporate alternatives and, boy, they get very thin on talent very quickly in terms of stimulating your own thinking.

The final obvious option is to leave Kline and start my own consulting company. I really do think I've got some concepts and ideas that are unique and for which there is a huge market. And I've only begun to develop this business at Kline.

We can afford a lower income while I get started. I could set up an office somewhere here near the house.

Unlike the other situations, I'd be in control. One of the beauties about consulting on your own is that if you get cross-wired with a client, or you don't like what he's doing or whatever, you can say forget it. You can afford a hell of a lot more risk. So I take a 10 or 15 or 20 percent cut in pay—big deal. Once you get to a certain level, an extra buck doesn't mean that much. Yet, if I do well, I could make a bundle at consulting.

One of the problems in sorting out these options is that I'm still not sure how important money is to me. Our family really never had a hell of a lot of money, but we were always reasonably well off. I can still remember selling Christmas cards and cutting lawns, caddying and working in the local gas station and all of that sort of thing. I guess I was 10 when I started selling Christmas cards. I sold vegetables around the neighborhood. The next-door neighbor had a big garden and I would go out and pick his vegetables. He knew that I was picking part of them. I don't know if he knew I was picking all of them. I would just go peddle them to all of the neighbors. It was really one of those jokes—what's Ben going to be selling next? I got a job working in a gas station in the summers when I was 13 and 14. The summer when I was 15 years old my dad got me a job as a laborer in a plant. I did the playboy kind of thing between 16 and 17, starting as a lifeguard at the country club swimming pool and ending up as manager of the pool. And there was always, you know, one kind of outside extracurricular deal or another like getting the flower concession and hamburger truck at college. I often say to myself that money isn't really important, but then, I look at my behavior pattern and I say—who are you kidding?

When I first joined Kline, Nancy and I sat down and tried to specify what an idealized life style would be in terms of how we would like to live. Then we translated that into dollars and totaled it up. And then we made an estimate of what that meant in terms of yearly income. We passed that figure three or four years ago. I'm doing everything I want to do. I'm not driving a Ferrari and no, I don't have an airplane, but I don't have enough time to fly one anyway. No, I don't have a yacht, but I decided I don't like sailing that well either. I'd rather play golf. So maybe the money doesn't really mean a hell of a lot other than as a scorekeeping thing.

There's one other factor that's probably important here. Nancy is the only child of a guy that runs one of the largest privately held real estate development companies in the world. So, she and the kids are going to come out all right financially. Her dad and I have never really talked about it, other than to say that they are in pretty good shape, and I don't really need to worry a hell of a lot about that.

Jerrow paused and stared out the living room window at the valley below. "I don't know. I wish one of the options looked very good and clearly better than the rest."

XX

Mid- and Late Career

Problems at Midlife

Between the ages of approximately 35 and 45, many people experience a difficult period associated with career, physical well-being, family, or the like, that can range in intensity from mild to very severe. During this period people often get divorced, change jobs, or significantly alter their relationships with their families and their work. On the average, this period is more unsettling, and lasts longer, than the time of questioning that occurs for many around age 30.

The severity of the so-called "midlife crisis"—if, indeed, one experiences it at all—seems to be a function of how many problems converge with what intensity on a person's life at the same time. A person who experiences each of the common midlife problems mildly but at different times—may wonder what all the talk about a midlife crisis is about. Another who simultaneously experiences each of these problems in a powerful way might change careers, have an affair, move to an entirely new place to live, or even commit suicide.

To understand why some people experience a major crisis at midlife, while others do not, we need to see how and why these problems develop.

Career Problems

By age 35 to 40 most professionals know whether they will achieve the vague and specific career objectives that they have set for themselves. For many, the answer is that they will not. The evidence piles up that they will never become a company president, or a U.S. Senator, or a Pulitzer Prize-winning writer, or even the key person in the X Division of Company Y; it becomes clear that they will never have much, if any, impact on the automobile indus-try, or U.S. housing policy, or the next generation of computers. The more such a person, consciously or unconsciously, wanted to achieve these career goals, the greater the loss, and the more intense this component of the potential crisis.

Somewhat ironically, not only does career "failure" often produce a problem at midlife, so does "success." People who have worked for years toward a single goal or set of goals often find themselves feeling very uncomfortable and disoriented after achieving the goal. The drive that for years has provided a key part of the structure for their lives is suddenly gone. The striving behavior that they have become so accustomed to, and often received great satisfaction from, is suddenly inappropriate. Having reached the top of the mountain, they find that there is nothing really there and they don't like just taking in the view. Moreover, they miss the climb.

This problem of career success and failure is rooted in the early career, when adult life goals are initially established. It would seem that the narrower a person's definition in career-oriented terms of success in life is, the greater are the chances that he or she will experience this component of the midlife crisis. Likewise, the person who defines success in broader terms—that is, with multiple career, family, and personal objectives that have different time horizons—seems to be less susceptible to this problem.

Physical Problems

Many people become increasingly aware of their physical aging at midlife.[1] And for some this awareness comes as an unwanted shock of serious proportions.

---

[1]For an informative and highly readable discussion of the aging process, see Margaret Huyck, *Growing Older* (Englewood Cliffs, N.J.: Prentice-Hall, Inc., 1974).

At midlife people often find that they are physically unable to do some things anymore; they can no longer read without glasses, play touch football effectively, or work for 20 straight hours. They sometimes find that on their jobs they are no longer treated as a young, "up-and-coming" star; new employees even treat them as members of the old guard. And suddenly the prospect of death becomes a reality; startlingly, over a period of just a few years, both parents may die, and friends of their own age are killed or have premature coronaries. These losses, combined with the recognition that at 40 they are probably in the second (and *last*) half of their lives, hit some people like an unexpected fist in the face.

Again, it is easy to see how this problem has roots earlier in life. People who develop self-concepts during their adolescence and early careers that include as central elements ideas such as "I am a young star" or "I am physically able to do" this or that are much more likely to experience this part of the midlife crisis than other people. The same is true for people who have not experienced the loss of a friend through death, or have just refused to think about death as an issue.

Family Problems

A person's family can, and often does, also contribute to a crisis at midlife. Those with teenage children must often put up with the younger generation's need for authority figures to rebel against. If such a parent has previously gained considerable satisfaction from relating to the children, and if all his or her children reach adolescence simultaneously, this too can be a very unsettling change.

Relationships between husband and wife sometimes explode at midlife. During the early career, goals of spouses often are focused heavily in very different worlds; traditionally the male has lived with his career while the woman raised a family. Under these conditions it is easy for people to grow apart. And at midlife, they sometimes suddenly find they no longer meet each other's needs.

A common contemporary pattern that leads up to such difficulties is shown in Figure 1. Here the seeds of problems felt at midlife are again sown long before. The very contract that is the basis of the marriage during the early career helps create the explosion at midlife. Many professionals make it through this difficult period only because the alternatives—divorce primarily—seem equally cumbersome and onerous.

Coping with the Crisis

"Making it through" the midlife crisis can be a difficult experience for an individual and all those close to him or her. The changes people make—in their work and family lives—sometimes are impulsive and not at all helpful. But sometimes the crisis, and whatever adjustments people do make in response to it, lead to a very happy and productive period in their lives. Indeed, some who have looked into this subject would go so far as to say that unless one experiences a crisis of some intensity and then comes to

FIGURE 1 One Typical Form of a Marriage Crisis at Midlife

Ages	Wife	Husband
25–37	Vicariously enjoys husband's career and its rewards, while providing support. Suppresses feelings and:	Suppresses feelings and focuses energy on career achievement.

Gives	Gets
Emotional, Housekeeping, Maternal, and Sexual Support	$, Status, Security, Children

Ages	Wife	Husband
38–40	Kids grow up. She decides vicarious rewards aren't really worth it and begins to feel "had." She withdraws support and puts energy into personal growth and achievement for herself.	He has either accomplished all his goals or discovers he can't; in either case he ends up saying, "Is there nothing more? Gasp!" His suppressed feelings explode. His need for support skyrockets.
At age 41–45 leads to:	Leads her to think: "Why can't he hold together like a good husband so I can go out and grow without feeling guilty?"	Leads him to think: "What the hell is she doing running off in other directions while I'm falling apart?"

EXPLOSION in the marriage

terms realistically with the forces creating it, it isn't possible to lead a really fulfilled life afterwards.

How well one copes with a crisis in midlife is undoubtedly a function of many factors. One in particular is worth noting; we will call it "personal support systems." It has often been said that "no man is an island." This is particularly true in times of personal crisis. We need the understanding, the empathy, the sympathy, and the support of other human beings to help us keep things in perspective and to help us move toward a realistic resolution of our problems. And whether one gets this support in a time of crisis is very much a function of whether one has previously developed the needed system of personal relationships.

In this highly mobile world in which we live, it takes a conscious effort to build and maintain a personal support system. Without the effort, our own movement across the country and up in organizaitons will automatically break personal supportive relationships but not build them. And that can leave us in the position of one very successful executive who at age 40 found that "there is not one single person in my life that I feel I can discuss a personal problem with."

Generativity

A major theme in the mid- (and late) careers of most healthy, happy, and successful people is generativity. Eric Erikson, who first identified this theme in people's lives, has defined it as "the concern in establishing and guiding the next generation." Erikson postulated that all adults had to come to grips with this development issue in their lives or face psychological stagnation.

The most direct way in which adults concern themselves with establishing and guiding the next generation is by bearing and raising children. There are, however, other ways that people deal with this concern. Professional people, in particular, often seem to do it through their careers.

Managers achieve generativity by building organizations, by coaching younger managers, and by serving as mentors to still others. It is not uncommon for a successful business person to spend the early career involved in personal achievement, to get to the point where he or she is running the business around age 40, and then after a mild to moderately intense crisis period shift activities more and more to developing and managing others who in turn run the business. This type of activity often peaks around age 50–55 and then lets up as the person begins to disengage from work in anticipation of retirement.

By taking advantage of the generativity period in people's lives, some organizations gain a very important and valuable resource. All organizations need to somehow continuously acquire and develop employees. They need some mechanism to help attract new employees, to help new employees "join up," and to aid young employees in adapting to the realities of organizational life. Professional recruiters, formal orientation courses, and the like, are expensive. Middle-aged and older professional employees can often perform these functions in a way that gives them considerable personal satisfaction while saving the organization a lot of money.

Retirement

Retirement, whether it comes at age 60, 62, 65, or 70 or whenever, can be a big shock for people, especially those who are heavily invested in their work and career. Numer-

ous cases have been reported of people who retire from their work and soon afterward die. Suddenly stripped of a large portion of their lives and the satisfaction they derived from it, they just wither away.

People who go through this phase in the late career with the least trauma and problems seem to be those who have consciously or intuitively prepared for it well in advance. For people who successfully retire at age 65, the three to five preceding years tend to be a period of disengaging and planned adjustment. Such people often systematically develop multiple sources of satisfaction and fulfillment that do not depend on their full-time job. They begin to participate more in activities that they like but have never had the time to pursue. They find ways to do voluntary work in their profession. In the final year before retirement they often cut down the number of hours a week they spend at their job. As a result, retirement for them, although sometimes a fairly large change in their activities, does not represent a large shift downward in the total satisfaction they receive from living. Retirement is not then a gigantic, sometimes lethal, loss.

Successful managers often take on more and more civic, charitable, and government tasks between 60 and 65. Some "retire" into a full-time portfolio of interesting and exciting part-time jobs. Others rely more and more on their spouse and families as sources of satisfaction by taking vacations, improving the home, and looking after the grandchildren.

As modern medicine continues to lengthen life expectancy and as pressures for earlier and earlier retirement continue, we are moving into a period of history in which more and more people will experience a large part of their lives after retirement. The implications of these changes are not entirely obvious yet. It is clear, however, that until our social institutions adjust to these changes, the burden is on the individual to plan carefully for his or her retirement.

Exercise

The case that follows describes one person's career up until age 52. After reading Jerrold Hirsch (A), ask yourself, what should he do? Why?

Jerrold Hirsch (A)

Jerrold Hirsch, President, the mastermind and guiding force behind Compass 360, sat with members of his top policy group listening to a presentation by a management consultant. The consultant had been asked, by Hirsch, to make an assessment of the highly successful real estate firm. In the last dozen years Compass 360 had grown from a small three-man group in Denver to a national corporation with offices in 30 locations around the U.S.A. Hirsch had been wondering how to keep the growth momentum going through internal development now that the acquisition program had slowed down.

Historically, Compass 360's growth strategy had been to acquire an interest in small, generally weak, companies around the country. These companies had been offered the resources of the national organization in a management package consisting of proven financial and marketing pro-

grams, control systems, management techniques, and a successful recruitment and training program for newcomers to the firm.

Hirsch and his two most senior executives had been responsible for locating companies for acquisition and then ensuring that the resources and management philosophy of Compass 360 were applied to aid in their growth. However, while the search for new companies and acquisition negotiations had consumed approximately 60 percent of the time of the three senior executives, they had spent most of the balance of their time maintaining prime management responsibilities of the local Denver office, its clients and projects.

In reviewing his analysis, the consultant told the policy group:

In effect, the network has been starved of your attention while the Denver office has been suffocated by your playing line managers and preventing the younger managers here from having real responsibility. The scope of operations around the country is now outreaching what you as a group can adequately cope with by your hands-on efforts. So the firm is hurting; the network isn't developing internally, and the Denver managers are being held back by your inability to relinquish control over local operations.

The consultant paused as the room grew silent. Hirsch was starting to exhibit signs of restlessness. He stared at the consultant, who continued:

What I suggest is that you formally split yourself off from the Denver office and form a corporate level of national executives. Denver then becomes another local office—at the moment the biggest and most profitable—and you treat it much the same as any other office. At the national level you concentrate on planning, policy, and strategy for the entire firm, new acquisitions and internal management development—in fact nothing much different from what you're doing now. You will have to develop programs for those green kids you've got out there who are trying to learn the Compass 360 way but have got no one to show them how. Their own managers don't understand your marketing and financing concepts, but you have all been too busy to help them because you've been playing nursemaid in Denver to some already competent local people.

What I'm saying is that if you want this company to grow internally you've got to do a full-time job for the entire organization, not just Denver. And I want to warn you—it isn't going to be easy psychologically or any other way to give up local involvement and turn the management of your projects over to someone else. But I believe it is essential. You've just spread yourselves too thin to be effective any more—and the numbers are starting to show it!

The atmosphere in the room became uncomfortable and the silence intensified. No one moved. Hirsch sat still, his face beginning to show signs of anger. He stared directly at the consultant. Then, in a controlled voice, he said: "What the hell am *I* supposed to do in this new setup—spend my time looking at reports and addressing Christmas cards to clients? You're trying to turn us into a bloody monolithic structured organization—and that goes against everything I believe in."

The Early Years

Jerry was a lonely child with few close friends. His father, who worked long hours trying to establish his real estate business, had little time for Jerry and for activities like fishing or playing softball. The Depression years did not help bring father and son together, as Hirsch senior fought for the survival of his business.

In 1940, as was expected by his parents, Jerry prepared to go to college. He didn't have any preferences either academically or vocationally. At best he was a halfhearted student and managed to flunk out of college in his first year.

The United States' entry into World War II gripped Jerry's imagination as nothing else had done. He rushed off to enlist. It was a crushing disappointment to find himself rejected because of a leaking heart valve, the aftermath of a bout with rheumatic fever at age 13. With the opportunity to do something "useful" so abruptly cut off, he groped around for something else that would give direction and meaning to his life. As friends around him went off into the service, Jerry found himself "the only 20-year-old guy in the world not in the war"—and his depression grew.

He found work as a cashier in a bank, but rapidly grew tired of it. When he went in to the bank manager to quit, he was asked why he wished to leave. Hirsch replied, "Because the job is very dull." "Young man," responded the bank manager, "one of the things you will learn in life, and you might as well learn it now, is that *all* jobs are dull."

Hirsch didn't believe that. He was certain that somewhere out there in the working world was something that would capture his fancy; but what was it? He didn't want to work for his father; however, to keep from starving while he looked for something better, he took a routine job in the real estate firm. Not exciting, but not horribly boring either; and it gave him time to think.

After some months Eleanor, whom he had been dating for several years, urged him to go back to school. She was pursuing a degree in education and felt further formal education would be a prerequisite to any career Jerry might later wish to enter. Having nothing better to do, he decided to return to night school. After a couple of semesters, he transferred back to day school and began full-time studies once again. He continued working in the real estate firm on weekends and occasionally at night. After three more years he finally completed the requirements for his bachelor's degree. Now, in 1945, he was back at the same place he'd been four years earlier—namely, what to do with himself?

Jerry and Eleanor decided to get married. When he announced this decision to his parents, they were vehemently antagonistic—Eleanor wasn't good enough for him. Her parents were immigrants, and although she had completed her bachelor's degree his parents felt she just wasn't a suitable partner for their son. Not deterred by this opposition, Jerry and Eleanor decided to go ahead. At their graduation ceremony, while both sets of parents sat (separately) in the audience waiting for the awarding of degrees and attempting to catch a glimpse of their robed offspring, Jerry and Eleanor slipped away from the campus, packed a few things at their respective homes, and eloped to San Francisco.

On their return to Denver, Jerry visited his parents. He was greeted by a demand for the return of his house keys and office keys—he was out of the house and out of a job. "You made your bed, now go sleep in it," were his father's parting words.

So once again Jerry had to look for work. He soon found a job with another real estate firm in town. But things were slow, and after a year he was becoming bored and frustrated. With some experience behind him, with his license in real estate, and with a pregnant wife, he sought a reconciliation with his father. In 1946 the firm of Hirsch and Hirsch was formed. Jerry took over the responsibilities of managing the office and tried to strengthen the organization.

The Middle Years

By the mid-1950s Jerry had gained confidence in his own abilities and experience in dealing with the business community. He had joined the Toastmasters' Club, a group that gave local managers help in improving their public presence by public speaking. He worked at learning as much as he could about the nuances of real estate.

During the decade of the '50s, Jerry continued working for his father. He was earning more money, and the practice, while not growing rapidly, was profitable. Jerry and Eleanor, now with two young daughters, were starting to enjoy the manifestations of middle-class affluence he had learned from his mother and father. By the time 1960 arrived, it appeared he had achieved most of what he had been striving for: two cars, house in the mountains, comfortable life style, etc. Jerry was determined not to deprive his children of emotional support as he had been deprived as a child. He devoted time to the family, to social activities ". . . to the garden, bowling, golf, bridge, and poker—the standard suburban shtick. It was a good time—we took a cruise to Europe which we loved. It appealed to my aesthetic side—I have read a lot of European history, philosophy, and art and for the first time it all came alive."

At the office, however, all was not going as well as it might. The first major setback started during the recession of 1957–58 and culminated in 1959, when the biggest client being serviced by the firm suddenly pulled out. Lacking the flexibility to cut overhead drastically, the firm suffered considerable loss of income. Jerry, however, experienced a sustained build-up of pressure and the arrival of an intense two-year-long depression. His attempts to build an organization that could shed the vulnerability of small companies to the loss of their better, more successful clients seemed to have failed. He was seriously concerned and began thinking about getting out of real estate completely and trying his hand at something else. But it wasn't so easy—the life style, the house in the suburbs, the teenage children approaching college age. . . . A period of intense self-evaluation followed:

I was 35 then. . . . I started looking around at what I had and what I had achieved. I asked myself what was it all worth? I really wanted to build something substantial, not a way of life subject to the loss of a major client. I had some ideas about motivating people, encouraging them to grow and find expression as the firm grew. But I just couldn't find the levers, I guess. I was completely demoralized and depressed. I talked it over with my doctor when I had my check-up. You know the kind of stuff: "I don't know what's wrong with me, doc, what the hell's it all about, the purpose of life." And you know what he said that straightened me up? He said, "There ain't no purpose to life!!"

Jerry started drinking. There had been some bouts of drinking before, dating back to his college days, but this time: "heavy . . . heavy . . . heavy. I mean, I just crawled right inside a scotch bottle and stayed there. It was brutal."

The Deals. On several occasions Hirsch had attempted to develop ventures outside the real estate business. In 1947, shortly after joining his father's firm, Jerry had met a man

with an idea for developing plastic furniture. It looked good and Jerry got together some financing—his own savings, some of his father's money, and bank loans. But the joint venture with the "ideas" man soured within a matter of months. The deal did not get off the ground, and Jerry, who had put almost no time into the venture, pulled out, a little wiser and a lot poorer.

In 1954, with the plastic furniture fiasco still fresh in his memory, Jerry once again launched himself into a part-time business venture. This time the product was printed circuitry, but the deal was essentially the same. Hirsch did the financing while his partner contributed the idea. Again, the venture lacked the necessary components to make it successful; his partner lacked sufficient technical expertise to continue development to a successful product and Hirsch was splitting his time between the real estate business and the new venture. After a year it was clear they were going nowhere. As he had done the last time, Hirsch attempted to pull out; but this time it wasn't so easy. In fact, he was unable to extricate himself and his interests before the venture went under. The consequence was a considerable loss of capital and a bruising learning experience. Laying people off, sealing off buildings, hiring guards to protect property, and encountering threats to life all proved to be difficult and painful experiences. Hirsch described the entire situation as "ugly." Once again his naivete about business ventures had been exposed. He vowed never again to go into another partnership deal.

But in 1960, with the real estate business apparently faltering and with Jerry feeling depressed and ready to quit, he found another deal. He went into partnership with a man who had a small manufacturing business making a product that promised to radically improve gas mileage in automobiles. Again, the deal was essentially the same; Hirsch would supply the financing and the other partner would supply the product. This time Hirsch checked out both the product and the man a little more carefully. He approached his father for capital; he sunk just about all his own net worth into the deal and secured additional loan financing. Hirsch hoped the venture would really fly and he could withdraw from the real estate business.

Within six months most of the capital had been eaten up and the business was practically on the rocks. Hirsch had spent considerable time away from the office and, with the loss of the major client, the real estate business was also in trouble. Hirsch was working flat-out 24 hours a day, 7 days a week, trying to save the automotive venture from bankruptcy. He was also hitting the bottle hard.

My back was really to the wall financially. You don't know the meaning of the word "overexposed." I mean things were a complete shambles. And in the middle of all this, while everything is caving in around my ears, Eleanor goes to see a lawyer. I felt completely betrayed, stabbed in the back. I'm in no condition for a divorce. So I make peace: "You want this—OK; you want that—OK." Man, I was really disgusted though and I wasn't about to forget this little piece of "loyalty."

Hirsch decided to put all his efforts into rescuing the automotive venture. He abandoned Hirsch and Hirsch to his father and to the three new managers who had joined in the late 1950s. Jerry felt that these managers would take over, allowing him to devote his energies entirely to the manufacturing business.

The automotive venture somehow survived the next few months. Then they came up with a new marketing and financing idea: they would franchise the distribution and sale of the product. The partners would continue production while organizing franchising sales meetings. They would be able to ship out the inventory, and at the same time get the franchisees involved in the business. The idea worked; sales began to pick up and the venture started to get itself out of financial difficulties. "The business was really moving. 1962 was our big year—sales of about a quarter of a million. We had a long margin on it, because when you're selling a franchise you mark up pretty good." However, the venture ran into a major legal problem that threatened to end it abruptly. Franchise holders were enjoined from selling the product to their customers.

So what happens is that all the franchise holders are stuck with the inventory, and potential new franchise holders want to check with the old franchise holders to find out how the stuff is selling before they accept the franchise. They find out there haven't been any sales, so all of a sudden both franchise sales and final sales of products drop off. By December of 1962 we were back in the same position as March of 1961, with the thing starting to go down the drain again.

Meanwhile, the real estate business of Hirsch and Hirsch was running into deep trouble. Jerry's lack of attention to the business was being felt.

The whole thing began to run downhill, increasing speed all the time. The managers just didn't seem to be able to put on the brakes or to figure out what exactly the hell was going wrong. So here I am with potential failures on both hands: on the one hand, the sales of this automotive accessory look like they're done forever; and on the other, the real estate firm, to which I'd devoted so much time and energy in the early 1950s, also looks like it's about to hit the skids. It all happens at the same time. I decide the only thing to do is try to wind down the franchise thing and see if I can get out without going through bankruptcy. That's where I spent the winter of 1962, while the managers were trying to get the real estate firm back on solid ground. I finally got the venture wound down with no bankruptcy, but at a horrible cost financially.

Building the Firm. Hirsch had some major decisions to make. The manufacturing business had collapsed, leaving him deeply in debt. The real estate business was suffering; its revenue had decreased substantially and was generating very little income for Hirsch. His marriage was on the rocks and his children were showing signs of emotional problems. And he was drinking very heavily and suffering from an acute depression. "I had the option of crawling away under a stone somewhere or grabbing hold of the situation. I guess I just figured it was really time to dig in my heels and get something going."

Drained by his experiences, Hirsch took his family off to Hawaii for a vacation. The desire to build something substantial and to put into practice some of his own ideas on management remained to be fulfilled. He decided to commit his physical and emotional energies to building Hirsch and Hirsch.

Back in Denver, Hirsch threw himself into the real estate business, working long hours, six days a week. He started to reorganize the office staff, began an intense review of all office practices and policies, established a client review to assess the quality and profitability of all current activities: "What they had been desperately wanting was strong leadership—and I am a good manager. I just crunched into everything and everyone pretty good. I felt great—I was really getting committed to something and it was fun."

With Jerry now firmly committed and in charge of the business, Hirsch senior decided to retire. Although in good health, he was approaching his 70th birthday, and was seeking to reduce his involvement in the firm.

It took about six months for Jerry to stop the decline and start to turn the office around. With the business now stabilized, he started implementing his building program. In Hawaii he had decided he was less interested in the real estate business as such and much more interested in applying the concept of franchising. His outside ventures had taught him a lot about partnerships—and he was determined not to make the same mistakes again! The franchising approach was sound, he felt, even though the previous experiment had run into legal problems. As Hirsch thought about building the real estate business, an idea hit: Why not build a national network of real estate acquisitions through a franchising package?

Something like this had never been tried before. Why the hell not? I wasn't prepared to sit on a small local business any more. I wanted to build an organization that had the potential of turning on and exciting those who worked in it. No standardized systems, no formality, just a bunch of bright young people being creative, growing, and helping the business grow.

Having cleared the legal position for the idea, Hirsch and his managers sat down and began working out a franchising package. For the next year they read books, discussed options, and sought outside assistance. Hirsch was doing what he enjoyed best—coming up with new ideas and convincing his more sceptical managers. Within a year, the group was holding franchise meetings in Denver and arranging contacts with acquisition prospects. "We were well received. It was fun polishing up our own concepts and attempting to excite others with our ideas. We were looking for established businesses that for one reason or another had stopped growing." In 1963 the first deal, in Miami, was consummated and the process of building a national network had begun. During the next seven years a series of franchises followed in rapid succession. The strategy was aimed at gaining minority interests in small real estate companies. These would then form a network across the United States operating under a unified corporate label.

We named the operation Compass 360 back in 1963. I knew I could really do it once I had swung the Denver office around simply by determination and lots of hours. Developing new concepts, influencing others, and putting it all into practice made those years particularly fulfilling ones for me.

Some of the early acquisitions were of marginal companies, because Hirsch felt it more important to build a national framework quickly rather than wait for the "right one" to come along. Occasionally, the acquired owners were content to move slowly, resisting the new concepts and programs they had acquired from Compass 360. On other occasions, when a location had been targeted for a Compass 360 office, but an acquisition prospect was unavailable, Hirsch and his fellow managers would attempt to open their own office. As the Denver office grew, younger employees, who had gained experience in the real estate business, were transferred to a new location to start an office. "Perhaps the biggest kick came when we sent out a couple of the younger guys from Denver to open a new office near Los Angeles—and they made the thing *fly*. It meant that my concepts really worked, and they worked Compass 360's way." Considerable effort was directed toward recruiting young staff who were prepared to grow with the firm and accept early responsibility.

I'm a strong believer in human potential. My resentment of huge structured organizations is that they stifle human growth and development. I wanted us to develop a philosophy that would encourage people to grow and not crawl into a box in an organization chart and stay there. When our Denver people went out and grew an office from nothing, it proved to me that our philosophy worked. All the hours I spent with those people were worth it.

By 1970, Compass 360 had attracted a sizable reputation in its industry. There were now 18 offices throughout the United States, with Denver the largest and most profitable and six others developing internally using the Compass 360 approach. However, many other offices remained shoestring operations and had not developed. In many cases this was due to a lack of attention from Compass 360 management. While Hirsch and his managers attempted to help these slow-moving offices grow, most of their time and energies were spent in looking for new acquisitions and managing the Denver operation.

By 1971 the merger program had dried up, owing partly to the economy and partly to the unavailability of suitable acquisition prospects. Compass 360 was now experiencing difficulties in generating growth. The weaknesses in the organization were becoming apparent: Real growth was coming from just a handful of offices in the network.

In response, Hirsch started to concentrate on the task of management development and specifically on devising a national training program. He read prolifically in the management literature to develop his ideas, and he called on outside consultants in management training. The purpose was to find a way of developing a common ideology.

There was nothing binding us together. We were a bunch of disparate groups coming from different backgrounds. We never deluded ourselves that we could convert all these people to the Compass 360 way. I wasn't looking for a vast homogenized organization—in fact, that goes against the grain. But we were emphasizing good recruitment procedures for new staff, and we had to sort of rescue the young potential from the old hacks. We started pouring enormous sums of money into this activity, hoping to develop a younger generation of good motivated managers.

In addition, Hirsch initiated activities to clean up the debris within the organization. This involved committing resources to organization development and to "pruning and clipping." A consultant was hired to monitor the offices needing help. An internal team of consultants, consisting of the most effective people in the organization, started attending to the improvement of technical, financial, and marketing skills in the offices around the country. Hirsch concentrated on neutralizing the negative effect of some of the older "died-in-the-wool" managers and on developing the skills of the younger members of management. But he accepted only with great reluctance the necessity to "neutralize" the older, acquired managers.

I have a real problem with the kind of confrontation that leads to me chopping a guy's head off. I figure there's something wrong with me if that's what it boils down to. I don't know if this is good business or not. Maybe it's just a matter of personal style. But I kind of have a moral hangup about that kind of thing. I keep working with the guy and working with the guy. . . .

A further move was a major reorganization of the acquisition arrangement. The franchising concept was terminated and the "franchised offices" were consolidated into a total corporation. Hirsch commented:

All my life I had this ambition to establish and build something. Now, with the entire organization consolidated, I felt as if I had achieved something. Call it a monument if you like, but for me it was the personal satisfaction of having had some ideas, sold them to others, and implemented them.

The decline of the economy in 1973 severely affected the real estate business, and Compass 360 was no exception. In fact, economic uncertainties only tended to show up the weaknesses in the organization. The pressure was on Jerrold Hirsch again:

You know, I'm seen as some kind of organizational guru, the ideas man, the philosophizer. I like coming up with ideas and I'm good at it. The convincing process I like, too—the motivation aspects of selling ideas to others. But when things turned sour more and more, I was thrust into the front line. The good guys wanted me to throw out the old-timers who hadn't produced. Everyone was on my tail. Everyone wanted Jerry to make it all better, and no one really wanted to stop bitching and get on the stick themselves.

In the spring of 1974, in the midst of these problems, the consultant reported back to the top management group and recommended the establishment of a corporate level of national executives to oversee the business. Hirsch was angry and over a few drinks shared his feelings with a friend.

I knew it was my initial concept that had founded the firm, and I also knew it was my day-to-day efforts that kept it going as well as it was. And now along comes this know-it-all consultant and tells me not to interfere with the day-to-day management here in Denver. Instead he wants us to structure our organization.

I enjoy the person-to-person contacts with the important clients, and I enjoy the day-to-day relationships required to make the business go. I don't like to be a figurehead; I'd rather work behind the scenes and make things happen. I've never been much for sitting out at the front desk to greet people when they come in and want to talk to the President or the Chairman of the Board. Nor do I like big organizations much. They're all controlled by systems. The personal touch is lost. The idea of heading up a large formal organization repulses me. I'd just be a figurehead in a corner office, and the real decisions would be made by the systems.

I don't believe in it—it's against everything I've tried to build. It would make Compass 360 just like any other large organization—and we're not. We've got something unique here in our philosophy. It's the people that count, and the informal interaction we have helps them learn and encourages them to grow. I'm not about to let this consultant turn us into a dehumanized straitjacket organization with levels and boxes. He says that's what happens when you grow, you need systems, but I don't want to lose what we've got—we manage by people not by control systems and structures.

The constellation of events—the decline in earnings, the consolidation program, the pressure to remove ineffective managers, the consultant's recommendations—had produced in Hirsch a reassessment of his current position and of the options available to him.

I'm 52 years old now, and the crack I made about the Christmas cards is no idle chatter. I mean I just can't see what my role would be. Do I want to get into a structured "corporate headquarters" situation—and give up building?

There's a fair amount of money I would get if I decided to get out now. I don't have to worry about eating. I could walk away from it; if it survives, I can get a pretty large payout from it, and I can go do something else, or I can go do nothing. At several points in my life, especially when I was younger, I've really enjoyed doing nothing. Haven't had a chance to do much fishing for the last twenty years or so. Maybe I'd enjoy getting back to that.

What I'm afraid of in a new role is that I would have to give up the building aspect that I so much enjoyed, and move on to some kind of stewardship position. Not necessarily a figurehead, but at least in order to be functioning in that category, I'd have to adopt a completely different kind of style, I'd have to learn new techniques, learn how to run a big company. And I don't know whether I want to do that. With ego and everything else, I still don't like to front for the firm. I'd rather have other people do that—people who like it. I don't like being the head in terms of everybody saying, "There's the Chairman of the Board." I just don't like it.

Look at my alternatives. One, I can stay with the business, and continue running it just the way I have in the past. After all, it's my business, and I'm under no obligation to accept the recommendations of this consultant, whose fee I'm paying to begin with. Or, two, I can accept the recommendations and start immediately to set up a national corporate office. Now, if I do this, I recognize that I am going to have to get out of the day-to-day active running of the business, because if I try to maintain that same management style after I set up a national office, the thing is just not going to fly. That style isn't compatible with a national, centralized office. Or, three, I can take my money and get out. Henry and Larry, the Vice-Presidents, are pretty competent. I don't think, if I got out, the thing would go down the tubes again. Maybe it would, I don't know. But at this point, let's assume that the thing will continue to run just fine without my daily attention. Well, if that's the case, then there is really nothing to prevent me from getting out. I can take my chips, cash them in, and live very comfortably, which gives me time to do nothing and enjoy myself—get some of the relaxation I'm overdue to have after all these years of nothing but work. I don't have to worry about my children—they're both grown and married, and anyway they'll inherit my father's dough. So they're pretty independent. My relationship with Eleanor is like a nonaggression pact. We stay together because it's easier that way.

I could probably use some rest. You know, a couple of years ago I went to my doctor for an exam. I've never told anyone this but he checked me over, shook his head, and said, "You amaze me. With your heart, I'd have bet you'd be dead by 40."

Another alternative I've got is to take my money and start looking for something else to get involved in that is going to provide the new challenges and the opportunity for hands-on management I've so much enjoyed in the past.

Well, as I say all this to you, it sounds like it's the kind of decision I should be able to make just based on logical, rational considerations. I can describe for you the alternatives, and I can describe for you the pros and cons of adopting each one. But what I can't describe so easily or so well is the big knot I feel down in my gut as I contemplate having to decide just exactly what the hell I'm going to do with myself at age 52. What we're talking about here is a complete change in what I do with myself 24 hours a day, a complete change in what I do with my mind; and I frankly don't know how good I'd be at doing anything else. It took me a long time to find my way to this business, which, as the record shows, has obviously been very successful. But suppose my management style, suppose my own personality, the way I'm put together, doesn't lend itself to a different kind of venture or a different kind of activity? Then what? Am I just setting myself up for yet another business failure? Remember now, I've had three serious failures on the way to my one success with Compass 360. At my age, I don't need another major failure. While it's easy to say I can take my money and run, I don't know if I can just take my money and sit on it; or go fishing, while I invest it in some very secure investment. After a week or a month or a few months, will I still find it possible to continue doing nothing, or will I have to get back into some activity? And, will I be able to find something at which I have as good a chance for success as I already have with the business I've built at Compass 360? I don't know. I really don't know what to do.

Hirsch fell very silent and ran his finger around the lip of the near-empty glass. Just then the waiter reappeared. "Another round please, Charlie."

XXI

Managing a Career over Time

A professional is called on to make decisions related to job and career throughout his or her life. From the time we leave school until the time we retire, we are faced with a continuous string of questions, such as:

- How should I approach my new assignment?
- Should I try to get the marketing research job when it becomes available next year?
- Am I spending sufficient time on my job now, or am I spending too much?
- Should I quit my job soon and go into business for myself?
- If the vice-president asks me to go to Europe to open up a new plant, should I accept?

The careers of Ben Jerrow and Jerrold Hirsch rather clearly illustrate that the quality of the answers to these questions is directly related to the quality of our lives.

The approach to making these job and career decisions so far is summarized graphically in Figure 1. In this final chapter we will discuss how this approach can be used, not only to make one or two important initial career decisions, but to effectively manage a career over time.

The Decision-Making Model

The approach to job/career decision making shown in Figure 1 begins with a self-assessment process characterized by

1. the use of multiple sources of data which have been carefully selected, and
2. thematic analysis, based on explicit logic.

This type of process can generate the accurate self-awareness which is the cornerstone to our whole approach. That self-understanding makes systematic and effective opportunity assessment, option generation, and option analysis all possible.

The approach to identifying, securing, and understanding opportunities shown in Figure 1 can be characterized as highly proactive and based on a reasonable understanding of the realities of job hunting, career development over time (e.g., career stages, adult development, etc.), and your own character. These processes can generate options that you will find attractive, and that you will understand.

The approach to the actual decision-making process shown in Figure 1 is made up of two components—analysis and choice. The analytical process is characterized by the rational examination of each option in terms of its impact on the various interdependent parts of one's life, and the projection of the most probable events into the future for each option. The choice process is then characterized by coming to grips emotionally with each of the options and then choosing one and building emotional commitments toward it. Together these processes lead to a rational decision which one is prepared to implement.

With one modification, this systematic approach to making job- and career-related decisions can be used throughout your career. And that modification relates to the self-assessment and opportunity-assessment processes.

It obviously is not necessary, every time you wish to make a job- or career-related decision, to do the type of self-assessment outlined in Part One of this book or the type of opportunity-assessment and option generation described at the beginning of Part Two. Those processes are designed to give you self-awareness and understanding of opportunities in general that can support decision making over a period of time. Only when those understandings grow out

FIGURE 1 Career and Job Decision Making

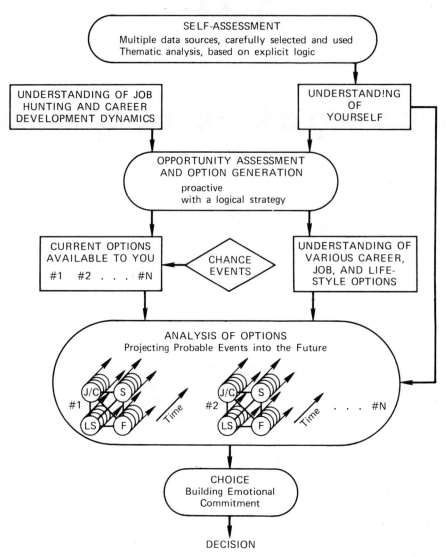

of date do the processes need to be repeated, in whole or in part.

Reassessment

Keeping an up-to-date assessment of yourself and your opportunities requires periodic reassessment. Our observations of people who seem to effectively manage their careers suggest that at least three different types of reassessments are needed (see Figure 2).

At least once a year it seems useful to sit down to systematically review your performance, the satisfaction gained from work and other parts of your life, and any indications of problems that are not being addressed. This one- or two-day review might usefully be scheduled soon after a formal job performance review if your organization has a performance appraisal and feedback system. If it does not, then the ball is squarely in your court to proactively seek out this information.

Once every three to four years, a more detailed analysis

of how you and the world around you are changing can be very useful. The questions you address here are: Do any of the assumptions about myself and my opportunities used in my last complete reassessment need to be altered because of changes in the last few years? If yes, what are the changes? Do they call for some type of change in my current career or life situation?

This type of assessment takes more than a day. In structuring it, three-day to one-week career planning seminars that are offered by some companies to their employees and by some consulting firms to the general public can be very helpful.

Finally, about every seven to ten years one needs to take the time to do a complete reassessment of the magnitude described in this book. Setting aside the time to do any of these reassessments and structuring them is extremely difficult, but this one is probably the most difficult of all. Assessment centers of the type that some companies are now developing can be helpful. So can professional career counselors and structured sabbaticals (such as to a three- to four-month program at a university).

FIGURE 2

Activity	Intensity	Frequency	Sources of Input and Help
General evaluation of year's performance and of satisfaction with various aspects of life. Any problems?	One or two days' worth of work.	Once a year.	Organization-initiated formal performance appraisal. Conversations with important others in your life.
Analysis of changes in you and your opportunities. Are changes needed?	Up to a week's worth of work, at one time or spread out over a few months.	Every three or four years.	Three- to seven-day career planning seminars.
Major reassessment of self and opportunities.	Of the magnitude described in this book.	Once every seven to ten years.	Assessment centers. Career counselors. Three- to four-month university programs.

The Challenge

Many professionals get on a track during their twenties as a result either of carefully made choices or of chance events and then chug along that track for a lifetime, never looking to the left or right or up. They don't ever stop the train to seriously reevaluate their situation, even if they recognize that the ride is not as much fun as it used to be. Some people go throughout life this way. Others, like Ben Jerrow and Jerrold Hirsch, have their trains derailed by a sudden boulder from the sky and are forced to do some reassessment. As you might expect, being forced into a major reassessment and change during one's mid- or late career can be a very painful experience.

It's amazing how many excuses people can invent to avoid reassessment exercises. And this tendency is exacerbated by most professions and organizations, which provide people with little or no help or encouragement for reassessment. Often both individuals and organizatons avoid the subject of individual career reassessment out of an uneasiness—let well enough along, don't open up Pandora's box.

One of the biggest challenges you face in your career is to use the tools and knowledge you now have regarding career management and not to let yourself slip into a self-induced career coma. Dealing with the challenge requires awareness and self-discipline on your part, because while you may receive some help from elsewhere (more and more organizations are providing career planning workshops, assessment centers, and counselors each year, but the total amount of such services is very low), the burden rests mostly with you.

Although the amount of available support for career management is not as great as we might like it from the point of view of society, it does make career planning in one sense even more attractive for the proactive individual. Today a person who is willing and able to use the ideas presented in this book to manage his or her career has a real competitive advantage. In a world that currently supplies considerably less money and fewer interesting jobs than people would like, competitive advantage is very important. The ideas here can give you an edge. Use them!

A POSTSCRIPT TO PART TWO

To help you use the information in Part Two of this book, turn to the career development paper assignment in the workbook. This assignment is designed to assist you in thinking out the job and career implications of your self-assessment paper. Like the self-assessment paper, this paper requires considerable effort, but it can be extremely rewarding. For an example of a good career development paper, see Appendix B on page 209.

A

An Example of a Self-Assessment Paper*

BY JOE BRUNSWICK

Introduction to Method and Mechanics

The first part of this assessment paper deals with the development of personal themes. Using the various data-generating instruments, I attempted to identify bits of information that, when viewed collectively, said something about who and what I am. For each group of data so collected I came up with a descriptive statement or phrase that attempts to capture some common thread in the data. My process was to assemble data from the instruments, label them, and then make a summary comment. This comment summarizes where the data came from and highlights any question or implication that I can see in them.

After each theme is a number indicating the number of data points comprising that theme—an indication of its importance. Before each data point is a code identifying where that datum came from. The first letters indicate the source document. The code used is as follows:

Code	Document
WI	Written Interview
HT	Hand Test[1]
AVL	AVL Study of Values
BSA	Graduate School Application[1]

D	24-Hour Diary
RT	Rorschach Test[1]
ST	Strong Vocational Test[2]
LS	Life-Style Diagram

The code "FR" indicates that the data came from the Feelings Record for the document identified by the initial code.

For the Written Interview, the second code indicates the question number from which the data came, and the third number indicates the page.

For the graduate school application, the second number indicates the page and the third number indicates the question number.

For all themes, a plus sign indicates positive supporting data, while a minus sign indicates contradictory evidence.

Part II of this paper uses these themes to make statements that have implications for job, career, and life-style decisions. After each statement the source themes used to derive it are identified by means of a parenthetical listing of theme numbers (the numbers refer back to the 26 themes listed in Part I).

---

[1] Joe Brunswick used some data-generating devices not specifically dealt with in this book. Chapter IX refers to a number of other data-generating devices.
[2] Joe Brunswick used the earlier version of the Strong-Campbell Interest Inventory.

*This has been chosen as an example of a good solid paper. It is not meant to represent the best that can be done nor even one of the best that we have ever received.

Part I: Thematic Analysis

1. Develop Special Competences/Be a Pro (21)

WI, I, 2	(+)	Biggest thing to happen during childhood was beginning to play baseball
WI, I, 4	(+)	Richmond Falls . . . open spaces . . . good place to develop my baseball skills
WI, I, 4	(+)	Must have practiced a million hours
WI, I, 4	(+)	First career aspiration . . . become a professional baseball player
WI, I, 7	(+)	Started to play pool . . . got good
WI, I, 8	(+)	Just seemed to search for special competences that would make me "attractive"
WI, I, 9	(+)	Learn how to play guitar
WI, I, 9	(+)	Decided realistically I wasn't a *pro calibre* ball player or guitarist
WI, I, 10	(+)	College . . . academically . . . I really wanted to do well
WI, I, 11	(+)	Felt I needed more technical competence to sell myself
WI, III, 1	(+)	Deciding on material, arranging, practicing, booking jobs . . .
WI, III, 2	(+)	Most professional band
WI, III, 4	(+)	I had to gain some work skills
WI, V, 1	(+)	I like the competence you feel when you have a lock on the financial numbers and angles
WI, III, 2	(−)	Field audit was very technical, accounting-oriented . . . (took other job)
WI, VII, 3	(+)	I was worried about whether I could master the chemistry needed to be a really good sales-man . . . if I couldn't be a *great* salesman I wasn't interested
WI, VII, 3	(+)	Grad school would give me technical marketing competences
WI, VIII, 1	(+)	Wouldn't have come if I hadn't gotten into a *good* school
WI, VIII, 2	(+)	Feeling of a lack of a marketable competence
BSA, 3, 6	(+)	Success in IRS schools was important . . . *skills* in income tax law, criminal law, detection of fraud
BSA, 5, 9	(+)	Joe, there's no percentage in being average at anything

Comment: Of the 21 data points, 19 or 90 percent came from the Written Interview; the other 10 percent came from my B-School application. The common thread seems to be to try to gain expert power—the power of being really good at something. I don't have to be the absolute best, but I'm not satisfied as long as I feel I could do better. This theme is quite strong because of the large number of data points and only one piece of contradictory evidence. This one point related to a competence that I feel represents a rather commonplace, unspecial, boring competence—accounting. I don't feel that the dependence on one instrument (Written Interview) distorts these data, since related data (e.g. athletics, active orientation) come out in other themes and from other instruments.

2. Logical, Pragmatic, Realistic Approach to Problem Solving (19)

WI, I, 9	(+)	Made realistic assessments . . . not *pro calibre* baseball player or guitar player
WI, I, 9	(+)	Super band . . . girlfriend . . . decided to go to local college
WI, I, 10	(+)	Rules of game—good jobs, good money
WI, I, 11	(+)	Made a "deal" with myself
WI, III, 2	(+)	Some of the guys got *carried away* by our success
WI, III, 2	(+)	Quit band for several reasons . . . we weren't good enough . . . doing well in college
WI, III, 2	(+)	Careful to ensure that band's goals were . . . *not* get off on some star trip
WI, III, 3	(−)	Decision wasn't because of any long-term appraisal of what I wanted my career to be
WI, V, 1-2	(+)	I like the competence you feel when you have a lock on the financial numbers and angles. Marketing to deal with people's motivations, and your product's niche in the market
WI, VII, 1	(+)	I decided I didn't want to leave home because . . . bands and money . . .
WI, VII, 2	(+)	Special Agent's job was something I could qualify for, whereas Audit's accounting requirement was more than I had . . . so I applied for Special Agent job
WI, VII, 3	(+)	I didn't feel I had the *information* to make that decision
AVL	(+)	Economic score #1 @ 58. Theoretical score tied for last @ 31
BSA, 2, 4	(+)	Emphasize practical over theoretical
BSA, FR	(+)	All entries on application were fitted into space provided; didn't feel free to use extra pages
D	(−)	Sat. 7:30: Concern over lack of big picture
RT	(+)	Start with Big W or D and proceed to little d and back to big D
RT, FR	(+)	Felt I had to be realistic. Limited by the data, I felt uneasy in trying to make something out of the entire image if I couldn't get everything to fit. This led to frustration. . . . Not being able to see the whole picture I resorted to trying to see a lot of smaller images, i.e., go for production
ST	(+)	Within Group II, Architect, which deals with application of sciences, was three times greater than the average score of the remaining theoretically oriented activities

Comment: 63 percent Written Interview, 5 percent AVL, Diary, and Strong, 11 percent B-School application and Rorschach. Perhaps the most interesting fact came from the Rorschach Test and the Feelings Record, in seeing the frustration I had from trying to make all the pieces fit and being limited by the data.

3. Money, Economic Success, and Security (18)

WI, I, 5	(−)	Family wasn't wealthy, but I can't remember wanting for anything
WI, I, 7	(+)	Kids who were popular were rich, pretty kids . . . Weejuns
WI, I, 10	(+)	Rules of game—good jobs, good money
WI, I, 10	(+)	Exposed to affluent living . . . came to accept these goals as desirable
WI, III, 2	(+)	We were all money oriented and businesslike
WI, III, 2	(+)	Careful to ensure that band's goals were only to make money . . .
WI, III, 3	(+)	I guess I decided to take the job because the money was good
WI, V, 1	(+)	Money is important because of the security and freedom it brings
WI, V, 2	(+)	Thinking about leisure-time industries, but I wonder about *growth* possibilities
WI, VII, 1	(+)	I decided to stay at home for several reasons . . . bands and money
WI, VII, 1	(+)	Didn't think there was enough money in education to want to be a teacher
WI, VII, 1	(+)	I didn't think about the job so much as I did about the fact that I could make more money
WI, X, 1	(+)	I just wanted to make money . . .
WI, XI, 1	(+)	Money became a major theme
WI, XI, 1	(−)	Money was important . . . but quality of work experience and perceived prestige of that job became crucial
AVL	(+)	Economic score the highest @ 58
BSA, 3, 6	(+)	Middle-income squeeze . . . realized lucrative potential in bands . . .
BSA, 4, 7	(+)	M.B.A. gives higher starting salary . . . greater salary potential

Comment: 83 percent from Written Interview. I feel that the theme relates strongly to a desire for security.

4. Small Groups, Friendly and Noncombative Relationships (18)

WI, I, 3	(+)	Felt need to give Harry a symbolic gesture of my leaving . . . important to me
WI, I, 5	(+)	Dad and interaction with other truckers . . . joke around . . . funny, good-natured
WI, I, 7	(+)	High school more difficult . . . instead of 40 people, you're thrown together with 400 people
WI, I, 10	(+)	Developed a lot of warm personal relationships with co-workers
WI, I, 10	(+)	Disliked role . . . dealing with people in an exclusively *combative* manner
WI, III, 1	(−)	Until I was let down a few times . . . then I was a real hard ass
WI, III, 4	(−)	I worked by *myself* and really got into the job
WI, IV, 2	(−)	Jay was kind of a guy who liked to take charge. So did I, and that caused problems
WI, IV, 2	(+)	Jay liked to take *charge* . . . *not* the kind of person I could confide my innermost feelings to. Dave was a very *philosophic* guy . . . he and I talked a lot about very *personal* things
WI, V, 1	(+)	I don't think I'd like a highly structured role . . . a technocrat . . . a computerlike servomechanism
WI, VII, 2	(+)	The guys I worked with were really fun to be around and there was great rapport . . .
WI, IX, 1	(+)	Knowing and liking these people was very important to me . . . realized that in any job I would ever have this would be important.
HT	(+)	Although people-related activities were not the largest category (39 percent), Affection was by far the largest component of the People category (almost half) Aggressive/People was only 10 percent of the People category
AVL	(−)	Social score near bottom
AVL, FR	(+)	Felt test was biased toward welfare of *large,* impersonal groups and didn't truly reflect my social inclination in smaller groups
BSA, 3, 6	(−)	Success in IRS program *important* because . . . competition among the agents was fierce
ST	(+)	Highest scores were in occupations that could be described as "face-to-face helping," e.g., YMCA Staff Member, Physical Therapist, Social Worker. Group I scores, representing predominantly human-helping services, was an average of 20 per item. Group II, which listed activities dealing with nonhuman sciences, averaged only 9.4 per item. In Group I, especially high scores are Psychiatrist and Psychologist, which deal with helping personal problems on a one-to-one or limited group basis
LS	(+)	Shows that relations with people I work with are an important component of my life

Comment: Of the 18 data points, 67 percent are from the Written Interview, 6 percent from the Hand Test, 11 percent from the AVL, and 6 percent from the B-School application and Strong Test. Over 25 percent of the data are contradictory, although data from the AVL and the B-School application (11 percent) are unreliable because of the social score bias, and garbage, respectively.

5. Athletic Interest/Active Involvement (15)

WI, I, 2	(+)	Biggest thing to happen during childhood was playing baseball
WI, I, 4	(+)	Richmond Falls . . . open spaces . . . develop my baseball skills
WI, I, 4	(+)	Practiced a million hours . . . throwing a ball against a wall
WI, I, 4	(+)	Baseball was first career aspiration
WI, I, 5	(+)	Always had all the baseballs, footballs, etc.
WI, I, 6	(+)	Played ball all the time in those days (growing up in Petersfield)
WI, I, 9	(+)	Liked for the *things* you can *do*
WI, III, 1	(+)	Lot of effort in deciding on material, arranging, practicing, booking jobs, and overall logistics . . .
WI, V, 2	(+)	Climate is important . . . all my outside interests center around warm weather . . . golf, tennis
WI, V, 2	(+)	I feel better and healthier when it is warm, and my personal attitude is directly related to the amount of sunlight
HT	(+)	Largest category was active environment with 50 percent of responses. Most of these responses centered around athletic activities
BSA, 2, 5	(+)	Long list of athletic hobbies
D	(+)	Most of activities deal with sports or watching action activities on TV
D	(+)	Sat. 10:30: Sunny California looked great
ST	(+)	High scores for adventure and recreational leadership on interest scale. Above-average scores on outdoor, active jobs, e.g., Forest Service Man, YMCA Staff Member

Comment: 67 percent Written Interview, 7 percent from the Hand Test, BSA, and Strong, and 13 percent from the Diary. This particularly has implications for geographic location of a job.

6. Quality of Life, Personal Development, Long-Term Viewpoint (12)

WI, I, 10	(+)	Realized rules of game for adult success—good jobs, good money
WI, III, 1	(+)	I realized I had to go to college to *escape a fate* like this
WI, III, 2	(+)	Quit band for several reasons . . . figured we'd end up playing in bars and clubs for the rest of our lives
WI, I, 4	(+)	Manual labor jobs . . . convinced me I had to gain some work skills that would keep me from having to do these things for the rest of my life
WI, V, 2	(+)	Couldn't think of anything worse than to spend my whole life in New York City, Boston, . . . or any other cold-climate business centers.
WI, V, 3	(+)	Greatest fear is that of getting *locked into* a job I don't like and not being able to get out
WI, VII, 1	(−)	Didn't start to think about college . . . until halfway through my senior year
WI, VII, 3	(−)	I knew that whatever decision I made probably wouldn't seem satisfactory for *quite a while* . . .
WI, VII, 3	(+)	I wanted to make sure the business I chose was the right one
WI, IX, 1	(+)	Led to concern about the quality of life
AVL	(−)	Aesthetic score tied for lowest score
BSA, 3, 6	(+)	Success in IRS schools important because . . . would have a profound effect on our subsequent work assignments and advancement

Comment: 83 percent from the Written Interview, 8 percent from the AVL and B-School application. The theme relates to taking a long-run viewpoint and an emphasis on gaining skills to aid in personal development and to allow me to have a *choice* in the matter.

7. Conscious of Self-Image (12)

WI, I, 8	(+)	I didn't think other people liked me very much
WI, I, 9	(+)	Decided that I wasn't a *pro calibre* ball player or guitarist—not result of bad self-image
WI, I, 10	(+)	Thing I disliked the most about job was "idea" of working for IRS
WI, I, 10	(+)	Concept of self-image through psychocybernetics
WI, I, 10	(+)	Didn't like myself in the role I had to play—exclusively combative
WI, V, 1	(+)	I want to feel important and to feel good about myself in the job, and good about the company I work for. I don't want to feel like a technocrat, a computerlike servomechanism
WI, IX, 1	(+)	I started to change my self-assessment from one of self-pity . . . improved self-image made me relax and enjoy things more
WI, IX, 1	(+)	The whole concept of self-image reappraisal pervades all the subsequent transitional periods

WI, X,1	(+)	Collection job . . . didn't like to play that kind of role
WI, X,1	(+)	Self-image and the way I felt about myself in the job role became critical
WI, FR	(+)	I like to feel that I'm more people oriented than that
ST, FR	(+)	Concerned over data pointing toward a staff inclination. "I don't like the impotent staff image"

Comment: Over 90 percent of the data came from the Written Interview. The data point out the importance of the way I feel about myself, my job role, and the organization. They also indicate that I like the image of being a friendly, strong, competent, people-oriented person.

8. Prestige (12)

WI, I, 10	(+)	Had a tough time finding job because I graduated from a "small school"
WI, I, 11	(+)	Would only do it (come to grad school) if I could get into the first-level business schools
WI, III, 3	(+)	Jobs seemed pretty rinky-dink, I had more prestigious things in mind
WI, V, 2	(+)	Side ventures . . . a *fine* New Orleans restaurant, or maybe a *fine* men's store . . .
WI, VII, 1	(+)	It was a more important job
WI, VII, 2	(+)	Both were considered the top-echelon jobs . . .
WI, VII, 3	(+)	I couldn't turn down the prestige that graduate school offers . . .
WI, VIII, 1	(+)	Wouldn't have come if I hadn't got into a good school . . . reputation and prestige
WI, X, 1	(+)	The name of the school you graduate from makes a big difference
WI, X, 1	(+)	Thought Special Agent job was going to be an important, prestigious job
WI, XI, 1	(+)	Perceived prestige of that job became crucial
BSA, 3, 6	(+)	My only regrets are that I could not afford to attend a more prestigious institution

Comment: Over 90 percent of the data came from the Written Interview. The important implication in this data is that I must perceive that both my job and the organizaton I work for are important and prestigious.

9. Don't Like Major Changes (12)

WI, I, 3	(+)	Moving away from Brinksville . . . gray day . . . I was feeling gray
WI, I, 3	(+)	Make a symbolic gesture of my leaving
WI, I, 5	(+)	Move to Petersfield was "traumatic" because I had to change schools
WI, I, 9	(+)	Decided to go to local college rather than leave area . . .
WI, I, 11	(+)	Deciding to come to business school was the "single most courageous decision I've ever made"
WI, III, 3	(+)	Decided to take job because . . . only 50 miles away
WI, IV, 4	(+)	My parents were really decent people . . . their relationship was always *stable*
WI, IV, 3	(+)	My wife and I . . . went together for about six years
WI, VII, 1	(+)	Big decision was whether I wanted to leave home or not
WI, VII, 2	(+)	I kept thinking about leaving the government . . . couldn't do anything about it . . . maybe a little apathy
WI, VII, 3	(+)	Lilly job . . . weeks of monumental indecision . . . probably the worst two weeks in my life
WI, VIII, 3	(+)	Fear of change

Comment: All data come from one source—the Written Interview. I don't feel that this reliance on one instrument is important because of the nature of the theme. This also relates to other themes in that major changes mean *uncertainty*.

10. Admiration of Physically, Technically, and/or Socially Competent People (11)

WI, I, 2	(+)	Idol was Tommy Littler . . . a great baseball player
WI, I, 3	(+)	Associate Tommy with baseball because he was really good
WI, I, 4	(+)	Lived next door to a kid who didn't like sports . . . figured he was a sissy . . . didn't play with him
WI, I, 5	(−)	Dad and I were good friends . . . physically big not aggressive . . . big teddy bear
WI, I, 6	(+)	Looking back at area I grew up in . . . super athletes
WI, I, 8	(+)	Didn't feel "adequate" until ninth-grade football
WI, III, 2	(+)	Best musicians . . . most professional band
WI, IV, 1	(+)	Dad was "John Wayne" type . . . expressed love through good-natured wrestling
WI, IV, 3	(+)	Father-in-law . . . really admire him for his social skills
D	(−)	Tues. 1 P.M.: Professor grabs people and pushes them . . . sadistic tendency
D	(+)	Tues. 2:30 P.M.: Professor is an incredibly sharp guy

Comment: Over 80 percent from the Written Interview. These data have implications for the type of authority figure I am likely to respond favorably to and also the kind of person I want to be.

11. Influenced by Other People (11)

WI, I, 4	(+)	Be good at things other people think are cool
WI, I, 5	(−)	Running around with hoods . . . but chickened out when they wanted to do something bad
WI, I, 6	(−)	Parents didn't like black friends . . . they couldn't convince me I was wrong
WI, I, 9	(−)	Too stubborn to say I'm sorry (to father)
WI, I, 10	(+)	Reaction that people give you
WI, I, 10	(+)	Recurrent theme . . . my reliance on other people's acceptance and what they think
WI, IV, 3	(+)	Father-in-law has had a lot of influence on me. . . . He's been a model for me
WI, VII, 1	(+)	Penn State . . . go there because a lot of people were going there . . .
WI, VII, 1	(+)	Choosing first job . . . under pressure from my parents to accept . . .
WI, XI, 1	(+)	Theme of letting other people influence my decisions . . . bent the way the wind was blowing
HT	(−)	Only 4 percent of responses relate to dependence on other people

Comment: Over 90 percent of data points came from the Written Interview. Thirty-six percent of the data are contradictory. I think it is important, because I'm prone to be influenced by others when I have a lot of *uncertainty*. Reliance on one instrument doesn't bother me, since no other instrument is likely to produce this kind of information.

12. Desire to Feel Acceptance for Personal Qualities Rather than Physical Abilities (10)

WI, I, 8	(+)	Didn't feel people liked me very much
WI, I, 8	(+)	I realized I wanted personal acceptance . . . not just athletic acceptance
WI, I, 8	(+)	Being star quarterback was fun, but not satisfying . . . couldn't get rid of feeling of personal inadequacy
WI, III, 3	(+)	Learned I could use my intelligence to gain a feeling of superiority . . . in retrospect, I wasn't any more satisfied by this tactic as I was with the jock approach, because more than *superiority* I needed *acceptance*
WI, IV, 2	(−)	Jay was kind of guy who liked to take charge and be the leader. So did I, and sometimes this caused problems
WI, IX, 1	(+)	Knowing and liking these people was very important to me
HT, FR	(+)	Concerned over lack of people responses (39 percent), like to feel I'm more people oriented than that
AVL	(−)	Low social score @ 34 (next to bottom)
AVL	(+)	Political score was second highest @ 55
AVL, FR	(+)	Felt test was biased toward concern for welfare of large, impersonal groups and didn't reflect my true social inclination

Comment: 60 percent of data points come from the Written Interview, 10 percent from the Hand test, and 30 percent from the AVL, 20 percent of the responses were contradictory. The clash tends to come from the fact that I sometimes want not only to be accepted but admired at the same time and I sometimes feel threatened by other strong personalities. I tend to discount any social inferences from the AVL test because of its focus on the welfare of large masses of people.

13. Self-Analytical, Introspective, Psyche-out (10)

WI, I, 4	(+)	Sets up recurrent theme: gain acceptance through skills
WI, I, 7	(+)	Look back on viciousness of cycle . . .
WI, I, 8	(+)	Same adaptive style persisted . . . looked for competences to make me attractive
WI, I, 11	(+)	Course in Self-Assessment finds me in a period of self-assessment. During past year, I've been trying to assess my own feelings, perceptions, and assumptions . . .
WI, IV, 2	(+)	Dave was a very philosophic guy and he and I talked a lot about very personal things
WI, V, 1–2	(+)	Marketing . . . enjoy opportunities to deal with people and their *motivations* . . .
WI, VII, 3	(+)	This quandary (Lilly job decision) led to a lot of introspection
WI, IX, 1	(−)	Started to become less introspective and hard on myself. . . . All my life I had been trying to analyze all my feelings
WI, FR	(−)	Began to wonder if I wasn't too introspective
ST	(+)	Highest average scores in Group I relate to Psychiatrist and Psychologist

Comment: 90 percent Written Interview, 10 percent from the Strong test. This has implications for any career choice, since I tend to constantly question and analyze my personal situation. Only 20 percent of the data contradict this theme.

14. Admiration of Hard Work/Work Ethic (10)

WI, I, 2	(+)	Tommy used to really work my ass off
WI, I, 4	(+)	Must have practiced a million hours
WI, I, 4	(−)	Did well in school but didn't study hard
WI, I, 7	(−)	Didn't study much at all
WI, I, 10	(+)	College . . . academically . . . wanted to do well . . . studied a lot
WI, IV, 1	(+)	Both my parents have worked hard all their lives
WI, IX, 1	(+)	Began to work very hard and to expect to do well
BSA, 5, 9	(+)	Parents instilled in me the desire to work and to succeed
RT, FR	(+)	Felt pressure to get a lot of images, i.e., production
LS	(+)	When work was not an important and central activity, I was not very happy

Comment: 70 percent from Written Interview. Data indicate that I'm not likely to be happy unless I think I'm working hard. I tend to equate hard work with personal development. It is also a means of dealing with uncertainty, i.e., if I can't make all the pieces fit, I'm likely to try to snow people with a lot of data or production.

15. Gain Acceptance or Domination through Special Skills, Especially Physical Abilities (9)

WI, I, 4	(+)	Since I was a good ballplayer . . . everybody thought I was OK. Set up recurrent theme: be good at things people think are cool
WI, I, 5	(+)	Being good at baseball made my acceptance at new school easier
WI, I, 7	(+)	Traditional means of gaining acceptance—athletics, baseball—was closed
WI, I, 8	(+)	Didn't feel "adequate" until ninth-grade football
WI, I, 8	(−)	Being star quarterback was fun, but not satisfying
WI, I, 8	(+)	Competences would make me "attractive"
WI, I, 9	(+)	Liked because of the *things* you *do,* not the kind of person you were
WI, III, 2	(−)	Do *not* get off on some star trip
WI, I, 3	(+)	In college . . . I learned that I could use my intelligence to gain a feeling of superiority over other people

Comment: 100 percent of these comments come from the Written Interview. Only two data points are contradictory. Both of these points relate to the theme of gaining acceptance by *personal* qualities. Therefore, this technique of mastery is still strong; it is just that sometimes it clashes with the need to be accepted as an individual. These contradictions usually occur *after* I've been accepted for special skills.

16. Influence People Without Using Formal Power (9)

WI, I, 2	(+)	Conned my mother and sister
WI, I, 10	(+)	Disliked role—dealing with people in an exclusively combative way
WI, III, 1	(−)	Management style was cooperative until I was let down once or twice by somebody . . . then I became a real hard ass
WI, III, 1	(+)	Learned best way to get people to help you is to show them how *they* can gain from it, or *think* they're gaining
WI, V, 2	(+)	Side ventures . . . owning a fine New Orleans restaurant, or maybe a fine men's store . . . (merchandising)
AVL	(+)	Political score was next to highest @ 55
BSA, 2, 4	(+)	Articulate my ideas and to influence my fellow students
ST	(+)	Group IX, and Advertising Man in Group X, average a score of over 33. This is high compared to the average of other scores. These jobs deal largely with people-related activities, where you are trying to influence behavior by other than formal power
ST, FR	(−)	Concerned that scores may be pointing toward a staff orientation. "I don't like the impotent staff image"

Comment: 56 percent Written Interview, 22 percent Strong, and 11 percent each for the AVL and BSA. Contradictory evidence does not seem that strong. Points toward a desire to be a leader because I'm respected, not because somebody gave me a title.

17. Make Work = Play (9)

WI, I, 9	(+)	Liked music a lot—started bands (to make money)
WI, III, 4	(+)	I really want to be involved in my work

WI, III, 4	(+)	I want work and play to be close together
WI, III, 4	(+)	I don't want to think of my job as work
WI, V, 1	(−)	I also want the freedom to live a personal life and to develop personal interests and avocations
WI, V, 2	(+)	I don't think I'd like a highly structured role
WI, VII, 1	(+)	Bands and money
ST	(+)	Very high score for YMCA Staff Member, who combines a job in a recreational setting
LS	(+)	Recreation and work are very much entwined

Comment: 78 percent of data are from the Written Interview. This may represent a "pie-in-the-sky" goal.

18. Variety—Excitement—Involvement (9)

WI, III, 1	(+)	Pennysform job . . . money was pretty good . . . but the work was extremely dull
WI, III, 4	(+)	I really want to be involved in my job. From what I've seen, the people whose lives and work are inextricably bound together are the happiest
WI, V, 1	(+)	I also want freedom to live a personal life and to develop personal interests and avocations. I also think I'd like to have other ventures on the side
WI, V, 2	(+)	About side ventures . . . fine New Orleans restaurant, or maybe a fine men's store . . .
WI, V, 3	(+)	My greatest fear is that of getting locked into a job and not being able to get out
WI, VII, 2	(+)	Field Audit was very technical . . . Special Agent job seemed more interesting . . . criminal fraud . . . carried a gun . . .
WI, VIII, 1	(+)	Many boring work experiences
WI, X, 1	(+)	Work turned out to be incredibly tedious at times
ST	(+)	High interest scales for almost all topics

Comment: 90 percent of data from the Written Interview. The data point toward a job with a lot of variety or compensating for it outside the job.

19. Like Responsibility/Expect It from Others (8)

WI, III, 1	(+)	Management style was cooperative until I had been *let down* once or twice by somebody . . . then I was a real hard ass
WI, III, 2	(+)	First kid in family ever to go to college
WI, III, 4	(+)	Liked print-room job . . . sense of responsibility . . . worked hard because I *wanted* to . . . kind of feeling I want in my career choice
WI, III, 4	(+)	Other jobs were only manual labor . . . no real responsibility
WI, IX, 1	(+)	Realization that the only person in this world with responsibility for my happiness is myself. A realization of personal responsibilities
WI, X, 1	(+)	You couldn't get any meaningful responsibility until you had about five years experience.
BSA, 3, 6	(+)	My parents were very proud . . . gratifying to me
BSA, 3, 6	(+)	Success in IRS schools important because . . . have a profound effect on our subsequent work assignments and advancement

Comment: 75 percent from Written Interview; 25 percent from the B-School application.

20. Entrepreneurial/Individual Leadership (8)

WI, I, 9	(+)	Bands were my own creation—I was leader
WI, III, 1	(+)	Formed my first band
WI, III, 1	(+)	Lot of effort in deciding on material, arranging, practicing, booking jobs, and overall logistics . . .
WI, V, 1	(+)	The idea of going into business for myself is also attractive
BSA, 3, 6	(+)	Realized lucrative potential of bands . . . organized my own band
ST	(−)	Below-average scores President-Mfg. and C.P.A. owner
ST, FR	(+)	Concern over whether the results might be pointing toward a staff orientation rather than line leadership. "I don't like impotent staff image"
LS	(+)	Outside venture

Comment: Only 50 percent of the data were from the Written Interview. Contradictory evidence comes from the Strong.

21. Take Easy Way Out (8)

WI, I, 4	(+)	Did well in school but didn't study hard
WI, I, 7	(+)	Didn't study much at all
WI, I, 9	(+)	Because I had great band and girlfriend—decided to go to a local college
WI, III, 3	(+)	Decided to take the job because . . . only 50 miles away
WI, VII, 1	(+)	Choosing first job . . . tired of looking
WI, VII, 2	(+)	I kept thinking about leaving the government . . . but didn't do anything about it . . . maybe a little apathy
WI, XI, 1	(+)	Most pervasive theme . . . doing what was easiest at the time
D	(+)	Tues. 5:30: Tempted to use excuse

Comment: 87 percent Written Interview, 13 percent Diary. I think this then is similar to the theme of Influence by Others in that I'm prone to do this when I'm dealing with uncertainty.

22. Concern over Lack of Social Skills (7)

WI, I, 7	(+)	I started to sense that I didn't really have any developed social skills
WI, I, 8	(+)	Feeling of personal inadequacy
WI, IV, 3	(+)	Father-in-law . . . I really admire him for his social skills. He has an extraordinary ability to meet and deal with people. He's been a kind of model for me
HT, FR	(+)	Concern over low score for people-related activities
AVL, FR	(+)	Concerned over low social scores
BSA	(+)	Deals quite a bit with personal interaction with other people, e.g., lasting friendships, interests of fellow students
D, FR	(+)	Concern over lack of people interaction in the Diary

Comment: 40 percent Written Interview, and 14 percent for the Hand test, AVL, B-School application, and Diary. I could find no contradictory evidence—this theme seems strong.

23. Passive Role/Things Should Take Care of Themselves (7)

WI, I, 5	(+)	Thought all I had to do was drink Ovaltine and I'd be super strong
WI, I, 7	(+)	Shy around girls . . . nothing happened unless they made the first move
WI, I, 7	(+)	Waiting for kids to be nice to me
WI, VII, 3	(+)	I figured the degree would *pay for itself* in time
WI, VIII, 1	(+)	College seemed like a *passport* to success
WI, IX, 1	(−)	Led to concern about quality of life and the *absolute importance* for the right career choice
WI, X, 1	(+)	Thought all I had to do was do well in college and the world *would beat a path to my door*

Comment: All data from Written Interview. Although there are only seven data points, I feel the theme is important because it makes establishing personal relationships more difficult.

24. Don't Show Emotions (7)

WI, I, 2	(+)	I felt bad about the superman scene—jealous and stupid
WI, I, 3	(+)	It feels "embarrassing" to think back to singing good-bye song
WI, I, 8	(+)	Risk being hurt (by showing a need for friendship)
WI, I, 9	(+)	Too stubborn to say "I'm sorry"
WI, IV, 1	(+)	My family . . . never much affection expressed, especially "touchy-touchy"
WI, IV, 2	(+)	Thought kissing and stuff like that was kind of embarrassing
WI, FR	(+)	Thought I was being very honest . . . started to wonder if I wasn't being too introspective

Comment: All data points are from the Written Interview. The theme seems to be related to wanting to maintain *control*. Emotions are equated with weakness. This sometimes clashes with the need for close interpersonal relationships.

25. Opportunistic (4)

WI, VII, 1	(+)	After going to work and finding out where the best jobs were, I immediately applied for another job.
WI, VII, 2	(+)	I knew I couldn't put up with that job very long so I started looking around

WI, VII, 3   (+)   Grad school would offer me more opportunities than I presently had
WI, IX, 1   (+)   Knew that the first job was only a prelude to a better job

Comment: All data come from the Written Interview. Although there are only four data points, I feel that it is a strong theme. Combined with a tendency to be introspective and limited by a dislike for major change, it points toward a tendency to feel that the grass is always greener on the other side of the fence. Where the opportunity does not involve major change (e.g., within-company changes) I am likely to make changes.

26. Loner Mystique/Rationalization of Rejection (3)

WI, I, 7   (+)   Became defiant during high school . . . rebel, nonconformist . . . difficult to adjust to new setting . . . couldn't show off any more
WI, I, 7–8   (+)   Compensate by telling myself I didn't need anybody . . . nobleness in loneliness
WI, III, 4   (+)   Worked in print-room by myself . . . really got into job

Comment: All data were derived from the Written Interview. The data points all relate to feelings when I was in my teens. Despite this and the fact that there are only three data points, I still feel that the theme is important because it represents a technique that I'm prone to use if I don't feel that I'm being accepted or appreciated.

Part II: Implications

1. Relationships with Other People

A. I have a desire to gain acceptance, recognition, status, and admiration within a group, or on a person-to-person level, by exhibiting special knowledge or skills that will be appreciated by these people. (1, 4, 11, 15)

B. I don't like to deal with large groups of people, but rather with small, informal groups, or on a one-to-one basis. (4, 22)

C. I will tend to equate personal happiness with the number and/or quality of personal relationships, even though my concern over social skills and tendency to act passively in social situations makes these relationships difficult to initiate. (4, 6, 7, 12, 13, 22, 23, 24)

D. I like people who don't pose a threat to my expert power and will therefore prefer to be around and work with people who are either team-oriented or personally noncompetitive. (1, 4, 15, 22)

E. My tendency to act passively in social settings makes work-related friendships a desirable and easy way to gain social expression. (4, 22, 23)

F. If I do not feel that I am accepted by the group, I will feel alienated and will probably become a loner. I will try to rationalize this by feeling that I don't really need the group's acceptance, or that I am better than the group—but I will be extremely unhappy and uneasy. (7, 12, 22, 24, 26)

2. Leadership Style

A. I prefer to dominate by expert power rather than formal power derived by a title. I want other people's admiration for my competence to be enough justification for them to do what I want them to do. I will feel very uncomfortable if all I have is formal power. (1, 15, 16)

B. I will expect people below me to be responsible and loyal to me. If they let me down without justification, I will resort to a real hard-ass management style. (12, 14, 15, 19)

C. I like people to seek my counsel in areas of my expertise, but I may become reluctant to give advice if I feel my power will be lessened by it, e.g., if they could use this information to become expert too, and compete with me. (1, 4, 15)

3. Task Preferences

A. I would like to work for someone whom I admire as physically and technically competent. I would hope that this management style was helpful and directive and that a mentor-protégé relationship would develop. (4, 6, 10)

B. I like a job that offers a lot of variety, i.e., I'm not doing the same thing day after day. Also, I like to be physically active and free to move around. I want to be actively involved and informed. (5, 18)

C. I want to feel that my job and the work I do is important to the organization and that I am a needed and appreciated part of the team. I want to be able to see a clear career path. (6, 7, 8, 12, 18, 19)

D. If I am left unsupervised or undirected I will initiate action of my own, but I am likely to feel restrained by not being sure how this action will be received by the organization. (2, 7, 20)

E. I would like to be in a field or functional area where a certain tangible competence or expertise can be developed. I also want to feel that my M.B.A. training gives me a better opportunity to acquire this competence. (1, 10, 15, 16)

F. If I am not able to interact with other people in my job, I am likely to feel isolated and unhappy. (7, 12, 13, 15)

4. Approach to Tasks and Problems

A. I generally approach a task by first trying to see how it is related to the organization or to other problems. If I cannot see this, I will break the problem down into smaller parts and will attempt to solve it by a logical, pragmatic process. If I am certain of my skills, I will proceed in a very aggressive way and will feel very powerful. If I feel uncertain, I will tend to concentrate on details and will feel limited in reaching conclusions using only what I can substantiate with facts. This inability to creatively assemble and analyze data to reach conclusions will make me feel very uneasy. In situations of uncertainty, I am likely to recommend the status quo or try to get the opinions of others on what I should recommend. (2, 7, 11, 21)

B. I will feel unhappy if I am not working hard and getting good feedback, but will feel overworked and that my life is passing me by if I don't have enough free time to pursue personal relationships or recreational diversion. A job that involves these two things, e.g., entertaining clients, may solve this conflict. (5, 14, 17)

C. I won't feel happy if my work role is in conflict with my personal self-image as a friendly, people-oriented, active, competent person. (6, 7, 8, 13)

D. I won't feel happy if I perceive that the organization that I work for is not prestigious or an enviable place to work at, i.e., a successful industry leader with a good reputation. (6, 7, 8, 13)

E. I want to feel that I am receiving an above-average salary and that my economic wealth level is great enough so that I am working for a company not because I have to, but because I want to. (3, 6, 7)

5. Attitude Toward Change

A. I dislike major disruptive changes that involve leaving a familiar environment of friends, or a job that requires new and untried skills. (9, 12, 15, 22, 23)

B. When faced with major change I am prone to maintain the status quo or to take the easy solution, unless I can see the change as crucial to personal success or development. (6, 9, 21, 25)

C. After making the change I usually feel very uneasy until I can see either that I am able to acquire the requisite new skills, or that the change actually will benefit me personally. (1, 6, 9, 15, 25)

6. Life Style

A. I prefer to be actively involved in my work and to feel that my work and personal life are entwined. (5, 18)

B. I want the personal freedom in my job to be able to get away from it if I feel the need. (3, 5, 6, 18)

C. I would prefer to live in a warm climate and an aesthetically stimulating area where I would be able to be physically active the year round. (5, 6, 17)

D. I would like to be able to get into some personal business ventures outside of my job, or as full time, after I have worked for someone else for a while. The image of a self-made, independent man is very appealing to me. (3, 6, 7, 14, 18, 20, 25)

B

An Example of a Career Development Paper*

BY KAREN ZUGAR

Career and Job Possibilities That I Have Tentatively Eliminated

A. Finance:
1. Commercial Banking (considered because commercial banking at present has many outstanding opportunities for women)
   (a) Low banker score on Strong test.
   (b) Dislike and lack of prowess in Management of Lending course.
   (c) Extensive discussions with an executive in banking (nothing he said about it appealed to me).
   (d) Self-Assessment paper:
      (i) Not wanting to work in a highly structured competitive atmosphere.
      (ii) Wanting an overview of the problem—not wanting to work on one part of a problem.
      (iii) Having an idealistic bent.
      (iv) Wanting to be "near the center of the decision-making power structure."
      (v) Fear of commitment.
      (vi) I do not like "keeping something going."
2. Financial Department of Corporation (considered because of my interest in Finance)
   (a) Dislike of previous job in a Treasurer's office.
   (b) Same as (d) under Commercial Banking.

3. Investment Banking or Management (considered because career counselor suggested it). After discussions with investment banking professor three negatives stand out:
   (a) My "salesmanship" attributes are not outstanding.
   (b) I would not like the complete emphasis on profits (idealism—Self-Assessment paper).
   (c) I would not like living in New York City.
   (d) Self-assesment paper:
      (i) I am risk averse.
      (ii) Wanting to work in a friendly, supportive, accepting atmosphere.
      (iii) Not wanting to be a woman "path-breaker."
4. Real Estate
   (a) Same as those negatives under Investment Banker and Management.
   (b) Also lack of entrepreneurial style (Self-Assessment paper).

B. Marketing:
1. Marketing Management (considered because of the project management implication from Self-Assessment paper)
   (a) Little encouragement from marketing professor.
   (b) When I thought carefully about what I liked about my marketing course, it was the "strategy" aspect of marketing rather than pricing, packaging, market research, or any of the other nitty gritty.

---

*This has been chosen as an example of a good solid paper. It is not meant to represent the best that can be done nor even one of the best that we have ever received.

(d) Self-Assessment paper:
   (i) Idealism—could I really devote my life to selling Life Cereal or Sanka Coffee? It just does not fit.
   (ii) Fear of commitment.
   (iii) Fear of failure.
   (iv) Need to feel I am having a direct impact on solving an "important" problem. (I am not sure whether I will consider all marketing problems "important.")

2. Advertising (considered because of its "glamorous" appeal):
   (a) Never had a particular talent for advertising.
   (b) Self-Assessment paper (same items as under Marketing).

3. Retailing (considered because of my high interest in merchandising on Strong test and my love of shopping and pretty things):
   (a) Self-Assessment paper:
      (i) Having "status" is important to me.
      (ii) Fear of commitment.
      (iii) My idealism.
      (iv) I enjoy putting something together, but I do not like being in role of keeping something going.

C. Business Policy:
1. Planning and Policy Department of Corporation
   (a) Self-Assessment paper:
      (i) Need for concrete accomplishments.
      (ii) Enjoy project management (I do not think there is very much of this in this field).
      (iii) Wanting to work on that which is considered to be the highest or almost highest priority in my environment.
      (iv) Wanting to be near the center of the decision-making power structure.

2. Acquisitions and Mergers
   (a) Self-assessment paper:
      (i) My idealism.
      (ii) Risk averse.
      (iii) Lack of initiative.
      (iv) Wanting to be in a friendly, supportive, not highly competitive atmosphere.

3. Assistant to a Principal Corporate Executive
   (a) My idealism.
   (b) I am afraid that many of these jobs are quasi-secretarial in content. If I were to be in an "assistant"-type role, it would be better, I think, if it were in government, where women having a professional status are more accepted (and there is a greater history of women in higher positions). It would depend on the executive and the firm, of course, so I am leaving this alternative open.

Career Choices I Have Decided to Pursue

A. Consulting. Smallish, international consulting firm (with an excellent reputation) that works on both government and corporate projects.

1. Why consulting?
   (a) Self-Assessment paper:
      (i) Having "status" in my environment is very important to me. Consulting provides me status.
      (ii) I have a fear of going a route that would involve a major commitment. Consulting can be used as a jumping-off point (if I ever so desired) to a government or corporate job or to teaching.
      (iii) I would not have to be an entrepreneur. If the firm has a strong enough reputation, clients will come to it rather than vice versa.
      (iv) I will have a direct impact on solving problems.
      (v) I will have the opportunity to indulge in project management from time to time, "directing an integrative situation, pulling things together, organizing and creating structures for other people to work in."
      (vi) I am comfortable in an advisor role.
      (vii) I will have the opportunity to be near the "center of decision-making power structure" by dealing with the top managers of government and corporations.
      (viii) I will be working on a problem that is considered to be high-priority in my job environment (by virtue of the fact the firm or government agency is paying a lot of money to have that problem solved).
      (ix) In many instances I will be able to get the overview of the problem. I will be able to look at my environment in terms of the big picture.
      (x) I will be able to work with bright people.
      (xi) This profession will provide me with a good standard of living.
      (xii) The firm will provide me with diversity.
      (xiii) My fear of failure may work to my advantage. I will work very hard trying to prove myself to firm and client and in the end then I might prove successful.

2. Why a "smallish" firm, and what kind of internal atmosphere in the firm am I looking for?
   (a) I am looking for a firm that:
      (i) Is not hierarchically structured (Self-Assessment paper "not highly structured").
      (ii) Small enough for everyone to know each other and fairly close-knit. (I need friends in and out of work—Self-Assessment paper.)
      (iii) Is not highly competitive (Self Assessment paper).
      (iv) Has people in it whom I really like and admire.
      (v) Work-pace pressure is from moderate to "medium-high." (Will allow me time to develop relationships outside of work—Self-Assessment paper.)

3. Why a firm that has government projects and international clients?
    (a) My previous job experience will no doubt be an asset to me.
    (b) I would have a chance to work out my idealistic bent (Self-Assessment paper).
    (c) I would have a chance for international travel (on company time).
4. Why a firm that is growing and financially stable?
    (a) One of my concerns is to have financial security (Self-Assessment paper). I want to make sure that the firm is financially stable and will be around through economic thicks and thins.
5. Contrary evidence to becoming a consultant.
    (a) I have a need for concrete accomplishment (Self-Assessment paper). Consultants are not always contracted to implement recommendations. Furthermore, consultants are not always able to see "the fruits of their labor."
    (b) Dissatisfaction of not having a deep enough knowledge of problem I am working on (Self-Assessment paper). Consultants are often forced by the very nature of their work to learn about a problem very quickly and come up quickly with a solution. They are instant experts. As my written interview repeated several times, I have always felt like a "dilettante" (very uncomfortable, almost dishonest) when I have been in this situation.
    (c) Dislike of my consulting job in London because I was off in a corner writing papers, I was not directly involved in what was going on, and I did not feel I had sufficient expertise (knowledge of the U.K. corporate system) to do a decent job.
6. How do I minimize these negatives?
    (a) As I have just mentioned, I would try to find a firm that is not a "flash-in-the-pan" type—one that runs in quickly, defines the problem, presents recommendations, and then runs out. In other words, I would be more comfortable working in a firm that worked with clients for *a long period of time* (1) to help them define their own problems and then (2) to work with them through their problem to the *final solution*. This is where I would get my satisfaction—seeing that the clients have their problem solved and that they are happy with the solution.
    (b) Find a firm that believes in constant client contact to solve the problem.

Other Job Possibilities and Why?

Working for the government again is, of course, a distinct possibility for me. My Self-Assessment paper points to it: (1) idealism, (2) risk aversion, (3) friendly, supportive, not highly competitive work environment, (4) wanting to be near the "center of decision-making power structure," (5) wanting to work on that which is considered of high priority, (6) needing to feel I am having a direct impact on solving an "important" problem. My Strong test blaringly points toward it.

However, there were some good reasons why I left government, and they are included in my Written Interview and Self-Assessment paper: (1) I was disillusioned with the political rather than social concerns for important decisions made (at the federal level), (2) limitations to my growth in compensation and career development, (3) unstimulating nature of most government agencies (I was lucky to be where the action was most of the time, but there was a limit to that), (4) lack of enough competent and committed employees in the city government, (5) enjoyment of "putting something together but not liking being in a role of keeping that something going" was going to keep me job-jumping for the rest of my government career, and somehow this made me very uncomfortable (6) not wanting to be in Washington, D.C., any more because of the "social" situation.

As an option to consulting, however, (because of my idealism) government cannot be overlooked. If I find a career in government that eliminates the negatives I just discussed, it will indeed be a viable option to consulting. Specific careers would include:

A. Aide to a top official (possibly even a mayor) in a city or federal government. Supported by elements of Self-Assessment paper:
    1. Desire for status.
    2. Diversity.
    3. Need to feel I am having a direct impact on solving an "important" problem.
    4. Enjoying putting something together but do not like being in a maintenance role.
    5. My idealistic bent.
    6. Often comfortable in the "assistant to" or advisor role—a sort of "Tonto to the Lone Ranger."
    7. Wanting "excitement" in the job, which means to me (a) being near the center of the decision-making power structure, (b) working on that which is considered to be the highest or almost highest priority in my job environment.
    8. I like the overview of a problem.
    9. Wanting to work in a highly supportive, friendly atmosphere.

Problems with this career route:

    1. To get these jobs, one often has to be politically connected to the official.
    2. They are insecure by their very nature, upon change of administration or elections.
    3. The possibilities would be limited in scope because of my life-style desires of being in a large city.
    4. To be an aide to someone in the federal government, I would have to live in Washington, D.C., which I am not sure I want to do.
    5. I have a need for concrete accomplishments. I am not sure that I, personally, would feel I accomplished something tangible in this position.

B. Financial department in the city government (if the financial department is the main source of power in the city government and if it is not highly structured) as an Assistant to the Budget Officer (having project management opportunities). Supported by:

1. My interest in finance.
2. Over time, satisfying my need to have a deep enough knowledge of the problem I was working on (Self-Assessment paper).
3. Wanting to be in a friendly supportive atmosphere (Self-Assessment paper).
4. Wanting status (Self-Assessment paper). Many financial departments have a great deal of status in a city government.
5. Having a direct impact on solving an "important" problem (Self-Assessment paper). I consider problems of the city as very important.
6. My idealistic bent (Self-Assessment paper).
7. I would have an overview of the problem (Self-Assessment paper).
8. Being comfortable in an "advisor role" or an "assistant to" (Self-Assessment paper).
9. Implications in Self-Assessment paper on project management.

Problems with this career objective:

1. I do not like being in a role of keeping something going, e.g., keeping the budget cycle going month after month, year after year. (This *might be* avoided, however, if the job entailed keeping "ı fingers in many pies" instead of just one.)
2. Foreign cultures' attraction and travel.
3. I want a good standard of living. (I anticipate salary levels not being high in this job function.)
4. Lack of enough competent and committed employees in city governments.

C. Federal government, which involves international travel and project management opportunities. Supported by:
1. Same as following for financial department in city government: 2, 3, 4 (if consider the job as having status); 5, 6, 7 (if the job gives me an overview).
2. Attraction to foreign cultures and international travel.

Problems:

1. I do not like being in a maintenance role.
2. Problems of working for the federal government and D.C. as outlined above.
3. Wanting to be in an unstructured work environment (some federal agencies are and some are not).

D. World Bank or other international development organizations (if they take new employees over 30). Supported by:
1. Same positive considerations as those listed for financial department of city government and international travel.

Problems:

1. Being in a maintenance role.
2. Being in highly structured atmosphere.

3. If I enter at a low level, not having an overview of the problem.
4. Working in Washington, D.C. (if the job is there).

Life Style for Next Year

A. Location: Because I am single, I would locate *in* (not near) a big city. I have listed some of the big cities I am interested in and the pros and cons (I can think of right now) of their attractiveness to me (see Figure 1). As time goes on, and as I gather more information, I will add to the pros and cons list.

FIGURE 1 Location

Washington

Pros	Cons
1. Have many established friendships.	1. Social scene limited.
2. Know city well.	2. Expensive housing.
3. Have contacts in many government agencies— might be valuable to firm.	3. No sense of adventure of going to new place.

Chicago

Pros	Cons
1. Housing expense still reasonable.	1. Away from East Coast, its culture, intellectual life, excitement.
2. Have two friends there.	2. Feel only mildly excited about city, restaurants, stores.
3. Near to sister and family.	3. Acceptability of an older single woman in Midwest?
4. Opportunity for a new "adventure."	
5. Female M.B.A.s relatively rare commodity in Chicago.	

Boston

Pros	Cons
1. Area is pleasant and comfortable.	1. A lot of M.B.A.s and general competition for jobs.
2. Have friends here.	2. Although like female friends in area feel slightly constrained by them.
3. Opportunity for a new adventure.	

New York

Pros	Cons
1. Lots of single people.	1. Bad experience in N.Y.C. previously.
2. Maybe negative feeling about city has more to do with personal circumstance at the time (1974).	2. Very expensive.
	3. Feel I am "too conservative" for social scene.
3. Best job opportunities may be here.	4. Feel midwesterners are looked down on.

San Francisco

Pros	Cons
1. City is very exciting; terrific in fact.	1. Far away from family and existing friends.
	2. No friends already there.

B. Style of Living: I want to live somewhat in style. If I am in an apartment, I want a fireplace and a view overlooking a body of water and generally a nice place to entertain (goes with consulting job and having lots of friends). Since my father has set up his own apartment in California, I have furniture from my parents (dining room suite, etc.) that I can move into whatever apartment or house I settle in come next September. I would live by myself.

C. Other Aspects of Life Style: To preserve my health and figure (this has been bugging me lately) I must reserve some time for a sport or other exercise. I am not particularly athletic, but I have in the past enjoyed horseback riding. Perhaps I can join a club and do this on the weekends.

D. Fit of Work Time with Life Style: I would limit my work week to 45–50 hours (excluding travel). Hopefully I would have most weekends free (with maybe 5 or 6 hours of weekend work at the most). I would choose a firm that did not require more. (There could be some real conflict here with a consulting firm's requirements.) During the week I would do most of my traveling and visiting of clients, realizing I will have little time then for my friends (outside of work) or for developing relationships. However, on weekends I would have dinner parties, go to plays, or participate in group activities where I could meet people—especially single people. (One of the things that also appeals to me about consulting is that I would have a lot of opportunity to meet a lot of different people.) During the week I could socialize with people at work (since they will also be my friends), and if these friendships develop sufficiently I could also socialize with them on the weekends.

E. Time to Refuel: I also want sufficient time for a vacation when I could go abroad. Hopefully, my job will at times be abroad, and then while I am there I could also squeeze in a few days in London, or the Spanish beaches, or whatever.

Job and Life Style after Next Year

I do not anticipate that my job or life style after next year will be any different, unless my first year out for some reason does not work out, e.g., dislike of firm or location. But I am anticipating doing everything in my power this year to choose the right firm and location.

If I am married, however, I do anticipate some changes. These changes will take the form of my cutting back on my work hours by exercising one of the following options: (1) working less hours in the consulting firm I am already in (by insisting on taking on less projects and taking a salary cut), (2) going into teaching, (3) going back to government work. I think I will do this because my family will take on added importance for me (my family is important to me—Self-Assessment paper) and I will want a 40-hour work week rather than a 45- to 50-hour work week plus travel. It all depends, however, on my then current financial situation, and whether I plan to have children. I can only say that I will reassess my position at that point in time.

My Plan of Attack

I have done considerable work thus far to assist me in finding a suitable consulting firm (see Figure 2), and these activities will be ongoing until graduation.

Based on my considerations of what type of consulting firm I would like, I have also developed a *tentative* check list (with a weighted number scale) to assist me in selecting a firm (see Figure 3).

I have also drafted a list of questions to ask of consulting firms at interviews (or if inappropriate to ask interviewers to ask of personnel in the firm on an informal basis) (see Figure 4). These considerations and list of questions will be modified over time.

FIGURE 2 Finding A Firm

What I have done thus far to find a suitable consulting firm:

A. Joined newly formed Management Consulting Club as an officer. As an officer of the club:
  1. I am invited to go to dinner with seminar speakers (consultants), giving me direct contact with consultants from many firms in an informal setting to ask questions of the consultant with the following purposes:
    (a) To decide whether I like the consultant personally, e.g., are our value systems consistent?
    (b) To assess the environment, e.g., competitive vs. cooperative style of the consultant's firm.
    (c) To assess whether I am the type of person, in terms of personality and background, that the firm might hire.
    (d) To find out the nature of the firm's clients and projects.
    (e) To find out the consultant's view of other firms.
    (f) To find out *exactly* what the consultant does.
    (g) To find out whether government consulting is as much fun as corporate consulting.
  2. I am in a better position to hear of openings in consulting firms.
  3. I am in a better position to hear about firms who do not normally recruit on campus.
  4. I am in a better position to sell myself as being interested in management consulting.
B. I have talked with my Business Policy professor (active in consulting) about my suitability as a consultant. I have given him a list of consulting firms who have recruited on campus. He has promised me to make comments next to the firms' names based on the following criteria:
  1. Atmosphere of the firm.
  2. Specialty of firm.
  3. Suitability to my personality and style.
  4. Turnover rate of firm's personnel.
  He also said that he will set up luncheon appointments for me with people from firms that I am interested in.
C. Career Resource Center. I have checked out the "consulting" folders and folders of three firms I am tentatively interested in.
D. I am taking a field study course in consulting next semester to make sure that I like consulting.

FIGURE 3 Tentative Criteria (Weighted) for Selection of Firms

Internal atmosphere 14
a. Fun
b. Cooperative
c. Unstructured
d. Proportion of single people
e. Values and personalities of employees
   (I like and admire them)
Reputation and quality of management 10
Beginning salary 6
Compensation growth 6
Promotion speed 4
Interesting projects 10
Has government clients 5
Chance for international travel 6
Location 14
Emphasis on management development 9
Likely growth and financial stability of firm 9
Nature of client contacts 7

   TOTAL 100

My schedule for job search over the next six months speaks for itself (Figure 5).

I anticipate coming up with a list in January of about 50 consulting firms (that match my criteria) and by March narrowing it down (I reject them or they reject me) to about 10 firms. By April I hope to consider five firms from which to choose.

Concurrently I will be developing my other options in government. Since my feelings about pursuing a job in government at this point are mixed, I will place my primary focus on consulting firms. However, I will do the following:

1. Interview with all government agencies of interest (including international organizations) coming to campus.

2. Follow up on correspondence opportunities coming to campus.

3. Write letters to Mayors, Deputy Mayors, and Budget Officers of large cities and five federal agency heads.

4. Answer solicitations dealing with jobs just outlined for government and possibly "assistant-to" jobs in corporations. (I am leaving the door *ajar* for this job possibility—see item C3 under "Career and Job Possibilities That I Have Tentatively Eliminated.")

5. Write letters to international organizations.

However, although my schedule says that I will be making the decision by the third week in May, if I do not find a suitable firm I *will* postpone making the decision.

FIGURE 4   Questions to Ask to Determine How Firm Will Fit Criteria

(Assisted by material provided by a consulting contact of mine).

Internal Atmosphere:

1. What kind of activities do you do as a group? Business and social.
2. How often do you work in a group vs. alone?
3. Are there formal training programs?
4. What happens if a consultant is "stuck" in solving a problem?
5. Staff and officer turnover: rates of voluntary and involuntary turnover.
6. How is performance measured? What are the feedback systems?
7. How are project teams organized?
8. How do you maintain a climate conducive to innovation and creativity?
9. What are typical jobs to which people leaving the firm have gone?
10. How is the firm "structured"? What is the seniority distribution of staff? What does the organizational chart look like?
11. What is management's philosophy? How do they feel they get best work from personnel? What kind of atmosphere do they try to create?

Reputation:

1. Ask professors.
2. If possible, contact former clients or ex-staff of firms.
3. Assess background of staff.
4. See if mentioned in newspapers or magazines (look in readers' periodicals and newspaper guides).

Beginning Salary:

1. Wait and see.

Compensation Growth and Promotional Speed:

1. What are the compensation policies of the firm? Compensation levels of staff, expected growth in compensation.
2. What is the actual and expected promotional sequence and timing for employees?
3. What is policy on "promotion from within"?
4. How many new employees are taken into the firm each year? At what levels do they enter?

Projects and Clients:

1. Define precisely businesses, products, and services.
2. Number and nature of clients, industries represented.

Emphasis on Management Development:

1. What percentage of business is devoted to this area?
2. What kind of programs and techniques do you use in this area?
3. What role does the consultant perform?

Quality of Management:

1. Assess management's business or government background.
2. What methods and criteria for selecting management?
3. How are management decisions made? Collectively or by individual managers?
4. Talk to them.

Chance for International Travel:

1. How often and under what circumstances do consultants based in U.S. travel abroad? How long?

Likely Financial Stability and Growth of Firm:

1. What is the ratio of proposals accepted to proposals made?
2. What is the percent of new business coming from former clients, current clients, and new clients?
3. Does the firm have a strategy for growth?
4. What is the percent of revenues accounted for by the three largest clients?
5. Look at annual report. Correct revenues for inflation rates. Look at historical achievement.

Nature of Client Contacts:

1. Ask to see calendar of consultant at the level I would enter and one at five years senior. Assess extent, frequency, level, timing, and nature of client contacts.
2. How are project teams organized? Who takes what role?
3. What are the methods of assigning consultants to clients?

FIGURE 5 Schedule for Job Search over the Next Six Months

December 18, January 4, 5	Construct list of alumni in consulting for Management Consulting Club (this will help me too).
Over Christmas vacation in Miami and Washington, D.C.	1. Construct letter for consulting firms and Alumni in consulting. 2. Construct letter to be sent to Mayors, Deputy Mayors, and Budget Officers of five large metropolitan cities. 3. Construct letters to heads of five federal government agencies of interest. 4. In Washington, D.C., get back in contact with old boss, D.C. Budget Officer. 5. Write letter to World Bank and other international organizations. 6. Firm up personal recommendations. 7. Send out letters to consulting firms and government agencies coming to campus.
January—first three weeks	1. Spend Saturdays in Career Resource Center. Comb every corner for appealing consulting firms. Find out which international organizations to write to. Also talk to professors. Goal: develop a list of 50 of the most suitable consulting firms. 2. Find out more about field of organization and management development within consulting firm. Find out from professors and firm brochures which firms emphasize this. 3. Contact a woman consultant I met at Women Students Association Career Seminar.
Last week of January	Send out letters. Check out correspondence opportunities. Talk to professors about consulting contracts. Interview consulting and government firms coming to campus.
February—first week	Send out letters. Check out correspondence opportunities. Talk to professors about consulting contacts. Interview consulting and government firms coming to campus.

February, March, April	1. Wait and interview.
	2. Carefully assess "social potential" of cities.
	   (a) Read local newspapers.
	   (b) Talk to friends.

Early May	Make decision. Make job starting date—September.
After Finals to Graduation	Make trip to firm. Contact every friend and friend of friends in city. Get placed on firm's mailing list. Ask for training material. Get local newspaper. Start to find house or apartment.
After Graduation June	Look for house or apartment.
First week of July	Find house or apartment.
Three weeks of July, first week of August	RELAX (VACATION)
Last three weeks of August	Move to new city and set up.
September	Start job.

C

Sources of Information on Selected Industries and Career Opportunities

The references[1] listed here represent a selected set of useful information that is readily available to you. Each reference can be located in any major library.

Titles are listed first according to industry or profession and then by type, e.g., Directory, Book, Periodical, etc.

Advertising and Consumer Marketing

Encylopedias and Dictionaries

1. *Ayer Glossary of Advertising and Related Terms*. Philadelphia: N. W. Ayer & Son, 1972.
2. *Encyclopedia of Advertising*, 2d ed. New York: Fairchild Publications, 1969.
3. Shapiro, Irving J. *Marketing Terms: Definition, Explanations and/or Aspects*, 3d ed. West Long Branch, N.J.: S-M-C Publishing Co., 1973.

Handbooks and Manuals

4. Barton, Roger, ed. *Handbook of Advertising Management*. New York: McGraw-Hill, 1970.
5. *Do's and Don'ts in Avertising Copy: A Looseleaf Service of Advertisers, Advertising Agencies, Broadcasters and Printed Media*. New York: Council of Better Business Bureaus, 1975. Successor to "A Guide to National Advertising."
6. *Handbook of Independent Advertising and Marketing Services*. New York: Executive Communications, 1974.
7. Stansfield, Richard H. *The Dartnell Advertising Manager's Handbook*. Chicago: Dartnell Corp., 1969.

8. Worcester, Robert M., ed. *Consumer Market Research Handbook*. New York: McGraw-Hill, 1972.

Bibliographies

9. Culley, James D., et al. *Current Sources of Marketing Information: An Annotated Bibliography of Major Data Sources*. Newark, Delaware: Bureau of Economic and Business Research, 1974.
10. *A Basic Bibliography on Marketing Research*, 3d ed. American Marketing Association, 1974. Includes material in the social sciences and other disciplines that have direct applicability to marketing research. Coverage is up to the end of 1973.
11. *Marketing Information Guide*. Monthly. Washington, D.C. Marketing Information.
12. "Marketing Abstracts," *Journal of Marketing*. Quarterly. Each issue contains an annotated bibliography covering selected articles of interest to marketers. It is arranged in 22 broad subject headings.
13. Steilen, Charles, and Roley Altizier. *Guide to Marketing/Advertising Information*. Atlanta: Admar Books, 1972. An annotated bibliography covering general as well as specific secondary sources of marketing and advertising information.
14. Thompson, Ralph B. *A Selected and Annotated Bibliography of Marketing Theory*. Austin, Texas: Bureau of Business Research, 1970.

---

[1]These references were compiled by the staff at Baker Library, Harvard Business School, whose help we appreciate.

Books

15. Crissy, W. J. E., and Robert M. Kaplan. *Salesmanship: The Personal Force in Marketing.* New York: John Wiley & Sons, 1969. Written primarily for students enrolled in courses in salesmanship, the majority of whom have career aspirations in business and particularly in marketing.

16. Dirksen, Charles J., and Arthur Kroeger. *Advertising Principles and Problems,* 4th ed. Homewood, Ill.: Richard D. Irwin, 1973.

17. Dunn, S. Watson, and Arnold M. Barba. *Advertising: Its Role in Modern Marketing,* 3d ed. New York: Dryden Press, 1974. An up-to-date introduction to the world of advertising for students.

18. Haas, Kenneth B., and John W. Ernest. *Creative Salesmanship; Understanding Essentials,* 2d ed. Riverside, N.J.: Glencoe Press, 1974. Includes chapters on "Opportunities in Selling" and "Selling as a Career."

19. Mandell, Maurice I. *Advertising,* 2d ed. Englewood Cliffs, N.J.: Prentice-Hall, 1974. An up-to-date source that includes chapter-length examples and good illustrations. It is an introductory overview of advertising intended for those who are interested in careers in advertising.

20. Zober, Martin. *Principles of Marketing.* Boston: Allyn and Bacon, 1971.

Periodicals

21. *Academy of Marketing Science Journal.* Monthly.

22. *Advertising Age.* Weekly. This journal publishes five annual surveys of special interest to advertisers: (1) Marketing Profiles of 125 Leading National Advertisers; (2) 100 leading National Advertisers; (3) AA's Yang Estimates—annual summary of the economy and estimates of advertising expenditures; (4) U.S. Agency Billings; and (5) New Market Data.

23. *Journal of Advertising.* Quarterly.

24. *Journal of Advertising Research.* Bimonthly.

25. *Journal of Marketing.* Quarterly. Features: book reviews, legal developments, and marketing abstracts.

27. *Marketing News.* Bimonthly.

28. *Marketing Times.* Bimonthly. Issues usually focus on one topic, e.g., "Women in Selling" and "How to Sell in a Recession/Inflation Era."

29. Special Libraries Association. Advertising and Marketing Division. *What's New in Advertising and Marketing.* Monthly.

Directories

30. American Business Press, Inc. *Leading Advertisers in Business Publications.* Annual. Ranks about 600 leading advertisers in business journals. Includes an alphabetical list of over 2,400 companies that spend $35,000 or more in business publications.

31. Bradford, Ernest S. *Bradford's Directory of Marketing Research Agencies and Management Consultants in the United States and the World.* Biennial. A list and description of reliable market research agencies in the U.S. and abroad.

32. *Commercial Atlas and Marketing Guide.* Skokie, Ill.: Rand McNally & Company. Lists of railroads, airlines, colleges, and universities (by state). Lists of top 50 (largest) corporations: advertising agencies, commercial banks, life insurance companies, retailing companies, transportation, utilities, and industrial corporations.

33. Marketing Economics Key Plants. *Guide to Industrial Purchasing Power.* New York: Marketing Economics Institute, Ltd., 1973. Directory of 40,000 plants with 100 or more employees. Useful as a statistical research tool, as a prospect list, and as a geographic guide to sales territories.

34. *Standard Directory of Advertisers.* Directory of 17,000 companies that advertise nationally, arranged by industry groupings, with alphabetical index. Gives officers, products, agency, advertising appropriations, media used, etc. Includes a "Trademark Index."

35. *Standard Directory of Advertising Agencies.* Skokie, Ill.: National Register Publishing Co., 1975. Covers 4,400 agency establishments, both National (4,000) and Foreign (400). Issued three times a year in February, June, and October. Supplements called "Agency News" are issued in the months between publications.

36. *Who's Who in Advertising,* 2d ed. New York: Derna V. Morgan, 1972. Index to company names. Limited to United States and Canada.

Statistics

37. *A Guide to Consumer Markets.* New York: The Conference Board, Inc., 1974/1975. Published annually since 1960. A standard source of statistical information concerning the consumer—his demographic and social profile and his economic behavior.

38. *Measuring Markets: A Guide to the Use of Federal and State Statistical Data.* Washington, D.C.: U.S. Dept. of Commerce, August 1974. Brings together in one convenient and concise package those materials published by the federal and state governments that would be useful in marketing research, especially consumer market research.

Career Information and Opportunities

39. Catalyst. *Advertising Career Opportunities.* Series C2. Prepared by Catalyst, the national nonprofit organization dedicated to expanding employment opportunities for college-edcuated women who wish to combine career and family responsibilities. A concise and simple overview of what advertising is and what opportunities are available. Good source of information for both women and men.

40. Gamble, Frederic R. *What Advertising Agencies Are: What They Do and How They Do It.* New York: American Association of Advertising Agencies, 1963. This pamphlet is also available from the AAAA at no charge.

41. Heidrick & Struggles, Inc. *Profiles of a Chief Marketing Executive: Findings of a Study of the Chief Marketing Executives of America's Largest Companies.* New York: H & S Inc., 1971.

Aerospace and Air Transportation

Reports

42. *Frost and Sullivan Reports: Transportation in the U.S.A. to 1990,* No. 315. A profile and projection of the aviation industry.

43. National Petroleum Council. *U.S. Energy Outlook: An Initial Appraisal, 1971–1985.* 2 vols. Includes projections and task force reports.

44. U.S. President. *Aeronautics and Space Report of the President.*

Abstracts and Indexes

45. *Air University Library Index to Military Periodicals.* Quarterly. See "Aerospace Industry" and "Aeronautical Research." See "Airlines" for articles on companies.

46. *Applied Science and Technology Index.* Monthly.

47. *Government Report Index.* Biweekly.

48. *International Aerospace Abstracts.*

49. *Scientific and Technical Aerospace Reports.* For NASA contractors, ongoing research projects and reports issued by the government.

Guides to Sources

50. Metcalf, Kenneth N. *Transportation Information Services.* Detroit: Gale Research Co., 1966.

51. Flood, Kenneth U. *Research in Transportation: Legal/Legislative and Economic Sources and Procedure.* Detroit: Gale Research Co., 1970.

52. Wasserman, Paul, Ed. *Encyclopedia of Business Information Sources.* Detroit: Gale Research Co., 1970.

Statistical Sources

53. *Aerospace Facts and Figures.* Annual. Aerospace Industries Association of America.

54. *Air Shippers Manual.* Annual. Import Publications.

55. *Air Transport Facts and Figures.* Annual. Air Transport Association of America.

56. *Air Transport World,* "Market Development Issue." Annual. May issue.

57. Aviation Daily. *Aviation Daily's Airline Statistical Annual.* Washington, D.C.: Ziff-Davis Publishing Company.

58. *Aviation Week and Space Technology,* "Forecast and Inventory Issue." Annual, e.g., March 17, 1975 issue.

59. *Business Flying.* Quarterly. National Business Aircraft Association.

60. U.S. Civil Aeronautics Board. *Handbook of Airline Statistics.* Biennial. Updated by *Air Carrier Traffic Statistics,* monthly; and *Air Carrier Financial statistics,* quarterly.

61. U.S. Federal Aviation Administration. *FAA Statistical Handbook of Aviation.* Annual.

Books

62. Aerospace Industries Association of America, Inc. *Aerospace and the U.S. Economy: Its Role, Contributions, and Critical Problems.* 1971.

63. Hoyt, Edwin Palmer. *The Space Dealers: A Hard Look at the Role of American Business in Our Space Effort.* New York: John Day Co. 1971.

64. Kane, Robert M., and Allan D. Vose. *Air Transportation.* Dubuque, Iowa: Kendall/Hunt Pub. Co. 1974.

65. Stekler, Herman O. *The Structure and Performance of the Aerospace Industry.* Berkeley: University of California Press, 1965.

66. Stratford, Alan H. *Air Transport Economics in the Supersonic Era.* New York: St. Martin's Press, 1967.

Directories

67. *World Aviation Directory.* Washington, D.C.: American Aviation Associates, Inc. Semiannual. Aviation/aerospace companies and officials.

68. *World Space Directory Including Oceanography.* Biannual.

General Investment Services

69. *Forbes,* "Annual Report on American Industry." First issue in January each year. Has section on aerospace.

70. Standard & Poor's Corporation. *Industry Surveys.* Coverage is separate for aerospace and air transportation; latest issue is in a separate folder.

Census Publications

71. *Census of Transportation.* Washington, D.C.: U.S. Bureau of the Census, Government Printing Office. 1972.

72. *Current Industrial Reports.* U.S. Bureau of the Census. Washington, D.C. Irregular. Contains pamphlets that are arranged alphabetically.

Related Bibliographic Aids

73. Harvard University Graduate School of Business Administration, Baker Library. *Energy Information Sources*. 1976, Mini-list # 14.

74. Harvard University Graduate School of Business Administration, Baker Library. *Sources of Information for Industry Analysis*. 1977, Mini-list # 15.

75. Harvard University Graduate School of Business Administration, Baker Library. *U.S. Transportation Statistical Sources*. 1976, Mini-list #8.

Annual

76. *The Aerospace Year Book*. This contains information on all phases of the aerospace industry.

Arts Management

Bibliographies

77. Georgi, Charlotte. *The Arts and the Art of Administration: A Selected Bibliography*. Los Angeles: UCLA Graduate School of Business Administration, Division of Research, 1970.

78. Georgi, Charlotte. *The Arts and the World of Business: A Selected Bibliography*. Metuchen, N.J.: Scarecrow Press, 1973. Supplement I. Los Angeles: UCLA Graduate School of Management, 1974.

79. Georgi, Charlotte. *Management and the Arts: A Selected Bibliography*. Los Angeles: UCLA Graduate School of Management, Division of Research, 1972.

80. Prieve, E. Arthur, and Ira W. Allen. *Administration in the Arts: An Annotated Bibliography of Selected References*. Madison, Wis.: University of Wisconsin Graduate School of Business, 1973.

81. Quint, Barbara, and Lois Newman. *Performing Arts Centers and Economic Aspects of the Performing Arts: A Selective Bibliography*. Santa Monica, Calif.: Rand Corporation, 1969.

82. Reich, Ann S. *Bibliography for Arts Administration*. n.p.: 1972. This paper is a master's thesis.

Directories

83. *American Art Directory*. New York: R. R. Bowker Company, 1974. Museums, art schools, and art associations in the United States; includes lists of art magazines, fellowships, and scholarships, art schools abroad, and other art resources.

84. *Annual Register of Grant Support*. Orange, N.J.: Academic Media. Annual. Architecture and Fine Arts, p. 100; Performing Arts, p. 162.

85. *Art Direction Buyer's Guide of Art and Photography*. Annual. New York: Art Direction. Lists approximately 2,500 suppliers of art for advertising, illustrations, design, photography, and graphic art services; includes classified listings, representatives, and studio listings, each giving address, telephone number, and services performed.

86. Associated Councils of the Arts. *Directory of National Arts Organizations: Membership Associations Serving the Arts*. New York: Associated Councils of the Arts, 1972.

87. *Fine Arts Market Place*. Annual. New York: R. R. Bowker Company. See Organizations and Associations.

88. *The Foundation Directory*. New York: Columbia University Press for the Foundation Center, 1971. Arranged by state; check subject index in back for various fields of interest, i.e., Performing Arts, Dance, etc.

89. *Who's Who in American Art*. New York: R. R. Bowker Company, 1973.

Indexes

90. *Art Index*. Quarterly. New York: H. W. Wilson Company. For relevant articles check under subject headings such as Museums and Art Galleries—Administration, Art Patronage, Art and State, Art and Society, Business Committee for the Arts, National Endowment for the Arts, etc.

91. *Business Periodicals Index*. Monthly. New York: H. W. Wilson Company. For relevant articles check under subject headings such as Art and State, Museums, Performing Arts, The Arts, Art and Industry, Art Patronage, Theater, Opera, etc.

92. *PAIS*. Weekly. New York: Public Affairs Information Service. For relevant articles check under subject headings such as Arts Market, Museums, Theater, Opera, Art and Industry, Art and State, Art and Society, Performing Arts, Art Patronage, etc.

93. *Reader's Guide to Periodical Literature*. Semimonthly. New York: H. W. Wilson Company. For relevant articles check under subject headings such as Art and Industry, The Arts, The Arts—Finance, The Arts—Federal Aid, Museums, Museum Directors, Theaters, Dance, Opera, Orchestras, etc.

Books

94. Baumol, William J., and William G. Bowen *Performing Arts: The Economic Dilemma*. New York: Twentieth Century Fund, 1966.

95. Chagy, Gideon. *Business in the Arts '70*. New York: P. S. Eriksson, 1970.

96. Chagy, Gideon. *The New Patrons of the Arts*. New York: Harry N. Abrams, 1972.

97. *Cultural Policy and Arts Administration*. Cambridge, Mass.: Harvard Summer School in Arts Administration, 1973.

98. Easton, Allan. *Community Support of the Performing Arts: Selected Problems of Local and National Interest*. Hempstead, N.Y.: Hofstra University, 1970.

99. Eells, Richard Sedric Fox. *The Corporation and the Arts*. New York: The Macmillan Company, 1967.

100. *The Finances of the Performing Arts*. New York: Ford Foundation, 1974.

101. Gingrich, Arnold. *Business and the Arts: An Answer to Tomorrow*. New York: P. S. Eriksson, 1969.

102. Henry, Austin H., and E. Arthur Prieve. *Improved Financial Management of Smaller Performing Arts Organizations*. Madison, Wis.: University of Wisconsin, 1973.

103. Kaderlan, Norman S. *The Role of the Arts Administrator*. Madison, Wis.: University of Wisconsin, Graduate School of Business, Center for Arts Administration, 1973.

104. Moore, Thomas Gale. *The Economics of the American Theatre*. Durham, N.C.: Duke University Press, 1968.

105. National Endowment for the Arts. *National Endowment for the Arts: Our Programs*. Washington, D.C.: U.S. Government Printing Office, 1972.

106. National Endowment for the Arts. *New Dimensions for the Arts, 1971–1972*. Washington, D.C.: U.S. Government Printing Office, 1973.

107. Osborne, Alan. *Patron: Industry Supports the Arts*. London: Connoisseur, 1966.

108. Raymond, Thomas Cicchino, Stephen A. Greyser, and Douglas Schwalbe. *Cases in Arts Administration*. Cambridge, Mass.: Institute of Arts Administration, 1971.

109. Reiss, Alvin H. *The Arts Management Handbook*, rev. 2d ed. New York: Law-Art Pub., 1974.

110. Reiss, Alvin H. *Culture and Company*. New York: Twayne Publishers, 1972.

Newsletters

Though no periodicals focus on this topic, many general art periodicals and business periodicals contain information on arts management. These are accessible through the indexes as mentioned above.

111. *Arts Business*. Quarterly. New York: Business Committee for the Arts.

112. *Arts Management*. 5 a year. New York: Radius Group. This newsletter is edited by Alvin H. Reiss.

113. *BCA News*. Quarterly. New York: Business Committee for the Arts. The editor and publisher of this newsletter is Gideon Chagy.

114. *Management in the Arts Program: Newsletter*. Irregular. Los Angeles: UCLA Graduate School of Management in cooperation with the College of Fine Arts.

Communications

Directories

115. *Broadcasting Yearbook*. Washington. Broadcast Publications. List of all TV stations and AM-FM radio stations in the United States and Canada, including addresses and telephone numbers, licenses and owner, representatives. Lists names and addresses of radio and TV commercial and program producers, news service distributors, network executives, and research services.

116. Weber, Olga S. *Audiovisual Market Place*, 3d ed. New York: R. R. Bowker Company. Company names, addresses, key personnel, and product lines for all active producers, distributors, and other sources of audiovisual learning materials. Includes national, professional, and trade organizations, educational, radio, and TV stations.

117. Weiner, Richard. *Professional Guide to Public Relations*. Englewood Cliffs, N.J.: Prentice-Hall, Inc. Lists 500 public relations services with names, addresses, phone numbers of firms, and key personnel. Services include: clipping bureaus; literary, mailing, radio, and TV public relations services; media directories, motion picture distributors; fine art and rare photo services.

The Computer Industry

Statistical Sources

118. *Computer Review*. Lists significant features of virtually all digital computers and related peripheral devices and indicates comparative prices. Updated every four months to include specifications of new equipment.

119. Lee, Wayne J., ed. *The International Computer Industry*. Washington, D.C.: Applied Library Resources, 1971. Surveys nations that are leading users of computer equipment and systems and provides information concerning the market, duties and trade restrictions, and technical requirements.

120. *Predicasts*. Provides forecast data by SIC number. Sources for each forecast are given.

121. *U.S. Industrial Outlook*. Annual. Pertinent forecast and statistical data in Chapter 29: "Computing and Calculating Equipment."

Investment Services

122. Smith, Barney & Company. *Subscription Research Service*. Provides financial data for specific companies within the industry; pertinent information listed in "Data Processing" section.

123. Standard & Poor's Corporation. *Industry Surveys*. Provides basic data with current updating. Check under "Computers" in index.

124. *Value Line Investment Survey*. Provides stock evaluation for specific companies.

Directories, Encyclopedias, and Yearbooks

125. *Computer Yearbook*. Triennial. Provides overview of the industry. Includes sections on state of the art, computer applications, and a computer language summary.

126. *Computers and People: Computer Directory and Buyer's Guide*. Annual. In addition to organizational listings, includes information on the industry as a whole: a world computer census, a comprehensive list of computer applications, and a roster of college and university computer facilities.

127. *Directory of the Computer Industry*. Washington, D.C.: Applied Library Resources, Inc. A list of over 25,000 computer organizations and computer users, their names and addresses and other information.

128. *International Directory of Computer and Information System Services*. Detroit: Gale Research Company. Alphabetical listing and addresses of all types of electronic data processing agencies.

129. Jordain, Philip B., ed. *Condensed Computer Encyclopedia*. New York: McGraw-Hill, 1969.

130. *Worldwide Directory of Computer Companies*. Four indexes provide extensive coverage of material included. Presents full financial profile of public, private, and nonprofit companies, when available.

Dictionaries

131. Berkeley, Edmund C., and Lovett, Linda L. *Glossary of Terms in Computers and Data Processing*. Newtonville, Mass.: Berkeley Enterprises, 1960.

132. Committee on Computers and Information Processing. *American National Standard Vocabulary for Information Processing*. New York: American National Standards Institute, 1970. Includes list of references used in compilation.

133. Sippl, Charles J. *Computer Dictionary and Handbook*. Indianapolis: Bobbs-Merrill Company, 1966. The several appendices provide general introductory information to the industry. Two specialized appendices provice mathematics and statistics definitions.

134. U.S. Bureau of the Budget. *Automatic Data Processing*. Washington, D.C.: U.S. Government Printing Office, 1972.

135. Weik, Martin H. *Standard Dictionary of Computers and Information Processing*. New York: Hayden Book Companies, 1969. Extensively illustrated.

Bibliographies and Guides to the Literature

136. Carter, Ciel. *Guide to Reference Sources in the Computer Sciences*. New York: The Macmillan Company 1974. Provides detailed annotations for industry information sources.

137. *Computing Reviews*. Monthly. A journal of reviews and abstracts of current publications in areas of the computing sciences.

138. *International Computer Bibliography*. Manchester, England: National Computing Centre, 1969.

139. *New Literature on Automation*. Monthly. A journal of abstracts of recent industry literature: books, reports, articles, works of reference, proceedings, standards.

140. Pritchard, Alan. *A Guide to Computer Literature*, 2d ed. Hamden, Conn.: Shoe String Press, 1972.

141. *Quarterly Bibliography of Computers and Data Processing*. Phoenix, Arizona: Applied Computer Research. Selection designed for use by those actively engaged in profession; highly research-oriented material not included.

142. U.S. Bureau of Domestic Commerce. *Data Communications: Market Information Sources*. 1972.

Trade Journals

143. *Communications of the ACM* (Assocation for Computing Machinery). Monthly.

144. *Computer Decisions*. Monthly.

145. *Computerworld*. Weekly.

146. *Data Processing Digest*. Monthly. "Alerting" service with summaries of selected articles.

147. *Datamation*. Monthly.

Access to information in trade journals is provided by periodical indexes such as *Applied Science and Technology Index*, *Business Periodicals Index*, *F & S Index of Corporations and Industries* (by SIC code number), and *Public Affairs Information Service Bulletin*. Appropriate headings to check are: Computer Industry, Computers, Electronic Data Processing, Information Processing Systems.

Books

148. Bassler, Richard A., and Edward O. Joslin. *An Introduction to Computer Systems*, 2d ed. Arlington, Va.: College Readings, Inc., 1972. Selected articles divided into three sections: background, technology, applications.

149. Billings, Thomas H., and Richard C. Hogan. *A Study of the Computer Manufacturing Industry in the U.S.* Springfield, Va.: National Technical Information Service, 1970. Presents history of the industry with emphasis on economic importance of its present structure. Bibliographical References, pp. 211–213.

150. Gruenberger, Fred, ed. *Expanding Use of Computers in the 70's: Markets, Needs, Technology*. Englewood Cliffs, N.J.: Prentice-Hall, Inc., 1971. Treats industry from viewpoint of market needs. Bibliographical references at end of some chapters.

151. *Frost and Sullivan Reports*. Reports provide detailed industry analysis.

152. Stern, Robert A., and Nancy B. Stern. *Principles of Data Processing*. New York: John Wiley & Sons, 1973. Presents overview of data processing as it specifically relates to the business world. Numerous illustrative aids.

153. Turn, Rein. *Computers in the 1980's*. New York: Columbia University Press, 1974. Discussion of industry potential with specific forecasts concerning hardware and software. Bibliographical references at end of each chapter.

Conservation and Environment

Directories

154. *Conservation Directory.* Annual. Washington, D.C.: National Wildlife Federation. Lists organizations and agencies concerned with the conservation, management, and use of this country's national resources.

155. *Directory of Organizations Concerned with Environmental Research.* State University College at Fredonia. Geographic and subject listing of organizations (governmental, university, and private) throughout the world involved in environmental research.

156. *Pollution Control Directory.* Volume 4, No. 11, of Environmental Science and Technology, American Chemical Society. Lists manufacturers and suppliers of pollution control equipment, products, and services.

Consulting

Bibliographies

157. Association of Consulting Management Engineers, Inc. *Selected References on Management Consultation.* New York: 1974. Excellent entry point to the current and retrospective literature in the field. Includes speeches, articles, pamphlets, books, etc.

158. Hollander, Stanley C. *Management Consultants and Clients.* Michigan State University Business Studies, 1972. An annotated bibliography of books and monographs.

Guides

159. Angel, Juvenal L., compiler. *International Marketing Guide for Technical, Management and Other Consultants.* 1971. Deals with the international aspects of consulting including management consulting.

160. Wasserman, Paul, and Janice McLean. *Who's Who in Consulting: A Reference Guide to Professional Personnel Engaged in Consultation for Business, Industry, and Government,* 2d ed. 1973. Biographical information on over 7,500 individuals engaged in consulting. Listed alphabetically with cross-reference through the subject index.

Directories

161. American Management Association. *Directory of Consultant Members.* Annual.

162. American Management Association. *Directory of Membership and Services.* Annual.

163. American Society for Training and Development. *ASTD Consultant Directory.* Madison, Wis. 1967.

164. Association of Consulting Management Engineers. *Directory of Membership and Services.* Annual. New York.

165. Association of Management Consultants. *Directory of Membership and Services.* Updated annually. Milwaukee.

166. *Directory of Management Consultants and Industrial Services.* Los Angeles Chamber of Commerce. Lists consulting firms, business and industrial services.

167. *Engineering Careers with Consulting Firms.* Resource Publications, D. R. Goldenson and Company. Page profiles describing the activities of the firm and the nature of engineering services, requirements for positions. Information arranged by specialty and geographic location.

168. *European Directory of Economic and Corporate Planning 1973–1974.* Penelope Lloyd, ed. Eppine, Essex, U.K.: Gower, 1974. Lists European management consultants among others. Use the unit index as an access point.

169. *Industrial Research Laboratories of the U.S.,* rev. ed. William Buchanan, ed. Washington: Bowker Associations. Irregular.

170. Institute of Management Consultants. *Directory of Members–Institute of Management Consultants.* New York: 1974. Contains Supplement I, August 19, 1974.

171. *National Roster of Minority Professional Firms.* U.S. Department of Commerce. February, 1973. Not limited to management consultants.

172. *New Consultants: A Periodic Supplement to Consultants and Consulting Organizations.* June 1973–January 1975.

173. Smith, Robert, ed. *Register of Management Consultants and Advisory Services to Industry.* Eppine, Essex, U.K.: Gower, 1972. Contains over 1,000 entries as well as many useful chapters such as "How to Select and Use a Management Consultant" and "Presentation and Layout of a Consultant's Report."

174. Wasserman, Paul, and Janice McLean, eds. *Consultants and Consulting Organizations: A Reference Guide to Concerns and Individuals Engaged in Consultation for Business and Industry,* 2d ed. Detroit: Gale Research Co., 1973. Lists over 5,000 individuals and firms. Contains a subject index and lists both U.S. and foreign firms.

Monographs and Conference Reports

Works dealing with various aspects of business or management consulting may be found by consulting the card catalog at a library under the subject heading "Business Consulting." A few examples are listed below.

175. Amon, Richard R., et al. *Management Consulting.* Management Consulting Report Associates, 1958. Although somewhat dated, this does contain a good history of consulting.

176. *Management Consulting in the 1970's: Proceedings North American Conference of Management Consultants*, January 25, 1972.

Periodicals

Articles on consulting appear in many different periodicals, but they can usually be located by using one of the various indexes such as *ANBAR Management Services, Business Periodicals Index, F & S Index to Corporations and Industries, Public Affairs Information Services Index,* and *Readers' Guide.*

177. *American Institute of Certified Public Accountants Management Advisory Services Guideline Series*. Irregular. New York.

178. Association of Consulting Management Engineers. *ACME Survey on Compensation for Professional Staff in Management Consulting Firms*. Triennial. New York. Excludes partners, officers, directors, and owners.

179. Association of Consulting Management Engineers. *Management Consultant*. New York. Irregular.

Books

180. Wasserman, Paul, and W. R. Greer, Jr. *Consultants and Consulting Organizations*. Ithaca, N.Y.: Graduate School of Business and Public Administration, Cornell University.

Educational and Library Administration

Indexes to Educational Information

181. Wasserman, Paul, ed. *Encyclopedia of Business Information Sources*. Detroit: Gale Research Co., 1970. Volume I. Includes references for educational information under the topic "Schools."

Directories

182. *A Directory of Educational Programs for the Gifted*, 1st ed. Lavonne B. Axford, ed. Metuchen, N.J.: Scarecrow Press.

183. *A Summary of Paraprofessional Training in Colleges and Universities*. Office of New Careers. Washington, D.C.: U.S. Government Printing Office. Geographical listing of opportunities for "new careers for the poor."

184. *Accredited Institutions of Postsecondary Education*, and Programs and Candidates, Washington, D.C. American Council on Education. Annual.

185. *American Junior Colleges*, 8th ed. Edmund J. Gleaser, Jr., ed. Washington, D.C.: American Council on Education.

186. *American Library Directory*, Helaine MacKeigan, ed. Biennal. New York: R. R. Bowker Company. Lists public libraries, county and regional systems, college and university libraries, and private libraries. Information includes names of key personnel and addresses.

187. *American Universities and Colleges*, 10th ed. Otis A. Singletary, ed. Washington, D.C.: American Council on Education.

188. *Barron's Guide to the Two-Year Colleges*. R. William Graham, ed. Woodbury, N.Y.: Barron's Educational Series.

189. *Barron's Profiles of American Colleges*. Benjamin Fine, ed. Woodbury, N.Y.: Barron's Educational Series. Detailed profiles on 1,350 colleges. Competitive ratings listed.

190. *Comparative Guide to American Colleges*. James Cass and Max Biernbaum, eds. New York: Harper & Row. Descriptions of U.S. four-year colleges, with indexes by state, religious affiliation, selectivity, and number of degrees granted in selected fields.

191. *Comparative Guide to Two-Year Colleges and Four-Year Specialized Schools and Programs*. James Cass and Max Biernbaum, eds. New York: Harper & Row.

192. *Directory of National Association of Schools of Music*. Washington, D.C.: National Association of Schools of Music.

193. *Directory of Accredited Institutions*. Washington, D.C.: United Business Schools Associations. Alphabetical and geographic listing of accredited business schools.

194. *Directory of Accredited Private Home Study Schools*. Washington, D.C.: National Home Study Council.

195. *Directory of Approved Counseling Agencies*. Washington, D.C.: American Board on Counseling Service, Inc., APGA.

196. *Directory of Catholic Special Facilities and Programs in the U.S. for Handicapped Children and Adults*. Washington, D.C. National Catholic Educational Association.

197. *Directory of Computer Education and Research*. Washington, D.C.: Science and Technology Press Inc. In two volumes; offers information on over 1,400 Institutions in the U.S. offering educational programs in computer and computer-related fields; their courses and research activities.

198. *Directory of Educational Statistics, A Guide to Sources*. Malcolm C. Hamilton, ed. Ann Arbor, Mich.: Piernan Press, 1974.

199. *Directory of Exceptional Children, A Listing of Educational and Training Facilities*, 7th ed. E. R. Young and Porter Sargent, eds. Boston: Porter Sargent, Annual. Lists private residential and day schools and treatment centers for the emotionally disturbed and socially maladjusted.

200. *Directory of Experimental Schools, Issue No. 57*. Pettigrew, Arkansas: New Schools Exchange.

201. *Directory of Free Schools*. Sebastopol, Cal.: Alternatives Foundation.

202. *Directory of Full-Year Head Start Programs.* Washington, D.C.: Office of Child Development, Project Head Start, U.S. Department of HEW. Geographic listing with key personnel of all the programs. Addresses of regional offices.

203. *Directory of Library Consultants.* John Berry III, ed. New York: R. R. Bowker Company. Lists qualified consultants in the United States and Canada and in every area of libarianship. Names, addresses, backgrounds. Listed alphabetically and by specialty.

204. *Directory of Member Colleges.* Washington, D.C. Council for the Advancement of Small Colleges.

205. *Directory of National Association of Trade and Technical Schools.* Washington, D.C.: Accrediting Commission of National Association of Trade and Technical Schools. Schools listed under subject headings, alphabetically, by state. Includes course descriptions and use of the school by public and private agencies.

206. *Directory of Predominantly Black Colleges and Universities in the U.S.A.* Washington, D.C.: National Alliance of Businessmen. Geographic directory, including enrollment, curricula, degrees offered, and description of each institution.

207. *The Academic Underachiever.* Triennially. Boston: Porter Sargent. Selective information on the classification and description of over 700 sources of help for the able student who needs special assistance in planning his educational career.

208. *Directory of Special Libraries and Information Centers.* Anthony Kruzas, ed. Detroit: Gale Research. Volume I lists information facilities in the United States and Canada: special libraries in colleges and universities, branches of public library concentrating on one group of subjects, company, government, and nonprofit-sponsored libraries; Volume II gives geographic and personnel listings.

209. *Directory of State and Local Resources for the Mentally Retarded.* Washington, D.C.: U.S. Department of HEW. List of state and local agencies, facilities, and other resources that serve the mentally retarded. Includes clinical programs and residential facilities, special rehabilitation facilities, and type of client served.

210. *The Directory of Traditional Black Colleges and Universities in U.S.* Detroit: Ford Motor Company & U.S. Plywood Champion Paper, Inc.

211. *Early Childhood Education Directory,* 1st ed. New York: R. R. Bowker and Co. Guide to approximately 2,000 schools devoted to the educational interests of preschool children.

212. *Education Directory. Education Associations.* Annual. U.S. Office of Education. Washington, D.C.: U.S. Government Printing office. Includes association's publications and frequency of issue.

213. *Education Directory—Higher Education.* Washington, D.C.: U.S. Department of HEW, National Center for Educational Statistics. Lists accredited institutions (alphabetically by state) in United States and its outlying areas.

214. *Education Directory. Public School Systems 1973–74.* Washington, D.C.: U.S. Government Printing Office, 1971.

215. *Education Directory—State Governments.* Washington, D.C.: U.S. Department of HEW. Lists principal officers of state agencies responsible for elementary and secondary education and vocational-technical education in United States.

216. *Encyclopedia of Associations.* Volumes 1, 3. Detroit: Gale Research Co. Volume 1 is an annual compilation of names and addresses for all types of national organizations arranged by broad index to provide easy access. Volume 3 is published quarterly and lists "new associations and projects." Section 5 of Volume 1 is "Educational Organizations."

217. *Directory of Facilities for the Learning Disabled and Catalog of Tests.* San Rafael, California: Academic Therapy Publications; New York: Harper & Row. Geographic listing of schools, learning centers, and clinics.

218. *Guide to Master of Arts in Teaching Program.* Anne M. Scott, ed. State University of New York at Binghamton. Programs, by state, described by level of specialization available; program length; intern and salary information.

219. *Hand Book of Private Schools.* Boston: Porter Sargent Publications. Schools and academies listed by geographical districts; leading private schools classified; summer academic and camp programs.

220. *Encyclopedia of Library and Information Science.* New York: Marcel Dekker, Inc. Lists alphabetically all information related to library and information science. Includes organizations, individuals, conferences, countries, libraries, systems, codes, copyright information, etc.

221. *Index of Opportunity in the Teaching Profession.* Employer profiles. Princeton, N.J.: Princeton University Press, 1970.

222. *Guide to the Two-Year Colleges.* Woodbury, N.Y.: Barron's Educational series.

223. *Lovejoy's Career and Vocational School Guide.* Clarence Lovejoy, ed. New York: Simon and Schuster. Private and public vocational school programs.

224. *Lovejoy's College Guide,* Clarence Lovejoy, ed. Annual. New York: Simon and Schuster. Entries for more than 3,368 American colleges, universities, junior colleges, and technical institutes; 500 programs geared to specific careers and discussion of new college board program.

225. *Private Independent Schools, The American Private Schools for Boys and Girls,* Annual. Wallingford, Conn.: Bunting and Lyon, Inc. Lists by state, summer programs.

226. *Requirements for Certification for Elementary, Secondary Schools and Junior Colleges.* Elizabeth Woellner and Maurilla Woods, eds. Chicago: University of Chicago Press. Listed for each state are

classifications of certificates and requirements for elementary and secondary, including special subject areas, guidance, supervisory, and junior college.

227. *Scholarship Program, Education of Handicapped Children*. Washington, D.C.: U.S. Office of Education.

228. *The Counselor Education Directory 1971*, 1st ed. Muncie, Ind.: Ball State University. Counselor education programs; lists institutions and the degrees, majors, and certificates available; lists 2,500 counselor educators, and state directors of counseling and guidance.

229. *Who's Who in American College and University Administration Annual*. New York: Crowell-Collier Educational Corporation. Presents biographical information on "11,000 administrators including presidents, deans, librarians, bursars and others."

Bibliographies and Guides

230. *Comparative Guide to American Colleges*. James Cass and Max Biernbaum, eds. New York: Harper & Row. Descriptions of U.S. four-year colleges, with indexes by state, religious affiliation, selectivity, and number of degrees granted in selected fields.

231. *Comparative Guide to Two-Year Colleges and Four-Year Specialized Schools and Programs*. James Cass and Max Biernbaum, eds. New York: Harper & Row.

232. Forrester, Gertrude. *Occupational Literature–An Annotated Bibliography*. New York: H. W. Wilson Company, 1971, p. 432. Information found under "School Administrator."

233. Pierce, Milo C. *Administration and Planning in Higher Education: A Bibliography of Books and Reports*. Monticello, Ill.: Council of Planning Librarians, 1972. Encompasses five aspects of administration and planning in higher education: Policymaking, Legal, Financial, Physical Plant, and Academic.

234. *School Executive's Guide*. Englewood Cliffs, N.J.: Prentice-Hall, Inc., 1965. A practical compendium for administering public schools in the United States.

Statistics

235. College and University Personnel Association. *Administration Compensation Survey*. Biennial. Washington, D.C.: C.U.P.A. Excellent survey including both fringe-benefit and salary analysis.

236. Harris, Seymour E. *A Statistical Portrait of Higher Education*. New York: McGraw-Hill, 1972.

237. National Education Association, Research Division. *Salaries Paid and Salary-Related Practices in Higher Education*. Washington, D.C.: NEA. Biennial. Includes salary and fringe benefits.

238. *Predicasts*. This publication gives forecast data by Standard Industrial Classification number. Education SIC number is 8200. Sources for each forecast are given. It is suggested that you check the original source for the most complete forecast information.

239. *Standard Education Almanac*. John S. Greene, ed. Indianapolis, Indiana: Academic Media, 1972.

240. U.S. Department of Commerce. *U.S. Industrial Outlook for 1975*. Washington, D.C.: U.S. Government Printing Office, 1975. "Educational Services" on pp. 413–415 with projections to 1980.

241. U.S. Office of Education. *Digest of Educational Statistics*. Annual. Washington, D.C.: U.S. Government Printing Office.

242. U.S. Office of Education. *Projections of Educational Statistics to 1982–83*. 1973 edition. Washington, D.C.: U.S. Government Printing Office, 1974.

Books and Pamphlets

243. Biegeleisen, J. I. *Careers and Opportunities in Teaching*, 1st ed. New York: E. P. Dutton and Co. 1972. Considerations about teaching at various levels or in related orientations; suggestions and list of accredited colleges with teacher education programs.

244. Bolin, James F., ed. *Management Information for College Administrators*. Atlanta: University of Georgia, 1971.

245. Carnegie Commission on Higher Education. *The More Effective Use of Resources: An Imperative for Higher Education*. New York: McGraw-Hill, 1972. A report and recommendations.

246. Committee for Economic Development, Research and Policy Committee. *The Management and Financing of Colleges*. New York: C.E.D., 1973.

247. Eisen, Irving. *Careers in Teaching and Education*. Washington, D.C.: B'nai B'rith Vocational Service, 1972. Descriptions of wide variety of professional jobs of a teaching nature within the school, college, or vocational school settings.

248. Getzels, Jacob W., James M. Lipham, and Roald F. Campbell. *Educational Administration as a Social Process—Theory, Research, Practice*. New York: Harper & Row, 1968.

249. Hefferlin, J.B. Lon, and Ellis L. Phillips, Jr. *Information Services for Academic Administration*. San Francisco: Jossey-Bass, Inc., 1971.

250. Hungate, Thad L. *Management in Higher Education*. New York: Bureau of Publications, Teachers College, Columbia University, 1964.

251. Lahti, Robert E. *Innovative College Management*. San Francisco: Jossey-Bass Inc., 1973. Includes annotated bibliography.

252. Minter, John, and Ben Lawrence, eds. *Management Information Systems: Their Development and Use in the Administration of Higher Education*. Boulder, Colorado: Western Interstate Commission for Higher Education, 1969. Seminar on the Advanced State-of-the-Art/The Sterling Institute, Washington, D.C.

253. Organization for Economic Cooperation and Development. *Institutional Management in Higher Education*. Paris: O.E.C.D. Publications, 1972. Four-day conference report; 21 countries and 83 institutions of higher education represented.

254. Richman, Barry M., and Richard N. Farmer. *Leadership Goals, and Power in Higher Education*. San Francisco: Jossey-Bass, Inc., 1974.

255. Wingfield, Clyde J., Ed. *The American University, A Public Administration Perspective*. Dallas: Southern Methodist University, 1970. Symposium on administration of higher education and presidential perspectives.

Indexes to Periodicals

256. *Business Periodicals Index*. New York: H. W. Wilson, Monthly except July (Cumulative).

257. *Current Index to Journals on Education* (CIJE).

258. *Educational Administration Abstracts*. Published three times a year by the University Council for Educational Administration, Columbus, Ohio. Abstracts approximately 100 journals.

259. *Educational Administration Quarterly*. Published three quarters a year by the University Council for Educational Administration, Columbus, Ohio.

260. *Education Index*. Bronx, N.Y.: The H. W. Wilson Co., Washington.

261. *Educational Resources Information Center* (ERIC). ERIC is a national information system established by the U.S. Office of Education in 1964. Its purpose is to collect, process, and make available a wide range of educational documents. These are four major parts to the ERIC system: (1) Thesaurus of ERIC Descriptors, (2) educational documents on microfiche, (3) abstract indices to microfiche—ex. RIE (Research in Education), and (4) machinery to read and reproduce microfiche. Initially, use the topic "Educational Administration"; for more in-depth research, check with Thesaurus of ERIC Descriptors.

Electronics and Engineering

Directories

262. *Electronic News Financial Fact Book and Directory*. New York: Fairchild Publishers. Annual. Lists officers and directors, products, and sales for electronic companies.

263. *Electronic Industries Association, Membership List, Trade Directory*. Annual. Washington, D.C.

264. *Science, Engineering, Research and Development Directory*. Annual. Small Business Administration (Regional Offices). Issued separately for each of the nine SBA regions.

Periodicals

265. *Electronics. Top 100*. A listing published each year in the July issue of *Electronics News* magazine.

Financial—Banking

Bibliographies

266. American Bankers Association. *Stonier Graduate School of Banking, Cumulative Catalog of Theses, Supplement*. New York. Annotated. Annual.

267. Federal Reserve Bank of Philadelphia. *The Fed in Print*. Quarterly. Current information of Federal Reserve publications.

Directories

268. *Who Owns What in World Banking*. London: Banker Research Unit. Annual. A guide to the subsidiary and affiliated interests of the world's major banks.

269. *Banking*. "A Bankers Guide to Washington." Annual. New York: Banking. Gives names, addresses, phone numbers of all federal agencies affecting banking, as well as key politicians, committees, and trade associations in the area.

270. *Banks of the World*. Frankfurt-am-Main: Fritz Knopp Verlag.

271. *Directory of American Savings and Loan Associations:* Baltimore: T. K. Sanderson Organization. Annual. Listing of 5,000 U.S. associations, with branches, key officials, officials, affiliations, etc.

272. *Financial Market Place*. New York: R. R. Bowker Company. Lists names and addresses (some foreign firms) of companies grouped by industry—such as banks, investment organizations, capital firms, credit and collection services, stock and commodity, and so on.

273. *International Bankers Directory*. Skokie, Ill.: Rand McNally & Company.

274. *Major Independent Finance Companies*. A listing published each year in the April issue of *Bankers Monthly* magazine.

275. *Polk's World Bank Directory*. Nashville, Tenn.: R. L. Polk and Company. Lists banks and information.

276. *Rand-McNally International Bankers Directory. Bankers Blue Book*. Biannual. Skokie, Ill.: Rand McNally & Company.

277. *Who's Who in Banking: The Directory of the Banking Profession*. New York: Business Press, Inc. Irregular.

Investment Services

278. *Frost and Sullivan Reports: Markets for Specialized Financial Services*, No. 221. Includes data on the banking industry.

279. Investors Management Sciences, Inc. *Financial Dynamics*. Gives financial analysis and comparisons, quarterly and annually, of individual industries, including banking and savings and loan associations.

280. Smith, Barney & Co. *Subscription Research Service*. Contains finance and research reports analyzing facts about banking.

281. Standard and Poor's Corporation. *Industry Surveys*. Includes current and basic analyses of the banking and savings and loan industries, with financial comparisons and outlook.

282. *Standard and Poor's Stock Reports.* Usually found in loose-leaf binder. Single page for each company listed on the New York, American, and over-the-counter stock exchanges. Each report gives fundamental position, recent developments, and so on, for companies.

283. *Value Line Investment Survey.* Includes ratings and reports on the banking industry, with special situation analysis.

284. *World Who's Who in Finance and Industry.* Career sketches of leading businessmen and others noteworthy in the fields of finance and industry. A selected index by company is at the front.

Additional Statistical Sources

285. Bank Administration Institute. *A Biennial Survey of Bank Officer Salaries.*

286. Federal Home Loan Board. *Savings and Home Financing Source Book.* Annual. Statistics on loans held, mortgages.

287. National Association of Supervisors of State Banks. *Profile of State-Chartered Banking.* Biennial. Includes statistics on state banking departments, number of banks, assets and liabilities, as well as operations, competition, etc.

288. *Predicasts.* Abstracts forecast statistics by SIC number, gives original sources of data.

289. Standard and Poor's Corporation. *Standard and Poor's Trade and Securities: Statistics.* "Banking and Finance." Current and basic statistical source.

290. U.S. Bureau of Domestic Commerce. *The U.S. Industrial Outlook.* Annual. Recent trends, with a brief outlook on commercial banking.

291. U.S. Bureau of the Census. *Statistical Abstract of the United States.* Annual. Includes government data on the banking industry, and a "Guide to Sources of Statistics."

292. U.S. Dept. of Commerce. *Survey of Current Business* (annual) with its biennial supplement, *Business Statistics.*

293. United States League of Savings Associations. *Savings and Loan Fact Book.* Annual.

Statistics on banking are published mainly by the various federal agencies: The Federal Reserve System (Assets and Liabilities of All Commercial Banks in the United States, etc.); The Federal Deposit Insurance Corporation; The Comptroller of the Currency of the Treasury Dept.; The Federal Home Loan Bank Board. The U.S. Savings and Loan League, the American Bankers Association, and various others also publish current material. For statistics in banking journals, see below. (Individual FRS banks also publish journals.)

Encyclopedia and Manuals

294. Bank Administration Institute. *Bank Administration Manual.* Park Ridge, Ill.: Bank Administration Institute, 1970. An aid in solving problems likely to arise in banking.

295. Ritter, Lawrence S. *Principles of Money, Banking, and Financial Markets.* New York: Basic Books, 1974.

296. Munn, G. G. *Glenn G. Munn's Encyclopedia of Banking and Finance,* 7th ed., revised by F. L. Garcia. Boston: Bankers Publishing Co.: 1973.

Journals and Magazines

297. *American Banker.* Daily.

298. *The Banker.* Monthly. London.

299. *The Banker's Magazine.* Quarterly. Includes a book review section.

300. *Banker's Monthly.* Monthly. National banking magazine.

301. *Banking.* Monthly. Journal of the American Banking Association.

302. *Burrough's Clearing House.* Monthly. Reports much S & L news, including annual meetings.

303. *Federal Reserve Bulletin.* Monthly. U.S. Board of Governors of the Federal Reserve Systems. Includes the FRS Directory, current events; one of the best sources of national and international banking statistics.

304. *Journal of Bank Research.* Quarterly. Bank Administration Institute.

305. *Journal of Commerce Bank Lending.* Monthly. Robert Morris Associates.

306. *Magazine of Bank Administration.* Monthly.

307. *Savings and Loan News.* Monthly. United States Savings and Loan League. Features a "Current Trends" section.

308. *United States Federal Home Loan Board Journal.* Monthly. Contains current statistics on savings and loan associations; annual reports in the April issue.

For recent articles in journals, magazines, and newspapers, see *Business Periodicals Index, Funk and Scott Index of Corporations and Industries, Funk and Scott Index International, New York Times Index, Public Affairs Information Service Bulletin, Wall Street Journal Index.*

Guides

309. Andriot, John L. *Guide to U.S. Government Serials and Periodicals.* McLean, Virginia: Documents Index.

310. Andriot, John L. *Guide to U.S. Government Statistics.* McLean, Virginia: Documents Index. Contains valuable sources of banking statistics published by the various federal agencies.

Lists of Largest Banks

311. *American Banker.* "500 Largest Banks in the Free World"; "300 Largest Banks in the U.S.," in last July issue each year; also "300 Largest Commercial Banks in the U.S.," each year in late January or early

February; "300 Top Savings and Loans," in the late February issue.

312. *The Banker*. "The Top 300 World Banks." Annual, June issue.

313. *Fortune*. "Directory of Largest Corporations." Annual, 4 parts. Part 3 (July) lists 50 largest commercial banks; part 4 (August) lists the 50 largest commercial banks outside the U.S.

314. *Moody's Bank and Financial Manual*. Annual, with biweekly supplements. Center blue pages include 300 largest banks in U.S. (by deposits), 50 largest banks (by amount of permanent capital funds), 100 largest savings and loan associations.

315. *Savings and Loan News*. "The Top 200 Associations." Annual, February issue.

Annual Surveys and Special Reports

316. *The Banker*. "International Banking Annual Review." August 1974, p. 891 ff.

317. *Business Week*. "A Close-up of How the 200 Top Banks Are Performing," "Annual Survey of Bank Performance." Mid-September issues (April 18, 1977).

318. *Business Week*. "New Banking," Special Report, Sept. 15, 1973, pp. 86–166. Tells of changes in the banking world, new operations and businesses.

319. *Forbes*. "Annual Report on American Industry." Includes section on Fianance—Banks. Always 1/1/—issue.

320. *Journal of Bank Research*. "The Changing Dimensions of Banking Structure." Autumn 1974, pp. 145–155.

321. *Management Controls*. Special Issue: "Bank Management," June 1974. Discusses issues, trends, and systems involved in improving organizational and operational efficiency; information on the computer process.

322. *World Banking Survey*. Annual. Includes list of the world's leading banks.

Recent Publications

323. Mayer, Martin. *The Bankers*. New York: Weybright and Talley, 1974. Report on the revolution in American banking and its possible consequences; examines most facets of banking today.

324. Prochnow, Herbert V., and Herbert V. Prochnow, Jr., eds. *The Changing World of Banking*. New York: Harper & Row, 1974. Survey of American banking; articulates numerous aspects of modern banking developments by authorities; includes bibliographical references.

Financial—Nonbanking

Directories

325. *Best's Digest of Insurance Stocks*. Morristown, N.J.: A. M. Best Company.

326. *Best's Life Insurance Reports*. Morristown, N.J.: A. M. Best Company.

Food Processing and Distributing

Directories

327. *Frozen Food Fact Book and Directory*. New York: National Frozen Food Association. Lists members of association by state. Lists are broken down into several different divisions (packers, brokers, warehouses).

328. *Grocery Distribution Guide*. Greenwich, Conn.: Metro Market Studies, Inc. Grocers listed by city and state.

329. *Supermarket Grocery and Convenience Store Chains*. New York: Business Guides, Inc. Chain Store Guide. Lists of supermarkets by city and state.

330. *Thomas Grocery Register*. New York: Thomas Publishing Company. Lists supermarket chains by states; exporters, importers, brokers; canners; frozen foods; packers; warehouse; trade associations.

Health Service Industries

Bibliographies

331. Davis, Morris E. *Planning Medical Care: Assessment of Distribution and Costs of Physician Services*. Monticello, Ill.: Council of Planning Librarians, Exchange Bibliography No. 475, November 1973.

332. Harrison, Fernande P. *Planning Health Care Facilities: A Bibliography*. Monticello, Ill.: Council of Planning Librarians, Exchange Bibliography No. 369, February 1973.

333. Sharma, Prakash C. *Health Services: A Selected Research Bibliography*. Monticello, Ill.: Council of Planning Librarians, Exchange Bibliography No. 586, June 1974.

334. Williamson, John W. *Health Services Research Bibliography*. Washington, D.C.: U.S. Department of HEW, 1972.

Statistical Sources

335. DMS, Inc. *Health Care Systems, 1972–1976*. New York: McGraw-Hill, 1971. Excellent basic source for cost estimates and outlook; division breakdowns with charts and tables, market outlook; directory of manufacturers of health industry equipment with description and use of instruments; directory of hospitals and of consultant assistance available in specialized clinical areas.

336. "1974 Salary Scoreboard." In *Modern Healthcare*, August 1974, pp. 19–24. Comparison charts and graphs of salary ranges in the field.

337. *Reference Data on Socioeconomic Issues in Health*. Annual. Chicago: American Medical Association.

Statistics and graphs on hospitals and nursing homes, health insurance, and personal and national health care expenditures.

338. Stewart, Paula A. *Health Manpower: A County and Metropolitan Area Data Book.* Washington, D.C.: U.S. Department of HEW, 1971.

339. Troy, Leo. *Almanac of Business and Industrial Financial Ratios.* Annual. Englewood Cliffs, N.J.: Prentice-Hall. Detailed listing of financial ratios for medical industry services operation; same for medical industry manufacturing.

340. U.S. Bureau of the Census. *Census of Manufacturers—Preliminary Reports.* 1972. Quinquennial. Uses Standard Industrial Classification (SIC). See Report Nos. 3841–42 for preliminary statistics on employment, payrolls, cost of materials, value added by manufacturer, and value of shipment.

341. U.S. Bureau of the Census. "Industry Series," *Census of Manufacturers.* 1972. Quinquennial. For operating ratios as well as an elaboration of *Preliminary Reports,* see SIC Industry Groups, pp. 384–387.

342. U.S. Social Security Administration. *Medical Care Expenditures, Prices and Costs: Background Book.* 1973. Overall view of operating costs and projections of hospital and nursing facilities.

Industry Information

343. DeSalvo, Robert J. "Medical Marketing Mixture." In *Medical Marketing and Media,* February 1974, p. 18. Structure of health care industry viewed.

344. Fritz, Eli. "Overview of the Hospital Marketing." In *Medical Marketing and Media,* November 1971, pp. 11–16. Comparisons of hospital expenditures in the years between 1946 and 1970.

345. Frost and Sullivan, Inc. *The Hospital Drugs, Supplies, Services, Equipment and Building Materials,* Report No. 333. New York, February 1975. Covers community hospital industry with projections to 1984.

346. Frost and Sullivan, Inc. *Markets for Health Care Equipment Leasing,* Report No. 264. New York. Covers present market, future trends with 10-year projections, opportunities, etc.

347. Gallop, Renee. "Health and Medical Services." In *U.S. Industrial Outlook, 1975, with Projections to 1980,* pp. 399–404. U.S. Bureau of Domestic Commerce, 1975. Annual. Broad-scoped article on the growing needs in health care industry as well as graphic depiction of present and projected costs. Brief explanation of health maintenance organizations.

348. *Health Care Facilities, Existing and Needed.* Washington, D.C.: Department of HEW, 1969. Dated but valuable, as projections of that year can be compared to actual current progress. Discussion of the Hill-Burton plan.

349. Industry File. *File I-80, Health Organizations.* For specific information on a number of hospitals and health service programs.

350. *Medical Marketing and Media.* Monthly. Stamford, Conn.: Navillus Publishing Corp. Up-to-date reports on advances in medical industry and manufacturing. Indexed in *F & S.*

351. *Nursing Home Fact Book, 1970–71.* Washington, D.C.: American Nursing Home Association, 1971.

352. Schiffman, Leon G., and Vincent Gaccione. "Opinion Leaders in Institutional Markets." In *Journal of Marketing,* 38(2):49, 1974. Impact of opinion leaders in health care institutional market.

353. *Sources of Medical Information.* New York: Exceptional Books, Inc.

354. Standard and Poor's Corporation. *Trade and Securities.* Monthly with annual cumulations. Industrial surveys on many aspects of health care industry. Reports accessible through subject index under "Medical Care" at the beginning of each year cumulation.

Administration/Management

355. *Comprehensive Health Care Centers Including HMO's.* Report No. 271. New York: Frost and Sullivan, Inc., June 1974. In-depth view of health care industry manpower resources, and supplies as well as the economics of health care including health care plans and HMOs.

356. DMS, Inc. *Health Care Systems, 1972–1976.* New York: McGraw-Hill, 1971.

357. Durbin, Richard L., and W. Herbert Springall. *Organization and Administration of Health Care: Theory, Practice, Environment,* 2d ed. St. Louis: C. V. Mosby Company, 1974.

358. Forsyth, G. C., and D. Glyn Thomas. "Models for Financially Healthy Hospitals." In *Harvard Business Review,* July/August 1971, pp. 106–117.

359. Griffith, John R., Walton M. Hancock, and Fred C. Munson. "Practical Ways to Contain Hospital Costs." In *Harvard Business Review,* November/December 1973, pp. 131–139.

360. Hepner, James O., and Donna M. Hepner. *The Health Strategy Game: A Challenge for Reorganization and Management.* Saint Louis: C. V. Mosby Company, 1973.

361. *Hospital Financial Management.* Monthly. Chicago: Hospital Financial Management Association. Current issues in hospital and health services management.

362. *International Journal of Health Services.* Quarterly. Westport, Conn.: Baywood Publishing, Co. Covers policy, planning, administration, and evaluation of health services.

363. Weber, James B., and Martha A. Dula. "Effective Planning of Committees for Hospitals." In *Harvard Business Review,* May/June 1964, pp. 113–142.

364. Wren, George R. *Modern Health Administration*. Athens, Ga.: University of Georgia Press, 1974.

Indexes and Abstracts

365. *Business Periodicals Index*. Articles on health services industry accessible through author and subject index. See subject heading "Medical Care" and its related subheadings and cross-references. Particularly good for articles on health maintenance organizations.

366. *F & S Index of Corporations and Industries*. Article citations accessible through numerically sequential Standard Industrial Classification (SIC) numbers; for "Health Services Manufacturing Industry," see SIC No. 3840; for "Health Services," see SIC No. 8000.

367. *Medical Care Review*. 11 per year. Ann Arbor, Michigan: Bureau of Public Health Economics. Includes abstracts of books, articles, and conferences.

368. Public Affairs Information Service (PAIS). Accessible through author and subject index.

369. Smithsonian Institution. Science Information Exchange. *Catalog of Health Services Research: Abstracts of Public and Private Projects, 1967–70*. Washington, D.C.: U.S. Department of HEW, 1971. Abstracts of 1,226 funded projects in all aspects of

health care including hospital and nursing home administration.

Directories

370. *Directory of Member Services*. Washington, D.C.: American Association of Psychiatric Services for Children. Geographic directory including names of key personnel, listing of approved training centers and programs in career child psychiatry.

371. DMS, Inc. *Health Care Systems, 1972–1976*. New York: McGraw-Hill, 1971.

372. *Guide to the Health Care Field*. Annual. Chicago: American Hospital Association. Directory of health care institutions, AJA membership, health organizations, agencies and educational programs; includes guide for hospital buyers.

373. *Health Organizations of the United States and Canada*. Ithaca, N.Y.: Graduate School of Business and Public Administration, Cornell University. Lists national, regional, and state organizations involved with health and related fields in the United States and Canada.

374. *Hospitals*. Guide issue of the Journal of the American Hospital Association, Parts 1 and 2. Chicago: American Hospital Association. Lists hospitals.

Leisure—Hotel and Motel Ventures; Entertainment

Bibliographies

375. Barsenik, Frank D. *Literature of the Lodging Market: An Annotated Bibliography*. East Lansing, Mich.: Michigan State University, 1966.

376. Bootle, Valerie, and Philip Nailon. *A Bibliography of Hotel and Catering Operation*. London: New University Education, 1970. A guide to books on operations, including some annotations.

377. Spinney, Katherine, and Blanche Fickle. "Bibliography Prepared for Hotel and Restaurant Related Subjects," in *Cornell Hotel and Restaurant Administration*, August issues. A list of books, pamphlets, and articles related to hotel administration.

378. Wasserman, Paul, et al. *Encyclopedia of Business Information Sources*. 2 vols. Detroit: Gale Research Company, 1970. Lists handbooks, manuals, bibliographies, periodicals, directories, statistics sources, financial ratios.

Books

379. Dukas, Peter. *Hotel Front Office Management and Operation*. Dubuque, Iowa: William C. Brown, 1970. An account of daily procedures and how to operate.

380. Gunn, Clare A., and Robert W. McIntosh. *Motel Planning and Business Management*. Dubuque, Iowa: William C. Brown, 1964.

381. Keister, Douglas Carlyle. *Selected Readings, for an Introduction to Hotel and Restaurant Management*. Berkeley, Calif.: McCutchen, 1971.

382. Lattin, Gerald W. *Careers in Hotels and Restaurants*. New York: Henry Z. Walch, 1967.

383. Lattin, Gerald W. *Modern Hotel and Motel Management*. San Francisco: W. H. Freeman, 1968. Tells about the industry, organization, career opportunities, future, and where to get training.

384. Lundberg, Donald Emil, and James P. Armatas. *The Management of People in Hotels, Restaurants, and Clubs*. Dubuque, Iowa: William C. Brown, 1974. Deals with screening, interviewing, managing, training; emphasizes the human aspect.

385. Lundberg, Donald E. *The Hotel and Restaurant Business*. Chicago: Institutions/Volume Feeding Management Magazine, 1971.

386. Pickering, J. F., J. A. Greenwood, and Diana Hunt. *The Small Firm in the Hotel and Catering Industry*. London: Her Majesty's Stationery Office, 1971. Covers structure, economics, changes, labor, and management of the industry.

387. Podd, George O., and John D. Lesure. *Planning and Operating Motels and Motor Hotels*. New York: Ahrens Publishing Co., 1964.

388. Scholz, William. *Profitable Hotel/Motel Management*. Englewood Cliffs, N.J.: Prentice-Hall, Inc., 1975. Techniques, employee relations, customer service, economy, hotel rules and laws.

389. Sonnabend, Roger P. *Your Future in Hotel Management*. New York: Richard Rosen, 1964.

390. Witzky, Herbert K. *Modern Hotel-Motel Management Methods*. New York: Hayden Book Companies, 1964.

Directories

391. *Celebrity Service International Contact Book*. Earl Blackwell, ed. International trade directory of the entertainment industry. Lists names, addresses, and telephone numbers in New York, Hollywood, London, Paris, and Rome. Stage, screen, radio, TV, dance, music agents.

392. *Directory of Hotel and Motel Systems*. Annual. New York: American Hotel Association Directory Corp. Hotel and motels and chain hotel and motel organizations owning or operating three or more properties.

393. *Hotel and Motel Red Book*. Annual. New York: American Hotel and Motel Association. Hotels in the United States, Canada, Central and South America, by state, size, cost and owner.

394. *Hotel and Travel Index*. Hollywood: Elwood M. Ingledue. Lists over 7,000 hotels and resorts throughout the world, travel agents, and other travel information.

395. *Hotel-Motel Buyers' Directory*. Annual. New York: American Hotel and Motel Association. Products and services used by hotel-motel industry.

396. *Leahy's Hotel-Motel Guide and Travel Atlas*. Annual. Chicago: American Hotel Register Co. Geographical list of inns, hotels and motels with locational sites for use with atlas, part 2.

Industry Statistic Sources

397. *Canada Bureau of Statistics, Hotels*. Annual. Ottawa: 1949–1968. Superseded by *Traveller Accommodation Statistics*.

398. *Hotels, Motels and Tourist Courts*. U.S. Bureau of the Census. Washington, D.C.: U.S. Government Printing Office, 1966.

399. *Investment Policy Review: Strategy Phase II*. Quarterly. Dean Witter and Co. Includes a section for the lodging industry.

400. Laventhol, Krekstein, Horwath, and Horwath. *Lodging Industry: Annual Report on Hotel and Motor Hotel Operations*. Annual. Trends, statistics, analysis.

401. Smith, Barney & Company. *Research Service*. Economic outlooks, statistics.

402. *Traveller Accommodation Statistics. Statistique de l'hebergement de Voyageurs*. Annual. Ottawa: Statistics Canada.

403. *Trends in the Hotel-Motel Business*. Annual. New York: Harris, Kerr, Forster and Company.

404. *U.S. Industrial Outlook*. Annual. U.S. Bureau of Domestic Commerce. Recent trends and ten-year outlook.

405. *Worldwide Operating Statistics of the Hotel Industry*. Annual. New York.

Periodicals

406. *Cornell Hotel and Restaurant Administration Quarterly*. Quarterly. Ithaca, N.Y.: School of Hotel Administration, Cornell University.

407. *Food and Lodging Hospitality*. Monthly. Chicago: Patterson Publishing Co.

408. *Horwath Accountant*. Monthly. New York: Horwath and Horwath, Public Accountants. Traces trends in the hotel business in various sections of the country and presents numerous statistics on hotel operations.

409. *Hospitality Magazines Lodging Combination*. Monthly. Chicago: Patterson Publishing Co.

410. *Hotel and Motel Management*. Monthly. Chicago: Clissold Publications Co.

411. *Hotel and Travel Index*. Quarterly. Hollywood: Elwood M. Ingledue.

412. *Hotel Bulletin*. Monthly. New York: Hotel Bulletin Inc.

413. *Hotel Industry*. Bimonthly. New York: International Geneva Association.

414. *Hotel Management Review*. Monthly. New York: Ahrens Publishing Co.

415. *Hotel-Motel Greeter*. Monthly. Denver: Allen Bell.

416. *Innkeeping*. Monthly. Chicago: Clissold Publishing Co.

417. *Motel News*. Semimonthly. Washington, D.C.: Motel Association of America.

418. *Tourist Court Journal*. Monthly. Temple, Tex.: Tourist Court Journal Co.

419. *Transcript*. Monthly. New York: Harris, Kerr, Forster and Co.

Trade Associations and Professional Societies

420. American Hotel and Motel Association. 221 West 57th Street, New York, N.Y. 10019.

421. Inter-American Hotel Association, P.O. Box 730, Harrisburg, Pa. 17108.

422. International Hotel Association, 89 rue du Faubourg Saint-Honore, Paris 8ᵉ, France.

Manufacturing

Directories

423. *Directory of Key Plants*. 2 vols. New York: Market Statistics, Inc. A directory of 41,000 plants with 100 or more employees. Volume I is by state and county and within each county, by SIC and employment size; Volume II is by SIC and then by state and country.

424. *Kelley's Manufacturers and Merchants Directory*. 2 vols. London: Kelley's Directories. Annual. World directory of merchants and manufacturers with comprehensive coverage for British Isles, and sections listing companies by major product for other countries. Includes a "Trades & Services Index."

425. *Thomas Register of American Manufacturers*. 10 vols. New York: Thomas Publishing Co. Annual. Volumes 1–6 list manufacturers by specific product; Vol. 7 is alphabetical list of companies, giving address, branch offices, subsidiaries, products, estimated capitalization, and occasionally, principal of-

ficers. Volume 9 is "Index" to product classifications and includes a list of leading trade names (pink),

boards of trade, chambers of commerce. Volumes 9–10 are "Catalogs of Companies."

Multinational Companies and International Business

Bibliographies

426. Lall, Sanjaya. *Foreign Private Manufacturing Investments and Multinational Companies.* New York: Frederick A. Praeger, 1975. An annotated bibliography.

427. Public Library of Newark. *Business Literature.* Irregular. Newark, N.J. Includes articles and books and has a section on job hunting.

428. Raine, John S. *Multinational Companies and Overseas Direct Investment.* Aberystwyth, Dyfed, U.K.: Business Information Press, 1975. A selected bibliography and books and reports.

Directories

429. *American Agencies Interested in International Affairs.* New York: Council on International Affairs. Lists approximately 300 organizations; gives the names of officers, purposes, founding dates, and other pertinent data.

430. *American Firms, Subsidiaries, and Affiliates.* Washington, D.C.: U.S. Bureau of International Commerce, 1972. Alphabetical by country list of 4,000 American corporations that operate foreign business enterprises.

431. *American Register of Exporters and Importers, Inc.* New York: American Register of Exporters/ Importers Corporation. Directory of over 30,000 manufacturers, export/import buying agencies, by product class. Also foreign offices of chamber of commerce and U.S. buying agencies.

432. *Bureau of International Commerce Trade Lists* (of every country). Annual. Washington, D.C.: United States Department of Commerce. Lists American firms, subsidiaries, and affiliates in country with brief descriptions and address.

433. *California International Business Directory.* Center for Advanced Studies in International Business. Los Angeles: Lists California companies in alphabetical order (description, imports, exports, addresses).

434. *Current European Directories.* G. P. Henderson, ed. Beckenham, Kent, England: CBD Research Ltd. Section 1 is an annotated guide, arranged by country in Europe, to general directories of associations, research organizations, biographical dictionaries, gazetteers, city directories. Section 2 is an alphabetical list of more specialized industry directories, incorporating title references to directories in Section 1.

435. *Directory of American Firms Operating in Foreign Countries,* 7th ed. Compiled by Juvenal L. Angel. New York: World Trade Academy Press. Section 1 lists companies alphabetically, giving name of officer in charge of foreign operations, and countries of operation; Section 2 lists companies by county of operation; Section 3 classifies the firms by product or industry.

436. *Directory of Corporate Affiliations.* Skokie, Ill.: National Register Publishing Co., 1976. Who owns whom—the family tree of every major corporation in America including foreign subsidiaries and affiliates.

437. *Directory of Foreign Firms Operating in the United States.* Compiled by Juvenal L. Angel. New York: World Trade Academy Press, 1971. Lists American companies that are affiliated or divisions of foreign countries.

438. *Directory of International Engineering and Construction Services.* Washington: National Construction Association. Information about each member company in the association and description of their particular interests in the construction industry.

439. *Directory of Opportunities for Graduates.* Annually in October. London: Cornmarket Press Ltd. Reference book for undergraduates and their advisers for work in Great Britain.

440. *Directory of Overseas Summer Jobs.* Charles James, ed. Cincinnati, Ohio: National Directory Service. Vacation work.

441. *Directory of United States Firms Operating in Latin America.* Washington, D.C.: Pan American Union. Company listings (including the name of each manager) arranged by country.

442. Dun and Bradstreet, *Principal International Business.* New York. A world marketing directory by country, by product classification, and alphabetically by business.

443. *Europe's 5000 Largest Companies.* New York: R. R. Bowker Company, 1975. Information on the top 4,000 industrials and the top 750 trading companies, ranked in terms of their latest declared annual sales.

444. *Federal Jobs Overseas.* Pamphlet No. 29. Washington, D.C.: U.S. Civil Service Commission. Describes overseas jobs in nine departments of the federal government. Included are Departments of Agriculture, Air Force, Army, Navy, Commerce, Interior, State, and the Agency for International Development, Panama Canal Company, Peace Corps, and the U.S. Information Agency.

445. *Foreign Direct Investors in the United States.* Washington, D.C.: U.S. Department of Commerce, Bureau of International Commerce, Oct. 1973, Mar. 1974, and Jan. 1975. Information on the parent company, American subsidiary, location, and product is given.

446. *Forbes,* "Annual Directory Issue," May 15 issue each year. The 500 largest corporations are ranked by revenues, assets, market value, and net profit. Each year the first January issue ranks companies by profitability, growth, and stock price gain.

447. *The Fortune Double 500 Directory.* Reprint of the annual May to August issues of *Fortune* Magazine.

The May issue lists the 500 largest U.S. industrial corporations; June, the second 500 largest; July, the 50 largest banks, life insurance companies, diversified—financial, retailing, transportation, and utility companies; and August, the 300 largest foreign industrial corporations and the 50 largest foreign banks.

448. *Guide to Foreign Information Sources*. Semiannual. Washington, D.C.: Chamber of Commerce of the United States. Contains sources of information on foreign nations, addresses of foreign embassies, organizations and services offering information, and annotated bibliography.

449. *International Almanac of Business and Finance*. Annual. *Finance* magazine. A list, by country, of U.S. corporations operating in that country, of U.S. banks, leading banks of the country, and of U.S. brokerage firms. Gives address and name of manager.

450. *Jaeger's Europa-Register: Teleurope*. Darmstadt: Deutscher Addressbach-Verlag. Addresses of European firms, in two parts: alphabetical list by country; classified trades section.

451. *Rand McNally International Bankers Directory*. Annual. Skokie, Ill.: Rand McNally & Company. Officers, directors, and balance sheet data for United States and principal foreign banks.

452. *Social Work Opportunities Abroad*. New York: National Association of Social Workers. A directory of over 100 organizations offering social work opportunities in foreign countries. Identifies the type of social work engaged in by the organization.

453. *Trade Directories of the World*. Compiled by U. H. E. Croner. New York: Croner Publications, Inc. This annotated list of business and trade directories is arranged by continent and then by country. Includes an index to "trades and professions" and a country index.

454. *U.S. Non-Profit Organizations in Development Assistance Abroad*. New York: Technical Assistance Information Clearing House. Comprehensive directory of information on over 400 nonprofit organizations, agencies, missions, and foundations and their work in 124 countries in Africa, East Asia and Pacific, Latin America, and Near East-South Asia. Alphabetical listing giving programs and objectives with cross-reference by region, country, and organization.

455. *Walker's Manual of Far Western Corporations and Securities*. Annual. Berkley: Walker's Manual, Inc. Lists corporations by city, state, and industry. A description of each is available. Aerospace, chemicals, computers, construction, merchandising, financial, food, utilities, real estate, entertainment.

456. *Who Owns Whom, Australia and the Far East*. Compiled by O. W. Roskill and Co., Ltd. London: 1976. A directory of parent, associate, and subsidiary companies for Australia and the Far East.

457. *Who Owns Whom, Continental Edition*. 2 vols. Compiled by O. W. Roskill and Co., Ltd. London: 1974. A directory of parent, associate, and subsidiary companies for the Continent.

458. *Who Owns Whom, North America*. Compiled by O. W. Roskill and Co., Ltd. London: 1974. A directory of parent, associate, and subsidiary companies for the United States, Mexico, and Canada.

Handbooks and Yearbooks

459. Angel, Juvenal L. *Looking for Employment in Foreign Countries Reference Handbook*, 5th ed. New York: World Trade Academy Press, 1972. Discussion of a vareity of topics in looking for foreign employment including markets, government work, and compensation.

460. Angel, Juvenal L. *Resumés for Overseas Employment*. New York: World Trade Academy Press, 1974. Offers sample resumés.

461. *The Financial Times International Business Yearbook*. London: Financial Times, Ltd., 1975. General information on countries around the world, and specific information on subsidiaries, officers, and capital of many industries.

462. *Informations Internationales*. Paris: DAFSA, 1975. Eight volumes and an index written in French, English, and German on specific companies giving background information, activity of the company, subsidiaries, and capital.

Indexes

463. Business International, *Master Key Index*. Quarterly. New York. Current information on international business concerning management techniques, country, and company.

464. *Business Periodicals Index*. Monthly. New York: H. W. Wilson Company. Look under "Corporations—Foreign Business" and "Corporations, International" and "Corporations—Subsidiaries."

465. *F & S Index International*. Monthly. Cleveland: Predicasts. Look under "International Groups" or by specific company.

466. *Index to Foreign Market Reports*. Monthly. Washington, D.C.: U.S. Department of Commerce, Bureau of International Commerce. Foreign market surveys on unclassified commodity, industry, and economic reports, including market research summaries and market surveys.

467. *Index to International Business Publications*. Washington, D.C.: U.S. Department of Commerce, Bureau of International Commerce, June 1975. Indexes *Overseas Business Reports* and *Foreign Economic Trends*.

468. *Public Affairs Information Service Bulletin*. Quarterly. New York. Under "International Business Enterprises."

469. *Public Affairs Information Service Foreign Language Index*. Cumulated annually. New York.

Investment Information

470. *Financial Dynamics.* 14 vols., loose-leaf. Denver: Investors Management Sciences. Detailed quarterly and annual analyses of major companies by industry.

471. *Jane's Major Companies of Europe.* Lionel F. Gray, ed. New York: Franklin Watts, 1975. Detailed financial and general information on major European companies.

472. *Standard and Poor's International Stock Report.* Monthly. Stock reports from major companies around the world.

Monographs

473. Brooke, Michael Z., and Lee Remmer. *The Multinational Company in Europe.* Ann Arbor: University of Michigan, 1972. Experts from five countries discuss the management problems of multinational corporations.

474. Haner, F. T. *Multinational Management.* Columbus: Charles E. Merrill Books, 1973. An overall picture of the problems of managing multinational companies due to differences in culture, attitudes, etc.

Books

475. Robbins, Sidney. *Money in the Multinational Enterprise.* New York: Basic Books, 1973.

476. Stopford, John M. *Managing the Multinational Enterprise.* New York: Basic Books, 1972.

477. Wortzel, Louis H. *Scientists and Salesmen.* New York: Basic Books, forthcoming.

Periodicals

478. *The International Executive.* Irregular—about 5 a year. Hastings-on-Hudson, N.Y. A bibliography of books and periodicals as well as a summarization of selected books.

479. *Mergers and Acquisitions.* Quarterly. Washington. General information on mergers and acquisitions and who is planning what. Also includes a roster of joint ventures and foreign acquisitions.

480. *Multinational Business.* London. Quarterly. A review of news and analysis on multinational business.

Reports and Articles

481. *The Conference Board Record,* "International Economic Trends to Watch in 1976," Alfred F. Miosi, XII (11): 37, November 1975. General article on multinational business.

482. *The Conference Board Record,* "Mini-Multinationals," John M. Roach, XI(2):27, February 1974. Fifty smaller companies report their experience in operating overseas.

483. *Forbes,* "Annual Report on American Industry," January issue. Measuring the management performance of the biggest public companies with articles on major industries.

Printing and Publishing Industry

Introductory Reading

484. Blum, Eleanor. *Basic Books in the Mass Media.* Urbana, Ill.: University of Illinois Press, 1972. An annotated bibliography covering source material about communications, including sections on book publishing, newspapers, advertising, indexes, etc.

485. Dessauer, John. *Book Publishing: What It Is; What It Does.* New York: R. R. Bowker, 1974. A general introduction to book publishing, with chapters on the creation of books, the history of the book trade, the manufacturing, marketing, storing, and delivering of books, and the general management theories of the industry.

486. Strauss, Victor. *The Printing Industry.* Washington: R. R. Bowker, 1967. A general introduction to the printing industry, with chapters on the printing process, theories of printing, and technical services (presses, inks, binding, graphics). Includes a selective bibliography.

Outlook for the Industry: Forecasts and Trends

487. *Census of Manufacturers.* 1972 Preliminary Report (Series MC 72). Washington, D.C.: U.S. Government Printing Office, 1975. SIC 2700 includes statistical information on the trends in growth of newspapers, periodicals, book publishing, book printing, miscellaneous publishing, commercial printing, etc. Data given for time span (1958–1972); geographic area; the value of receipts of products, of materials consumed; the number of employees; costs, etc.

488. J. S. Eliezer Associates. *The New Dynamics of Book Publishing: An Analysis of Trends 1967–1980.* New York: Eliezer Associates 1973. Includes chapters on the economic trends affecting book sales, external forces affecting the industry, trends in book clubs and mail order sales, the future outlook for juvenile, trade, text, professional and reference books.

489. Frost and Sullivan. *Graphic Art Supply Market,* Report No. 265. New York: Frost and Sullivan. August 1974. Forecast data for the printing and publishing market as it relates to the graphic arts.

490. Smith, Barney & Company. *Subscription Research Reports.* Volume 5. Under "Publishing and Broadcasting," includes current and selective research reports about trends and forecasts of specific companies within the industry. Data given on growth trends, current assets of the company, analysis of revenues, etc. Special features include "Reviews and Outlook Analysis" and a discussion of the factors affecting stock market activitiy.

491. *U.S. Industrial Outlook.* Annual. Washington, D.C.: G.P.O. Under "Printing and Publishing" gives the recent developments and projections for the

industry, with a brief outlook for newspapers, periodicals, book publishing, commercial printing, graphics, etc. Projections to 1980.

492. *Union Wages and Hours: Printing Industry.* Washington, D.C.: U.S. Government Printing Office. July 1, 1972. Cites the average salary scales of employees in the printing industry as of July 1, 1972. Data broken down by specific job function, age of employee, city and population statistics, etc. for 68 selected cities. Overall analysis given for the nation as a whole. Abbreviated version in *Printing and Publishing*, January 1974, pp. 7–13.

Investment Advisory Services

493. Investment Management Sciences, Inc. *Financial Dynamics.* Quarterly, with annual cumulations. Quarterly and annual financial analyses of selected leading publishing companies, with annual industry comparisons. Tab indexed under "Publishing." Includes information on income, expenses, invested capital, market data, assets, marketability, etc., for each company listed.

494. Standard and Poor's Corporation. *Industry Surveys: Communication.* Gives the latest current and basic analyses of the industry, with brief information on the industry and financial comparisons of leading companies. Includes a comparative stock analysis for selected companies. Offers a brief outlook, choices of favored issues, statistical comparisons of stocks. Also general information about industrywide trends and individual trends (e.g. newspapers, magazines, etc.)

495. *Value Line Investment Survey.* Weekly. Under "Publishing and Advertising Industry" has analysis of the publishing industry for newspapers, with information for specific publishers on their financial outlook, and their current assets and liabilities. Also, an analysis of their monthly situation, and fortnightly commentaries appraising the political and economic conditions affecting the industry.

Ratios for the Industry

496. Printing Industry of America. *Ratios for the Use of Printing Management.* Arlington, Virginia. Annual.

Directories

497. *American Book Trade Directory.* Biennial. New York: R. R. Bowker and Co. List of 4,000 publishers and booksellers with addresses and areas of interest, affiliated companies, subsidiaries, special distributions, mergers, foreign representatives, etc. Includes mainly American firms, with British and Canadian publishers and their American representatives. No personnel information.

498. *Ayer Directory; Newspapers, Magazines and Trade Publications.* Philadelphia: N. W. Ayer & Son. Firm, newspaper advertising agents.

499. *Ayer's Directory of Newspapers and Periodicals.* Philadelphia: N. W. Ayer & Son.

500. *Directory of Scholarly and Research Publishing Opportunities.* Indianapolis, Ind.: Academic Media. Lists magazines and other publishing concerns by subject category.

501. *Editor and Publisher International Yearbook.* Annual. New York: Editor and Publishing Co. "The Encyclopedia of the Newspaper Industry." Worldwide data on newspapers with information on dailies, association and club papers, supplies, equipment, awards, foreign language papers, Negro news in the U.S., listing of journalism schools and standards of education, etc. Statistical information includes a brief summary of circulation trends, a review of the British newspaper year, etc.

502. *Literary Market Place.* Annual. New York: R. R. Bowker Company. "The Bible of American Book Publishing." Directory of American book publishers and personnel. Subject arrangement by book publishers, associations, trade events, services and suppliers, free-lance editors, book manufacturers, magazine publishers, U.S. publishers' imprints, etc. Includes addresses and personnel information. See also the *International Literary Market Place* (annual) for similar information about European publishers.

503. *Names and Numbers.* 21st ed. New York: R. R. Bowker Company. Provides an alphabetical index to over 17,000 names of publishers with phone number, street address, city, zone. Companion to *Literary Market Place.*

504. *Newspaper International.* Published annually in January, plus updating supplements. Skokie, Illinois: National Register Publishing Company. Lists newspapers and newsweeklies in over 90 countries.

505. *Publisher's International Directory.* 4th ed. New York: R. R. Bowker Company. Directory gives names and addresses of 20,000 active publishers in 144 countries.

506. *Standard Periodical Directory.* Annual. New York: Oxbridge Communications, Inc. A subject listing of 53,000 U.S. and Canadian periodicals, giving address, scope, year founded, frequency, subscription rate, circulation, and one basic advertising rate. Alphabetical index at end.

507. *Who's Who in Publishing—An International Biographical Guide.* Quinquennial. New York: R. R. Bowker Company. Contains detailed biographical data of 3,500 leading persons in the publishing field.

508. *Writer's Market.* Annual. Cincinnati: F & W Publishing Corporation. Lists over 3,000 possible markets for writers, photographers, and artists. Requirements and other pertinent information are included.

Professional Associations

509. *Encyclopedia of Associations.* Volume 1, *National Organizations of the United States.* Volume 3, *Sup-*

plement. Irregular. Alphabetical and keyword indexes provide access to all types of national associations under "Print" and "Publishers." Provides the name of the chief officers, a brief statement of activities, committees, number of members, and names of publications.

510. *Encyclopedia of Business Information Sources*. Volume 1 under "Printing" and "Publishing Industry" provides a selective list of professional associations, as well as suggested sources for statistics, periodicals, directories, financial ratios, price sources, and general readings.

Journals

511. *Book Production Industry*. Bimonthly. General news and articles of interest to book manufacturers and publishers. Includes book reviews, concentrating on the format and textual quality of the book.

512. *Editor and Publisher*. Weekly. General news and articles in the newspaper medium. Special features include reprints of statistical studies done by Media Records, Inc.

513. *Folio: The Magazine for Magazine Management*. Monthly. General management articles for the publishing industry.

514. *Inland Printer/American Lithographer*. Monthly. General articles of interest to the printing industry. Emphasis is on changing trends and technology within the industry. Special feature appearing semiannually is "Forecast."

515. *Knowledge Industry Report*. Semimonthly. Newsletter with tidbits of information and gossip on the publishing world. Acts as a source of current awareness information.

516. *Printing and Publishing*. Quarterly. Offers miscellaneous articles on the printing and publishing industries. Its regular feature is a Statistical Series, with comparisons of principal markets, imports and exports of books and other printed matter, economic indicators, percentage changes on a quarterly and yearly basis, etc.

517. *Printing Management*. Monthly. Articles about printing management, with an emphasis on forecasts and changes in technology. Special feature: "Forecast."

Public Administration in City Government

Almanacs and Handbooks

518. *Directory of Urban Corps Programs*. Washington, D.C.: National Development Office. Alphabetical and state listing of urban corps programs.

519. *Municipal Yearbook*. Annual. Chicago: International City Management Association. An authoritative resumé of activities and statistical data of American cities. It is also the source for annual reviews for all significant developments, problems, and conflicts in the field of local government.

Bibliographies

520. Government Affairs Foundation, Inc. *Metropolitan Communities: a Bibliography with Special Emphasis Upon Government and Politics*. Chicago: Public Administration Service, 1956–1972. A series of 5 volumes containing listing of books, periodical articles, and government reports dealing with (1) the functions, problems, and the organization of metropolitan governments, and (2) the socioeconomic background of metropolitan areas.

521. Holler, Frederick L. *The Information Sources of Political Science*. Santa Barbara, Calif.: ABC-Clio, Inc., 1975. Consult the local government section of Vol. 3 of the 5-volume set.

522. Joint Reference Library. *Recent Publications on Governmental Problems*. Semimonthly. Chicago. References are listed under the heading "municipal government" in some issues.

523. McCurdy, Howard E. *Public Administration: A Bibliography*. Washington, D.C.: College of Public Affairs, The American University, 1972.

Indexes and Abstracts

524. *Index to Current Urban Documents*. Westport, Conn.: Greenwood Periodicals Co. A quarterly and annual publication that indexes official documents on urban affairs issued in 154 cities and 24 counties. All documents cited in the index are made available by the publisher either individually or in regional sets.

525. *Sage Public Administration Abstracts*. Beverly Hills: Sage Publications.

Journals

526. *Public Administration Review*. Bimonthly.
527. *Public Personnel Management*. Bimonthly.
528. *Urban Research News*. Bimonthly.
529. *Urban Affairs Quarterly*. Quarterly.

Books

530. Banovetz, James M. *Managing the Modern City*. Washington, D.C.: International City Management Association, 1971.

531. Bish, Robert L., and Vincent Ostrom. *Understanding Urban Government: Metropolitan Reform Reconsidered*. Washington, D.C.: American Enterprise Institute for Public Policy Research, 1973.

532. Bollens, John C. *The Metropolis: Its People, Politics, and Economic Life*, 2d ed. New York: Harper & Row, 1970.

533. David, Stephen M., and Paul E. Peterson. *Urban Politics and Public Policy: The City in Crisis*. New York: Frederick A. Praeger, 1973.

534. DeTorres, Juan. *Government Services in Major Metropolitan Areas; Functions, Centers, Efficiency.* New York: The Conference Board, 1972.

535. Drake, Alvin W. *Analysis of Public Systems.* Cambridge, Mass.: MIT Press, 1972.

536. Goodman, Jay S. *The Dynamics of Urban Government and Politics.* New York: The Macmillan Company, 1975.

537. Hawley, Willis D. *Improving the Quality of Urban Management.* Beverly Hills: Sage Publications, 1974.

538. Kotter, John P., and Paul R. Lawrence. *Mayors in Action: Five Approaches to Urban Governance.* New York: John Wiley & Sons, 1974.

539. Martin, Michael. *Management Science and Urban Problems.* Lexington, Mass.: Lexington Books, 1974.

540. Rosenbloom, Richard S. *New Tools for Urban Management: Studies in Systems and Organizational Management.* Boston: Graduate School of Business Administration, Harvard University, 1971.

541. Russell, John R. *Cases in Urban Management.* Cambridge, Mass.: MIT Press, 1974.

542. Stillman, Richard J. *The Rise of the City Manager: A Public Professional in Local Government.* Albuquerque: University of New Mexico Press, 1974.

543. Sweeney, Stephen B. *Governing Urban Society: New Scientific Approaches.* Philadelphia: American Academy of Political and Social Science, 1967.

Public Administration in Federal and State Government

Directories

544. *A Directory of Public Management Organizations.* Washington, D.C.: U.S. Government Printing Office. National organizations of state and local governments and associations of public officials with an interest in public employee-management relations.

545. *Directory of Government Agencies.* Littleton, Colorado: Libraries Unlimited, Inc. Lists department and description.

546. *Directory of Information Resources in the United States: Federal Government.* Rev. ed., 1974. Washington, D.C.: Library of Congress. Lists information offices and information analysis centers for various agencies and programs.

547. U.S. Civil Service Commission. *Federal Career Directory.* Annual. "Specific information about federal careers and the agencies that employ college graduates for these positions."

548. U.S. Civil Service Commission. *Guide to Federal Career Literature.* Annual. Note chart, "The Federal Job System," explaining how to apply for a federal job.

549. U.S. Civil Service Commission. *Summer Jobs in Federal Agencies.* Annual.

550. *United States Government Manual.* Annual. Describes federal agencies and programs. Provides listings of key personnel, regional offices, and organization charts.

Books

551. Adrian, Charles R. *Governing Our Fifty States and Their Communities,* 3d ed. New York: McGraw-Hill, 1972.

552. Smoot, Dan. *Business End of Government.* Belmont, Mass.: Western Islands, 1973.

553. Steiss, Alan W. *Public Budgeting and Management.* Lexington, Mass.: Lexington Books, 1972. First 6 chapters deal with public management.

554. Van Dersal, William R. *The Successful Manager in Government and Business.* New York: Harper & Row, 1974.

555. Wamsley, Gary L. *Political Economy of Public Organizations: A Critique and Approach to the Study of Public Administration.* Boston: D. C. Heath & Company, 1973.

Magazines and Journals

556. *CG Weekly Report.* Weekly. Weekly coverage of government and congressional activities.

557. *Government Executive.* Monthly.

558. *Public Administration Review.* Bimonthly.

559. *Public Personnel Management.* Bimonthly.

560. *Public Policy.* Quarterly.

561. *Trends in Federal Hiring.* Quarterly. U.S. Civil Service Commission.

Articles

562. Bowman, James S., and David L. Norman, Jr. "Attitudes Towards the Public Service: A Survey of University Students." In *Public Personnel Management,* March-April 1975, pp. 113–121.

563. Buchanan, Bruce II. "Government Managers, Business Executives, and Organizational Equipment." In *Public Administration Review,* July/August 1974, pp. 339–347.

564. Graham, G. A. "Ethical Guidelines for Public Administrators: Observations on the Rules of the Game." In *Public Administration Review,* January/February 1974, pp. 90–92.

565. Imundo, Louis V., Jr. "Ineffectiveness and Inefficiency in Government Management." In *Public Personnel Management,* March/April 1975, pp. 90–95.

566. Malek, Frederic C. "Managing for Results in the Federal Government. . . ." In *Business Horizons,* April 1974, pp. 23-28.

Bibliographies and Guides

567. Andriot, John. *Guide to U.S. Government Publications.* Mclean, Va.: Documents Index 1972 and supplements. Lists publications by issuing agency.

568. Joint Reference Library. *Recent Publications on Governmental Problems.* Semimonthly. Chicago.

569. U.S. Superintendent of Documents. *United States Government Publications, Monthly Catalog.* Monthly. Indexes government publications by author, title, and subject.

Public Utilities

Directories

570. *Brown's Directory of North American Gas Companies.* Annual. Philadelphia: Harcourt, Brace, Jovanovich. Provides lists of gas utilities by state plus extensive company information. Also includes information on state public utility commissions.

571. *Electric World Directory of Electric Utilities.* Annual. New York: McGraw Hill. Lists of electric utilities by state and company information, including officers and major department heads, etc.

572. *Moody's Public Utilities Manual.* Annual. New York: Moody's Investors Service, Inc. Extensive company and financial information, including historical financial tables for the industry. City index lists names of utilities serving different areas. Updated by *Moody's Public Utilities News Reports.*

Periodicals

573. *American Gas Association Monthly.* Monthly. Reports the activities of the various sections of AGA in sales promotion, research, and public relations. January issue provides a 25-year industry forecast.

574. *Bell Journal of Economics.* Biannual. Scholarly articles on public utility economics and management.

575. *Bell Telephone Magazine.* Quarterly. Articles of interest to Bell management.

576. *Edison Electric Institute Bulletin.* Monthly. Reports EEI activities in research, sales promotion, accounting, and public relations.

577. *Electrical World.* Weekly. Technical and business articles on the electric power industry. Regular statistical review issues.

578. *Land Economics.* Quarterly. Includes scholarly articles on public utility economics.

579. *Public Power.* Monthly. January issue has a directory of publicly owned electric utilities. Includes articles of interest to the management personnel of municipal and federal power agencies.

580. *Public Utilities Fortnightly.* Biweekly. Feature articles on current news and issues in public utilities. Regular columns on government regulations, financial analysis of selected utility companies, and industrial progress. First January issue contains "Washington Outlook for Utilities," which projects current government regulation and ratemaking trends.

581. *Telephony.* Weekly. Telephone industry news, management information, and regulation news. Regular statistical reviews.

Conference Proceedings

582. *AGA-EEI Accounting Conference Proceedings.* Annual. Arlington, Virginia: American Gas Association and Edison Electric Institute. Papers on various aspects of public utility accounting and related areas.

583. *National Association of Regulatory Utility Commissioners Convention Proceedings.* Annual. Washington, D.C.: Papers on different topics relating to public utilities. Also includes brief biographical sketches of attending public utility commissioners.

584. *New Challenges to Public Utility Management: Proceedings of the Sixth Annual Conference 24-25 April 1973.* Institute of Public Utilities, East Lansing, Mich.: Michigan State University, 1974.

585. *Now, a New Generation in Utility Marketing: Proceedings of the 17th Public Utilities Marketing Seminar.* Denver, 1971. Colorado Springs, Colorado: Public Utilities Seminar, Colorado Interstate Gas Co.

586. *Today's Challenge, Tomorrow's Opportunity: Proceedings of the 18th Public Utilities Marketing Seminar.* New Orleans: 1972.

Books

587. Farris, Martin T. *Public Utilities: Regulation, Management, and Ownership.* Boston: Houghton Mifflin Company, 1973.

588. Garfield, Paul J. *Public Utility Economics.* Englewood Cliffs, N.J.: Prentice-Hall, Inc., 1964.

589. Haring, Joseph E., and Joseph F. Humphrey, eds. *Utility Regulation During Inflation.* Los Angeles: Occidental College, Economics Research Center, 1971.

590. Hayden, Howard R., ed. *Risk and Regulated Firms.* East Lansing, Mich.: Michigan State University, Graduate School of Business Administration, 1973.

591. Phillips, Charles F. *The Economics of Regulation.* Homewood, Ill.: Richard D. Irwin, 1969.

592. Samuels, Warren J., and Harry M. Trebling, eds. *A Critique of Administrative Regulation of Public Utilities.* Ann Arbor, Mich.: Michigan State University, Graduate School of Business Administration, 1972.

593. Shepherd, William G., and Thomas G. Gies. *Regulation in Further Perspective: The Little Engine that Might.* Cambridge, Mass.: Ballinger, 1974.

594. Shepherd, William G., and Thomas G. Gies. *Utility Regulation: New Directions in Theory and Practice.* New York: Random House, 1966.

595. Sichel, Werner, and Thomas G. Gies, eds. *Public Utility Regulation: Change and Scope.* Lexington, Mass.: Lexington Books, 1975.

596. Turvey, Ralph. *Public Enterprise*. Baltimore: Penguin Books, 1968.

Rates and Regulations

597. *A.G.A. Rate Service*. Loose-leaf. American Gas Association. Rates for various types of service by state, updated periodically.

598. *Federal and State Commission Jurisdiction and Regulation of Electric, Gas and Telephone Utilities*, 6th ed. U.S. Federal Power Commission, 1973. Comprehensive information on government regulation of utility rates, accounting forms and requirements, financial and corporate regulation, licenses and permits, etc.

599. *National Electric Rate Book*. Loose-leaf. U.S. Federal Power Commission. Rate schedules for electrical service by state, updated periodically.

600. *Public Utilities Reports*. Issued periodically. Opinions of commissions and courts on public utility cases.

601. *Typical Electric Bills for Residential, Commercial, and Industrial Services*. Annual. Washington, D.C.: U.S. Federal Power Commission. Consumer costs for representative amounts of electricity for different types of service and for different areas in the country.

602. *Uniform System of Accounts Prescribed for Public Utilities and Licensees Subject to the Provisions of the Federal Power Act*. Loose-leaf.

Statistics

603. *Electric Power Statistics*. Monthly. U.S. Federal Power Commission. Various statistics, including monthly operating and income statements of privately owned electric utilities.

604. *Electric Utility in New England Statistical Bulletin*. Annual. Electric Council of New England. Industry statistics on supply, uses, sales and revenues, finances, operations, etc.

605. *Gas Facts: A Statistical Record of the Gas Utility Industry*. Annual. American Gas Association. Contains statistical data on energy reserves, production, transmission, distribution, storage, sales, labor, and finance.

606. *Historical Statistics of the Electric Utility Industry*. Decennial. Edison Electric Institute. Information on electrical utility generating capacity; sales, customers and revenues; financial and operating data and ratios, etc.

607. *LP-Gas Market Industry Facts*. Annual. LP-Gas Association. Industry statistics on production, transportation, storage, sales, etc.

608. *Statistical Yearbook of the Electric Utility Industry*. Annual. Edison Electric Institute. Annual updates of the information contained in the *Historical Statistics of the Electric Utility Industry*.

609. *Statistics of Communications, Common Carriers*. Annual. U.S. Federal Communications Commission. Includes financial and operating data for telephone and telegraph companies.

610. *Statistics of Privately Owned Electric Utilities in the United States*, annual, and *Statistics of Publicly Owned Electric Utilities in the United States*, annual.

611. *Statistics of the Telephone Industry*. Annual. U.S. Independent Telephone Association.

612. *U.S. Federal Power Commission Annual Report*. Annual. Industry statistics. Also reviews electric power and natural gas developments for the year, including regulation and legislation.

613. *World's Telephones*. Annual. American Telephone and Telegraph Co. Statistics on number of telephones and types of calls made in the world.

Industry Outlook/Investment Advisory Services

614. *A.G.A. Report of Gas Industry Operations*. Quarterly. New York: American Gas Association. Various information on the gas industry: income statements, operating trends, customers, sales and revenues, etc.

615. *Business Week*. Weekly. Quarterly covers sales and profitability of large public utility companies.

616. *Financial Dynamics*. Loose-leaf. Investor's Management Services, Inc. Comparative company financial analyses in Vol. 10 for telephone companies and in Vol. 13 for electric utilities.

617. *Forbes*. Weekly. January 1 issue contains information on the industry outlook and on the growth and profitability of major public utility companies.

618. *Fortune*. Monthly. August issue contains "The Fifty Largest Utilities Ranked by Assets."

619. *Gas Utility Industry Projections*. Annual. American Gas Association. Industry sales outlook, projected 15 years, by various regions in the U.S.

620. *Industry Surveys*. 3 times a year. Standard and Poor's Corporation. Industry outlook and comparative company appraisals listed under "Telephone," "Utilities—Gas," and "Utilities—Electric."

621. *Quarterly Survey of Utility Appropriations*. Quarterly. Conference Board. Capital appropriations and expenditures of investor-owned gas and electric utilities.

622. *Subscription Research Service*. Periodically updated. Smith, Barney & Co. Volume 5 contains industry and individual company information for gas and electric utilities.

623. *Value Line Investment Survey*. Loose-leaf. Arnold Bernhard & Co. Industry analysis and company data for electric utilities and telecommunications.

Career Information

624. Bowman, Dean O. "Executive Development for Public Utilities," *Public Utilities Fortnightly* 89:39-43, March 16, 1972. Results of a survey on participants in the Public Utility Executive Program.

625. Byars, Lloyd L. "What Others Think: Management Training in Public Utilities," *Public Utilities Fortnightly* 88:58-60, December 9, 1971. Outlines some in-house management development programs within public utilities.

626. Easlick, D. K. "The New Face to the World of Work," *Public Utilities Fortnightly* 90:24-26, October 12, 1972. Examines equal opportunity in the Bell System.

627. Garlinghouse, F. Mark. "Employment Discrimination Law and Equal Employment in Public Utilities," *Public Utilities Fortnightly* 92:83-84, September 13, 1973.

628. Holmberg, Stevan R. "Integrating Manpower and Corporate Strategic Plans," *Public Utilities Fortnightly* 94:31-35, November 21, 1974. Survey of manpower planning systems in public utilities.

629. King, Sandra L. "Occupational Pay Benefits in Electric and Gas Utilities," *Monthly Labor Review* 97:53-54, November 1974. Survey of wages and benefits for hourly employees.

630. Smith, Chesterfield H. "Management Responsibility—Past, Present and Future," *Public Utilities Fortnightly* 91:32-35, June 21, 1973. Discusses the general concept of public utilities serving the public interest.

631. *Encyclopedia of Business Information Sources.* Volume 1. Detroit: Gale Research Company, 1970.

632. Hunt, Florine E. *Public Utilities Information Sources.* Detroit: Gale Research Company, 1965. "An annotated guide to literature and bodies concerned with rates, economics, accounting, regulation, history, and statistics of electric, gas, telephone, and water companies."

633. Lapinsky, M. "Guide to the Sources of the Economics of Regulation Literature," *Public Utilities Fortnightly* 96:21-29, July 17, 1975.

Retail Trade Industry

Directories

634. Aspley, J. C. *The Dartnell Sales Manager's Handbook,* Ovid Riso, ed. 11th ed. Chicago: Dartnell Corp., 1968. A list of directories, by key word, is in each edition of this handbook.

635. *Directory of Department Stores.* Annual. New York: Chain Store Guide.

636. *Directory of Franchising Organizations.* New York: Pilot Books. Lists franchise opportunities with concise descriptions and required investment. Includes a franchise evaluation checklist.

637. *Directory of National Trade and Professional Associations of the United States.* Washington, D.C.: Columbia Books, Inc. Alphabetical list of 4,300 national trade and professional associations, with key word and executive indexes. Gives chief officer, number of members, annual budget, publications.

638. *Encyclopedia of Associations,* 9th ed. M. Fisk, ed. Detroit: Gale Research Co., 1975. See items 2380–2389, p. 200.

639. *Fairchild's Financial Manual of Retail Stores.* Annual. New York: Lists names of officers and directors. Includes basic financial information about each store.

640. *Retailer Owned Cooperative Chains; Wholesale Grocers; Wholesaler Sponsored Voluntary Chains.* Business Guides, Inc. Lists companies by country and state.

641. *Sheldon's Retail Directory of the United States and Canada,* 88th ed. New York: Phelon, Sheldon & Marsar, Inc. Annual. Formerly *Sheldon's Retail Trade of the United States.* Includes chain, independent, department, junior department and speciality stores. Lists executives, general and divisional managers, department buyers.

642. *Shopping Center Directory (United States and Canada).* Burlington, Iowa: National Research Bureau, Inc. Lists shopping centers by city and state.

643. *Stores of the World Directory.* Biennial. London. Includes list of retail trade journals with addresses.

644. U.S. Department of Commerce. *Franchise Opportunities Handbook, 1973.* Complete guide to franchises. Bibliography.

Retail Trade Statistics

645. *A Guide to Consumer Markets 1974/75.* New York: The Conference Board. A standard source of statistical intelligence concerning the consumer and his relation to retail trade. Of special interest are the sections "Expenditures," pp. 158–206, and "Production and Distribution," pp. 207-232.

646. Marketing Economics Institute. *Marketing Economics Guide, 1973–74.* New York. In three sections. Includes SMSA rankings, population estimates, households, incomes for 1,500 cities, metropolitan areas, and retail sales data for nine retail store groups.

647. *Sales Management.* "1974 Survey of Buying Power," October 28, 1974. Includes market rankings as well as national, regional, and metropolitan area market data. Projections are made up to 1978.

648. U.S. Bureau of the Census. *Annual Retail Trade Report.* Statistics include per capita sales of five basic types of retail stores by geographic division as well as total annual sales.

649. U.S. Bureau of the Census. *Monthly Retail Trade Reports.* Has estimates of retail sales and accounts receivable listed by type of business. Firms with 11 or more retail stores are listed individually. These reports include data on department store sales, all retail stores, and major types of businesses such as furniture, lumber, and auto retailers.

650. U.S. Bureau of the Census. *Weekly Retail Sales Reports.* Estimates volume of sales, but considered less reliable than *Monthly Retail Trade Reports,*

since they are made on a small sample and on estimated (vs. actual) sales.

651. U.S. Dept. of Commerce. *U.S. Industrial Outlook.* Annual. Describes recent developments and gives a 10-year projection.

Operating Ratios

652. *Department and Specialty Store Merchandising and Operating Results.* 4 vols. Annual. New York: National Retail Merchants Association, Financial Executives Division.

653. *Financial and Operating Results of Department and Specialty Stores.* Annual. New York: National Retail Merchants Association, Financial Executives Division.

654. National Cash Register. *Expenses in Retail Business.* Dayton, Ohio. Annual. Operating ratios for 50 lines of retail business.

655. *Operating Results of Self-Service Department Stores.* Annual. Ithaca, N.Y.: New York State College of Agriculture and Life Sciences, Cornell University, in cooperation with the Mass Merchandising Research Foundation. Provides financial history and performance indicators for 47 self-service department store companies.

656. Urban Land Institute. *The Dollars and Cents of Shopping Centers.* Washington, D.C. Triennial. Provides benchmark figures against which operating results for individual shopping centers can be compared with those that are typical for the industry on a uniform basis.

Investment Services for Retail Trade

657. Investors Management Sciences, Inc. *Financial Dynamics.* Multivolume set giving financial analysis of leading companies in major industries. For retail trade see Vols. 8 and 9.

658. Smith, Barney & Company. *Subscription Research Service.* Research reports about trends and outlook in the retail trade industry as a whole with analysis of selected large companies.

659. Standard and Poor's Corporation. *Industry Surveys.* Current analysis of retail trade market, with specific company stock analysis.

Journals

660. *Discount Merchandiser.* Monthly. Issues annual *Discount Merchandiser: True Look at the Discount Industry,* June. Includes operating ratios.

661. *Economics Priorities Report,* Vol. 5, No. 3, 1974. Council on Economic Priorities. "Minorities and Women in Retail Industry." Entire issue devoted to analysis of employment opportunities in five major retail chains: Sears Roebuck, J. C. Penney, Ward's, Kresge, and Grant's.

662. *Footwear News.* Weekly. Issues annual *Footwear News Fact Book.* Includes statistics concerning marketing information as well as consumer market data.

663. *International Association of Department Stores–Retail News Letter.* Monthly. Covers trends in international department stores.

664. *Jewelers' Circular Keystone.* Monthly. Each issue includes statistical indicators for imports, exports, monthly sales trends.

665. *Journal of Retailing.* Quarterly. New York: New York University Institute of Retailing Management. Book reviews.

666. *Mass Retailing Merchandiser.* Monthly. Special reports include: "How Much Do You Earn? An Industrywide Salary Survey of Mass Retailing," December 1974, pp. 10–16, and "General Merchandise Share of the Market Report," January 1975, pp. 8–15.

667. *Men's Wear.* Semimonthly. Special report: "Who's Gaining Share of the Men's Wear Market?" February 14, 1975, pp. 59–88.

668. *Modern Retailer.* Monthly. Concerned with consumer goods market, marketing and management and distribution in the United Kingdom. Special issue: March 1975, "Annual Review of Retailing," pp. 5–18.

669. *Shopping Center World.* Monthly. Special issues include January 1975 "State of the Industry," pp. 19–30: includes statistics for United States (by state) and Canada—update of 1972 survey; and February 1975 "Annual 1975 Regional Roundup."

670. *Stores.* Monthly. International coverage of department, chain, variety, mass merchandising, and specialty stores. August issue annually has special report, "100 Top Volume Department Stores."

Books

671. Boone, Louis E., and James C. Johnson. *Marketing Channels.* Morristown, N.J.: General Learning Press, 1973. Includes bibliography.

672. Duncan, Delbert J., and C. Phillips. *Modern Retailing Management: Basic Concepts and Practices,* 8th ed. Homewood, Ill.: Richard D. Irwin, 1972. Includes annotated bibliography.

673. Harvey, Reed A. *Managerial Need Satisfaction in the Retailing Environment.* New York: National Retail Merchants Association, 1971. Retail trade as a profession. Includes bibliography.

674. Rachman, David J. *Retail Strategy and Structure: A Management Approach,* 2d ed. Englewood Cliffs, N.J.: Prentice-Hall, Inc., 1975. Includes annotated bibliography.

675. Walter, Bruce, and J. B. Haynes, ed. *Marketing Channels and Institutions.* Columbus, Ohio: Grid, Inc., 1973.

Small Business and Entrepreneurial Prospects

Bibliographies

676. Center for Venture Management. *The Entrepreneur and New Enterprise Formation: A Resource Guide.* Compiled by James W. Schreier and John L. Komives. Milwaukee: Center for Venture Management, 1973.

677. Dun & Bradstreet. *Management Source Publications for Small Business.* New York: 1972.

678. "Resources." An annotated bibliography that appears in each issue of the *Journal of Small Business Management.* Quarterly.

679. U.S. Small Business Administration. *Small Business Bibliographies.* A series of pamphlets that list sources of information on the management of specific types of small businesses.

General Books

680. Baty, Gordon B. *Entrepreneurship: Playing to Win.* Reston, Va.: Reston Publishing Co., 1974.

681. Baumback, Clifford M., comp. *Entrepreneurship and Venture Management.* Englewood Cliffs, N.J.: Prentice-Hall, Inc., 1975.

682. Baumback, Clifford M., et al. *How to Organize and Operate a Small Business,* 5th ed. Englewood Cliffs, N.J.: Prentice-Hall, Inc., 1973.

683. Broom, H. N., and J. G. Longenecker. *Small Business Management,* 4th ed. Cincinnati: South-Western Publishing Company, 1975.

684. Cohn, Theodore, and R. A. Lindberg. *Survival and Growth: Management Strategies for the Small Firm.* New York: AMACOM, 1974.

685. Dible, Donald M. *Up Your Own Organization. A Handbook for the Employed, the Underemployed, and the Self-Employed on How to Start and Finance a New Business.* Santa Clara, Calif.: The Entrepreneur Press, 1971. Includes a list of seminars on small business management, Small Business Administration office locations, and business and financial periodicals. Also includes "Recommended Reading" at end of each chapter.

686. Goodman, Sam R. *Financial Manager's Manual and Guide.* Englewood Cliffs, N.J.: Prentice-Hall, 1973. Includes a section on "Cash Management for Small and Medium-Sized Companies."

687. Greene, Gardiner G. *How to Start and Manage Your Own Business.* New York: McGraw-Hill, 1975.

688. Griffen, Barbara C. *A Successful Business of Your Own.* Los Angeles: Shelbourne Press, 1974.

689. Klatt, Laurence. *Small Business Management: Essentials of Entrepreneurship.* Belmont, Calif.: Wadsworth Publishing Co., 1973.

690. Klein, Howard J. *Stop! You're Killing the Business.* New York: Mason & Lipscomb, 1974.

691. Lasser (J. K.) Institute, *How to Run a Small Business,* 4th ed. New York: McGraw-Hill, 1974.

692. Lilies, Patrick. *New Business Ventures and the Entrepreneur.* Homewood, Ill.: Richard D. Irwin, 1974. Contains a note on the legal forms of business.

693. Markstein, David L. *Money Raising and Planning for the Small Business.* Chicago: Henry Regnery Company, 1974.

694. Nicholas, Ted. *How to Form Your Own Corporation Without a Lawyer for Under $50.00.* Wilmington, Del.: Enterprise Publishing Co., 1972.

695. Petrof, John W., P. S. Carusone, and J. E. McDavid. *Small Business Management: Concepts and Techniques for Improving Decisions.* New York: McGraw-Hill, 1972.

696. Roberts, E. Wilson. *How, When and Where to Go Public with a Small Company.* New York: Exposition Press, 1973.

697. Small, Samuel. *Starting a Business after Fifty.* New York: Pilot Books, 1974.

698. Steinhoff, Dan. *Small Business Fundamentals.* New York: McGraw-Hill, 1974.

699. Tate, Curtis E., et al. *Successful Small Business Management.* Dallas: Business Publications, 1975.

700. U.S. Internal Revenue Service. *Tax Guide for Small Business.* Annual.

Venture Capital and Small Business Investment Companies

701. Dominquez, John R. *Venture Capital.* Lexington, Mass.: Lexington Books, 1974. Includes a list of venture capital firms by investment limit.

702. Kelley, Albert J., F. F. Campanella, and J. McKiernan. *Venture Capital: A Guidebook for New Enterprises.* Chestnut Hill, Mass.: School of Management, Boston College, July 1971. Includes a selected list of venture capital sources.

703. New Enterprise Systems, Inc. *Venture Capital in the U.S.: An Analysis.* Wellesley, Mass., 1972.

704. Noone, Charles M., and S. M. Rubel. *SBIC's: Pioneers in Organized Venture Capital.* Chicago: Capital Publishing Co., 1970. Background on the development of the SBIC industry and a directory of a few firms.

705. Rubel, Stanley M. *Guide to Venture Capital Sources,* 3d ed. Chicago: Capital Publishing Co., 1974. Biennial. Presents an analysis of the venture capital industry and includes a directory of venture capital companies in the U.S., Canada, Puerto Rico, France, United Kingdom, and South Afirca.

706. Rubel, Stanley M., and E. G. Novotny. *How to Raise and Invest Venture Capital.* New York: Presidents Publishing House, 1971.

707. U.S. Small Business Administration. *List of Small Business Investment Companies.* Irregular.

708. *Venture Capital.* Chicago: S. M. Rubel & Co.

Monthly. Presents news of new venture groups and financial performance of venture capital firms.

709. Western Association of Venture Capitalists. *Directory of Members*. San Francisco, 1974/75.

Management Guides

710. *How to Start Your Own Small Business*. New York: Drake Publishers. Volumes 1–3, 1973–1975. Information is given on starting specific types of small businesses.

711. *Small Business Reporter*. Issued periodically. San Francisco: Bank of America. A collection of reports on starting and managing specific types of small businesses. Also booklets on specific management problems in small business management.

Publications of the Small Business Administration

712. 115A *Free Management Assistance Publications*. Lists titles in the following series: *Management Aids and Small Business Bibliographies*.

713. 115B *For-Sale Booklets*. Lists the contents of the *Small Business Management* and *Starting and Managing* Series as well as the annual issues of *Management Aids for Small Manufacturers* and *Small Marketers Aids*.

714. *Management Aids for Small Manufacturers*.

715. *Small Business Management Series*. Irregular.

716. *Small Marketers Aids*.

717. *Starting and Managing Series*. Irregular.

Journals and Magazines

718. *Journal of Small Business Management*. Quarterly. West Virginia University: Bureau of Business Research, College of Business and Economics.

719. *NASBIC News*. Washington, D.C.: National Association of Small Business Investment Companies.

720. *Quarterly Economic Report for Small Business*. San Mateo, Calif.: National Federation of Independent Business. A series of quarterly economic reports based on survey data from members of the National Federation of Independent Business.

721. *Small Business News*. Monthly. Waltham, Mass.: Small Business Administration of New England.

Social Service

Directories

722. *Community Action Agency Atlas*. Washington, D.C., Office of Economic Opportunity. Geographic listing of all agency offices, regional, state, local, and those in Indian land areas.

723. *Conservation Directory*. Annual. Washington, D.C.: National Wildlife Federation. Governmental and private organizations concerned with natural resource use and management.

724. *Directory of Agencies Serving Blind Persons*. Revised biennially. New York: American Foundation for the Blind. Lists 500 American agencies and schools serving blind.

725. *Directory of Approved Counseling Agencies*. Washington, D.C.: American Board on Counseling Services, Inc., American Personnel and Guidance Association. Directory of counseling agencies that have been evaluated and approved. Includes sponsor, clientele, fees, and professional staff. Arranged geographically for the United States and Canada.

726. *Directory of Full-Year Head Start Programs*. Washington, D.C.: Office of Child Development, U.S. Department of HEW. Geographic listing of the programs including the names of directors.

727. *Directory of Spanish Speaking Community Organizations*. Washington, D.C.: U.S. Government Printing Office. Listing of national, state, and city organizations.

728. *Directory of State and Local Resources for the Mentally Retarded*. Washington, D.C.: U.S. Department of HEW. List of state and local agencies, facilities, and other resources that render services to the mentally retarded.

729. *Directory–United Way of America*. Alexandria, Va.: United Way of America. Listing of United Funds, Community Chests, and Community Health and Welfare Councils that are members of United Way of America. Address and name of executive included.

730. *Encyclopedia of Social Work*. Quinquennial. New York: National Association of Social Workers. International indexed directory of social welfare agencies.

731. *JWB Personnel Reporter*. Biannual. New York: National Jewish Welfare Board. Listing of current job openings in Jewish community centers and other personnel and training information.

732. *Public Welfare Directory*. Washington, D.C.: American Public Welfare Association. Lists all federal, state, local, and territorial public welfare agencies throughout the United States and Canada. Lists other related public agencies—federal and state level.

D

Sources of Information on Developing Job Opportunities

- Resumé writing, cover letters, and follow-up
- Interviewing
- Executive recruiting search firms
- Salaries in different industries and jobs
- Job opportunities: geographic sources
- Life-style information in specific geographical areas
- Geographic relocations outside the U.S.
- Dual-career families

The references listed here represent a selected set of useful information that is readily available to you.[1] Each reference can be located in any major library.

Titles are listed under subject headings and then by type of publication where appropriate.

Resumé Writing, Cover Letters, and Follow-up

Books

1. Alumni Advisory Center, Inc. *How to Write Your Resume.* New York: 1970.
2. Angel, Juvenal L. *Specialized Resumes for Executives and Professionals.* New York: Regents Publishing Co., 1967.
3. Angel, Juvenal L. *Why and How to Prepare an Effective Job Resume,* 5th ed. rev. and enl. New York: World Trade Academy Press; distributed by Simon and Schuster, 1972.
4. Biegeleisen, Jacob I. *Job Resumes: How to Write Them, How to Present Them.* New York: Grosset & Dunlap, 1969.
5. Boll, Carl. *Executive Jobs Unlimited.* New York: The Macmillan Company, 1965.
6. Bolles, Richard Nelson. *What Color Is Your Parachute?* Berkeley, Calif.: Ten Speed Press, 1972.
7. Black, James Menzies, and Edith M. Lynch. *How to Move in Management.* New York: McGraw-Hill, 1967.
8. Brennan, Lawrence David, Stanley Strand, and Edward C. Gruber. *Resumes for Better Jobs.* New York: Simon and Schuster, 1973.

9. Cass, Frank. *Recruitment Advertising.* New York: American Management Association, 1968.
10. Dickhut, Harold W. *Professional Resume/Job Search Guide,* 3d ed. Chicago: Management Counselors, 1975.
11. Greco, Benedetto. *How to Get the Job That's Right for You.* Homewood, Ill.: Dow Jones/Irwin, 1975.
12. Gruber, Edward C. *Resumes That Get Jobs.* New York: Arco, 1963.
13. Irish, Richard K. *Go Hire Yourself an Employer.* Garden City, N.Y.: Anchor Books, 1973.
14. Johnson, Gil. *How to Prepare Your Job Resumé,* 2d ed. Monrovia, Calif.: Association Writers, 1971.
15. Mandell, Milton. *The Selection Process: Choosing the Right Man for the Job.* New York: American Management Association, 1964.
16. Schrameck, Carolyn F. Nutter. *The Resume Workbook. A Personal Career File for Job Applications.* Cranston, R.I.: Carroll Press, 1970.
17. Uris, Auren. *The Executive Job Market.* New York: McGraw-Hill, 1965.

[1]These references were compiled by the staff at Baker Library and the Office of Career Development, Harvard Business School, whose help we appreciate.

18. Vogel, Erwin. *How to Write your Job-Getting Resume and Covering Letter*. Brooklyn, N.Y.: Copy-Write Creations, 1971.

Guides and Handbooks

19. Angel, Juvenal L. *Looking for Employment in Foreign Countries Reference Handbook*, 6th ed. Volume 7 of *Encyclopedia of International Information*. New York: World Trade Academy Press, 1972.

20. Employment Management Association. *Job Hunting Guide*. John D. Erdlen, ed. Boston: Herman Publishing, Inc., 1975.

Interviewing

Popular Works

25. Boll, Carl. *Executive Jobs Unlimited*. New York: The Macmillan Company, 1965. See Chapter 6. Very basic, introductory source. Material is sometimes dated but still useful. Good for beginners.

26. Bolles, Richard N. *What Color Is Your Parachute?* Berkeley, Calif.: Ten Speed Press, 1973. Emphasis is on self-analysis as preparation for job search. Information on interviewing is scattered throughout.

27. Crystal, John C., and Richard N. Bolles. *Where Do I Go from Here with My Life?* New York: Seabury Press, 1974. See Chapter 14. Stresses self-evaluation and analysis. Contains brief but unusual approach to interviewing.

28. Dauw, Dean C. *Up Your Career*. Prospect Heights, Ill.: Waveland Press, 1975. See Chap. 7. Mainly a list of questions most frequently asked by interviewers as well as a sample of questions that are illegal.

29. Dickhut, Harold W., and Marvel J. Davis. *Professional Resume/Job Search Guide*. Chicago: Management Counselors, 1975. See Section 12. Brief discussion of interview preparation, types of questions asked, conduct, and follow-up.

30. Djeddah, Eli. Moving Up: *How to Get High-Salaried Jobs*. Philadelphia: J. B. Lippincott, 1971. See Chapters 7, 9, and 10. A popular work, easy reading, many helpful hints.

31. Erdlen, John D., ed. *Job-Hunting Guide: Official Manual of the Employment Management Association*. Boston: Herman Publishers, 1975. See Chapter 6. Very brief section that includes crucial points in interviewing and follow-up evaluation.

32. German, Donald R., and Joan W. German. *Successful Job Hunting for Executives*. Chicago: Henry Regnery Company, 1974. See Chapter 13. Informative chapter designed for individuals in management. Includes information on planning and analysis of interviews.

33. Greco, Benedetto. *How to Get the Job That's Right for You*. Homewood, Ill.: Dow Jones/Irwin, 1975. See Chapter 9. Includes discussion of handling job interview, selling yourself, and sample of tough questions.

Periodicals

21. Dortch, R. N. "What Businessmen Look for in the Resume." *Personnel Journal*, 54:516, October 1975.

22. Hayden, R. L., and J. H. Jackson. "Behavioral Research and Computer Methods Applied to Managerial Resumé Design." *Personnel Journal*, 51:728-732ff, October 1972.

23. Perham, J. C. "What's Wrong with Executive Resumes?" *Duns Review*, 105:50-52 ff, May 1975.

24. Smith, L. "Notes from the Job Underground." *Duns Review*, 106:46-48, August 1975.

34. Hopke, William E., ed. *Encyclopedia of Careers and Vocational Guidance*. Chicago: J. G. Ferguson Publishing Co., 1972.

35. Irish, Richard K. *Go Hire Yourself an Employer*. Garden City, N.Y.: Anchor Press, 1973. See Chapter 4. Very readable, popular book offering a variety of hints for the job search.

36. Jameson, Robert H. *The Professional Job Hunting System: World's Fastest Way to Get a Better Job*. Verona, N.J.: Performance Dynamics, 1972.

37. Kent, Malcolm. *Successful Executive Job Hunting*. New York: Laddin Press, 1967. See Chapter 5. Aimed at business professionals; seems to be on a higher level than some of the other popular works. Discusses stress interviewing, executive search firms, and psychological testing along with preparing for and conducting interview.

38. Powell, C. Randall. *Career Planning an Placement for the College Graduate of the '70s*. Dubuque, Iowa: Kendall/Hunt Publishing Co., 1974. See Chapters 4 and 5. Discusses all aspects of job search. Very good introductory source. Includes information on screening, preparation, first interviews, frequently asked questions, illegal questions, and how to handle job offers.

39. Snelling, Robert O., Sr. *The Opportunity Explosion*. New York: The Macmillan Company, 1969. See Chapter 10. Written by executive of well-known placement firm. Heavy emphasis on appearance and luck in interviewing. Author presents different approach to topic.

Especially for Women

40. Bird, Caroline. *Everything a Woman Needs to Know to Get Paid What She's Worth*. New York: David McKay Company, 1973. Questions and answers, some dealing with topic.

41. Higgenson, Margaret V., and Thomas L. Quick. *The Ambitious Woman's Guide to a Successful Career*. New York: American Management Association, 1975. Deals primarily with career development. Contains chapter on job hunting with subsection on interviewing. Helpful for men as well as women.

42. Krohn, Miriam. *Your Job Campaign*. New York:

Catalyst. A workbook in the Catalyst Self-Guidance Campaign Series, 1974. See Chapter 7. Designed to address the ''unique problems of adult women.'' Very helpful section on preparing, conducting, and evaluating the interview. Definitely useful to men as well.

Periodicals

43. Clarke, John R. ''Landing that Right Executive Job.'' *Management Review*, August 1975, pp. 31–36. Contains small section on interviewing within article about job searching.

44. Costello, John. ''Executive Trends: Playing the Interview Game.'' *Nation's Business*, September 1974, p. 6. Very brief discussion of stereotypes who interview and tips on avoiding becoming one.

45. ''Finding a Job in the Recession.'' *Business Week*, January 11, 1975, pp. 101–106. A supplement to the regularly featured Personal Business section. Contains several paragraphs on interviewing as well as information on other aspects of job search. Includes bibliography.

46. Flanagan, William, ed. ''How to Keep Bias Out of Job Interviews.'' *Business Week*, May 26, 1975, p. 77. Discusses what an interviewer may not ask.

47. Keyser, Marshall. ''How to Apply for a Job.'' *Journal of College Placement*, Fall 1974, pp. 63–65. Discusses qualifications most often desired by employers as expressed in a survey of Los Angeles businessmen.

48. Kohn, Mervin. ''What Off-Campus Interviewers Look for in Young Job Seekers.'' *S.A.M. Advanced Management Journal*, vol. 40, pp. 59–62. Lists qualities considered important by campus recruiters. Moderately helpful to M.B.A. students.

49. Luk, Henry. ''Interviewing: A Statistical Look at Columbia '74.'' *MBA*, November 1974, pp. 43–45. Investigates and records statistics resulting from a study of aggressiveness in interviewing using students from Columbia.

50. Lumsden, Howard, and James C. Sharf. ''Behavioral Dimensions of the Job Interview.'' *Journal of College Placement*, Spring 1974, pp. 63–66. Types of

behavior influence job interviews. Could be a helpful list to use in preparation.

51. Shaw, Edward A. ''Behavior Modification and the Interview.'' *Journal of College Placement*, October/November 1973, pp. 52–57. Designed mainly for counselors, but students would find it quite helpful. Discusses pros and cons of being coached or even acting natural at interviews.

52. Welch, William F. ''A Professional Approach to Job Hunting.'' *Public Relations Journal*, October 1972, pp. 22–24. Section on interviewing has helpful hints. Aimed at those in public relations but so general as to be useful to anyone.

Several periodicals frequently offer information related to this topic, and new issues should be checked:

53. *Business Week*. Personal Business section.

54. *Journal of College Placement*.

55. *MBA*. Career Tactics column—new in January 1976.

56. *Nation's Business*. Executive Trends column.

Miscellaneous Sources

57. Amsden, Forrest M., and Noel D. White. *How to Be Successful: Step by Step Approach for the Candidate*. Cheney, Wa.: Interviewing Dynamics, 1974. Recommended for beginners as a practical reference book in interviewing by *Journal of College Placement*, Fall 1975.

58. McDonald, Stanleigh. *Ten Weeks to a Better Job*. Garden City, N.Y.: Doubleday & Company, 1972. See Chapter 4. Popular but thorough work that includes sample questions from interviews.

59. Noer, David. *How to Beat the Employment Game*. Radnor, Pa.: Chilton Company—Book Division, 1975. Discusses use and misuse of interview. Author believes it is much overrated. Has innovative viewpoint.

60. ''The Interview Game.'' University Park, Pa.: Career Development and Placement Center, Pennsylvania State University. Color video tape cassette. Teaching aid to interview process; uses game-show technique to introduce humor. Material discussed is helpful.

Executive Recruiting Search Firms

These selected sources provide information about executive recruiting search firms, commonly called recruiters or headhunters. They are frequently retained and paid by employers. Their job is to find qualified candidates for specific positions that their clients have available. Recruiters do not hire people; they only recommend them for hire to their clients. The two professional associations to which recruiters belong are:

Association of Executive Recruiting Consultants (AERC)
347 Madison Avenue, New York, N.Y. 10017. Phone: (212) 686-7194.

Association of Consulting Management Engineers (ACME)

347 Madison Avenue, New York, N.Y. 10017. Phone: (212) 686-7338.

Guides and Directories

61. American Management Association. *Executive Employment Guide*. New York: AMA, 1975. Excellent directory also including a guide indicating 150 firms' positions, salary levels, resumé and interview policies. Bibliography.

62. Consultant News. *Directory of Executive Recruiters*. Fitzwilliams, N.H.: 1976. Lists over 1,000 firms retained by management to locate executives.

63. Erdlen, John D. *Job Hunting Guide: Official Manual of the Employment Management Association*. Bos-

ton: Herman Publishing Co., 1975. Contains a directory section, by states, of both employment agencies and executive search consultants.

64. Executive Selection Institute. *Handbook of Executive Recruiters, 1967–68.* Detroit, 1967. An alphabetical list of firms practicing executive recruitment.

65. National Survey Information Co. *The National Service Directory of Executive Employment Research, 1972–73.* Lake Bluff, Ill., 1972. Lists, geographically, by state, firms and individuals participating in recruiting.

International Reference Sources

66. Angel, Juvenal L. *Looking for Employment in Foreign Countries Reference Handbook,* 6th ed. Volume 7 of *Encyclopedia of International Information.* New York: World Trade Academy Press. Provides guidelines for overseas employment, employment agencies, and sources of employment abroad.

67. *European Executive Position Information Guide.* Geneva. Enables the user to assess the job market. A source of information for those who may be looking for a chance to live and work in another country; lists executive recruiters, alphabetically, by country.

68. Jameson, Robert J. *Worldwide Directory of Employment Recruiters.* Verona, N.J.: Performance Dynamics, 1975. Executive search firms listed geographically by state and country; covers 3,000 recruiters.

Books

69. Bolles, Richard N. *What Color Is Your Parachute?* Berkeley, Calif.: Ten Speed Press, 1972. Contains a discussion and bibliography of periodical literature on the pros and cons of using executive job counselors.

70. Cox, Allan J. *Confessions of a Corporate Headhunter.* New York: Trident Press, 1973. Personal reminiscences.

71. Jameson, Robert J. *Professional Job Changing System: World's Fastest Way to Get a Better Job.* Verona, N.J.: Performance Dynamics, 1975. Helpful hints.

72. Johnson, Miriam. *Counterpoint: The Changing Employment Service.* Salt Lake City: Olympus, 1973. Background notes.

73. Ruttenberg, Stanley H. *Federal-State Employment Service.* Baltimore: Johns Hopkins Press, 1970. An overview.

74. Sweet, Donald H. *Modern Employment Function.* Reading, Mass.: Addison-Wesley Publishing Company, 1973. "How-to" for the recruiter.

75. Uris, Auren. *Executive Job Market.* New York: McGraw-Hill, 1965. A guide for executive job seekers and employers.

76. Williams, Roger K. *How to Evaluate, Select, and Work with Executive Recruiters.* Boston: Cahners, 1974. An overview.

Periodicals

77. Browdy, J. D. "The Personnel Man and the Headhunter." *Personnel Journal,* November 1974, pp. 46–52.

78. "Executive Recruiting: A Growth Business Week, January 26, 1973, pp. 58–59.

79. Kleinschrod, W. A. "What You Always Wanted to Know About Executive Recruiters . . . But Were Afraid to Ask." *Administrative Management,* February 1972, pp. 24–26 ff.

80. Newman, Barry. "The Rite of Spring: Recruiting of MBAs by Firm Is a Game with Strange Rules." *Wall Street Journal,* April 9, 1974.

81. Pfeffer, J. "Executive Recruitment and the Development of Interfirm Organizations." *Administrative Science Quarterly,* November 4, 1973, pp. 46–52.

82. "A Peek at the Money in Headhunting." *Business Week,* July 29, 1972, pp. 22–23.

83. Porter, K. "He Finds Jobs for Executives." *Duns,* June 1974, pp. 78–81.

Salaries in Different Industries and Jobs

Bibliographies

84. Mohn, N. Carroll. *Compensation of Professionals: A Selected and Annotated Bibliography.* Austin: Bureau of Business Research, Graduate School of Business, University of Texas, 1972. Mostly reference materials pertaining to theory of compensation.

Statistical Surveys

85. Crystal, Graef S. *Compensating U.S. Executives Abroad.* 1972. Based on a survey of 28 companies in 14 industries.

86. Dartnell Corporation. *Dartnell Survey of Executive Compensation.* Biennial. Chicago. Extensive statistics, charts, graphs, comparisons of compensation components by functional areas. Includes a section on Salary Administration.

87. *1970 Census of Population: Earnings by Occupation and Education.* Subject Report PC (2)-8B. Extensive Census Bureau report on wages, earnings, and income, classified by various demographic, social, and economic statistics.

88. Powell, C. Randall. *MBA Career Performance 10 Years after Graduation.* St. Paul, Minn.: Midwest College Placement Association, 1974. Includes tables giving salary statistics.

89. Powers, Janet T. *Executive Compensation in Retailing.* New York: National Retail Merchants Association, 1973. Excellent survey of salary and compensation trends in retailing.

90. *Report on Executive Compensation.* Prepared by the Executive Compensation Office of Wage Stabilization, Cost of Living Council, May 1974. Mostly textual, includes tables, graphs, etc. Also includes detailed analysis of changes and trends. Covers manufacturing and nonmanufacturing companies.

91. *Salary Survey of Business Economists.* Washington, D.C.: National Association of Business Economists.

Quadrenniel. 1972 report includes tables, statistics, charts and graphs for Business Economists, salary comparisons by industry, functions, size of firm, years of experience, education, etc.

92. Teague, Burton W. *Compensating Key Personnel Overseas.* New York: The Conference Board, 1972. Analysis of compensation structure of 267 of the largest U.S.-based international companies.

Job Opportunities: Geographic Sources

Directories

93. *Career Opportunity Index.* Huntington Beach, California: Career Research Systems, Inc. Professional edition, biannually with weekly supplements. California. Alphabetical listing of companies with job openings—descriptions of openings.

94. Los Angeles Times. *California's Leading Companies.* 1974. Directory listing.

95. *Organization Members of Chamber of Commerce of*

the U.S. Directory of local and state Chambers by state. Chambers sometimes publish listings of job opportunities.

96. *Standard and Poor's Register.* Volume 3, *Indexes.* 1975. Yellow pages list companies by major cities within states.

97. State Industrial Directories. Consult *CPP*—blue-edged pages for specific titles. Listings of companies within the state, mostly manufacturing or industrial.

Life-Style Information in Specific Geographic Areas

Bibliographies

98. *Encyclopedia of Business Information Sources.* Volume 2, Geographical Sources. Detroit: Gale Research Co. Pages 652–684 list bibliographic references to consult for life-style and business information by state.

Directories

99. *Almanac of American Politics.* Boston: Gambit. Biennial. State-by-state listing of senators and representatives, their records, states, and districts. Includes political background, census data, economic base, and voter statistics.

100. *Commercial Atlas and Market Guide.* Annual. New York; Chicago: Rand, McNally & Co. Useful for

checking map locations and gives useful geographic, social and economic synopses.

101. *Ayer Directory of Publications,* Annual. Philadelphia: Ayer Press. City within state listing of newspapers and magazines (consumer, business, technical, trade, and farm).

102. *Organization Members of Chamber of Commerce of the U.S.* Annual. Washington. Alphabetical listing of state and local chamber organizations, arranged by state. Many of these organizations will be quite happy to furnish life style information to prospective residents.

103. *Sales Management.* "Survey of Buyer Power." Annual. Chicago. Features population, income, retail sales, and merchandise line sales of all U.S. markets. Section D gives county-city data by states.

Geographic Relocations Outside the U.S.

This list provides material helpful to a family or individual making a geographic relocation outside of the U.S. Information is given about those aspects of relocation, such as taxation, adaptation, etc., that would be common to all moves, regardless of country. Attention is also given to the process of finding a job abroad.

gives an excellent run-down on the new tax laws governing most U.S. citizens abroad, by which the $20,000 exemption is expected to be phased out over the 1976–1980 period.

General Background

104. Prendergast, Curtis. "If You're Transferred Abroad," *Money,* December 1975, pp. 91–98. This is an excellent source for weighing the pros and cons of living abroad in terms of taxation, family life style, family considerations, etc. A graphic cost-of-living chart indicates the relative expensiveness of various cities around the world, and the author cites the personal experience of his family and friends.

105. *Wall Street Journal,* October 2, 1975. This article

Encyclopedias

106. Angel, Juvenal L. *Looking for Employment in Foreign Countries.* New York: World Trade Academy Press, 1972. Volume 7 of *Encyclopedia of International Information.* This is an excellent source of information about passports, visas, work contracts, and specific information about various countries. Some warnings about cultural acclimatization are given, and a list of American firms operating overseas is provided. Types of compensation policies are detailed.

107. Wasserman, Paul, ed. *Encyclopedia of Business Information Sources.* Detroit: Gale Research Com-

pany, 1970. This is a useful reference tool for books, government documents, and periodicals about international business and specific places, although the emphasis is on corporate rather than individual situations. Most useful as a guide to getting a job overseas.

Guides and Directories

108. *Directory: Public Elementary and Secondary Day Schools*. Vol. IV. Office of Education. Washington, D.C.: U.S. Government Printing Office. At the end of the directory is a list of schools in various countries with a brief reference to grade spans and types of programs.

109. *Europa Yearbook, 1975*. London: Europa Publications, Ltd. The emphasis is on the various organizations of the U.N. and different countries. Economic, historical, and cultural information is given, and there is a directory section regarding newspapers, periodicals, publications, trade associations, etc., for each country.

110. *Fodor's Modern Guides*. New York: David McKay Company. Although geared to tourists, these guides to various countries are excellent for explicit details about various countries, highlighting cultural and entertainment opportunities.

111. *Schools Abroad*. Anne Maher, ed. Boston: Porter Sargent Publishing, 1975.

112. *The World of Learning*. London: European Publications, 1975.

Journals

113. Krause, David, and Patrick Stewart. "International Executive Compensation—Unmanaged or Unmanageable?" *Business Horizons*, December 1974, pp. 45–55. Although the tax structure has changed somewhat since this was written, the article gives an excellent outline of the various complexities of company compensation polities and their hazards and recommends lump-sum inducements to executives being considered for overseas transfers.

Books

114. Casewit, Curtis W. *Overseas Jobs: The Ten Best Countries*. New York: Warner Paperback Library, 1972. Aside from detailed information about ten selected countries, this book covers issues including visas and entry permits, life styles, salaries, opportunities, and employment leads.

115. Hopkins, Robert. *I've Had It–A Practical Guide to Moving Abroad*. New York: Holt, Rinehart and Winston, 1972. This book covers the many aspects of moving abroad and also serves as an excellent bibliography. Chapters on such topics as climate and maps give numerous references to other materials published on the topics. Twelve countries are selected for more detailed treatment.

116. Winfield, Louise. *Living Overseas*. Washington, D.C.: Public Affairs Press, 1962. Although dated, this well-written book by the wife of a Foreign Aid official is highly informative on the daily details of establishing a home in a foreign country. Everyday realities such as medical treatment, marketing, what to bring and what to leave behind are treated in detail and with humor. An excellent source from the housewife point of view.

Government Publications and Company Documents

117. Arthur Anderson and Co. *U.S. Taxation and Its Citizens Overseas*. Chicago: Arthur Anderson and Co.

118. Price Waterhouse Company. *Information Guide for Citizens Abroad*. New York: Price Waterhouse Company, 1975.

119. U.S. Department of Labor. *U.S. Department of State Indexes of Living Costs Abroad and Living Quarters Allowances*. Quarterly. Washington, D.C.: U.S. Government Printing Office.

120. U.S. Department of State. International Development Agency. "Helpful Information Excerpted from *Living Abroad*," by Eleanor B. Pierce, March 1969.

Dual-Career Families

Dual-career families are a growing trend in western society. The references cited here represent the major studies and findings of recent years.

Books and Excerpts

121. Fogarty, Michael. *Sex, Career and Family*. London: George Allen and Unwin, 1974. See especially Chapter 9, "the Reconciliation of Work and Family Life—The Dual-Career Family."

122. Hoffman, Lois, and F. Ivan Nye. *Working Mothers: An Evaluative Review of the Consequences for Wife, Husband, and Child*. San Francisco: Jossey-Bass, 1974. Jossey-Bass Behavioral Science Series.

123. Holmstrom, Lynda Lytle. *The Two-Career Family*. Cambridge, Mass.: Schenkman Publications, 1972.

124. Morgan, James N., and Gred J. Duncan, eds. *Five Thousand American Families–Patterns of Economic Progress*. Volume 3, Dynamics. Ann Arbor, Mich.: Survey Research Center, Institute for Social Research, University of Michigan, 1974.

125. Ohio State University, Columbus, Center for Human Resources Research. *Dual Careers: A Longitudinal Study of Labor Market Experience of Women*. Washington, D.C.: U.S. Department of Labor, Manpower Administration, 1970.

126. Rapoport, Rhona, and Robert Rapoport. *Dual-Career Families*. Baltimore: Penguin, 1971. Case studies done in England.

Journal Articles

127. Bailyn, Lotte. "Career and Family Orientation of Husbands and Wives in Relation to Marital Happiness." *Human Relations*, 22(1):3-29, 1969.

128. Barlove, Mary. "Working Partners: For Married Couples, Two Careers Can be an Exercise in Frustration." *Wall Street Journal*, 185:1ff, May 13, 1975.

129. Bebbington, A. C. "The Function of Stress in the Establishment of the Dual-Career Family." *Journal of Marriage and the Family*, 35(3):530-537, August 1973.

130. "Family Trends Now Taking Shape." *U.S. News and World Report*, 79:32, October 27, 1975. (General overview, including dual-career families.)

131. Hedges, Janice N., and Jeanne K. Barnett. "Working Women and the Division of Household Tasks." *U.S. Labor Statistics Monthly Labor Review*, 95:9-14, April 1972.

132. Linn, Erwin L. "Women Dentists: Career and Family." *Social Problems*, 18(3):393-403, Winter 1971.

133. "Marital and Career Characteristics of the Labor Force." *U.S. Bureau of Labor Statistics Monthly Labor Review*, 98:52-56, November 1975.

134. *New York Times*, April 22, 1975, p. 26, column 1. (News article covering colloquia held at Princeton concerning the lives of dual-career couples.)

135. Poloma, Margaret M., and T. Neal Garland. "On the Social Construction of Reality: Reported Husband-Wife Differences." *Social Focus* 5(2):40-54, Winter 1971/1972.

136. Propper, Alice Marcella. "The Relationship of Maternal Employment to Adolescent Roles, Activities, and Parental Relationship." *Journal of Marriage and the Family*, 34(3):417-421, August 1972.

137. Rapoport, Rhona, and Robert Rapoport. "The Dual-career Family: A Variant Pattern and Social Change." *Human Relations*, 22(1):3-29, 1969.

138. Safilios-Rothchild, Constantina. "The Influence of the Wife's Degree of Work Commitment upon Some Aspects of Family Organization and Dynamics." *Journal of Marriage and Family*, 32(4):681-691, November 1970.

SELF-ASSESSMENT
AND
CAREER DEVELOPMENT
WORKBOOK

<u>Note to Readers</u>: Tear out the pages of this "workbook" section and put them in a large (1½-2 inches thick) binder. If you are using this workbook as a part of a course, your instructor will tell you how to use it and when. If you are using the workbook on your own, refer to the textbook for a recommended manner in which to proceed. In either case, DO NOT under any circumstances look through the text or the workbook until you have received instruction regarding how to proceed.

Data Generating Instruments and Your Responses

FEELINGS RECORD

Make a record below of any strong reactions you have while generating data by means of the instruments that follow or while analyzing and interpreting those data. For example, you may find yourself surprised, or happy, or annoyed, or angry or whatever. Make a note of both the feeling and the context in which it occurred.   Later on, this feelings record may be useful in helping you better understand yourself and in helping you to make more personally satisfying career and job choices.

The Written Interview

The AVL

24-Hour Diaries

The Strong-Campbell

The Life-Style Representations

The Background Fact Sheet

Other Device

Other Device

Other Device

260

Do not look at any of the pages that follow until you are ready to begin this exercise. When you are ready to begin, first look at the previous section, the "Feelings Record" (if you have not done so already).

WRITTEN INTERVIEW

<u>DO</u> <u>NOT</u> TURN PAGE UNTIL THIS ASSIGNMENT HAS BEEN MADE AND YOU ARE READY TO BEGIN WRITING

Our goal in this exercise is to create a written interview. We'd like to interview you on paper, wherever you are as you read this.

Your responses should be handwritten or typed, preferably, though if you want to reply to a person or a machine that can take dictation, that's up to you. The end product should be a typed transcript that, later on, you can read and we can read, so we all can perform some intellectual operations on the raw material. Rough typing will do; neither you nor we are going to be focusing on editorial exactness. Rough typing is likely best; stopping to correct the spelling or style will only break your flow of ideas, and it will help if you flow.

Write as you talk.

The point of using these 11 separate pages is that our dialog is going to proceed in stages, as a good dialog should. Verisimilitude will improve if you don't look ahead. Read the contents of each page only after you have responded completely to the previous question posed by the "interviewers." The point is not to spring any great surprises, but to facilitate an interviewlike sequence in your ideas as they flow. To do that, we have to provide a series of cues, one at a time, so that the effect is of Question, then Reply, then Question, then Reply.

The Replies will be much, much longer than the Questions, of course.

Like any good interview, this one is going to consist of a hundred times as much of your talk as of our talk. When you finish what you have to say in response to our question, please turn to the next page, so we can get a few remarks of our own into the conversation.

When you are ready to start this "interview," please turn to question number one.

QUESTION NUMBER ONE

DO NOT TURN PAGE UNTIL YOU HAVE READ THE PREVIOUS PAGE

To generate good data from which you can make valid inferences about your own career is the goal you and we now share.
In the end, it is you who make the inferences, so in one
sense, all through this exercise, or even all through this
course, you will be talking to yourself. We are, however, going
to listen in. Our presence may enable you to talk to yourself
in a more useful way. We will try to steer your soliloquy away
from running around in circles. Which direction its tangent
should take is not, however, something we intend to dictate or
direct. Our job is to show you how to generate good information
about yourself, for yourself.

For openers, we, your silent partners, need to hear something
about the story of your life. As of this moment, we know nothing
about you. What has happened to you thus far? What were the
twists and turns in the winding road of your life?

What you are going to need is an account of your life more
structured than free association, more personal than a resumé or
vita. The level of discourse will be that of personal history
- an overview of all those years' diaries that you didn't keep
(or at least the parts suitable for public consumption).

Just let it flow. If you belatedly realize you've left
something out, put it in when you think about it. This is a
rough manuscript! Order and method come later.

How long should your story be? As long as it takes to tell.
Although an autobiography is usually book length, you may be
able to tell your story in the equivalent of a chapter or two.

Tell away!

QUESTION NUMBER TWO

<u>DO</u> <u>NOT</u> TURN PAGE UNTIL YOU HAVE FINISHED QUESTION NUMBER ONE
AND ARE READY TO CONTINUE WRITING

How late did you start your story? Most people get themselves
born and then jump to age twenty, when they began their official
"career." In a resumé, you would lump all the distant past into
a few lines under "miscellany," but if you want to collect the
facts that you'll need later to analyze your own career path,
you should fill in some of the things that went on back before
you were an adult.

Not that we care if you fell in love with your rocking horse
at the age of four. But if your story begins with "I graduated
at Michigan and...," it probably leaves out some facts
that are both public and pertinent - such as the years of secondary school. Or even primary school, at least its name and
nature. Or early avocations. (Chemists and engineers often
receive their calling before puberty.) Or those most cordially
hated activities imposed by the community on the readily turned-
off young. Or . . . you tell us. This is your life.

What else went on back there?

Set aside your rambling account of your life from question
number one and go ahead and write some more about the beginning
of your life story.

Unless you've already said all that need be said. If so, go
on to the next question.

QUESTION NUMBER THREE

○ <u>DO</u> <u>NOT</u> TURN PAGE UNTIL YOU HAVE FINISHED QUESTION NUMBER TWO
AND ARE READY TO CONTINUE WRITING

269

Please fill in the cracks. Maybe you already have, but if you did you are unusually thorough. People's lives are full of temporariness. What went on during your summers? Was there a two-month gap between graduation and a first job? Did those four years at school include one spent abroad? Were there jobs that filled your evenings or weekends?

These odds and ends of living often teach lessons that matter. They often contain data you can use now, even though you saw no relevance in the experience back then.

Set aside question number two and write some bits and pieces about the little odds and ends of living that got tucked in between the major activities that you already have described.

Of course, if you have already covered everything, you won't have much work to do for this step in our conversation.

DO NOT TURN PAGE UNTIL YOU HAVE FINISHED QUESTION NUMBER THREE
AND ARE READY TO CONTINUE WRITING

Talk a little, if you already haven't, about the people in your life. At least the public facts. Was Uncle Louie a graduate of this school? A drop-out? What has become of your brothers and sisters? Did your mother work, or go to school? What was your spouse doing before you married? How have you two arranged your lives since then? And your friends, what of them?

All these are data - later on, you will make use of them. We beg no conclusions about how, or even whether, all these folks mattered. But they were there.

Put them in the picture.

QUESTION NUMBER FIVE

DO NOT TURN PAGE UNTIL YOU HAVE FINISHED QUESTION NUMBER FOUR
AND ARE READY TO CONTINUE WRITING

What about the future? Of course, that's the question we are
both laboring to answer, but what reading do you take of your
future now? Perhaps you've already said. If you haven't,
please do. Or state the ins and outs of your uncertainty.

One subquestion surely deserves your attention: what future
would be ideal? If all went as well as possible, what would be
the Happy Ending?

Or maybe you could dream of more than one? Or more than two?

When you have completed your reply, do not go on to the next
question. You deserve a rest. Allow at least a few hours before you read question number six and continue our interview.
Think about something else in the interim.

QUESTION NUMBER SIX

DO NOT TURN PAGE UNTIL YOU HAVE FINISHED QUESTION NUMBER FIVE
AND ARE READY TO CONTINUE WRITING

If we read back over the exchanges in your written interview, we surely can find a series of moments when your situation changed. You left secondary school to go to college, college to go to graduate school. You may have entered one or another of the Armed Services, from which you subsequently departed, presumably making a decision not to stay when your hitch was over. Perhaps during your college years you transferred, took a year elsewhere, or dropped out. Or simply changed major field. At the very least, you picked a summer job or school or vacation spot. Some of these changes were in good part forced on you. Each put you into a new situation.

Before we go on with our written exchanges, please go back over your story and pick out these points of change. Make a list of them. Add some others we haven't discussed, if others now occur to you. This list will be the backbone of our discussion as we continue our written interview.

Please set your list aside and read question number seven.

QUESTION NUMBER SEVEN

DO NOT TURN PAGE UNTIL YOU HAVE FINISHED QUESTION NUMBER SIX
AND ARE READY TO CONTINUE WRITING

Even though you may have said something about them before, there is much to be learned by talking at greater length and in a more systematic way about the turning points you have listed.

For instance, at each point there were other options. Even in situations in which you thought you had no choice at all, in all likelihood you did. Maybe you applied only to one college; even so, what others did you consider? Did you have more than one acceptance? One's major field is not usually the one and only possibility ever thought about.

Please tell us about your discarded options. Go back systematically and write an account of how it looked back there at each of those times just before your road forked.

What were for you the paths not taken?

QUESTION NUMBER EIGHT

DO NOT TURN PAGE UNTIL YOU HAVE FINISHED QUESTION NUMBER SEVEN
AND ARE READY TO CONTINUE WRITING

You may already have mentioned them, but it would be useful to review more thoroughly and to collect in one discourse the pros and cons that led to each of these decisions. The real reasons and the official reasons. Yours and other people's.

It usually wasn't entirely simple. "Why did you come to this school?" may evoke a blank stare and an astonished "Where else?" from some of us - but most of us can say a lot more. "My father got in and never had enough money to come and that influenced me a little, I guess, but the main reasons were what I wanted to get out of it for myself." Or, "The fact that my husband came from this part of the country was part of it," or, "I liked what I saw when I visited . . . . " All these things can be threads in the story behind a decision - even one so apparently obvious. Thin threads, perhaps. You tell us what were the main ones.

Please write, then, a full description of the warp and woof from which each of your decisions was woven. (In part, you may want to refer back to what you've already said; in part, there's probably also more to each little story.) What were the important parts of the tale, what the trivial, as you look back now on the way it was spun?

QUESTION NUMBER NINE

<u>DO</u> <u>NOT</u> TURN PAGE UNTIL YOU HAVE FINISHED QUESTION NUMBER EIGHT
AND ARE READY TO CONTINUE WRITING

After each of these turning points, what was the transition like? What new things had saliency? How was the living different than it had been before? What new things stood out for you?

External circumstances presumably differed in obvious ways. A dormitory is not the same as your own home. But the point is, what changed for you? Was there in some ways a new you? More subtly, was there a new texture of living?

Perhaps a further question would be: are there any pieces of each of these new stages in your past life still living in you today?

<u>DO</u> <u>NOT</u> TURN PAGE UNTIL YOU HAVE FINISHED QUESTION NUMBER NINE
AND ARE READY TO CONTINUE WRITING

What disillusionments did you suffer? Can you recall your expectations about college, or the Army, or a job, and how these expectations contrasted with the event? Perhaps you were utterly realistic in advance - if so, that is a datum about you well worth recording!

Please cast your mind back - as you have already been doing - and set aside your 20-20 hindsight long enough to recreate what you (perhaps vaguely) thought each situation was going to be like before you confronted it, then how it in fact turned out. Perhaps your expectations were dead wrong, perhaps they were right on target. Likely there were aspects of the new situation that would never have occurred to you even in your wildest imaginings!

At any rate, please try a little retrospect on the before-and-after view of each listed event. Perhaps even a table is indicated: As Seen Before and After. But a little narrative will serve.

The emphasis here is on cognitive awareness, not on values. Did you know the facts?

<u>DO</u> <u>NOT</u> TURN PAGE UNTIL YOU HAVE FINISHED QUESTION NUMBER TEN
AND ARE READY TO CONTINUE WRITING

By now you must be aware of some repetition in what you've
been saying. There probably are themes. In the past you have
been basing your actions on certain kinds of considerations.
What patterns do _you_ see?

If you want to be systematic, you can make some tables showing the plus and minus factors - and perhaps also their weight -
in each decision. What entries recur? Can you conceptualize a
factor underlying apparently distinct entries? If you arrange
the decisions chronologically, do the entries evolve with time?

This last point is of special interest, since being able to
observe yourself acting as if you held consistent values and
beliefs is one thing and deciding to base your next decision
on these same considerations is quite another. There are two
sides to a career: both where it has been and where it is going.

Can the array of ins and outs of your actions in the past reveal to you something of the direction of time's arrow?

When you have completed this reply, you are done. Put your
replies here in the notebook. We've enjoyed listening to you.
Thank you for your time and effort.

If you are using this book as a part of a course, your instructor will provide you with an AVL booklet and tell you when and how to use the score sheet on the following two pages. If you are working on your own, you can obtain an AVL through any reputable career counseling service (on campus or in private business) or by writing to

Houghton Mifflin
Pennington-Hopewell Road
Hopewell, New Jersey 08525

Enclose $1.35 and ask for an AVL examination kit.

After you have filled out the AVL, read Chapter IV in this book, and then use the following score sheet to score the test. Do not use the score sheet which is on the last two pages of the test booklet itself.

AVL STUDY OF VALUES

SCORE SHEET FOR THE STUDY OF VALUES

DIRECTIONS:

1. First make sure that every question has been answered. Note: If you have found it impossible to answer all the questions, you may give equal scores to the alternative answers under each question that has been omitted thus: Part I. 1½ for each alternative. The sum of the scores for (a) and (b) must always equal 3. Part II. 2½ for each alternative. The sum of the scores for the four alternatives under each question must always equal 10.

2. Add the vertical columns of scores on each page and enter the total in the boxes at the bottom of the page.

3. Transcribe the totals from each of the foregoing pages to the columns below. For each page enter the total for each column (R, S, T, etc.) in the space that is labeled with the same letter. Note that the order in which the letters are inserted in the columns below differs for the various pages.

Page Totals	Theoret-ical	Econom-ic	Aesthe-tic	Social	Politi-cal	Reli-gious	The sum of the scores for each row must equal the figure given below
PART I Pge 3	(R)	(S)	(T)	(X)	(Y)	(Z)	24
Pge 4	(Z)	(Y)	(X)	(T)	(S)	(R)	24
Pge 5	(X)	(R)	(Z)	(S)	(T)	(Y)	21
Pge 6	(S)	(X)	(Y)	(R)	(Z)	(T)	21
PART II Pge 8	(Y)	(T)	(S)	(Z)	(R)	(X)	60
Pge 9	(T)	(Z)	(R)	(Y)	(X)	(S)	50
Pge 10	(R)	(S)	(T)	(X)	(Y)	(Z)	40
TOTAL							240

4. Add the totals for the six columns.

5. Check your work by making sure that the total score for all six columns equals 240.

6. List your scores on the accompanying chart, Figure 1.

7. Remember to record your reactions, if any, in the Feelings Record at the beginning of your workbook.

Figure 1

AVL SCORES

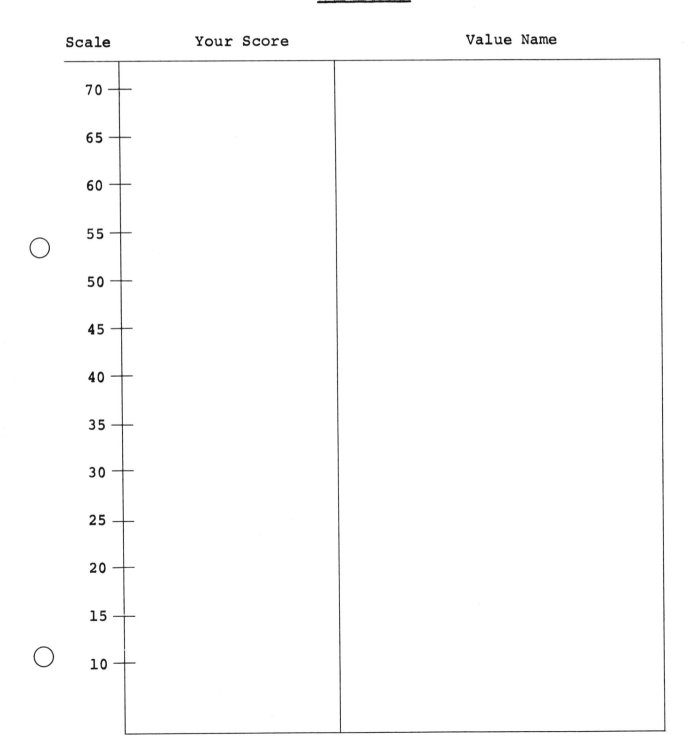

Scale	Your Score	Value Name
70		
65		
60		
55		
50		
45		
40		
35		
30		
25		
20		
15		
10		

Keep a diary of your activities for a 24-hour period on a weekday and on either a Saturday or a Sunday. Do not put off writing the diary until the 24 hours are over. If your memory is like most people's, you will have difficulty recalling accurately what happened more than two or three hours ago. Make notations as often as possible to capture the fine details of your day and provide more substantial data. Remember to record any reactions you may have had in the Feelings Record.

Put the completed diaries here in the workbook.

24-HOUR DIARY

If you are using this book as a part of a course, your instructor will provide you with a SCII. If you are using this book on your own, you can obtain an SCII and have it scored through any reputable career counseling service (on campus or in a private business), or by sending $6.00 to either:

Consulting Psychologists
  Press, Inc.
577 College Avenue
Palo Alto, California 94306
(415/326-4448)

National Computer Systems, Inc.
4401 West 76th Street
Minneapolis, Minnesota 55435
(612/920-3670)

The results of the Strong Vocational Interest Inventory which you completed at the beginning of the course will be returned to you. Place the profile in this section of the workbook; use the following page to analyze your results.

Be sure to record any reactions you may have had in the Feelings Record.

THE STRONG-
CAMPBELL

LIFE-STYLE REPRESENTATIONS

○ This assignment is explained in Chapter VIII of the textbook.

○

○

○ <u>FAMILY</u>

1. When were you born? _____

2. Where did you live before college?

City, State	Dates (from-to)
_____	_____
_____	_____
_____	_____
_____	_____
_____	_____
_____	_____
_____	_____

3. List your brothers and sisters and their ages relative to your own (e.g., one year older).

○

Brothers	Sisters
_____	_____
_____	_____
_____	_____
_____	_____

4. What jobs did your parents hold while you were growing up?

Father	Mother
_____	_____
_____	_____
_____	_____
_____	_____
_____	_____

5. What religion did your family practice? _____

○

EDUCATION

1. Did you attend private or parochial schools before college? If yes, which, when? _____

2. Please list all colleges attended, degrees received, and areas of specialization.

College	Specialty	Degree	Date
_____	_____	_____	_____
_____	_____	_____	_____
_____	_____	_____	_____

3. List any courses or training programs that you have completed besides those taken as a part of a program leading to a bachelor's, master's, or doctoral degree.

4. Please attach a transcript for all college and graduate work.

5. In what extracurricular activities did you participate in high school or college?

Activity	When	Your role in it
_____	____	_____
_____	____	_____
_____	____	_____
_____	____	_____
_____	____	_____
_____	____	_____
_____	____	_____
_____	____	_____

6. List any awards or honors you received in school.

7. Please attach a copy of your college and graduate school Board scores.

SUMMER AND PART-TIME JOB EXPERIENCE

	Organization	Position	Description of what you did	Dates (from-to)
a.				
b.				
c.				
d.				
e.				
f.				
g.				
h.				
i.				
j.				

FULL-TIME WORK EXPERIENCE (INCLUDING MILITARY)

	Organization	Job title	Description of what you did	Dates (from-to)
a.				
b.				
c.				
d.				
e.				
f.				
g.				
h.				
i.				
j.				

2. List any honors or awards you have won.

ORGANIZATIONAL MEMBERSHIP

1. What organizations have you belonged to and participated in outside of school (e.g., professional associations, churches, amateur sports teams, country clubs, etc.)?

Organization	Nature of your involvement	Dates from-to
a. _____	_____	_____
b. _____	_____	_____
c. _____	_____	_____
d. _____	_____	_____
e. _____	_____	_____

2. List any honors or awards you have won.

CURRENT FAMILY

1. Are you married _____   When _____

           single _____

           divorced _____   When _____

           other (specify) _____

2. Does your spouse work? If so, describe job.

3. Do you have children? If "yes," fill in below.

Age	Sex
_____	_____
_____	_____
_____	_____
_____	_____
_____	_____

4. Where do you live currently? _____

   Do you rent? _____ or own? _____

Dyad Exercise

Purpose

The purpose of this exercise is to (1) give you some practice in doing a Self-Assessment, and (2) allow for an external (to you) check of your preliminary analysis of your own data.

Procedure

1. Select someone who is also taking this course or doing a Self-Assessment.

2. Exchange notebooks. That is, give the person all of your data.

3. Each do an assessment of the other person's data, using the methods outlined in the Self-Assessment and Career Development textbook. That is, identify as many supported themes as you can.

4. You need not write up your assessment formally (as shown in Appendix A of that book). Instead, simply prepare some charts or exhibits from which you can talk.

5. Meet with your partner and take turns verbally presenting your assessments. Allow about a half-hour for each presentation and 10 or 15 minutes for questions afterward.

6. Insert all the materials, exhibits, etc. from your partner's assessment of you in this section.

7. Remember to record in the Feelings Record at the beginning of your workbook any reactions you may have had.

Your Self-Assessment Paper

SELF-ASSESSMENT PAPER ASSIGNMENT

Your Self-Assessment represents a written record of your efforts to assess yourself in relationship to work and a career, using the method we have developed to make sense of the data in the personal documents you have generated. This is a difficult task, both intellectually and emotionally. It is the purpose of this assignment sheet to clearly describe the structure of that task so that (hopefully) it won't get in your way.

Personal Documents

The data you have generated have been derived from at least the following:

1. A written interview
2. AVL responses
3. 24-hour diaries
4. Strong-Campbell profile
5. Current and desired life-style representations
6. Background facts
7. The dyad exercise
8. A record of your feelings and reactions to generating the above data

The paper should be based on these data. You can also include other data if you want, providing that you clearly state their source and explain how and why you are interpreting them as you are.

Content

The paper should include the following two elements:

1. Themes that you have found in your data, including a description of the data on which each theme is based.
2. Implications about yourself for a job/career life style, including a description of how you have drawn them (what themes and data they are based on).

CRITERIA FOR A GOOD SELF-ASSESSMENT PAPER

1. The data from each device are used carefully with a clear understanding of the nature of the device and the way in which it was employed.

2. A maximum of useful data are identified in each device.

3. A general sensitivity to contradictory evidence is exhibited.

4. A sufficient number of themes are identified (approximately 15-30), each supported by convincing evidence from as many sources as possible.

5. Themes are labeled precisely and nonevaluatively.

6. Implications are developed that overlap minimally while taking into account all the themes and their own inherent overlap.

7. Implications are expressed concisely as statements revealing characteristics, behavior, and preferences that have fairly obvious job/career/life-style implications.

8. The paper shows a general sensitivity in drawing inferences to the assumptions upon which they are based.

GENERAL REQUIREMENTS FOR THE PAPER

1. The paper must be typed and double-spaced.

2. It should not exceed 20 pages.

3. It can be organized as you see fit and written in a style you feel is appropriate (for you), as long as the reader can follow your train of thought. (That is, your logic should be explicit.)

Data on Specific Careers, Jobs, and Organizations

JOB-SEARCH DATA

As you gather information on career opportunities, industries, and specific organizations and jobs, you may find it useful to organize and file it here in the notebook.

Practice for Interviewing

AN INTERVIEWING EXERCISE

It is probably a good idea for most people to do some practice interviewing before undertaking any serious job interviews. There are any number of ways in which you can practice, but let us suggest the following exercise.

Participants: 4 people

Time: 3 hours

Preparation:

1. Each participant should give a resumé, a brief description of a type of job he or she would like to interview for, and a description of the interviewer and the interview location to one of the other three people.

2. To prepare for being an interviewee, each participant should think about the kinds of questions that may be asked (see Chapter XIII in the textbook) and the kinds of questions he or she may wish to ask in return. (It may be useful to write out some of these questions and answers.)

3. To prepare for being an interviewer, each participant should look over the resumé and job description he or she has been given and consider how to conduct the interview.

The Exercise:

The exercise will consist of four 30-minute interviews (each involving an interviewer, an interviewee, and two observers), each followed by a 15-minute debriefing.

1. The interviewer should start and stop the interviews.

2. The observers should use the forms on the following pages to record their observations.

3. At the conclusion of each interview the observers should share their observations with the others, and everyone should discuss them.

You may find it useful to enter in this notebook any feedback you receive plus answers to common questions.

OBSERVER FORM

Interviewer: _____

Interviewee: _____

Observer: _____

Date: _____

Brief description of

interview situation and

job opening: _____

_____

_____

_____

Observations: Record here any specific behavior on the part of the interviewee that you think helped or hurt the interview	Comments: Note here whether the behavior helped or hurt and (very briefly) why

OBSERVER FORM

Interviewer: _____

Interviewee: _____

Observer: _____

Date: _____

Brief description of

interview situation and

job opening: _____

_____

_____

_____

Observations: Record here any specific behavior on the part of the interviewee that you think helped or hurt the interview

Comments: Note here whether the behavior helped or hurt and (very briefly) why

Your Career Development Paper

CAREER DEVELOPMENT PAPER ASSIGNMENT

Content

The paper should include the following four elements:

1. A statement of your position regarding job possibilities for next year, including a careful description of how you have reached that position.

2. A statement of your conclusions regarding a life style for next year, including a justification for that position.

3. A statement regarding a job and a career after next year, including an explanation of how you reached that position.

4. A set of concrete plans as to how you will approach the job-hunting process, with a careful justification for all parts of the approach.

General Requirements

1. The paper must be typed and double-spaced.

2. The paper should not exceed 20 pages.

3. It can be organized as you desire and written in whatever style you feel is appropriate.

Criteria for Evaluating the Paper

1. How clear is the logic that links each of the four main parts of the paper (see content) to the person's Self-Assessment paper?

2. Are there parts of the person's Self-Assessment paper, the implications of which have been ignored in the Career Development paper?

3. How clear is the logic that links each of the four main parts of the paper to the content of the second half of the textbook?

4. Are there ideas and lessons from the second half of the textbook that are being ignored in the paper?

A Job-Hunting Diary

Beacuse job hunting can be hectic and confusing, some people find that keeping a diary (see Chapter XVI in the textbook) is very useful. Periodically reading back over the last week's or month's entries often helps one put things in their proper perspective and conduct the whole job-hunting process more dispassionately.

You might wish to keep a diary yourself and write your entries in this section of the workbook. If you do so, may we suggest the following:

1. Make entries as often as you can (preferably once a day).

2. When making an entry ask yourself:

   a. What has happened today of importance with respect to job hunting?

   b. How has this changed my strategy and plans (if at all)?

   c. How do I feel about today's events?